COMPANION

TO

Hymnbook for Christian Worship

COMPANION

TO
Hymnbook for Christian Worship

ARTHUR N. WAKE

THE BETHANY PRESS ✔ ST. LOUIS, MISSOURI

© 1970 by The Bethany Press
Library of Congress Catalog Card Number 72-129621

MANUFACTURED IN THE UNITED STATES OF AMERICA

Preface

This book is intended to be a companion to *Hymnbook for Christian Worship*. It is unique only in that the information given here is related to this specific hymnal and not to hymnody in general. I have carefully avoided the inclination to write a commentary on the contents of the hymnal but have endeavord to bring together historical facts normally scattered about in a wide variety of books, periodicals, newspapers, and reference works so that the users of *Hymnbook for Christian Worship* will have a capsule account of each hymn and tune at his fingertips.

Space and time have precluded a comprehensive or exhaustive presentation of the story of hymnody. It has been my aim to provide basic information to ministers, organists, choirmasters, choir members, directors of Christian education, church school teachers, and other interested laymen, which will assist them in making more intelligent use of the hymnbook in all areas of church life. I have made every effort to be accurate despite the knowledge that errors will doubtless be found. My research has revealed certain discrepancies in information relative to dates, names, places, and spelling. Resolution of these problems has been determined by accepting majority opinion of scholars in some instances and arbitrary decision by the writer in others. Experience has taught that there is a remarkable similarity in the way information is related by the authors of various handbooks, and I have concluded that there is a limited number of ways to write a brief biographical sketch or present certain other facts without unconsciously using words or phrases easily found elsewhere. I have endeavored to avoid any infringement on copywrited material. If I have failed in this, I offer humble apologies and will make proper acknowledgment in future editions of this work.

I wish to acknowledge my debt to numerous scholars of the past and present who have shared their research and thought with readers through their publications. The principal authors consulted are given in the bibliography. Readers who are interested in a more comprehensive study of specific hymns, and of hymnody in general, will profit from careful reading of these references. The original research contained in this companion was acquired primarily through correspondence with authors and composers. In several instances the information they gave appears for the first time in this book. We express our deep appreciation to all authors and composers who responded to our letters of inquiry. Various publishing houses, colleges, and universities have been most helpful in supplying addresses which expedited correspondence. We are especially grateful to Mrs. Josephine Williams, secretary to The Hymn Society of America, for her assistance in locating a number of hymns and authors.

I respectfully acknowledge and express appreciation to the Board of Trustees, President W. A. Welsh, and the faculty of Lexington Theological Seminary for granting the sabbatical leave during which the major portion of this book was written. Special appreciation is expressed for the expert assistance provided so generously by Professor Roscoe Pierson, Miss Gladys Scheer, and the staff of Bosworth Memorial Library at Lexington Theological Seminary, and to Mrs. Jack Obenshain who typed the manuscript.

Finally, I wish to thank my family and especially my wife, Jean, for the patience, encouragement, and gentle prodding which played no small part in bringing this book into being.

Arthur N. Wake

Lexington Theological Seminary
Lexington, Kentucky
January 12, 1970

Contents

HYMNS AND
SERVICE MUSIC

1   *Joyful, Joyful, We Adore Thee*

HYMN TO JOY 8.7.8.7.D.

> Henry van Dyke, 1852-1933
>
> Arr. from Ludwig van Beethoven, 1770-1827

    Written while the author was visiting Williams College as guest preacher and inspired by the beautiful Berkshire Mountains, this hymn is from the third edition of *Poems of Henry van Dyke,* 1911, and was dated 1908. The hymn was presented to the president of the college one morning at the breakfast table with the comment that it was to be sung to Beethoven's tune.

    Henry van Dyke was one of the great Presbyterian preachers, scholars, teachers, and authors. Born in Germantown, Pennsylvania, November 10, 1852, he was educated at the Brooklyn Polytechnic Institute, Princeton, and Princeton Theological Seminary. He was ordained in 1879 and began his ministry at the United Congregational Church, Newport, Rhode Island. For a number of years he was the pastor of Brick Presbyterian Church in New York City. In 1900 he became Professor of English Literature at Princeton and was elected Moderator of the General Assembly in 1902. During the year 1909 he was the American lecturer at the University of Paris and the following year was elected Fellow of the Royal Society of Literature and granted an honorary degree by Oxford University. In 1912 he was President of the National Institute of Arts and Letters. His close personal friendship with President Woodrow Wilson led to his appointment as United States Minister to the Netherlands and Luxemburg, a position he held from 1913 to 1916. In 1918 he became a member of the Legion of Honor. During his career he received many honors from American universities. His service to the Presbyterian church was extensive and significant. He died at Princeton, New Jersey, on April 10, 1933.

    HYMN TO JOY is adapted from Beethoven's mighty Symphony No. 9 in D minor, Opus 125, which was composed between 1817 and 1823 for Grand Orchestra, soprano, alto, tenor, bass, and chorus. The text for the work was selected from Schiller's *Ode to Joy* and proclaims with glorious vigor the brotherhood of man.

As early as 1846 the theme was used as a hymn tune in a work edited by Elam Ives, Jr. entitled *The Mozart Collection*. An arrangement by Edward Hodges is also found in Tuckerman's *Trinity Collection of Church Music*, 1863. The present arrangement seems to be a composite adaptation by an unknown person. The tune is also known as BONN, and JOY.

Ludwig van Beethoven's life and work is much too complicated and prolific to be treated fully here. In terms of his personality and musical productivity he stands as one of the most colorful figures in all of musical history. He was born in Bonn in 1770 and received his early musical training from his father and other court musicians in that city. He went to Vienna and studied with Mozart for a short time. Haydn heard one of his cantatas when he stopped in Bonn in 1792 and gave the young composer encouragement. Later that year Beethoven moved to Vienna where he studied with Haydn and remained until his death in 1827.

At the age of twenty-eight the first signs of deafness appeared and by 1815 he was unable to hear without artificial aid and was forced to give up public performances. Shortly afterward Beethoven became completely deaf and fell into ill health. During his final years of affliction he composed his most magnificent music including string quartets, the incomparable *Missa Solemnis,* Ninth Symphony and *Diabelli* variations. Beethoven's inventive genius was the capstone of the classical era and guidepost for developments in the nineteenth-century musical world.

2   *All Things Bright and Beautiful*

ROYAL OAK 7.6.7.6. with Refrain

Cecil Frances Alexander, 1818-1895
Traditional English Melody
Adapt. Martin Shaw, 1875-1958

Mrs. Alexander has been called the finest of all hymn writers for children. She wrote four hundred hymns and poems and most of these were for the teaching and edification of youngsters.

She was born Cecil Frances Hymphreys at Wicklow, Ireland. Her father was Major John Humphreys. In 1848 she published a book entitled *Hymns for Little Children*. John Keble wrote the preface to the collection which was of such quality that it went through one hundred editions. Two years after the publication of this book Miss Humphreys married William Alexander, Bishop of Derry and Raphoe. She gained the reputation for being the perfect minister's wife because of her great interest in the worship and general life of the parish and especially for her devotion to the care of all those in need. One example of her concern is found in her willingness to give all of the profits from the sale of her *Hymns for Little Children* to a deaf-mute school in Ireland.

As a poet she was known and loved throughout the British Isles. She counted among her close friends such people as Matthew Arnold.

This hymn is based on Genesis 1:31 and the phrase "Maker of heaven and earth" in The Apostle's Creed. As was the case with many of her hymns it was intended to explain an article of the creed in language the children could understand and appreciate. She was perhaps the most successful hymnist in this field simply because she did understand the needs and capabilities of children and was very much opposed to using a "namby-pamby childish style" of writing for them.

Among the author's other hymns, three stand out in popularity in American churches. They are:

"Once in Royal David's City"
"There Is a Green Hill Far Away"
"Jesus Calls Us O'er the Tumult"

The tune is a seventeenth-century traditional melody. It seems to have been published first in the 1686 edition of Playford's *English Dancing Master* under the title "The Twenty-ninth of May." In his *Hymn Tune Names,* Robert Guy McCutchan [Abingdon Press, 1957, p. 122] tells an interesting story relative to the probable origin of the Royal Oak tune. Charles II, in his flight after the Battle of Worcester, found it necessary to hide in an oak tree at Boscobel, Shropshire, England. This tree came to be known as the Royal Oak. McCutchan conjectures that the tune name is connected with this incident since "The Twenty-ninth of May" was a loyalist song related to the restoration of Charles II on May 29, 1660.

This arrangement is by Martin Shaw who distinguished himself as an organist, composer, and compiler of church music. Born in London, March 9, 1875, he studied at the Royal College of Music. In 1900 he founded the Purcell Society. From 1908 he was organist at St. Mary's, Primrose Hill. It was here that he worked with Percy Dearmer with whom he later compiled several hymnals. From 1920-1924 he was choirmaster at St. Martin-in-the-Fields. He has made many excellent contributions to modern hymnbooks.

3 *Let Us with a Gladsome Mind*

INNOCENTS 7.7.7.7.

Based on Psalm 136
John Milton, 1608-1674, alt.
The Parish Choir, 1850

The author of this paraphrase of Psalm 136 lived during the turbulent years of England's civil war and restoration. Complete details of his life and work can be found elsewhere. For the purpose of this brief hymnological review the following comments are sufficient. Born a Londoner on December 9, 1608, he spent his life there and died on November 8, 1674. He was educated at St. Paul's School and Christ College, Cambridge. In all he made nineteen paraphrases of various psalms. The present hymn was written in 1623 when he was but fifteen years of age and a student at St. Paul's School. It was published in his *Poems in English and Latin,* 1645. His contributions to hymnody are few indeed when compared to his other literary achievements. Despite this he did exert an important influence on the thought and expression of the Wesleys. His finest literary works were written after he became totally blind at the age of forty-four. These include *Paradise Lost,* 1667, *Paradise Regained,* 1671, and *Sampson Agonistes,* 1671. Milton was unorthodox in his theology, leaned toward the Independents regarding church government, and the Baptists concerning baptism. He was a convinced and outspoken exponent of democracy and Puritanism, the consequences of which he luckily escaped after the Restoration. His active support of Oliver Cromwell and his position as Cromwell's Latin secretary could easily have led to imprisonment or even death on the gallows in those days.

For a note on the tune and its source see No. 24.

4 *We Sing the Mighty Power of God*

ELLACOMBE C.M.D.

Isaac Watts, 1674-1748, alt.
Gesangbuch, Wirtemberg, 1784

This hymn of "praise for creation and providence" first appeared in Isaac Watts' *Divine and Moral Songs,* 1715.

For comments on Isaac Watts see No. 48.

ELLACOMBE came from a collection of German Roman Catholic hymns entitled *Gesangbuch der Herzoglichen Wirtembergischen Katholischen Hofkapelle*, 1784. This book was used in the private chapel of the Duke of Würtemberg. The tune was introduced into England through *Hymns Ancient and Modern*.

5   *This Is My Father's World*

TERRA BEATA S.M.D.

> Maltbie D. Babcock, 1858-1901, alt.
> Transitional English Melody
> Adapt. Franklin L. Sheppard, 1852-1930

The original sixteen-stanza poem from which these lines are taken appeared in Dr. Babcock's *Thoughts for Everyday Living*, 1901. This is his best-known and most widely used hymn.

Maltbie Davenport Babcock, born on August 3, 1858, was a native of Syracuse, New York. He was educated at Syracuse University and Auburn Theological Seminary and afterward began his ministry in the First Presbyterian Church at Lockport, New York. He accepted a call to serve the Brown Memorial Church in Baltimore, Maryland, where he remained fourteen years, serving the entire community with great distinction. In 1899 he became the pastor of the Brick Presbyterian Church in New York City where he ministered for eighteen months before his untimely death at Naples, Italy, on May 18, 1901. He was a man with exceptional gifts in music, athletics, scholarship and was a beloved pastor to young and old alike.

TERRA BEATA is translated "blessed earth." Another name for this tune is TERRA PATRIS or "Father's earth." Both are descriptive of the spirit of this hymn. A number of writers have assigned the music to Franklin L. Sheppard but Albert C. Ronander and Ethel K. Porter, in their *Guide to the Pilgrim Hymnal*, present a good argument for its English origin. Mrs. Porter presents a tune she found in the *English Hymnal* designated "From an English Traditional Melody" which is indeed remarkably similar to the tune used here.

Franklin Lawrence Sheppard, born in Philadelphia, Pennsylvania, August 7, 1852, was educated at the University of Pennsylvania where he graduated at the head of his class in 1872 and became a charter member of the Delta Chapter of Phi Beta Kappa. He became the manager of the Baltimore, Maryland, foundry of his father's stove and heater firm in 1875. His interest in the church developed early in life through his confirmation in the Zion Protestant Episcopal Church. Later he served as a vestryman in that church. He became an active Presbyterian upon his removal to Baltimore and served as an elder, Sunday school teacher, and director of music in the Second Presbyterian Church. He was frequently a lay delegate to the General Assembly and was elected to membership of the Board of Publication and Sabbath-School Work over which he later presided. It was through his leadership that the Presbyterian headquarters, Witherspoon Building, was built. He was an organist of considerable talent, serving at one time as organist of the Zion Protestant Episcopal Church. He was the editor of *Alleluia,* 1915, a Sunday school songbook, and served on the editorial committee for the Presbyterian *Hymnal,* 1911. He died at Germantown, Pennsylvania, February 15, 1930.

6 *The Spacious Firmament on High*

CREATION: L.M.D.

Joseph Addison, 1672-1719
Franz Joseph Haydn, 1732-1809

Published in conjunction with "An Essay on the Proper Means of Strengthening and Confirming Faith in the Mind of Man" this version of Psalm 19 appeared in *The Spectator* on Saturday, August 23, 1712.

Joseph Addison is remembered today primarily as a writer of essays and his numerous contributions to *The Spectator, The Tatler, The Guardian,* and *The Freeholder.* He was a son of an Anglican clergyman and was himself educated for the clergy. Born at Milston, Wiltshire, May 1, 1672, Addison was educated at Charterhouse, Queen's College, and Magdalen College, Oxford. Rather than taking Holy Orders, he turned to literature, law, and politics. His literary success was by far more important than his political accomplishments. For a time he held such positions as Commissioner of Appeals, Under Secretary of State, Secretary to the Lord Lieutenant of Ireland and Chief Secretary for Ireland. He entered into an unhappy marriage with the Dowager Countess of Warwick in 1716. Illness, controversy, and family hostility beclouded his final years. He died at Holland House, Kensington, London, on June 17, 1719.

CREATION is an abbreviated version of "The heavens are telling," a chorus from Franz Joseph Haydn's famous oratorio *The Creation*. It has been used extensively in America since an early appearance in Baker and Woodbury's, *The Choral*, 1845.

For a note on Franz Joseph Haydn see No. 354.

7   *For the Beauty of the Earth*

DIX 7.7.7.7.7.7.

Folliott S. Pierpoint, 1835-1917, alt.

Abridged from a chorale by Conrad Kocher, 1786-1872

Originally written as a hymn for Holy Communion, it was first published in the second edition of Orby Shipley's *Lyra Eucharistica*, 1864. It was eight stanzas in length but over the years has been reduced to the four or five stanzas now used almost entirely as a children's hymn and for flower services.

Folliott Sandford Pierpoint was born in Bath, England, October 7, 1835. He was graduated in classical honors from Queen's College, Oxford, becoming for a time classical teacher at Somersetshire College. He published *The Chalice of Nature and Other Poems* which was republished later as *Song of Love, The Chalice of Nature, and Lyra Jesu*. He died at Newport, England, on March 10, 1917.

For a comment on DIX and Conrad Kocher see No. 141.

8   *Men and Children Everywhere*

ROCK OF AGES 7.7.7.7.5.7.4.7.

John J. Moment, 1875-1959

Ancient Hebrew Melody
Arr. Charlotte M. Lockwood, 1903-

Originally written as an anthem accompanied by Charlotte Mathewson Lockwood's arrangement of the present tune and published by the H. W. Gray, Co., this hymn appeared in *The Hymnal*, 1933 (Presbyterian), *Christian Worship, a Hymnal*, 1941, and *The Methodist Hymnal*, 1964.

John James Moment was born in Orono, Ontario, Canada, in 1875. He was educated at Princeton University, A.B., 1896; Hartford Theological Seminary, B.D., 1906; and was the recipient of an honorary D.D. degree from Washington and Jefferson College. He taught several years at the Lawrenceville School near Princeton, New Jersey, before embarking on a career as a minister. From 1906 to 1908 Dr. Moment was assistant pastor of the First Presbyterian Church, East Orange, New Jersey. For the next three years he was associate pastor of the Bergen Reformed Church, Jersey City, New Jersey, and in 1911 became the minister of the High Street Presbyterian Church, Newark, New Jersey. He began his ministry at Crescent Avenue Presbyterian Church, Plainfield, New Jersey, in 1918. He died May 11, 1959.

ROCK OF AGES, MOOT ZOOR, MA'OZ TZUR, or FORTRESS ROCK is a traditional Hebrew melody used at the Festival of Lights and means (literally) "He is the fortress of my salvation."

Charlotte Mathewson Lockwood, F.A.G.O., S.M.M., was organist at the Crescent Avenue Presbyterian Church while Dr. Moment was pastor. She was a native of Granby, Connecticut, but spent her childhood in Reidsville, North Carolina, where at the age of twelve she was playing the organ at the Methodist Church. She was the organ student of Clarence Dickinson, Charles-Marie Widor in Paris, and Günther Ramin in Leipzig. For a number of years she was a member of the faculty of the Union School of Music, New York City.

9 *O God, Thy Great Creation*

MUNICH 7.6.7.6.D.

Edward E. Chipman, 1901-
Adapt. from *Gesangbuch*, Meiningen, 1693
Harm. adapt. from Felix Mendelssohn, 1809-1847

The author entitled this hymn, "Hymn of the Scientists" when he wrote it in 1947. At the time he was instructor in Bible and college pastor at Keystone Junior College, LaPlume, Pennsylvania. He tells us ". . . I was concerned with hymns for college chapel that would speak to students in terms of strong affirmation because of close relations to their experience and to which they could give full mental assent, as well as make some emotional response." The hymn was included in his privately published, *Hymns for the Space Age*, 1969.

Edward E. Chipman was born in Providence, Rhode Island, in 1901. He was educated at Colgate University (B.A.), Colgate-Rochester Divinity School (B.D. and M.Th.), and studied as a Fellow in New Testament at the University of Chicago Divinity School. He was ordained to the Baptist ministry in the Roger Williams Baptist Church, Providence, Rhode Island, and has served churches in New York state, Pennsylvania, and Illinois. For many years Mr. Chipman was involved with the national work of his denomination in the area of church extension. He is currently chairman of the Windham Area Community Action Program (the Economic Opportunity Board for twenty towns in Northeastern Connecticut), and a member of the Department of Christian Mission Support of the Connecticut Baptist Convention.

MUNICH has appeared in various melodic forms and with various harmonizations and under different names. The present form is an adaptation of the *a capella* quartet number from Felix Mendelssohn's oratorio *Elijah* which was performed at the Birmingham Festival in 1847. Although parts of the melody have been traced to earlier collections, the basic form as it now appears is from the *Neu-vermehrtes Gesangbuch,* Meiningen, 1693. In some German hymnals of recent dates, it still appears with Johann Heerman's *"O Gott, du frommer Gott."* The tune was introduced to America in Mason and Webb's *The National Psalmist,* 1848, under the name ELIJAH.

For a comment on Mendelssohn see No. 328.

10   *My Shepherd Will Supply My Need*

RESIGNATION C.M.D.

Psalm 23
Para. Isaac Watts, 1674-1748
Southern Harmony, 1855

This paraphrase of Psalm 23 first appeared in Isaac Watts' *The Psalms of David, Imitated in the Language of the New Testament, And Apply'd to the Christian State and Worship,* 1719.

For a comment on Isaac Watts see No. 48.

George Pullen Jackson gives both tune and text in his *Down-East Spirituals and Others* and indicates his source as *Southern Harmony,* 1854. William Walker of Spartanburg, South Carolina, was the compiler and editor of this famous collection of hymns and tunes which appeared as early as 1835. The last edition appears to have been published in 1854. The composer of the tune is not given. The present harmonization of the tune is from the *Hymnal for Colleges and Schools,* 1956.

11   *I Sought the Lord, and Afterward I Knew*

PEACE 10.10.10.6.

Unknown
The Pilgrim Hymnal, 1904
The Revivalist, 1869
Adapt. George Brandon, 1924-

The authorship and date of this hymn are unknown. It appeared in *The Pilgrim Hymnal,* 1904.

PEACE was adapted by George Brandon from an anonymous tune he selected from *The Revivalist,* 1869, edited by Hillman and Hartsough. He submitted the adaptation to the committee preparing a revision of *Pilgrim Hymnal,* and it was first published in the 1958 edition of that book, as an alternate setting of these words.

George Brandon is a native of Stockton, California. He was educated at the College of the Pacific, A.B., 1945, and Union Theological Seminary, M.S.M., 1952, M.R.E., 1957. He grew up in the Christian Church (Disciples of Christ), and was baptized in the First Christian Church of Stockton, California. Mr. Brandon has taught at Eureka College in Eureka, Illinois, and William Penn College in Oskaloosa, Iowa, and has been organist and/or choir director for churches in California, New York, North Carolina, and Iowa. He is currently devoting his efforts to composing and arranging music, much of it based on his research into old American sacred music, especially that of the early "Disciple" movement. He has published more than one hundred choral pieces with more than thirty publishers, as well as various organ compositions and a number of articles on church music.

12   *Immortal Love, Forever Full*

BISHOPTHORPE C.M.

John G. Whittier, 1807-1892
Attr. to Jeremiah Clark, c. 1670-1707

Under the heading, "The Love of Christ," and entitled, "Our Master," this hymn is a cento taken from Whittier's *Tent on the Beach, and Other Poems,* 1867.

For a comment on John G. Whittier see No. 85.

BISHOPTHORPE is also known as ST. PAUL'S, REPENTANCE, and CHARMOUTH. In Bridges' *Yattendon Hymnal,* 1899, there is a three-part setting taken from the Foundling Hospital's manuscript part-books. In both instances, the music is ascribed to Jeremiah Clark, *c.* 1670-1707. The music has also been found in the second edition of *Select Portions of the Psalms of David,* 1786, and in Edward Miller's *Psalms of David,* 1790. It is found in many major hymnals.

Jeremiah Clark made his first appearance as a musician in the capacity of chorister in the Chapel Royal under John Blow. For a time, he served as organist at Winchester College and subsequently at St. Paul's Cathedral, London. In 1700 he and his fellow student, William Croft, were made gentlemen-extraordinary of the Chapel Royal and in 1704 became joint organists of the chapel. Clark was a versatile musician, publishing a variety of church music, music for the stage, and a series of harpischord lessons. Becoming despondent over a thwarted love affair, he committed suicide, December 1, 1707, in his house on the grounds of St. Paul's Cathedral and was buried in the New Crypt in the Cathedral.

13   There's a Wideness in God's Mercy

WELLESLEY 8.7.8.7.

Frederick W. Faber, 1814-1863
Lizzie S. Tourjée, 1858-1913

These lines are from Faber's thirteen-stanza hymn beginning, "Souls of men, why will ye scatter?" which appeared in his *Hymns,* 1862.

For a note on Frederick William Faber see No. 253.

WELLESLEY was composed by Lizzie S. Tourjée when she was a senior in high school. She had been requested to write the music for a classmate's hymn which was to be used at the graduation exercises, and, after overcoming her feelings of despair, she created the tune which in America is used extensively with the present text. Her father named the tune for Wellesley College. It was published in the *Hymnal of the Methodist Episcopal Church with Tunes,* 1878.

Lizzie S. Tourjée was the daughter of Dr. Eben Tourjée who founded the New England Conservatory of Music. She was born in

1858, attended Wellesley College briefly, and married Franklin Estabrook in 1883. Nothing more is known of her except that she died in 1913.

14   *Great Is Thy Faithfulness*

FAITHFULNESS 11.10.11.10.

Thomas O. Chisholm, 1866-1960
William M. Runyan, 1870-1957

Thomas Obediah Chisholm was born near Franklin, in Simpson County, Kentucky, July 29, 1866. He received his education in a small country school where he became the teacher at the age of sixteen years. Five years later, he became the associate editor of the weekly newspaper, *The Franklin Favorite*. In 1893 he was converted to Christianity by the preaching of Dr. H. C. Morrison who prevailed upon him to move to Louisville, Kentucky, to become the manager and editor of the evangelist's *Pentecostal Herald*. This led to his ordination as a Methodist minister and after a brief pastorate at Scottsville, Kentucky, his health failed and he moved to Winona Lake, Indiana, in order to be near the headquarters of Billy Sunday and Homer Rodeheaver. He entered the insurance business while at Winona Lake and continued the same work upon his removal to Vineland, New Jersey, in 1916. He found time to write and preach until he entered the Methodist Home for the Aged at Ocean Grove, New Jersey, in 1953. He died at the age of ninety-three on February 29, 1960. His obituary appears in the March 2, 1960, issue of the *New York Times*, p. 37.

Chisholm wrote more than 1,200 hymns and devotional verses. About 800 were published and many of these were set to music. "Living for Jesus," "Great Is Thy Faithfulness," and "The Prodigal Son," his most popular hymns, have been translated into many foreign languages and appear in a number of hymnals.

William M. Runyan composed the tune for this text. It was first published in *Songs of Salvation and Service,* 1923. The refrain has been omitted here. FAITHFULNESS is the name given the tune in *The Baptist Hymnal* published by the Southern Baptist Convention of America, 1956.

Runyan, the son of a Methodist minister, was born at Marion, New York, January 21, 1870. When he was fourteen, his parents moved to Kansas. Here he studied and taught music until he was ordained to the Methodist ministry in 1891. After serving various pastorates for twelve years he became the evangelist for the Central Kansas Methodist Conference. For several years Runyan was pastor of the Federated Church and associated with John Brown University at Sulphur Springs, Arkansas. In 1925 he moved to Chicago where he did editorial work at the Moody Bible Institute, and for a few years at the Hope Publishing Company.

Runyan composed more than three hundred "gospel songs," edited magazines, compiled and edited songbooks. Wheaton College recognized his contributions to the spiritual life of America by granting him an honorary Doctorate of Letters degree. He died at Pittsburg, Kansas, July 29, 1957.

15   Strong Son of God, Immortal Love

DEO GRACIAS L.M.

Alfred Tennyson, 1809-1892
The Agincourt Song, 15th century

These words are stanzas 1, 5, 6, and 7 from the Prologue to Tennyson's famous *In Memoriam, A. H. H.* It was begun in 1833 on the occasion of the untimely death of his dearest friend, Arthur Henry Hallam (1811-1833), but was not completed until 1850. The poem represents the author's attempt to work through the spiritual upheaval he experienced at that time. His conclusion was that one's answer to suffering, doubt, and fear can be found only through faith in a God of love. Tennyson wrote no hymns as such. Those now used are all extracts from other poems.

Alfred, Lord Tennyson was a native of Somersby, Lincolnshire, England. He was born August 6, 1809, in the Somersby rectory, the fourth son in the family of eight sons and four daughters. He was educated at Trinity College, Cambridge, where he participated in a group of poets, critics, and intellectuals called "The Apostles" and developed his deep friendship with Hallam. His poem, *Timbuctoo,* won the chancellor's prize during his second year at Cambridge (1830). His works are too numerous to list here but the quality of his poetry is well known and earned him the reputation of being the most representative voice of the Victorian Age. In 1850 he succeeded Wordsworth as Poet Laureate, completed his *In Memoriam,* and married Miss Emily Sellwood. From that year until his death on October 6, 1892, he enjoyed a popularity afforded few men. He is buried in Westminster Abbey.

For a note on DEO GRACIAS see No. 146.

16   O Love of God, How Strong and True

EISENACH L.M.

Horatius Bonar, 1808-1889
Melody by Johann H. Schein, 1586-1630

This hymn first appeared under the heading "The Love of God" in Bonar's *Hymns of Faith and Hope,* Second Series, 1861. The original consisted of ten stanzas but underwent deletions until only the present four stanzas remain.

For a comment on Horatius Bonar see No. 185.

EISENACH was composed for the hymn *"Mach's mit mir, Gott"* and was first published as a fly sheet to be used in conjunction with Schein's *Cantional,* 1627. It later appeared in the 1645 edition of the same work. It has been used by Bach in his *St. John's Passion* and appeared in England with Bach's harmonization in *Hymns Ancient and Modern,* 1861. A simplified version was made in 1875 upon which the harmonies of the present version are based.

For a note on the composer see No. 350.

17   O Love That Wilt Not Let Me Go

ST. MARGARET 8.8.8.8.6.

George Matheson, 1842-1906
Albert L. Peace, 1844-1912

According to the author of this hymn it was written very rapidly on June 6, 1882, at a time when he was suffering from "extreme mental stress" in the Clydeside Manse at Innellan, Argyllshire, Scotland. It first appeared in the Church of Scotland publication *Life and Work,* January, 1883.

For a note on George Matheson see No. 215.

ST. MARGARET was composed in 1884 for this hymn at the request of the committee preparing the *Scottish Hymnal,* 1885. Dr. Peace was the musical editor of that work.

Albert Lister Peace was the most revered organist of his day and was in great demand as a recitalist. He was born in Huddersfield,

England, in 1844. His unique musical ability came to light when he was but a child and by the age of nine became the organist at the Holmfirth parish church. His talents were developed by some private lessons but for the most part he was self taught and devoted his entire life to playing the organ. He received his Bachelor of Music and Doctor of Music degrees from Oxford. His positions include: organist at Trinity Congregational Church, Glasgow; St. Andrew's Hall; Glasgow Cathedral; and St. George's Hall, Liverpool. He played organ dedication recitals at Canterbury Cathedral, Victoria Hall, and New Castle Cathedral. He performed other valuable service to the church as musical editor of a number of Church of Scotland hymnals. Dr. Peace died at Blundellsands in 1912.

18   O God Whose Love Compels Us

ROCKPORT 7.6.7.6.D.

Daniel B. Merrick, Jr., 1926-

T. Tertius Noble, 1867-1953

This hymn was the winning entry for a theme hymn to be used by the American Baptist Convention held at Pittsburgh, Pennsylvania, May 17-21, 1967. It was first sung at a worship service at the Union Church Pastor's Conference of the Caribbean Area, Bogota, Colombia, in January, 1967.

Daniel B. Merrick, Jr. was born April 29, 1926, in Bloomington, Illinois. He is a graduate of Phillips University and the Graduate Seminary of Phillips University of Enid, Oklahoma. He has held pastorates at Sandoval, Illinois (Christian, 1948-51), and Milwaukee, Wisconsin (The United Church, Baptist and Disciples of Christ, 1954-62). He became the pastor of Margarita Union Church, Canal Zone, in 1962 and continues his work there. At the present his hymns have been published by The Hymn Society of America; in *In Harmony,* a United Christian Youth Movement songbook; *Hymns and Songs of the Spirit;* and various religious periodicals.

ROCKPORT was composed in 1938 in Rockport, Massachusetts, the home of Dr. Noble. It was set to James Montgomery's hymn, "Hail to the Lord's Anointed" in *The Hymnal* (Evangelical and Reformed), in 1941.

For a note on T. Tertius Noble see No. 338.

19 O Father Above Us

MADDERMARKET 11.11.11.9.

Percy Dearmer, 1867-1936
Martin Shaw, 1875-1958

These stanzas are from a thirty-three stanza processional hymn which appeared under the heading *Onward Ever (For the Young, and others)* in *Songs of Praise for Boys and Girls,* 1930, and again in *Songs of Praise,* 1931. The hymn was arranged in four parts with a conclusion. The present hymn represents stanzas one and two from Part I, stanza thirteen from Part II, and stanza thirty-two from the Conclusion.

For a comment on Percy Dearmer see No. 107.

MADDERMARKET was composed especially for this hymn by Martin Shaw for use in *Songs of Praise for Boys and Girls,* 1930.

For a note on Martin Shaw see No. 2.

20 All My Hope on God is Founded

NEANDER 8.7.8.7.6.7.

Joachim Neander, 1650-1680
Para. Robert Bridges, 1844-1930
From Chorale *Unser Herrscher* by Joachim Neander, 1650-1680

Under the heading "Thanksgiving," and entitled "Grace after Meat" the text appeared as *"Meine Hoffnung stehet feste"* in a book published at Bremen entitled *A* and *Ω Joachimi Neandri Glaub-und Liebesübung:—auffgemuntert durch einfältige Bundes Lieder und Danck-Psalmen,* 1680.

The translation used here is by Robert Bridges as found in his *Yattendon Hymnal,* 1899. Perhaps it would be more accurate to list this as free poem based on the spirit of the original rather than either a translation or paraphrase of it. Our hymn consists of the first three stanzas of the original from the *Yattendon Hymnal.*

It was Joachim Neander's grandfather who assumed the Greek form of the family name Neumann or Niemann. Neander was born in

Bremen in 1650 and, except for brief sojourns in Heidelberg, Frankfurt, and Düsseldorf, lived and died there. As a young man he was given to wild and riotous living. During the summer of 1670 he and several friends went to St. Martin's Church not to worship but to amuse themselves and find fault. The pastor, Theodore Under-Eyck, thwarted the original intentions of these young men and was responsible for Neander's subsequent conversion to a meaningful Christianity.

After having served as a private tutor at Frankfurt-am-Main, and as rector of the Latin School in Düsseldorf, he returned to Bremen as an assistant to Under-Eyck. He died there on May 31, 1680.

Contrary to stories, Neander never spent any time as a recluse in caves. His temperament made it impossible for him to adhere to religious points of view held by some of his superiors, especially one Reformed Church minister by the name of Sylvester Lürsen who was over him at the school at Düsseldorf. He was suspended for a brief time because of his unorthodox activities but was subsequently reinstated. His conflicts prevented him from achieving significant standing within the church community.

He has been called the "foremost hymn writer of the German Reformed Church." He wrote more than sixty hymns and composed the tunes for many of them.

For a note on Robert Bridges see No. 162.

NEANDER, named for the composer, is sometimes called UNSER HERRSCHER because it was taken from another Neander hymn, "*Unser Herrscher, Unser König*" with which the tune appeared in the 1680 edition of the *Glaub-und Liebesübung*. Our text originally was set to the tune MEINE HOFFNUNG which is similar to UNSER HERRSCHER except in that it was cast in a minor mode. This similarity is particularly evident in the last line of the music. Both tunes can be found in *Songs of Praise, Enlarged Edition* at 442 and 477.

21   *Unto the Hills Around do I Lift Up*

SANDON 10.4.10.4.10.10.

From Psalm 121
John Campbell, Duke of Argyll, 1845-1914
Charles Henry Purday, 1799-1885

This is a metrical version of Psalm 121 which is often referred to as the traveler's Psalm.

John Campbell wrote this hymn before becoming a public figure. He was born August 6, 1845, the ninth Duke of Argyll, and became a chieftain of the Scottish Highlands. On March 21, 1871, he married Princess Louise, a daughter of Queen Victoria at St. George's Chapel, Windsor. He succeeded to the dukedom, November 1, 1900. His court and public life were marked by distinctive service as governor-general of Canada, commander-in-chief of Prince Edward Island, the keeper of the great seal of Scotland, and scepter bearer at the coronation of both Edward VII and George V. He died, May 2, 1914.

For a comment on SANDON and Charles Henry Purday see No. 28.

22 God of Our Fathers, Whose Almighty Hand

NATIONAL HYMN 10.10.10.10.

Daniel C. Roberts, 1841-1907
George W. Warren, 1828-1902

In writing an autobiographical letter which Louis F. Benson quotes in his *Studies of Familiar Hymns* (second series) 1923, the author of this well-known text says his "personal history is of little account," and "I remain a country Parson, known only within my own small world." Such modesty is refreshing especially when one considers how this hymn has fared over the years.

Daniel Crane Roberts was born November 4, 1841, at Bridge Hampton, Long Island. Educated at Kenyon College, Gambier, Ohio, he served in the Civil War with the 84th Ohio Volunteers. He was ordained deacon in 1865 and a year later became a priest and began his ministry at Christ Church, Montpelier, Vermont. For a time he was at St. John's, Lowell, Massachusetts, and then returned to Vermont. The last twenty years of his life were spent as Vicar of St. Paul's Episcopal Church, Concord, New Hampshire.

In 1885 Norwich University honored him with a Doctor of Divinity Degree. He was active in the New Hampshire branch of the Grand Army of the Republic and Knights Templar in which he served as their national grand prelate from 1901 until 1904. He died at Concord, New Hampshire, October 31, 1907.

This hymn was written for the observance of the centennial celebration of the Declaration of Independence while Roberts was rector of

St. Thomas' Episcopal Church, Brandon, Vermont. It was later selected as the hymn for the centennial celebration of the adoption of the Constitution.

The music was composed by George W. Warren especially for this text. NATIONAL HYMN reflects the spirit of the text and the historical aspect of its use. Warren was born at Albany, New York, on August 17, 1828. He was a composer of anthems, hymn tunes, and services and served as the editor of *Warren's Hymns and Tunes as Sung at St. Thomas' Church,* 1888. During his career as an organist he served churches in Albany, New York; Brooklyn; and finally at St. Thomas' Church in New York City. Warren was granted an honorary Doctor of Music degree from Racine College, Racine, Wisconsin. He died in 1902.

23   *O God, Our Help In Ages Past*

ST. ANNE C.M.

Based on Psalm 90
Isaac Watts, 1674-1748
William Croft, 1678-1727

This is the most common form of this hymn and consists of stanzas 1, 2, 3, 5, 7, and 9 of the original which first appeared in Watts' *Psalms of David,* 1719 under the title "Man frail and God eternal." Watts' original began with "Our" which was changed to "O" by John Wesley in 1737. The hymn is often called the greatest hymn of all times and among the best to come from Watts. It is sung on important special occasions throughout the English-speaking world.

For a note on Isaac Watts see No. 48.

ST. ANNE first appeared in *A Supplement to the New Version of Psalms by Dr. Brady and Mr. Tate. . . . The Sixth Edition, Corrected and Much Enlarged . . .,* 1708. Several authorities say the first line of the tune was in general use before Croft but Moffatt and Patrick in their *Handbook to the Church Hymnary, Revised Edition,* present a strong case for assigning the tune to Croft.

William Croft, one of England's great organist-composers, was born at Nether Ettington in Warwickshire where records indicate he was baptized on December 30, 1678. He was a chorister in the Chapel Royal and studied organ under John Blow, organist at Westminster Abbey. In 1708 he succeeded his teacher at Westminster and received a Doctor of Music degree from Oxford in 1713. His early years as a composer were devoted primarily to music for the theatre but even then he excelled in his anthems and services for the church. He is often referred to as the originator of the English Psalm tunes in contrast to the Genevan style. Dr. Croft died August 14, 1727, and was buried beside his teacher, John Blow, in Westminster Abbey.

For an additional reference to Croft see No. 12.

24   As the Sun Doth Daily Rise

INNOCENTS 7.7.7.7.

Latin: *Matutinus altiora*
Tr. O.B.C.
The Parish Choir, 1850

This hymn was included in Horatio Nelson's *Hymn for Saint's Day, and Other Hymns,"* 1864. The title is taken from the opening words of a Latin hymn translated by an unknown O.B.C. Upon its first appearance it was called King Alfred's Hymn and was translated as "As the sun to brighter skies." Competent researchers have found no connection between King Alfred and this hymn.

The tune INNOCENTS came to us through *The Parish Choir,* a monthly periodical published by The Society for Promoting Church Music, which was another by-product of the Oxford Movement. The tune was found in Volume 3, No. 59, November, 1850, and was called *An Ancient Litany.* It was set to the text "Little flowers of martyrdom" commemorating Herod's massacre of the children of Bethlehem. The Feast of Holy Innocents falls on December 28. The present form of the tune has been attributed to William Monk who was editor of *The Parish Choir* in 1850.

25   Through All the Changing Scenes

CONSOLATION C.M.

Based on Psalm 34
New Version, 1696
John Wyeth's *Repository of Sacred Music, Part Second,* 1813

This version of Psalm 34 is from Tate and Brady's *A New Version of the Psalms of David Fitted to the Tunes Used in Churches,* London,

1696. This Psalter, called the *New Version* served England for over one hundred years. Julian has categorized Psalm 34 as "sweet and simple verse."

For a further comment on Tate and Brady see No. 80.

CONSOLATION is an anonymous tune from John Wyeth's *Respository of Sacred Music, Part Second,* 1813. In the *Original Sacred Harp, Revised, Corrected and Enlarged, c.* 1911, it is attributed to one "Dean" of whom nothing is known. The tune appears in several early American hymnbooks with Isaac Watt's text beginning "Once more, my soul, the rising day." It appeared with the same text in Wyeth's *Repository,* second edition, 1820.

John Wyeth was born March 11, 1770, in Cambridge, Massachusetts, and is noteworthy because his *Repository of Sacred Music* contains examples of early American folk hymns and tunes. He was among the earliest and most successful publishers of the folk hymnody which developed out of the great religious revivals of the 1700's and early 1800's. Wyeth was active in the printing and publishing business all of his life and at one time was appointed postmaster at Harrisburg, Pennsylvania, by George Washington. He did not hold the position very long due to a conflict-of-interest charge. He died in Philadelphia, Pennsylvania, January 23, 1858.

26   *Sing Praise to God who Reigns Above*

MIT FREUDEN ZART 8.7.8.7.8.8.7.

Johann J. Schütz, 1640-1690
Tr. Frances E. Cox, 1812-1897
Bohemian Brethren's *Kirchengesänge,* 1566

This is a translation of four of the nine stanzas of Schütz's *Hymns of Thanksgiving, "Sei Lob und Ehr dem höchsten Gut."* The original was first published in his *Christliches Gedenckbüchlein,* Frankfurt am Main, 1675. Miss Cox contributed her translation to *Lyra Eucharistica,* 1864, and included it in her own *Hymns from the German,* the same year.

Johann Jakob Schütz was a lawyer by profession and a Lutheran Pietist and Separatist by religious conviction. He was an intimate friend of Phillipp Jakob Spener, the founder of the Pietist movement for the German Lutheran Church, and it was at Schütz's suggestion that Spener began the now famous *Collegia Pietatis* or prayer meetings. The fervor of his Pietism eventually caused him to leave the Lutheran church and cease communion. He died at Frankfurt, May 22, 1690.

Frances Elizabeth Cox was born at Oxford, England, May 10, 1812, and became another of her country's most famous women translators of German hymns. She published her translations as *Sacred Hymns from the German,* 1841, and the second edition, enlarged and revised, as *Hymns from the German,* 1864. She contributed other translations and original hymns to various magazines. Miss Cox died at Headington, September 23, 1897.

MIT FREUDEN ZART is also known as BOHEMIAN BRETHREN and is thought to be considerably older than the Bohemian Brethren's *Kirchengesänge* of 1566 in which it first appears in print. Several authorities list it as a pre-Reformation tune of the type Martin Luther found useful in his compilations, others point out similarities between the tune's original form and that of Psalm 138 in the *Genevan Psalter* and a French secular tune published in 1529-30. The joyous character of the tune precludes singing it too slowly.

27   Golden Breaks The Dawn

LE P'ING 5.5.5.5.D.

T. C. Chao, 1888-
Tr. Frank W. Price, 1895-

Chinese Folk Melody Adapt. Hu Te-ngai, c. 1900
Arr. Paul E. Koch, 1929-

This hymn was one of sixty-two written by Chinese Christians and published in the Chinese hymnbook, *Hymns of Universal Praise,* 1936. Frank W. Price translated twenty-three of this group into English and published them as *Chinese Christian Hymns by Chinese Writers, with Chinese Tunes,* 1953. The second stanza is omitted here.

T. C. Chao (Chao Tzu-Ch'en) was born in 1888. He has become one of the most important Chinese scholars and theologians of the present century and has been active in the Christian movement in China and around the world through the Missionary Council which met in Jerusalem in 1928 and in Madras in 1939. At the World

Council of Churches meeting in Amsterdam, 1948, he was elected one of the vice-presidents. He wrote many of his hymns during a period of imprisonment by the Japanese. Dr. Chao served as dean of the School of Religion of Yenching University from 1928 until 1953 after which he remained a faculty member until his retirement several years later. Since the Communist take-over no one appears to know his fate. He was given an honorary doctorate by Princeton University.

Frank W. Price was born in Kashing, Che., China, on February 25, 1895, the son of U. S. missionaries. He received a broad education as a student at Davidson College, Southeastern University, Nanking, China, Yale (B.D., 1922, Ph.D., 1938) and Columbia (M.A., 1923). He was awarded the Doctor of Divinity degree by Davidson College in 1940. He was ordained a Presbyterian minister in 1922. Dr. Price has devoted his life to theological education and the rural church in China. For a period of three years he was held in detention by the Chinese Communists after which he returned to America where he became pastor of a church in Lexington, Virginia (1953-1955). He was elected Moderator of the General Assembly of the Presbyterian Church, U.S. (1953-1954). Since then he has been director of the Missionary Research Library, New York City, and research secretary of the Division of Foreign Missions of the National Council of Churches of Christ in the U.S.A. (1956-1961). He has recently served as Professor of International Studies at Mary Baldwin College (1961-66). Dr. Price is the author of a number of books dealing with Christianity in China. He is presently living in Lexington, Virginia.

LE P'ING is a Chinese folk melody adapted by Hu Te-ngai and arranged by Paul E. Koch. We have been unsuccessful in finding information on Hu Te-ngai. Mr. Koch says the "harmonization was intended to reflect a small measure of oriental flavor by having a very simple, even barren, harmonic accompaniment."

Paul E. Koch was born in Ohio on May 24, 1929, was graduated from Ohio Wesleyan University, B.M., 1951. After spending three years in the army as a chaplain's assistant, he entered Union Theological Seminary School of Sacred Music and was graduated with a Master of Sacred Music degree in 1956. After serving the First Presbyterian Church, Oak Park, Illinois, for three years as organist-choirmaster, he moved to the First Methodist Church, Springfield, Illinois. He is currently serving that church as organist-choirmaster and has developed a musical program involving ten choirs which have been heard in concert throughout the North Central states. Mr. Koch has studied under Searle Wright, Leo Sowerby, Charlotte Garden, and Mildred Andrews and has published anthems, bell choir music, and flute and organ pieces.

God of Our Life, Through all the Circling Years

SANDON 10.4.10.4.10.10.

Hugh T. Kerr, 1872-1950, alt.
Charles H. Purday, 1799-1885

This hymn was written for the fiftieth anniversary celebration of the Shadyside Presbyterian Church, Pittsburgh, in 1916 where Dr. Kerr began his ministry in 1913. A Canadian by birth, he was born February 11, 1882, educated at the University of Toronto, and took his ministerial training at Western Theological Seminary at Pittsburgh. He was ordained as a Presbyterian minister in 1897 and began his career in Hutchinson, Kansas. For a time he held a pastorate in Chicago, Illinois, before moving to the Shadyside Church in Pittsburgh. Kerr was the recipient of several honorary doctorate degrees and became an outstanding leader of Presbyterian work in the United States. In 1930 he served as the Moderator of the General Assembly of the Presbyterian Church in the U.S.A.

SANDON was composed by Charles Henry Purday for the hymn, "Lead Kindly Light" and appeared in *Church and Home Metrical Psalter and Hymnal,* 1860, which he edited.

Purday was born in Folkstone, England, January 11, 1799. He was a vocalist of some repute and was among those who sang for the coronation of Queen Victoria. During his career he was a publisher of music, a lecturer on subjects relating to the art of music, the conductor of psalmody, and a lively advocate of reform of the copyright laws as they related to music. Among his publications is a book entitled, *Copyright, a Sketch of Its Rise and Progress,* 1877. He was also a contributor to the first edition of Grove's *Dictionary of Music and Musicians.* He died in London, April 23, 1885.

29   *God Moves in a Mysterious Way*

DUNDEE C.M.

William Cowper, 1731-1800
Scottish Psalter, 1615

The author of this justly famous hymn was born at Berkhamstead, England, November 26, 1731, the son and descendant of a distinguished family. Educated at Westminster he was destined for a life before the bar which he began in 1754. Always a keenly sensitive person, Cowper was plagued throughout his life with periods of depression and despondence. On the occasion of his nomination for the Clerkship of the Journals of the House of Lords and discovering he would have to stand for an examination, Cowper became so disturbed he lost his reason and attempted suicide. From this ordeal he never fully recovered and became so incapacitated he was dependent upon his friends for support.

During this tragedy and a period of convalesence he lived with the Morley Unwin family and established a relationship which lasted for the remainder of his life. After Mr. Unwin's death, he and Mrs. Unwin went to live at Olney where he came under the influence of John Newton whose extreme Calvinistic theology played havoc with any possibility of a full and complete mental and emotional recovery from his illness. Despite this Cowper and Newton were great friends and worked together in the parish at Olney and produced the now famous *Olney Hymns.* Insanity struck again, and he was forced to give up his parish work and retire to a life of simple tasks around the home. Gardening, carpentry, glazing and tending to rabbits occupied his time until his health improved to the point where he could attempt writing again. During periods of rationality he wrote some of his greatest poetry, all of which reflect his dreadful internal struggle and his dependence upon those whom he loved. Such works as *The Task, John Gilpin, On the Receipt of My Mother's Picture, Out of Norfolk, To Mary, The Castaway,* and a number of his contributions to the *Olney Hymns,* have given him a permanent place in the annals of English Literature and distinctive consideration as the "greatest English poet of his age."

Cowper died on April 25, 1800, at East Dereham.

For a comment on the tune DUNDEE see No. 324.

30   *Children of the Heavenly Father*

SANDELL (TRYGGARE KAN INGEN VARA) L.M.

Caroline V. Sandell Berg, 1832-1903
Tr. Ernest William Olson, 1870-1958
Swedish Melody

This hymn is originally from *Sacred Hymns for the Children of God in the Days of Their Pilgrimage,* by Cennick, 1742. It apparently is well known and loved in Scandanavia and among Lutherans of America. The words and music appeared as *Guds barnstrygghet* in the Swedish-American hymnal, *Sionsharpan,* 1890, and in English translation in *Service Book and Hymnal,* 1958.

Caroline (Lina) Vilhelmina Berg (nee Sandell) was born October 3, 1832, in Fröderyd, Sweden and died in Stockholm on July 27, 1903. She was the child of a wealthy family and enjoyed the best possible religious, literary, and artistic experiences and was influened by the leading personalities of Sweden's cultural and religious life between 1850 and 1860. Her father died in 1858 and this tragedy was followed by her mother's death in 1860. In 1861 she took up residence in an *Evangelische fosterlandstiftelsen tjanst,* a home sponsored by a religious group. Her creative period followed the death of her parents when she wrote a large quantity of poetry and literature. She married a merchant by the name of Carl Oscar Berg on May 21, 1867. Jenny Lind financed the first edition of *Ahnfelt's Sanger* which contained mostly songs by Miss Sandell.

Ernest William Olson was at one time secretary of literature for the Augustana Book Concern. He was a layman who played an important part in the publication of *The Hymnal,* 1925, translating a number of Swedish hymns into English.

SANDELL or TRYGGARE KAN INGEN VARA is a Swedish folk melody which has long been associated with Mrs. Berg's hymn.

31   *A Mighty Fortress Is Our God*

EIN' FESTE BURG 8.7.8.7.6.6.6.6.7.

Martin Luther, 1483-1546
Trans. Frederick Henry Hedge, 1805-1890

Martin Luther, 1483-1546

Once called the "Battle Hymn of the Reformation," "A Mighty Fortress" is sung by Christian people of all faiths the world over. John Julian lists sixty-three English translations of which eighteen were in common usage in the nineteenth century. The two most common translations in current use are those of Thomas Carlyle and

Frederick Henry Hedge. As one would suspect Carlyle's is the favorite of English churches and that of Hedge the favorite in America.

Luther used Psalm forty-six as a starting point for his text. Unlike a great number of later hymns this is not a paraphrase of the Psalm but rather a freely composed text derived from the inspiration of scripture. It was probably written during the time of the Diet of Speyer in 1529.

The life and work of Martin Luther are available in numerous books. Here we will present a brief outline of some of the most important events in his life. He was born at Eisleben, November 10, 1483, and received his education at the University of Erfurt (B.A., 1502, M.A. 1503). After he became an Augustinian monk in 1505, Luther was ordained priest (1507) and appointed Professor at the University of Wittenberg (1508). In 1517 he published the famous *95 Theses* which heralded open conflict with the pope. He attended the Diet of Worms in 1521, and translated the Bible into German, a task begun in 1521 and completed in 1534. The great teacher, priest, and reformer died at Eisleben on February 18, 1546. His contributions to hymnody may be summed up in such phrases as "the first evangelical hymnist," and the "Ambrose of German hymnody." Luther began writing hymns in 1523 and by 1543 had written about thirty-seven. His hymns began appearing in print in the first German evangelical hymnbook called *Achtliederbuch,* 1524, and were contained in the *Erfurt Enchiridion,* 1524, Walther's hymnbook of 1524, Klug's *Gesangbuch,* 1529, and others until Luther's death. In these books, we become aware of the steady increase in the number of German hymns in the vernacular.

The translator was a graduate of Harvard College and Divinity School. Dr. Frederick Henry Hedge (1805-1890) was a Unitarian minister who served churches in Maine, Rhode Island, and Massachusetts. During the years 1872-1876 he served Harvard as professor of church history. From 1872 to 1881 Dr. Hedge was also professor of German literature.

Dr. Hedge's version of the Luther text first appeared in Dr. W. A. Furness' *Gems of German Verse* in 1852. The following year it was included in Hedge's own *Hymns for the Church of Christ* (Boston, 1853).

The tune EIN' FESTE BURG is probably the work of Martin Luther himself. At any rate it is one of the truly great tunes of all time and has been used in every conceivable manner by composers such as Bach, Mendelssohn, and Meyerbeer. Unfortunately the manner in which many congregations sing it today robs it of much of its rhythmic force and interest.

RICHTER 8.4.7.8.4.7.

> *Seele, du musst munter werden*
> Friedrich von Canitz, 1654-1699
> Tr. Henry J. Buckoll, 1803-1871
> J. A. Freylinghausen's *Geistreiches Gesang-
> Buch,* 1704

The hymn beginning with the words *"Seele, du musst mun-
ter werden"* was written by the well-known and beloved poet, officer of
the court, philanthropist, and diplomat, Friedrich Rudolph Ludwig
von Canitz. Born in Berlin, November 27, 1654, he was educated at the
Universities of Leyden and Leipzig. He traveled Europe extensively
with and as an envoy of Elector Friedrich Wilhelm and was made a
baron by Emperor Leopold I in 1698. Tragedy plagued him with the
loss of six children, his wife, and a fire which destroyed his home. He
died at the age of 44, August 11, 1699. His hymns were published posthumously and without his name in 1700 in *Nebenstunden unterschied-
ner Gedichte,* a work edited by Joachim Lange.

This hymn appeared as an anonymous translation in English in the
British Magazine, July, 1838. Authorities now accept Henry James
Buckoll as the translator. Its second appearance in slightly altered form
was in Buckoll's *Hymns Translated from the German,* 1842. Buckoll
was born at Siddington, England, September 9, 1803, and died at
Rugby, June 6, 1871. He was educated at Rugby and Queens College,
Oxford, taking his M.A. in 1826 and the same year became assistant
headmaster of Rugby.

The tune name is that of one C. F. Richter, author of the hymn
"Meine Armuth macht mich schreien" with which the tune appeared
in Johann Anastasius Freylinghausen's *Geist-reiches Gesang-Buch,*
1704. This book contained 683 hymns and 173 tunes. The composer of
this tune is unknown.

Freylinghausen was born at Gandersheim, December 2, 1670. He
was a pastor, private tutor, hymn writer (forty-four of his hymns
were published in *Geistliche Lieder* in 1855), composer, (about twenty-
two tunes), and compiler. His fame rests primarily on his compilations,
Geist-reiches Gesang-Buch, 1704, and *Neues Geist-reiches Gesang-
Buch,* 1714. From 1695 Freylinghausen was associated with A. H.
Francke as his assistant at Glaucha, his colleague at St. Ulrich's, Halle,
and his son-in-law, 1715. He became subdirector of the Paedagogium
and Orphanage in 1723 and after Francke's death assumed full re-

sponsibility for both the church and institutions. In 1728 he had the first of a series of strokes which finally claimed him on February 12, 1739. As a hymn writer he has been called the "best of the Pietistic school" and "first among his contemporaries" (Julian p. 396).

33 *God the Omnipotent*

RUSSIAN HYMN 11.10.11.9.

Sts. 1, 2 Henry F. Chorley, 1808-1872
St. 3 John Ellerton, 1826-1893
Alexis Lvov, 1799-1870

Written in 1842 and beginning "God the All-Terrible" this hymn has undergone obvious revision and addition. The first two stanzas are from the pen of Henry Fothergill Chorley who was a well-known English literary and music critic. Chorley was born at Blackley, Lancashire, England, December 15, 1808, and died in 1872. From 1830 he was the musical editor for *The Athenaeum* and during his final years held the similar position for *The Times*. The hymn first appeared in John Hullah's *Part Music,* 1842, and bore the title "In Time of War." His literary interests brought him into contact with the leading literary figures of his time, and he counted Charles Dickens as one of his closest friends.

The third stanza given here is from John Ellerton's hymn, "God, the Almighty One, Wisely Ordaining" which was written several days before the Battle of Sedan in the Franco-German War.

For a note on Ellerton see No. 231.

RUSSIAN HYMN is so named from its history as the former Russian National Hymn composed by Alexis Lvov at the request of Emperor Nicholas I. It was composed for "God Save the Czar" in 1833.

Alexis Lvov, the son of the conductor of the imperial choir at St. Petersburg, was born June 6, 1798, and died December 28, 1870. He was an amateur violinist and composer who became a major-general in the Russian Army and adjutant to the Emperor. Upon the death of his father he became the conductor of the court choir, a position he held from 1836 to 1855. Lvov composed several unsuccessful operas, a quantity of excellent liturgical music and violin concerti. Deafness forced him to withdraw from all musical activities in 1867. His fame rests today solely on this tune.

34 God Hath Spoken

HYMN TO JOY 8.7.8.7.D.

George Wallace Briggs, 1875-1959
Arr. from Ludwig van Beethoven, 1770-1827

As one of the founders of the British Hymn Society of Great Britain and Ireland, Briggs gave evidence of his deep interest in the hymnody of the church. He was the author of many hymns, composed hymn tunes, and published several volumes of prayers and hymns. He collaborated with Percy Dearmer, Vaughan Williams, and Martin Shaw in the publication of several hymnbooks based on *Songs of Praise,* 1925. In 1945 Briggs published *Songs of Faith* in which the present hymn appears.

George Wallace Briggs was born December 15, 1875, at Nottingham. He was educated at Emmanuel College, Cambridge, and served successively as a chaplain in the Royal Navy, vicar of St. Andrew's, Norwich, rector of Loughborough College, canon of Leicester, and from 1934 to 1956 as canon of Worcester. One of his prayers was a part of the ceremony on the occasion of the historic meeting of President Franklin D. Roosevelt and Prime Minister Winston Churchill aboard the H.M.S. *Prince of Wales,* August 10, 1941, at which time the Atlantic Charter was adopted.

For a comment on HYMN TO JOY and Ludwig Van Beethoven see No. 1.

35 How Firm a Foundation

FOUNDATION 11.11.11.11.

"K" in Rippons *Selection of Hymns,* 1787
Early American Melody
Harm. Charles H. Heaton, 1928-

This might be called the "mystery hymn" since there is no positive identification of the original source of either text or tune. The text first appears in the John Rippon's, *A Selection of Hymns from the best authors,* London, 1787. At the time Rippon was pastor of the Carter Lane Chapel, London. The author of the hymn was listed simply as "K" which has been interpreted to mean Keen, Keith, or Kirkham. Robert Keene was the precentor of the Carter Lane Church and may have composed several tunes for Rippon's *Selection,* but it is considered unlikely he would have contributed this one text. Whatever its origin or whoever its author, the hymn has enjoyed great popularity in America for over a hundred years and has been the favorite hymn of such notables as Andrew Jackson, Theodore Roosevelt, and Robert E. Lee.

The tune FOUNDATION is also called BELLEVUE in *The Sacred Harp*, 1844, and in its revised and enlarged edition of 1911. William Jensen Reynolds in his *Hymns of Our Faith, A Handbook for the Baptist Hymnal*, 1964, informs us that the tune's first appearance was apparently in William Caldwell's *Union Harmony*, 1837. It is generally agreed now that the tune is definitely of "folk" origin, probably from Southeastern United States.

The present harmonization is the work of Charles Huddleston Heaton, editor of the *Hymnbook for Christian Worship*. Dr. Heaton is organist and choirmaster at the Second Presbyterian Church, and Director of Music at Eden Theological Seminary, Saint Louis, Missouri. He has contributed significant leadership to the musical life of the Christian Churches, Disciples of Christ, especially to the Association of Disciples Musicians.

He was born at Centralia, Illinois, November 1, 1928. He was educated at DePauw University, Greencastle, Indiana (B. Mus. 1950) and the School of Sacred Music of Union Theological Seminary (M.S.M., 1952; D.S.M., 1957) in New York City. From 1952-1954 he served in the United States Army. He became a Fellow of the American Guild of Organists in 1957.

Dr. Heaton is the author of two books, *How to Build a Church Choir*, 1958, and *A Guidebook to Worship Services of Sacred Music*, 1962, and has contributed articles to various magazines, including *The Christian, Pulpit*, and *The Diapason*. In 1969 he became a book reviewer for *Music/The A.G.O. Magazine*, and has served a term as a National Councilor for the American Guild of Organists.

36 *Father, Lead Me Day by Day*

ORIENTIS PARTIBUS 7.7.7.7.

John Page Hopps, 1834-1912
Adapted from Pierre de Corbeil, *d.* 1222

The author published this hymn under the heading "Child's Prayer for Divine Guidance" in his *Hymns, Chants and Anthems for Public Worship*, 1877. Hopps was born November 6, 1834, in London and studied for the Baptist ministry at the Baptist College, Leicester. After completing his work there he served the Baptists for two years and then was drawn into the Unitarian movement. He was the editor of a monthly magazine called, *The Truthseeker*, editor of several hymnals in which he included his own work, and the author of many books and pamphlets. Hopps died at Shepperton, Middlesex, in 1912.

Omitted stanzas are:

> When my work seems hard and dry,
> May I press on cheerily:
> Help me patiently to bear
> Pain and hardship, toil and care.

> May I see the good and bright,
> When they pass before my sight:
> May I hear the heavenly voice,
> When the pure and wise rejoice.

The tune name is the first line of an old carol called the "Hymn of the Ass" which began *"Orientis Partibus adventavit asinus"* which has been translated "From the eastern regions the Ass is now come." The piece has been traced to a prose believed to have been written by Pierre de Corbeil, Archbishop of Sens and is found in a manuscript in the library of Sens. It appears also in a similar manuscript in the British Museum. The story deals with the flight of Mary and Joseph into Egypt and was not intended as a parody. Traditionally the piece was dramatized at Beauvais at the festival known as the Feast of the Ass on January 14.

The tune has been adapted to various meters but its most popular form is in three which seems more in keeping with the dance rhythm of many of the early carols.

37   God of the Moving Years

CENTRALIA 6.6.12.6.6.6.6.6.4.

Kenneth I. Morse, 1913-

George Brandon, 1924-, based on a tune in *The Christian Psalmist,* revised (1854)

This hymn appeared in *The Brethren Hymnal,* 1951. According to Mrs. Ruth B. Statler, a Brethren historian, poet, and biographer, Mr. Morse was inspired to write the hymn as a result of the work he was doing on the hymnal.

Kenneth I. Morse was born in Altoona, Pennsylvania, in 1913. He was educated at Juniata College, Huntingdon, Pennsylvania (A.B.) and Pennsylvania State College, (M.A., 1940) and also studied at Princeton University and Bethany Theological Seminary. He is active in the Church of the Brethren and has served on the editorial staff of the Brethren General Board and was one of the editors of *The Brethren Hymnal,* 1951, in which six of his hymns appeared. He has been the editor of *Messenger,* the official organ of the Church of the Brethren, since 1950.

CENTRALIA was named by the composer after Centralia, Illinois. Mr. Brandon writes that he made the arrangement in 1966 for the *Hymnbook for Christian Worship* from an anonymous tune called REDEMPTION which he found in an old Disciples' book, *The Christian Psalmist,* revised edition, 1854, by Silas W. Leonard. Centralia, Illinois, was the home of Silas W. Leonard from 1856 until his death in 1870.

For a comment on George Brandon see No. 11.

38   *The Day Thou Gavest, Lord, Is Ended*

ST. CLEMENT 9.8.9.8.

John Ellerton, 1826-1893
Clement C. Scholefield, 1839-1904

Written in 1870 for *A Liturgy for Missionary Meetings,* it was revised the following year and appeared in *Church Hymns* (S.P.C.K.). Queen Victoria requested its use for her Diamond Jubilee in 1897.

For a comment on John Ellerton see No. 231.

ST. CLEMENT was composed for this text and was published in *Church Hymns with Tunes,* 1874. The composer probably had no ulterior motive for so naming the tune.

Clement Cotterill Scholefield, English clergyman, was born June 22, 1839, at Edgbaston (Birmingham). He was educated at Pocklington, Yorkshire, and St. John's, Cambridge. After his ordination in 1867 he was curate at Hove and St. Luke's, Chelsea. For ten years, between 1880 and 1890, he was Eton's chaplain. For a brief period he was associated with Arthur Sullivan at St. Peter's Church, Kensington, during which time Sullivan was the musical editor of *Church Hymns,* 1874. Scholefield died September 10, 1904, at Godalming.

39 *The Day Thou Gavest, Lord, Is Ended*

LES COMMANDEMENS DE DIEU 9.8.9.8.

John Ellerton, 1826-1893
Attr. to Louis Bourgeois, c. 1510-1561
Genevan Psalter, 1543

For a note on this hymn see No. 38.

For a note on John Ellerton see No.231.

LES COMMANDMENS DE DIEU is the tune used for Clément Marot's metrical version of the Ten Commandments in an early edition of the *Genevan Psalter.* As in the case of numerous other tunes from these Psalters the name of the composer remains in doubt. Most authorities say it was composed or adapted by Louis Bourgeois. Conflicting dates are given for the specific edition of the *Genevan Psalter* in which it is found, varying from 1540 to 1547 [Lightwood gives French Psalter, 1540; Dearmer and Jacob, 1543; Rowander and Porter, 1547]. The tune appeared in many later psalters and was introduced into England in *One and Fiftie Psalmes,* 1556 edition.

For a comment on Louis Bourgeois see No. 412.

40 *The Lord's My Shepherd*

CRIMOND C.M.

Based on Psalm 23
Scottish Psalter, 1650, alt.
Melody by Jessie S. Irvine, 1836-1887

This is said to be a composite version of Psalm 23. In 1641 Francis Rous published a paraphrase of the Psalm which found favor with and was altered by the Westminster Assembly, 1646. This form was again revised by a committee of the Church of Scotland and published in *The Psalms of David in Meeter* or the *Scottish Psalter* of 1650. It is probably accurate to say the authorship of this version is unknown. Like the *Genevan Psalter,* the *Scottish Psalter* passed through many editions after its beginning in 1564. The 1650 edition of the *Scottish Psalter* has been cited as a classic in English Protestant literature, taking its place beside the *King James Version of the Bible* and *The Book of Common Prayer.*

CRIMOND was attributed to David Grant (1833-1893) when it first appeared in *The Northern Psalter,* 1872. It is now generally agreed that Jessie Seymour Irvine composed the melody in 1871 and that it was harmonized by Grant. "Crimond" was the name of the parish in Aberdeenshire where Miss Irvine's father ministered for many years.

Jessie Seymour Irvine was born at Dunotter, Scotland, in 1836. She accompanied her father to Peterhead and to Crimond. She probably died at Crimond in 1887.

David Grant (1833-1893) was a friend of Williams Carnie, editor of *The Northern Psalter,* 1872. He was the proprieter of a tobacco shop and an amateur musician and is known today for his two tunes, CRIMOND and RALEIGH.

41 *The Lord's My Shepherd*

EVAN C.M.

From Psalm 23
Scottish Psalter, 1650
William H. Havergal, 1793-1870

For a note on this text see No. 40.

EVAN was originally composed for Burns' poem "O Thou Dread Power Who Reigns't Above" and was published in 1847. The tune was arranged by Lowell Mason who published it under the name of "Eva" in *New Carmina Sacra,* 1850. Havergal disapproved of Mason's arrangement and subsequently reworked the tune himself in 1846. Mason's version has remained the popular arrangement in America.

For a note on William H. Havergal see No. 94.

42   O God, in Whom We Live and Move

SALVATION CMD

George Wallace Briggs, 1875-1959

Ananias Davisson's *Kentucky Harmony*, c. 1815

This hymn was written for *Songs of Praise,* 1931.

For a comment on the author see No. 34.

SALVATION has been ascribed to one Robert Boyd and was one of the popular melodies of the early years of the nineteenth century in the South. It found a place in a number of the early American songbooks and appeared in several forms set to a variety of texts. The present form is from Ananias Davisson's *Kentucky Harmony* which was published *circa* 1815 in Harrisonburg, Virginia. In his *White Spirituals in the Southern Uplands,* 1964 (reprint of the 1933 edition, p. 30) George Pullen Jackson calls this book and its *Supplement,* 1820, "pioneer repositories of a sort of song that the rural south really liked."

Ananias Davisson was born February 2, 1780, somewhere in northern Virginia. He was a ruling elder in the Presbyterian Church, a singing-school master, compiler and sometimes printer of songbooks. He died near Wyer's Cave, Virginia, on October 21, 1857, and was buried in the cemetery of Union Church near the town of Dayton, Virginia.

43   God Be with You Till We Meet Again

RANDOLPH 9.8.8.9.

Jeremiah E. Rankin, 1828-1904

R. Vaughan Williams, 1872-1958

This familiar hymn was written by Jeremiah E. Rankin while he was the pastor of the First Congregational Church in Washington, D. C., a position he held for fifteen years. Before being called to the pastorate in the Capital City, Rankin had graduated from Andover Theological Seminary and served Congregational churches in New York, Vermont, and Massachusetts. According to the author, the hymn was not written for any specific occasion, but rather to show the derivation of the word "good-bye" from the phrase "God be with you." It was published in his *Gospel Bells,* 1883. Rankin was also president of Howard University, Washington, D. C. for a number of years.

RANDOLF was composed for this tune by Ralph Vaughan Williams and published in the *English Hymnal,* 1906. According to the instructions in that book the first two and the last two measures should be sung in unison. All the rest should be sung in harmony.

For a comment on the composer see No. 98.

44 *God Be with You Till We Meet Again*

GOD BE WITH YOU 9.8.8.9.

Jeremiah E. Rankin, 1828-1904
William G. Tomer, 1832-1896

For a note on the author of this hymn see No. 43.

GOD BE WITH YOU is the tune commonly sung to this text in American churches. Here it is improved by the omission of the refrain. Rankin requested the composer, who was then in charge of music at the Grace Methodist Episcopal Church, in Washington, D. C., to set his text to music when it was first introduced to the First Congregational Church in Washington, D. C. This was the tune Rankin used in his *Gospel Bells,* 1883.

William G. Tomer seems to have had scant musical training other than that received in public schools and practical experience singing in choirs. He was a school teacher in New Jersey, served as a Union Army soldier during the Civil War under General Oliver O. Howard, after whom Washington's Howard University was named. Tomer worked in Washington as a clerk in the Treasury Department and also as a newspaperman. After seventeen years in Washington he returned to New Jersey and became editor of the *Hunterdon Gazette.* He died in New Jersey in 1896.

45 *He Leadeth Me, O Blessed Thought*

HE LEADETH ME L.M. with Refrain

Joseph H. Gilmore, 1834-1918
William B. Bradbury, 1816-1868

Following his lecture on Psalm 23 at the First Baptist Church, Philadelphia, in 1863, Joseph Henry Gilmore continued his reflection on the idea of God's leadership, took pen in hand, and wrote this well-known text as it now stands and handed it to his wife. Without his knowledge she submitted it to *The Watchman and Reflector* in which it was first published with the title, "He Leadeth Me Beside Still Waters."

Gilmore was a prominent Baptist minister, preacher, teacher, and author. He was born at Boston, April 29, 1834, and died at Rochester, July 23, 1918. He received his education at Phillips Academy, Andover, Massachusetts, Brown University, and Newton Theological Seminary. Following his graduation from Newton he remained at the seminary for one year teaching Hebrew. The following year he was ordained and began a pastorate at Fisherville, New Hampshire. From 1863 to 1865 his father was governor of New Hampshire and Gilmore served as his private secretary. During this period he also served as editor of *The Concord Daily Monitor*.

He became the pastor of the Second Baptist Church, Rochester, New York, in 1865. After two years he became acting professor of Hebrew at the Rochester Theological Seminary. In 1868 he was appointed professor of logic, rhetoric, and English literature at the University of Rochester, a position he held until his retirement in 1911.

William Batchelder Bradbury read this text in *The Watchman and Reflector* and composed this tune for it. It was published in one of Bradbury's collections of Sunday school hymns and tunes, *The Golden Censer*, 1864. Bradbury wrote most of his tunes for use with children in the Sunday schools of America and never intended them to be used in public worship. He is sometimes called the originator of this particular style of religious song and set the pattern for the flood of "Gospel Song" tunes which became so popular from 1860 onward.

William Bradbury, a native of York, Maine, was born October 6, 1816. After his family moved to Boston in 1830 he studied music at the Boston Academy of Music and sang under the leadership of Lowell Mason at the Bowdoin Street Church. While at Boston he studied under Sumner Hill and Lowell Mason. In 1840 he became the organist for the First Baptist Church, Brooklyn, but the following year took up his duties as organist of the Baptist Tabernacle in New York City. His free singing classes were organized after the pattern of those conducted by Lowell Mason in Boston and led to the introduction of music in the curriculum of the New York public schools.

From 1847 to 1849, he and his family lived in Leipzig, Germany, where he studied under Hauptmann, Moscheles, and Böhme. Upon his return to the United States and until 1854 he taught, wrote, and conducted musical conventions. In 1854 he helped form a piano manufacturing company which became a part of the Knabe firm in 1917.

Bradbury edited more than fifty collections of music and composed numerous tunes for his collections. Missionaries have taken his songs to the far corners of the earth. He died at Montclair, New Jersey, January 7, 1868.

Lead, Kindly Light

SANDON 10.4.10.4.10.10.

John H. Newman, 1801-1890
Charles H. Purday, 1799-1885

This hymn was written aboard an orange boat bound from Palermo to Marseilles and during a week it was becalmed in the Straits of Bonifacio. Newman gives the date as June 16, 1833. The hymn was the result of his deep concern over the state of the church in general and the English church specifically. He was ill, homesick, and struggling for an inner peace. It was first published in *The British Magazine,* March, 1834, and became one of the finest of the nineteenth-century hymns.

Born in London on February 21, 1801, John Henry Newman was educated at Trinity College, Oxford, took Holy Orders in 1824, and for a time was Vice-Principal of St. Alban's Hall and Tutor of Oriel. He was appointed to serve St. Mary's Church, Oxford, in the spring of 1828. Newman was a close friend of John Keble and others connected with the Oxford Movement, a contributor to the Tractarian Movement through the *Tracts for the Times,* all of which led to his resignation from the Church of England and association with the Roman Catholic Church. In 1848 Newman became Father Superior of the Oratory of St. Philip Neri in Birmingham and in 1879 became a Cardinal. Cardinal Newman wrote considerable verse but the present hymn is one of the few that has been universally adopted. He translated a number of Latin hymns from the *Roman* and *Paris Brevaries* which were published as *Hymni Ecclesiae* in 1838 and 1865. He died at Birmingham in 1890.

For a note on SANDON and Charles Purday see No. 28.

47 *Abide with Me, Fast Falls the Eventide*

EVENTIDE 10.10.10.10.

Henry Francis Lyte, 1793-1847
William Henry Monk, 1823-1889

The author of this hymn was born at Ednam, Scotland, on June 1, 1793. Orphaned at an early age he knew sorrow, poverty, and ill health most of his life. Despite his many handicaps he struggled for an education and was graduated from Trinity College, Dublin, in 1814.

His early ambition was to become a doctor of medicine but during his college years decided in favor of theology and the ministry. After taking Holy Orders in the Church of England in 1815 he served parishes in Wexford, Marazion, Lymington, finally settling in Lower Brixham, Devonshire, where he served until September 4, 1847. He died at Nice, France, on November 20, 1847.

Lyte wrote more than eighty hymns and paraphrases of Psalms. Compilers have drawn the majority of his work from his Poems Chiefly Religion (1833) and Spirit of the Psalms (1834). The best-known hymns in use today are: "Abide with Me," "Jesus, I My Cross Have Taken," "Praise My Soul the King of Heaven," "Praise the Lord, His Glories Show," "Pleasant Are Thy Courts Above," "God of Mercy, God of Grace," "Far from My Heavenly Home," and "When at Thy Footstool, Lord, I bend."

"Abide with Me" is by far his best-known hymn. The circumstances surrounding its writing are uncertain. Two stories persist. The first tells us that he wrote it after visiting a dying friend who was a fellow clergyman by the name of William Augustus Le Hunte in 1820. It is said that his friend kept repeating the words "abide with me, abide with me," and when Lyte left him he closeted himself and wrote the hymn. The second story is that Lyte composed the hymn after his final service with the congregation of the Brixham church. He was preparing to leave for southern Europe in order to improve his health and in the afternoon he and his wife walked down to the water's edge to watch a particularly beautiful sunset.

Whatever the circumstances, the hymn is one of great beauty. Both stories show us clearly that Lyte was not contemplating the evening of the day but rather the evening of life. The hymn is not particularly appropriate for evening services unless certain stanzas are ommitted.

Stanzas not to be found in our hymnal are:

3. Not a brief glance I beg, a passing word,
   But as thou dwell'st with thy disciples, Lord.
   Familiar, condescending, patient, free,
   Come not to sojourn, but abide with me,

4. Come not in terrors, as the King of kings,
   But kind and good, with healing in thy wings:
   Tears for all woes, a heart for every plea.
   Come, Friend of sinners, thus abide with me.

5. Thou on my head in early youth didst smile,
   And though rebellious and perverse meanwhile,

Thou hast not left me, oft as I left thee.
On to the close, O Lord, abide with me.

7. I fear no foe with thee on hand to bless;
   Ills have no weight and tears no bitterness.
   Where is death's sting? where, grave, thy victory?
   I triumph still if thou abide with me.

Lyte also composed a tune for the hymn, but it is awkward both harmonically and melodically. The Lyte tune can be found in H. Augustine Smith's *Lyric Religion* (p. 8). Frederick Cook Atkinson (1841-1897) composed the tune Morecambe for his text in 1880 but it never replaced the tune Eventide to which it is almost universally sung today.

EVENTIDE was composed by William Henry Monk (1823-1889) in 1861. It was written specifically for this text for inclusion in the famous *Hymns Ancient and Modern*. Monk was the musical editor of *Hymns Ancient and Modern* and felt that the hymn needed a better tune. His tune was composed in a matter of ten minutes following a committee meeting concerned with the new hymnal. Monk's widow presented a different version of its composition. She said the tune was composed immediately after she and her husband watched a sunset "in a time of great sorrow."

William Henry Monk, born at Brompton in 1823, was an organist, choirmaster, composer, editor of hymnbooks, professor of vocal music, and lecturer, who is remembered today as the first musical editor of *Hymns Ancient and Modern,* and for his influence on the quality of hymnbooks from that time to this. He was organist at St. Matthias, Stoke Newington, and at the same time organist-choirmaster at King's College, London. In 1874 he became professor of vocal music at King's College and two years later professor at the National Training School for Music and at Bedford College, London. He died at Stoke Newington in 1889.

48 *Before Jehovah's Aweful Throne*

WINCHESTER NEW L.M.

Based on Psalm 100
Isaac Watts, 1674-1748
Adapted from *Musicalisches Handbuch,* Hamburg, 1960

Isaac Watts' contributions to English hymnody cannot be adequately described in the space allotted here. Suffice it to say that his influence on hymnody was felt throughout the history of congregational praise in both England and America up to the present.

Watts was born at Southampton, July 17, 1674. His father was a devout Nonconformist who suffered imprisonment several times for his deep religious convictions. The young Watts followed his father's footsteps by refusing a university education which would have ultimately led to his ordination in the Church of England. He choose rather to enter a Nonconformist academy. Upon completion of his academic work he became a tutor to the son of a Puritan. He began preaching at the age of twenty-four years and was eventually ordained as pastor of the Mark Lane church in 1702, a stronghold of the Independents. He was honored by the University of Aberdeen and University of Edinburgh in 1728 when he was granted a Doctor of Divinity degree. His interests included all facets of church worship, praise, and theological pursuits and philosophy as well as other academic disciplines. His book, *Logic,* was used as a text for a number of years at Oxford.

Although he remained a Nonconformist throughout his life, a monument was erected in his honor at Westminster Abbey. Isaac Watts died at Stoke Newington November 25, 1748. H. Leigh Bennett writing in Julian's *Dictionary of Hymnology* says of him: "His learning and piety, gentleness and largeness of heart have earned him the title of the Melanchthon (Phillip, 1497-1560, German Lutheran reformer and scholar) of his day" [p. 1236].

"Before Jehovah's Aweful Throne" is a version of Psalm 100, and was originally embodied in Watts' *Psalms of David,* 1719. John Wesley altered it somewhat for use in the hymnbook he published in Charles Town, South Carolina, 1737. The original first stanza has been omitted for obvious reasons. It reads:

> Sing to the Lord with joyful voice.
> Let every land his name adore;
> The British Isles shall send the noise
> Across the ocean to the shore.

WINCHESTER NEW was originally a German Chorale tune to which Georg Neumark's text *"Wer nur den lieben Gott lässt walten"* was sung. John Wesley is credited with its introduction into English hymnody through his *Foundry Tune Book,* 1742. William H. Havergal utilized it in approximately the present form in his *Old Church Psalmody,* 1847. Since its appearance in early English hymnals its popularity has continued to grow and is now generally found in many modern hymnals. It has been variously called SWIFT GERMAN TUNE, FRANKFORT, WINCHESTER TUNE, CRASSELIUS, and BARRE.

49   *The King of Love My Shepherd Is*

DOMINUS REGIT ME 8.7.8.7.

Based on Psalm 23
Henry W. Baker, 1821-1877
John B. Dykes, 1823-1876

Written for the appendix to the first edition of *Hymns Ancient and Modern,* 1868, this hymn is an interesting rendering of Psalm 23. Note the allusion to the parable of the lost sheep in the third stanza and the use of the word "cross" in stanza four.

For a comment on Henry W. Baker see No. 209.

DOMINUS REGIT ME are the first three words of Psalm 22, Vulgate version of the Scriptures. John B. Dykes composed the music for Baker's text for use in the appendix to *Hymns Ancient and Modern,* 1868.

For a note on John B. Dykes see No. 195.

50   *With Broken Heart and Contrite Sigh*

BABYLON'S STREAMS L.M.

Cornelius Elven, 1797-1873
Thomas Campian, 1567-1620

This Lenten hymn was written by Cornelius Elven for use at special services with his own congregation in January of 1852. It was first published in the English Baptist hymnal, *Psalms and Hymns,* 1858. The hymn is based on Luke 18:13.

Cornelius Elven was born February 12, 1797, at Bury St. Edmunds, Suffolk, England, where he lived his entire life and died on August 10, 1873. His family were members of the Congregational Church but he became a Baptist at the age of twenty-four. When the pastor of the Baptist church retired in 1823, Elvin was ordained and ministered to the congregation for the following fifty years. He was a close and beloved friend of Charles H. Spurgeon.

BABYLON'S STREAMS was composed for voice, lute, and viola and set to a metrical version of Psalm 137 in Thomas Campian's *First*

Booke of Ayres, c. 1601. This is, of course, a much altered form of the melody. The name became associated with the tune in Gawthorn's *Harmonia Perfecta,* 1730.

Thomas Campian (or Campion), English physician, composer, dramatist, and poet, was born in London, February 12, 1567. He studied at Cambridge but did not take a degree. He lived abroad for several years and upon his return entered the medical profession. No record of his education for this vocation has been found, but by 1602 he was calling himself a Doctor of Physic. His principal contribution to the world was his musical compositions which consisted primarily of songs or airs and songs for masques. He died in London on March 1, 1620.

51   If Thou but Suffer God to Guide Thee

WER NUR DEN LIEBEN GOTT 9.8.9.8.8.8.

Georg Neumark, 1621-1681
Tr. Catherine Winkworth, 1827-1878
Georg Neumark, 1621-1681

This is considered to be the best of Neumark's thirty-four hymns. The author's life seems to have been beset by troubles and misfortunes. He was born in Langensalza on March 16, 1621, and received his early education at Schleusingen and Gotha. His ambition in life was to attend the University at Königsberg and study for a career in law. He joined a group of travelers for the purpose of reaching the University but along the way they were set upon by robbers and Neumark was relieved of all his possessions except his prayer book and a bit of money which was sewn in his clothing. The following months were spent in wandering and seeking work, food, and shelter. Destitute he moved from one city to another without finding relief from his plight until he finally arrived in Kiel where he found employment as tutor to the family of Judge Stephan Henning. It was the sudden and unexpected change in his fortune that prompted him to write this hymn. His title reads, "A Song of Comfort." God will care for and help everyone in his own time. "Cast thy burden on the Lord, and he will sustain thee" (Psalm 55:22). After saving enough money to matriculate at the University, Neumark made his way to Königsberg and began his study of law on June 21, 1643.

During his five years at Königsberg disaster struck again in the form of a fire which destroyed everything he owned. Once more he was destitute, but managed to complete his work. Afterward, unable to find work, he moved from city to city until he came to Weimar where he eventually received an appointment as court poet, librarian, registrar, and ultimately, secretary of the Ducal Archives. Blindness struck him in 1681 and he died at Weimar on July 18 of that year.

The present translation is that of Catherine Winkworth who included it in her *Chorale Book for England,* 1863.

For a note on Miss Winkworth see No. 58.

The name of the tune is taken from the opening words of Neumark's hymn. The tune itself is attributed to Neumark who published it in his *Fortgepflantzter musikalisch-poetischer Lustwald,* Jena, 1657. The melody has been used extensively by compilers of hymnbooks, by J. S. Bach in various contatas and organ books, and by Mendelssohn in his oratorio, *St. Paul.*

For a note on the composer see above.

52 Depth of Mercy

HEINLEIN 7.7.7.7.

Charles Wesley, 1707-1788
Attr. to Martin Herbst, c. 1654-1681

This text was first published in Wesley's *Hymns and Sacred Poems,* 1740, in thirteen stanzas of four lines under the heading "After a Relapse into Sin."

For a note on Charles Wesley see No. 180.

The tune name is from that of one Paul Heinlein, 1626-1686, a composer who lived in Nuremberg, Germany, who at one time was credited with the composition of the tune. The tune came from the *Nürnbergisches Gesangbuch,* 1676, where the composer is indicated as M. H., which is believed to be Martin Herbst of whom there is no record as a musician. In his short lifetime Herbst was pastor of St. Andreas' Church in Eisleben. He was born in Nürnberg and studied in Altdorf and Jena. His life was cut short by the plague in 1681.

53   *Day is Dying in the West*

CHAUTAUQUA 7.7.7.7.4. with Refrain

Mary A. Lathbury, 1841-1913
William F. Sherwin, 1826-1888

This beautiful vesper hymn was written in 1880 for the vesper services held at Chautauqua Institute. The original contained two stanzas but two others were added later at the insistence of the author's many friends. Here we are using only the first and fourth stanzas.

For a note on the author see No. 327.

The tune is named for the famous Chautauqua Institute at Chautauqua, New York, where both author and composer were employed during the summer seasons for many years.

For a note on the composer see No. 327.

54   *All Creatures of Our God and King*

LASST UNS ERFREUEN 8.8.4.4.8.8. with Alleluias

St. Francis of Assisi, 1182-1226
Tr. William Henry Draper, 1855-1933

Melody from *Geistliche Kirchengesäng*, 1623
Harm. and Arr. R. Vaughan Williams, 1872-1958

This hymn is based on the St. Francis canticle variously known as "Cantico del Sole," "Cantico della Creature," and "Sun Song." St. Francis, the founder of the Franciscan Order, wrote his canticle in the final years of his life when extremely ill and almost blind. Its spirit is closely akin to Psalm 145.

The translator, William Henry Draper, was born at Kenilworth, Warwickshire, December 19, 1855. He was educated at Cheltenham College and Keble College, Oxford. After being ordained in 1880 he served churches in Shrewsbury, Alfreton, Leeds, and Somerset, as curate, vicar, and rector. For a time he was Master of the Temple in London.

"All Creatures of our God and King" was written especially for the school children's Whitsuntide Festival while he was rector of Adel, Leeds. When someone asked him about the date it was written, the author said he could not remember.

Dr. Draper translated other hymns from the Greek and published *The Victoria Book of Hymns* (1897), *Hymns for Holy Week* (1898), and *Hymns for Tunes by Orlando Gibbons* (1925). He died at Clifton, Bristol, August 9, 1933.

The name of the tune, LASST UNS ERFREUEN, is derived from the first line of the Easter hymn with which it appeared in Brachel's *Geistliche Kirchengesäng* (1623). The composer is unknown. It is also known by the names EASTER ALLELUYA, and VIGILES ET SANCTI. The tune has become popular in the United States and is practically always used with "All Creatures of Our God and King." It is also used for Watts' "From All that Dwell Below the Skies" and Riley's "Ye Watchers and Ye Holy Ones."

For a comment on R. Vaughan Williams see No. 98.

55   *O God, We Praise Thee, and Confess*

TALLIS' ORDINAL C.M.

Based on *Te Deum Laudamus*, 5th century?
A Supplement to the New Version, 1700, alt.
Thomas Tallis, c. 1505-1585

Legend attributes the *Te Deum Laudamus* to Sts. Ambrose and Augustine. Some scholars, however, are inclined to discredit this story by saying it is a composite hymn of unknown origin and authorship while others ascribe it to Niceta, Bishop of Remesiana from 392 until 414. Whatever its origin it is one of the earliest and perhaps the most famous of the Latin hymns.

The present anonymous metrical paraphrase of the first part of the English prose translation of the *Te Deum* appeared in the *Supplement to the New Version*, circa 1700. Julian suggests it was a rewritten form of the same hymn found in Dr. J. Paterick's *Psalmes of David in Metre, etc.*, 1679.

The term "New Version" refers to the *New Version of the Psalms of David*, etc. published by Nahum Tate (1652-1715) and Nicholas Brady (1659-1726) in contrast to the "Old Version" published by Sternhold and Hopkins in 1562. The latter version was the first metrical psalter published in England.

TALLIS' ORDINAL was the last of nine tunes composed in four parts which appeared at the end of Matthew Parker's *The Whole Psalter translated into English Meter, which contaynes an hundred and fifty Psalmes,* circa 1561. Originally it was set to the ordination hymn

VENI CREATOR SPIRITUS. The tune may have been based on the carol tune set to THIS ENDRIS NYGHT. (For comparison see *The Oxford Book of Carols*, No. 39.)

For a comment on Thomas Tallis see No. 68.

56 *Praise the Lord, His Glories Show*

GWALCHMAI 7.7.7.7. with Alleluias

Henry F. Lyte, 1793-1847
Joseph D. Jones, 1827-1870

"Praise the Lord, His Glories Show" is Lyte's paraphrase of Psalm 150 which appeared in his *Spirit of the Psalms*, 1834. The Alleluias were added to fit the tune LLANFAIR to which the text is often sung in England.

For a note on Henry Francis Lyte see No. 47

GWALCHMAI was composed by Joseph David Jones and published in Stephen's *Llyfr, Tonau ac Emynau,* 1868.

Joseph David Jones, a Welsh amateur musician, was born in 1827. He composed hymn and psalm tunes, and a cantata entitled *Llys Arthur.* His first publication, a small collection of psalm tunes entitled *Y Perganiedydd* earned enough money to take him to London for musical training. For a time he was a teacher of singing and from 1857 to 1866 taught music in the British School at Ruthier. He died September 17, 1870.

57 *Praise to the Lord, the Almighty*

LOBE DEN HERREN 14.14.4.7.8.

Joachim Neander, 1650-1680
Tr. Catherine Winkworth, 1827-1878, alt.
Stralsund Gesangbuch, 1665

Since its introduction to England about 1848 this hymn of praise has found its way into most of the major hymnbooks on both sides of the Atlantic. It is based on Psalms 103 and 150. The present translation is based primarily on that of Miss Winkworth which appeared in her *Chorale Book for England,* 1863, but contains alterations made by various hymnbook editors.

For a note on Joachim Neander see No. 20

Miss Winkworth is noted under No. 58.

LOBE DEN HERREN is Neander's adaptation of a tune which appeared in the *Stralsund Gesangbuch,* 1665, and is believed to be of secular origin. It has been associated with the above text since 1680 when they were published together in Neander's *A und Ω Glaub-und Liebesübung.* The harmonization is basically that which appeared in the *Chorale Book for England* and is the work of Sterndale Bennett and Otto Goldschmidt according to Erik Routley in *Companion to Congregational Praise,* p. 29.

58 *All Glory Be to God on High*

ALLEIN GOTT IN DER HÖH' 8.7.8.7.8.8.7.

Nikolaus Decius c. 1485-1541
Tr. Catherine Winkworth, 1827-1878, alt.

Geistliche Lieder, Leipzig, 1539
Harm. Hieronymus Praetorius, 1560-1629

Founded on the angel's song as found in Luke 2:14, and better known as the "Gloria in Excelsis," this hymn is from the Low German rendering of the text in four stanzas of seven lines by Decius which began *"Alleine God jn der höge sy ëre."* According to Julian it first appeared in the Rostock *Gesangbuch,* 1525, and later in V. Schumann's *Gesangbuch,* Leipzig, 1539. The latter was given in High German from which Miss Winkworth made her translation for the *Chorale Book for England,* 1863.

Nikolaus Decius was born at Hof in Franconia, Bavaria, circa 1485. He received his education in a Latin school at Hof and the University of Leipzig where he took his B.A. degree in 1505.

During his early years he became a monk but soon left his home for Brunswick to become the spiritual leader of the Benedictine nunnery at Steterburg. It was here that he became involved with the Lutheran movement and contributed to the cause by writing some of the first Lutheran hymns, predating those of Martin Luther himself. In 1523 he entered the University of Wittenberg in order to study theology.

Duke Bogislas of Pomerania, upon Luther's recommendation, appointed him to the position of second pastor in the town of Stettin. Shortly thereafter he was made first pastor of the Nikolaikirche, Stettin.

He remained in this position until 1527. He served briefly in Leibstadt, East Prussia, and in 1534 settled in Muehlhausen, near Elbing. This area was heavily populated with Calvinists from Holland and Decius became sympathetic to their cause and was drawn ever closer to Calvinistic thought. Walter E. Buszin has suggested that this development explains why Luther never recognized the work of Decius or ever included any of his hymns in his collections.

After moving about frequently in other positions he finally returned to Muelhausen. He died suddenly at Stettin on March 21, 1541.

Despite his restlessness and theological instability he left Protestantism two beautiful hymns which are still found in nearly every Lutheran hymnal and those of other denominations—"All Glory Be to God on High" and "O Lamb of God Most Holy."

The translator of this hymn from the German is probably the best-known English translator. Catherine Winkworth was born September 13, 1827, in London, the fourth daughter of Henry Winkworth, a silk merchant. Most of her education was received at home by governesses and private tutors. The Reverend William Gaskell and Dr. James Martineau were tutors who became lifelong friends of the Winkworth family.

After her mother's death in 1841 and her father's remarriage in 1845 she went to live briefly with an aunt in Dresden. Her stay in Germany aroused her interest in the study of German which remained with her throughout her life.

In 1853 Miss Winkworth published her first series of translation of German hymns then in common use. The series was called *Lyra Germanica*. That book became very popular in England and went through thirty editions. A second series published in 1858 enjoyed similar popularity and saw twelve editions. It was the extremely popular reception of her work that inspired William Sterndale Bennett and Otto Goldschmidt to publish in 1862 *The Chorale Book for England,* to which a supplement was added in 1865.

After 1862 when her family moved to Clifton, Miss Winkworth devoted her life to a movement promoting higher education for women. She joined the committee in 1868 and became the secretary in 1870. It was largely by her effort that a number of schools were established for women. She wrote voluminously and lectured on behalf of the cause. Miss Winkworth died suddenly of a heart attack July 1, 1878, at Monnetier in Savoy. She was buried there.

John Julian writing in his *Dictionary of Hymnology* toward the end of the nineteenth century says of her on page 1287:

> although not the earliest of modern translators from the German into English, [she] is certainly the foremost in rank and popularity. Her

translations are the most widely used of any from that language, and have had more to do with the modern revival of the English use of German hymns than the versions of any other writer.

ALLEIN GOTT IN DER HÖH' is taken from the first line of the hymn. The music is probably derived or adapted from an old Gloria tune from an Easter Mass and is attributed to Decius.

Hieronymus Praetorius, German organist and composer, was born in Hamburg on August 10, 1560, and died there on January 27, 1629. He studied under his father, Jacob Schultze. "Praetorius" is an assumed surname used by several families of German musicians and is reputed to be the latinized form of "Schultz." His first position was as town cantor at Erfurt, but he served in that capacity only briefly before becoming assistant to his father and succeeding him as organist for the church of St. James in Hamburg in 1582, where he remained until his death. H. Praetorius was a follower of the Venetian School of composition and composed numerous choral pieces for five or more voices, sometimes as many as twenty, utilizing several choirs. His major works reveal his mastery of the contrapuntal technique of the period but at the same time he could produce effectively in the more limited requirements of the chorale style. Twenty-one of his chorale settings were given in simple four-part counterpoint in the *Hamburg Meladeyen—Gesangbuch,* 1604.

59 *All Praise to Thee, for Thou, O King Divine*

NATIONAL CITY 10.10.10. with Alleluia

F. Bland Tucker, 1895-
Lawrence P. Schreiber, 1933-

This hymn was written in 1938 and was first published in *The Hymnal,* 1940.

For a note on F. Bland Tucker see No. 169.

NATIONAL CITY was composed for this hymn in 1965 for use in *Hymnbook for Christian Worship.* The tune name is derived from The National City Christian Church where Mr. Schreiber is Minister of Music.

Born in 1933, Lawrence Patrick Schreiber was educated at Texas Christian University, Fort Worth, and at the School of Sacred Music, Union Theological Seminary, New York City. Among his teachers were

Robert Baker, Margaret Hillis, Elaine Brown, and Searle Wright. His vocal solo "St. Francis' Prayer" won first prize in the Union Seminary composition contest in 1961 and it was published by Mercury (Presser) in 1964. Mr. Schreiber is active as a conductor, accompanist, organ recitalist, lecturer, and author. He is a member of the American Guild of Organists, and was one of the founders of the Association of Disciples Musicians (ADM) in 1962, serving as its president in 1966-1967. Since 1960 Mr. Schreiber has held the position of Minister of Music at the National City Christian Church in Washington, D. C.

60 Come, O Come, in Pious Lays

ALLE MENSCHEN 7.7.7.7.D.

George Wither, 1588-1667, alt.
Jakob Hintze, 1622-1702
Harm. by J. S. Bach, 1685-1750

This hymn is based on Psalm 148 and appeared in Wither's *Halelujah*, 1641. It sometimes appears as "Come, O Come, with Sacred Lays."

The author was a prolific writer of prose and poetry as well as a colorful figure in the annals of seventeenth-century English history. George Wither was born June 11, 1588, at Bentworth near Alton, Hampshire, England. In 1604 he entered Magdalen College, Oxford, but withdrew before earning his degree.

In 1613 Wither wrote *Abuses Stript and Whipt* which so aroused the wrath of James I that he threw Wither into prison. He was released shortly after 1615 after having written "A Satyre to the King" and signing it with these words, "his Majesty's most loyal subject, and *yet* Prisoner in the Marshalsey." He served Charles I as captain of horse and quartermaster of his regiment under the Earl of Arundel. Later, however, he decided to sell all his possessions in order to raise a troop for Parliament. Once again he was taken prisoner and eventually released. Oliver Cromwell made him a Major-General in his army but at the restoration his pen once more sent him to prison as a result of his plea for "popular rights and liberties" in his *Vox Vulgi*. In 1661 he wrote *Prisoner's Plea humbly offered* which led to his removal from Newgate prison to the Tower of London.

He married Elizabeth Emerson, a writer in her own right, who was of the same ancestoral family as Ralph Waldo Emerson. Wither wrote more than a hundred books and pamphlets of poetry and prose, many in the confines of prison. He died a free man on May 2, 1667, at London.

The tune, ALLE MENSCHEN MÜSSEN STERBEN, was originally composed as a funeral hymn in 1652 and was published anonymously in Crüger's *Praxis Pietatis Melica* (19th edition, 1678) and again in the twenty-fourth edition with the name J. Hintze appended to it. It should not be confused with a tune by Haydn having the same name. ALLE MENSCHEN is also called SALZBURG in some books.

The composer was born at Bernau, Brandenburg, September 4, 1622, and in 1662 succeeded Crüger as editor of *Praxis Pietatis Melica* which contained best of Reformation hymnody. He became a court musician to the Elector of Brandenburg in 1666 and died on May 5, 1702.

The harmonization is from Bach's *Choralgesäng*.

For a note on Bach see No. 193.

61   God Himself Is with Us

ARNSBERG 6.6.8.D.3.3.6.6.

Gerhard Tersteegen, 1697-1760
Tr. Frederick W. Foster, 1760-1835
and John Miller, 1756-1810; alt. 1932
From Joachim Neander's *Bundes-Lieder,* 1680

This is a translation of Gerhard Tersteegen's hymn, *"Gott ist gegenwärtig"* from his *Geistliches Blumen-Gärtlein,* 1729, where it appeared under the title "Remembrance of the Glorious and Delightful Presence of God."

Born in Westphalia on Nov. 25, 1697, Gerhard Tersteegen was to have become a minister of the Reformed church, but the early death of his father and lack of funds altered plans and he was apprenticed to a relative who kept a shop in Mülheim. After a period of depression and spiritual crises, he earned his living weaving ribbons. He had dissociated himself from the organized church because he could not "in conscience communicate along with open sinners" (Julian). This did not deter him from conducting prayer meetings, preaching, and counseling those in spiritual need. He established a *Pilgerhütte* or Pilgrims' Cottage where his followers could retreat for spiritual renewal and "awakened souls" could receive further guidance from Tersteegen. His influence spread and eventually led him to make regular visits to Holland to preach to and visit with his followers there.

From 1730 to 1750 a law against conventicles forced him to curtail his activities and so he removed himself to the house of a former friend where he preached and ministered to the poor and sick by distributing food and medicine. For several years after the law was abandoned he preached publicly but his health began to fail and he was once again forced to limit his ministry to very small groups. He died on April 3, 1769.

Tersteegen is considered one of the great German hymnists and spiritual leaders. He was never ordained nor really recognized by the church, and his simple, devout, and mystical faith constrained him from establishing a separate sect.

The translation here given is again a sort of composite. Major credit has been given to Frederick W. Foster and John Miller, both Moravian ministers, and the name of William Mercer (1811-1873) is often mentioned as the translator of stanza three. Mercer was an English scholar. The hymn is found in a number of books as "God Reveals His Presence" and there is a translation by John Wesley which begins, "Lo, God is here! Let Us Adore."

ARNSBERG is also known as WUNDERBARER KÖNIG and GOTT IST GAGENWÄRTIG, the latter being the first line of this hymn. The tune was found in Joachim Neander's *Glaub-und Liebesübung*, Bremen, 1680, where it was set to a hymn beginning *"Wunderbarer König."*

For comment on Joachim Neander see No. 20.

62 Father, We Praise Thee, Now the Night Is Over

CHRISTE SANCTORUM 11.11.11.5.

Latin: *Nocte surgentes*
Attr. to Gregory the Great, 540-604
Tr. Percy Dearmer, 1867-1936
La Feillée's *Méthode-du Plain-chant* 1781

Whether or not Pope Gregory the Great ever wrote any hymns is not known. Through the years Benedictine editors have however ascribed eight hymns to him and this one beginning *"Nocte surgentes vigilemus"* has enjoyed a long history of usage in various breviaries and has been translated in different ways.

Gregory the Great was a man from a family of great wealth and was known for his learning. His importance here lies in the fact that his interest in liturgy and the music of the church has influenced the church's worship for twelve centuries. He is credited with codifying the chant of the church and the style of singing he advocated still bears his name.

For a note on the translator see No. 107.

The tune is from La Feillée's *Nouvelle Méthhodedu Plain Chant,* 1782, the fourth edition of the book first published in 1748. Despite the title of the book, this tune appeared with the text beginning *"Christe sanctorum"* in measured form.

63 Sing to the Lord a Joyful Song

SCHÜTZ 81 L.M.

John Samuel Bewley Monsell, 1811-1875
Heinrich Schütz, 1585-1672

One of Monsell's most popular hymns, this appeared in his *Hymns of Love and Praise for the Christian Year,* 1863. It is based on Psalm 145:1-2.

For a note on Monsell see No. 256.

SCHÜTZ 81 is the four-part setting published in the composer's *Psalmen Davids,* 1628. It was composed for Psalm 81 in Becker's *German Psalter,* 1602.

For a comment on Heinrich Schütz see No. 91.

64 Come, Thou Almighty King

ITALIAN HYMN 6.6.4.6.6.6.4.

Anonymous, c. 1757
Felice de Giardini, 1716-1796

This popular hymn first appeared as one of two hymns in a tract bound with the sixth edition of George Whitfield's collection, 1757, hence the date given here. The other hymn was portions of Charles Wesley's hymn "The Backslider," and began with the words, "Jesus, let thy pitying eye." The tract was bound with Whitfield's collection in its eighth and ninth editions but commencing with the tenth edition both hymns were incorporated in the body of the work. It was sung to the tune we call AMERICA which, of course, is the British National Anthem.

Martin Madan included the hymn in his *Collection,* 1763, and from these two sources it has made its way into the hearts of Christian worshipers around the world. It is interesting to note the variety of appelations given to God: King, Father, Ancient of Days, Word, Spirit, Comforter, and One in Three. All are given in the classical Trinitarian formula.

The tune was written by Felice de Giardini at the request of Martin Madan for inclusion in his collection of psalm and hymn tunes, 1769, which has come to be known as the *Lock Collection,* so called because it was intended to be used at the Lock Hospital where Madan was chaplain. The tune is variously known as MOSCOW, BENDTINCK, FAIRFORD, FLORENCE, TRINITY, and of course, ITALIAN HYMN.

Felice de Giardini was born in Turin, April 12, 1716. He was an accomplished violinist and earned his living playing in theater orchestras in Rome and Naples and by giving concerts. He appeared in London with great success and after a short sojourn in Paris returned to London and became the leader of Italian opera. After becoming manager of the organization he suffered severe financial difficulties and returned to concertizing. It was during this time of crises that Madan commissioned him to write hymn tunes for his collection. This is one of the results of the commission. Giardini returned to Italy for six years and then returned to London to try to reestablish Italian opera there but was unsuccessful. He went to Moscow hoping to find success, but found instead more poverty, disillusionment, and distress. He died in Moscow on December 17, 1796.

65   *It Is Good to Sing Thy Praises*

HASTINGS-ON-HUDSON 8.7.8.7.D.

From Psalm 92
The Psalter, 1912
Harold W. Friedell, 1905-1958

This metrical version of selected verses from Psalm 92 first appeared in *The Psalter,* 1912, published by the United Presbyterian Church Board of Publication. It appeared under the heading "Joyful Worship," set to the tune ELLESDIE which was adapted from Mozart.

66

HASTINGS-ON-HUDSON is one of thirteen original hymn tunes Friedell contributed to *Hymns for Children and Grownups,* 1953, which was edited with Lee Hastings Bristol, Jr. Hastings-on-Hudson was Friedell's home in New York.

For a note on Harold W. Friedell see No. 316.

66 Glad Hymns and Songs Will I Recite

OMNOM KAYN L.M.

> Author unknown, 13th century
> Tr. from the Hebrew by Alice Lucas
>
> Traditional Hebrew melody

We have found no information on the hymn, author, or translator used here. Both text and tune appear in the 1914, 1936, and 1957 editions of the *Union Hymnal* published by The Central Conference of American Rabbis. Alice Lucas contributed more hymns to these hymnals than any other person, a total of twenty-one poems in the 1936 and 1957 editions. The present hymn consists of stanzas 1, 2, 5, and 6 of the six stanzas given in the 1936 edition of the *Union Hymnal.* We have substituted "Glad" for the original opening word "Sweet."

OMNOM KAYN, according to Professor Eric Werner of Tel-Aviv University, is the nucleus of a fifteenth-century *Bergamasca* from Northern Italy which was taken up by the German Jews. He informs us that "a variant of it is in use for the beginning of Psalm 144 on Sabbath afternoon."

67 O Worship the King

LYONS 10.10.11.11.

> Based on Psalm 104
> Robert Grant, 1779-1838
>
> Arr. from Johann Michael Haydn, 1737-1806

This version of Psalm 104 is an adaptation of an earlier setting by William Kethe which appeared in the *Anglo-Genevan Psalter,* 1561. Grant's hymn has appeared in numerous American and British hymnbooks since its first printing in Edward Bickersteth's *Christian Psalmody,* 1833.

Robert Grant was born in Bengal, India, in 1779. He became a great scholar, statesman, jurist, and philanthropist. Educated at Magdalen College, Cambridge, he was called to the bar in 1807 and became King's Sergeant in the court of the Duke of Lancaster. The following year he entered Parliament where he rendered significant service for many years. In 1831 he was made a Privy Councilor, in 1832, Judge Advocate General, and in 1833 was sponsor of the bill which emancipated the Jews. Grant was knighted on the occasion of being appointed Governor of Bombay in 1834. He died at Dalpoorie, India, July 9, 1838. A memorial hospital was built and named in his honor in Bombay.

LYONS is generally attributed to Johann Michael Haydn, younger brother of Franz Joseph. No one knows for a certainty whence came the tune or its name. It appears to have been introduced into English churches through Volume 2 of William Gardiner's *Sacred Melodies,* 1812-15 and American churches through the *Boston Handel and Haydn Society's Collection of Church Music,* edited by Lowell Mason in 1822.

Johann Michael Haydn was born September 14, 1737, and died August 10, 1806. He began his musical life as a chorister at St. Stephen's, Vienna. He studied violin and organ and became assistant organist at the church. In 1757 he became kapellmeister at Grosswardein and five years later was appointed Concertmeister and director of music to Archbishop Sigismund of Salzburg, a position he held until his death. Like his brother Franz Joseph, Michael was a prolific composer. The bulk of his output was for the church and included about 360 masses, cantatas, oratorios, and graduals, much of which remains unpublished. He was held in high esteem by Empress Maria Theresa, Prince Esterházy, his brother Franz Joseph, and his distinguished pupil Carl M. von Weber. His modesty and the shadow of his illustrious brother probably deprived him of the recognition he deserved.

68 *All Praise to Thee, My God, This Night*

TALLIS' CANON L.M.

Thomas Ken, 1637-1711, alt.
Thomas Tallis, c. 1505-1585

This hymn was written by one of the most colorful men in the history of the English church. His deep religious convictions compelled him to defy kings and sustained him with strength enough to withstand the consequences. James II called him the "most eloquent preacher among the Protestants of his time" (Julian, p. 611).

Ken was born at Berkhamstead in July, 1637. He grew up under the care of Izaak Walton, who had married Ken's eldest sister, Ann. He was educated at Winchester College and New College, Oxford. His entire life was spent in the service of the church in one way or another. He began as curate and rector and was appointed chaplain to Princess Mary at The Hague. After a conflict with William of Orange he was sent back to England where he became chaplain to Charles, II.

Charles II made Ken Bishop of Bath and Wells after he had refused to permit Nell Gwynne, the king's mistress, to stay in his home at Winchester. After Charles' death Ken was imprisoned in the Tower in 1688 for having refused to read the Declaration of Indulgences set forth by James. When William III came to the throne, Ken was deprived of his bishopric in 1691 because he refused to take the oath. Left with little more than his library he spent the remainder of his life in study and writing. He died at Longleat, March 19, 1710 or 11.

Bishop Ken's fame continues today as the author of two hymns, a morning hymn and an evening hymn. These were part of a trilogy written for private devotion of the scholars at Winchester in which he exhorted the students to sing these hymns at morning, evening, and midnight devotions. "All Praise to Thee, My God, This Night" was designated as the evening hymn and is here taken from the 1695 edition of his *Manual of Prayers*.

The words we sing as the Doxology were added at the end of each hymn by Ken. If for no other reason we can be eternally grateful to Bishop Thomas Ken for these wonderful words of praise.

Thomas Tallis [Tallys or Talys] has been called the "father of English cathedral music." Whether or not this is an accurate ascription, the fact is that Tallis was one of the truly great musicians of his day. He has the distinction of having served under Henry VIII, Edward VI, Mary, and Elizabeth I. This was no small feat considering the fortunes of the church in England during those troubled times.

Tallis was born sometime between 1505 and 1512 but the exact date is unknown. He held some sort of official position at the Abbey of the Holy Cross at Waltham, Essex. Henry VIII appointed him as one of the gentlemen of the Chapel Royal and Tallis continued his association with the royal family through the reign of Elizabeth. Tallis worked closely with William Byrd, another of the great musicians of the period. Elizabeth granted both men a license which gave them the exclusive right to print music and music paper in England. It is said that Tallis was among the very first to set English words to music for use in the English church. This must have come quite naturally for him when one considers the necessity laid upon him by the fluctuation between the Roman and Protestant factions of the church.

Tallis wrote nine tunes for Archbishop Parker's *Psalter* of 1567. The famous Canon we use was an adaptation of the eighth tune and is now his best-known tune. He died in Greenwich, November 23, 1585.

69   *Holy God, Thy Name We Bless*

GROSSER GOTT, WIR LOBEN DICH 7.8.7.8.7.7.

Attr. to Ignaz Franz, 1719-1790
Tr. R. Birch Hoyle, 1875-1939
and Clarence A. Walworth, 1820-1900

Katholisches Gesangbuch, c. 1774

This is an English version of the German translation of the *Te Deum Laudamus.* Most authorities agree that the author of the German version is unknown but because it first appears in the *Katholisches Gesangbuch* c. 1774, edited by Ignaz Franz, it is sometimes attributed to him. The present version is the work of R. Birch Hoyle (Stanzas 1 and 3), and Clarence A. Walworth (Stanza 2).

Ignaz Franz, a Roman Catholic hymnologist, was born October 12, 1719. He was ordained a priest in 1742. He published about ten books, most of which were hymnals. The *Katholisches Gesangbuch* was his most ambitious undertaking and was done at the request of Empress Marie Theresa.

Clarence Walworth, a native of Plattsburg, New York, received his first theological training at the General Theological Seminary in New York City. He became a Roman Catholic in 1845 and assisted in founding the order of Paulist Fathers.

For a comment on R. Birch Hoyle see No. 181.

GROSSER GOTT, WIR LOBEN DICH is the first phrase of the text with which the tune appeared in the *Katholisches Gesangbuch.* The composer is unknown. The original six-eight meter and dancelike rhythm was altered to the present form in Schicht's *Choralebuch,* 1819, to which we owe its introduction into Protestant worship. This is the obvious source of the tune HURSLEY.

70 *Holy, Holy, Holy! Lord God Almighty*

NICAEA 11.12.12.10.

Reginald Heber, 1783-1826
John B. Dykes, 1823-1876

This is perhaps Bishop Heber's best-known and most widely used hymn. Written for Trinity Sunday, it is an excellent paraphrase of Revelation 4:8-11. It was first published in the *Selection of Psalms and Hymns for the Parish Church of Banbury*, 1826, and the following year in Heber's posthumous hymns.

For a note on Reginald Heber see No. 304.

NICAEA was composed for this text by John B. Dykes and appeared in the first edition of Hymns Ancient and Modern, 1861. The name of the tune is appropriate for this text in that it is derived from the Council of Nicaea which convened A.D. 325 and formulated the Trinitarian dogma in answer to the Arian heresy.

For a note on John B. Dykes see No. 195.

71 *All People That on Earth Do Dwell*

OLD HUNDREDTH L.M.

William Kethe, d. 1593
Genevan Psalter, 1551

Little is known of the author of this paraphrase of Psalm 100. During the persecutions of Bloody Queen Mary (1553-1558) Kethe is known to have been among the exiles in Europe. He spent some time in Frankfurt, 1555, and in Geneva, 1557. In 1558 he was sent on a special mission to other exiles in Strassburg and Basel, returning to Geneva in 1559.

The refugees were not idle during their exile. They were actively engaged in translating the Bible and translating the Book of Psalms into English metrical form. They published *One and Fiftie Psalms* in 1556, 1560, and again in 1561. William Kethe contributed twenty-five metrical Psalms to the 1561 edition. Psalm 100 was one of these and it was set to the Bourgeois tunes.

Kethe seems to have reestablished himself with the English sometime before 1563. At that time he is known to have been chaplain to the Queen's forces at Havre under the Earl of Warwick but James Mearns writing in Julian's *Dictionary of Hymnology* [p. 623] tells us that one John Hutchins wrote in his County history of Dorset that Kethe was made Rector of Childe Okeford, near Blandford, in 1561. Mearns believes Kethe's activity at Okeford "ceased by death or otherwise about 1593."

Whatever the romance connected with this hymn the fact remains that it has outlived most of the metrical Psalms of England and continues to be in demand for all major denominational hymnals even to the present.

For a comment on OLD HUNDREDTH see No. 412.

72   O for a Thousand Tongues to Sing

AZMON C.M.

Charles Wesley, 1707-1788
Carl G. Gläser, 1784-1829
Mason's *Modern Psalmody*, 1839

This well-known text is from an eighteen-stanza hymn Charles Wesley wrote celebrating the first anniversary of his Aldersgate experience (May 21, 1738) entitled "Glory to God, and Praise, and Love." The full hymn was included in his *Hymns and Sacred Poems,* 1740, under the heading "For the Anniversary Day of One's Conversion." R. Conyers is said to have been among the first to adapt it for use in congregational praise. The present form is a favorite hymn of all denominations and especially of the Methodists.

For a note on Charles Wesley see No. 180.

Lowell Mason introduced this German tune to America through his *Modern Psalmist,* 1839, where it was set to Isaac Watts' hymn "Come, Let Us Lift Our Joyful Eyes" in 4.4 meter. Two years later the tune appeared in the present 3.2 meter in his *Carmina Sacra.* AZMON was a place name used in describing the boundaries of Canaan in Numbers 34:4-5. Its connotation has to do with strength, might, numbers, and abundance. The passive form of the word means strong defense or fortress. The tune is sometimes called ASMON, DENFIELD, DEERFIELD, and GASTON.

For a note on Lowell Mason see No. 273.

A native of Weissenfels, Germany, Carl G. Gläser was born May 4, 1784. In his early years he studied music under his father but later became a student of piano and violin at the Thomasschule in Leipzig. In 1801 he entered the University of Leipzig as a student of law but discontinued this pursuit in favor of music. He settled in Barmen and spent the rest of his life teaching violin, piano, and voice, directing choirs, and operating a music store. His compositions include motets, school songs, and piano music. He died April 16, 1829.

73   *Praise My Soul, the King of Heaven*

PRAISE MY SOUL 8.7.8.7.8.7.

> Based on Psalm 103
> Henry Francis Lyte, 1793-1847, alt.
> John Goss, 1800-1880

This is the second of two paraphrases of Psalm 103 Henry Francis Lyte published in his *Spirit of the Psalms,* 1834, which presented over 280 new paraphrases of various psalms. Queen Elizabeth II used this as the processional hymn for her wedding on November 20, 1947. The version used here is slightly altered from the original.

For a note on Henry Francis Lyte see No. 47.

PRAISE MY SOUL, also called LAUDA ANIMA, was composed for this text by John Goss and was first published in the third edition of Robert Brown-Borthwick's *Supplemental Hymn and Tune Book,* 1869.

John Goss, born in Hampshire, began his illustrious musical career as a chorister in the Chapel Royal where he studied under Thomas Attwood. After serving as organist for Stockwell Chapel and St. Luke's, Chelsea, he became professor of harmony at the Royal Academy of Music in 1827, a position he held for forty-seven years. He succeeded Attwood as organist of St. Paul's Cathedral in 1838, was appointed composer to the Chapel Royal in 1856, and was knighted by Queen Victoria on the occasion of his retirement in 1872. Cambridge University awarded him an honorary Mus. D. in 1876. Dr. Goss died in London on May 10, 1880. He was the composer of many anthems, chants, services, and hymn tunes.

74 I'll Praise My Maker While I've Breath

OLD 113TH 8.8.8.8.8.8.

Psalm 146
Isaac Watts, 1674-1748
Alt. by John Wesley, 1703-1791
Strassburger Kirchenamt, 1525
Probably by Matthäus Greiter, c. 1500-1552
Harm. V. Earle Copes, 1921-

This hymn was first published in Isaac Watts' *Psalms of David,* 1719 as "I'll Praise my Maker with my Breath." John Wesley made several alterations including the first line of the stanza given here. In this form Wesley published it in his *Psalms and Hymns,* Charleston, South Carolina, 1736-1737 and in his subsequent collections.

For a note on Isaac Watts see No. 48.

The story of John Wesley's life and work is well known. Born at the Epworth Rectory in Lincolnshire in 1703, he was educated by his mother and at Charterhouse, and at Christ Church, Oxford. He received Holy Orders in the Church of England from the Bishop of Oxford in 1725, became a Fellow of Lincoln College, Oxford, the following year, and in 1727 returned to Lincolnshire as an assistant to his father. In 1729 he returned to Lincoln College as a teacher. The Oxford Methodist Movement had already begun and John now assumed its leadership. He was sent to Charleston, Georgia, to be the resident minister and missionary to the Indians in 1735. It was while on the voyage to the New World that he heard the singing of a group of Moravians which impressed upon him the efficacy of hymn singing and which led him to begin translating their hymns into English. Discouraged with his work in Georgia, Wesley returned to London where he again came under the influence of the Moravians, especially one Peter Böhler. This led to his memorable Aldersgate conversion experience on May 24, 1738, which started him on his way to a life of fervent evangelism. He was one of the world's greatest peripatetic preachers and prolific authors. He wrote hymns and translated more than thirty from the German and French.

OLD 113TH was a favorite tune of John Wesley. It has been traced from the *Teusch Kirchenamt*, Strassburg, 1525 to John Calvin's *Aulcuns Pseaulmes*, 1539, and the French and Genevan psalters. Its first English use seems to be in the *Fourscore and Seven Psalmes*, 1561. John Wesley included it in his *Foundery Collection*, 1742, and subsequent tune books. It is said that this hymn and tune were on the lips of John Wesley when he died.

Matthäus Greiter, German composer, singer, and poet, was born at Aichach, Bavaria, c. 1500. He was a monk and singer in Strassburg Cathedral before becoming involved in the Lutheran cause in 1524. Greiter wrote numerous tunes and texts which were sung by Lutherans for many years, including free metrical versions of several of the psalms. He is best remembered today for the tune to *"Es sind doch selig alle"* which became associated with the hymn *"O Mensch, bewein dein' Sünde gross"* which, in turn, J. S. Bach used so significantly in his *Passion According to St. Matthew*. Greiter is believed to have died of the plague on December 20, 1550.

For a note on V. Earle Copes see No. 309.

75 *Immortal, Invisible, God Only Wise*

ST. DENIO 11.11.11.11.

Walter Chalmers Smith, 1824-1908, alt.
Welsh hymn melody
John Roberts' *Caniadau y Cyssegr*, 1939

Based on 1 Timothy 1:17, this powerful hymn first appeared in Smith's *Hymns of Christ and the Christian Life*, 1876. Walter Chalmers Smith was born in Aberdeen, Scotland, December 5, 1824, and died in Kimbush, Perthshire, September 20, 1908. He was educated at the University of Aberdeen and New College at Edinburgh. After his ordination in 1850 he held pastorates in several Free Churches in England and Scotland, ending his career as pastor of the influential Free High Church in Edinburgh. He was the moderator of the Free Church of Scotland in 1893. Some of his contributions to poetical literature were *The Bishop's Walk*, 1860, *Olrig Grange*, 1872, *North Country Folk*, 1883, and *Hymns of Christ and Christian Life*, 1876.

ST. DENIO or JOANNA seems to have appeared as early as 1839 in John Roberts' *Caniadau y Cyssegr* where it is called PALESTINA. Some authorities believe the tune is founded upon an early nineteenth-century Welsh folksong "Can Mlynedd i 'nawr.' " *The English Hymnal* was the first to carry the tune with this text.

76 *Ye Servants of God, Your Master Proclaim*

HANOVER 10.10.11.11.

Charles Wesley, 1707-1788
William Croft, 1678-1727

First published in *Hymns for Times of Trouble and Persecution,* 1744, this hymn is sometimes listed under "Missions" and in the first publication appeared in a section of "Hymns to be sung in Tumult." It was written during the time of England's persecution of Methodists.

For a note on Charles Wesley see No. 180.

HANOVER is the tune generally associated with "O Worship the King" in English churches. It first appeared in the sixth edition of *A Supplement to the New Version of Psalms,* 1708, and has been attributed to William Croft, who is believed to have had a part in editing the collection. The tune is also called ST. GEORGE'S, ST. MICHAEL'S, and OLD 104TH. In *A Supplement,* etc. it appeared with Psalm 67 and included a note to the effect that it was a new tune for the *New Version* Psalm 149 and *Old Version* Psalm 104.

For a note on William Croft see No. 23.

77 *O Be Joyful in the Lord!*

FINLAY 7.7.7.7.5.7.6.7.

Based on Psalm 100
Curtis Beach, 1914-
Harold W. Friedell, 1905-1958

Dr. Curtis Beach informs us he wrote this hymn for a Thanksgiving service in 1954 which coincided with "the 300th anniversary of the first Jewish settlement in North America." In his sermon that day, he drew a parallel between the experiences which brought both the Pilgrims and the Jewish colonists to this land. The hymn was first published in *The Pilgrim Hymnal,* 1958, and has subsequently appeared in the *Catholic Hymnal,* 1966, and the hymnal of the United Church of Japan.

Curtis Beach was born in Cambridge, Massachusetts, in 1914. He was educated at Harvard College (1935), Boston University School of Theology (1941), and the University of Southern California (Ph.D. 1957). He served the Neighborhood Church, Pasadena, California, from 1943 until 1959 and has been serving the Smithfield Congregational Church in Pittsburgh since then.

FINLAY was composed for "O Be Joyful in the Lord" in 1957. It is named in honor of Terence J. Finlay, rector of St. Bartholomew's Church in New York City.

For a note on Harold W. Friedell see No. 316.

78 *With the Morn in Radiance Breaking*

SANDELL (TRYGGARE KAN INGEN VARA) L.M.

Karpínski, 1741-1825
Tr. W. J. Rose, 1922
Swedish melody

This hymn was included in early editions of the World Student Christian Federation's hymnbook *Cantate Domino.* The date of translation suggests that it was included in the first edition, 1924. No information has been found on either the author or the translator.

For a note on Miss Sandell and SANDELL see No. 30.

79 *Praise the Lord! Ye Heavens*

HYFRYDOL 8.7.8.7.D.

Based on Psalm 148
Stanzas 1, 2:. Foundling Hospital Collection, c. 1801
Stanza 3: Edward Osler, 1798-1863
Rowland Hugh Prichard, 1811-1887

The first two stanzas of this hymn are by an unknown author. They were first found in a pamphlet appended to copies of the musical edition of *Psalms, Hymns, and Anthems of the Foundling*

Hospital, 1796, under the title, "Hymn From Psalm CXLVIII, Haydn." Erik Routley suggests the indication "Haydn" refers to the tune AUSTRIA which was introduced into England in 1802. The third stanza is by Edward Osler and was added to the hymn in Hall's *Mitre Hymn Book,* 1836.

Edward Osler was born in Falmouth, England, in January of 1798. He was educated for the medical profession and devoted several years to its practice before turning to religious and literary pursuits. He was associated with the Society for Promoting Christian Knowledge for a number of years before becoming editor of the *Royal Cornwall Gazette,* a position he held for twenty-two years until his death at Truro, March 7, 1863. Dr. Osler wrote on a variety of subjects including natural science, natural history, travel, and biography. His contributions to hymnology were mainly through the *Mitre Hymn Book, Psalms and Hymns adapted to the Services of the Church of England,* and monthly numbers of his *Church and King.*

HYFRYDOL literally means "good cheer." The tune was composed about 1830, but did not appear in a collection until 1855. This collection was compiled by Griffith Roberts under the title *Haleliwiah Drachefn.* It has had a long association with Wesley's "Love Divine, All Loves Excelling."

Rowland Hugh Prichard was born in 1811, near Bala, Holywell, Wales, where he lived much of his life. His tunes were published in various Welsh periodicals, and he was well known as a precentor. HYFRYDOL was written when he was twenty years old. In 1844 he published a collection of tunes entitled *Cyfaill y Cantorion,* the singer's friend. Most of these tunes were his own compositions. When sixty-nine years of age, he became assistant loom tender at Holywell Mill with the Welsh Flannel Manufacturing Company. He died at Holywell in 1887. The present tune appears to be his only claim to fame.

80   *As Pants the Hart*

IRISH C.M.

Based on Psalm 42
A New Version of the Psalms, 1696, alt.
Hymns and Sacred Poems, Dublin, 1749

Although Percy Dearmer in *Songs of Praise Discussed* suggests both the Old and New Versions of the Psalms of David "seem like national disasters" (p. 242), these two historic metrical versions of the Psalms have played a significant role in the development of English and American hymnody. Thomas Sternhold (d. 1549) was among the first to cast some of the Psalms into English meters for use in private and public devotions. The *Old Version,* as it was called, made its debut sometime before 1548 and survived through 600 editions. The second edition was published in 1549 and contained the metrical version of Psalm 42 which has been attributed to John Hopkins (d. 1570?). The *New Version* was published in 1696 by Nahum Tate (1652-1715) and Nicholas Brady (1659-1726) with a corrected version following in 1698. Many of the Psalms from the *Old Version* were included in a much improved form, Psalm 42 being one of them. Tate and Brady's *New Version* served the church well for a hundred years or more.

For a comment on Nahum Tate see No. 126.

The tune IRISH is one of those tunes whose origin is difficult to trace. Since the composer is unknown some authorities conjecture that it may be either an Irish or Scottish folksong. About the only thing about it for a certainty is that it appeared without a name in *Hymns and Sacred Poems,* published in Dublin, 1749. It was not until about 1760 that it was called IRISH TUNE in Caleb Ashworth's *Collection of Tunes.* It is sometimes called DUBLIN.

81   *The God of Abraham Praise*

LEONI 6.6.8.4.D.

Yigdal elohim chay veyishtabach
Daniel ben Judah Dayyan, c. 1400
Tr. Max Landsberg, 1845-1928 and
Newton Mann, 1836-1926

Hebrew Tradition, 17th century?
Transcribed by Meyer Lyon, 1751-1797

This hymn is based on the thirteen articles of the Jewish faith, a summation of essential doctrines of Judaism begun by Moses Maimonides (1130-1205) and put in metrical form by Daniel ben Judah Dayyan, circa 1400. A Welsh Wesleyan preacher by the name of Thomas Olivers (1725-1799) rendered an English version of the *Yigdal* or (Doxology) after hearing it sung in a synagogue in London. Its acceptance and popularity was instantaneous following publication in 1772. The present rendering of the *Yigdal* is the work of a Jewish rabbi, Max Landsberg (1845-1926) and a Unitarian minister, Newton Mann (1836-1926), both from Rochester, New York.

Thomas Olivers (1725-1799), orphaned at four, became an apprentice shoemaker. He was converted by the preaching of Whitefield and became an enthusiastic follower of John Wesley. In the course of twenty-five years he traveled more than 100,000 miles on horseback preaching the Gospel in England and Ireland. For a time he was editor of *The Arminean Magazine* but was relieved of his position by John Wesley because of his ineptitude in dealing with matters of topography and policy. He died in London.

Max Landsberg, born in Berlin, Germany, on February 26, 1845, was educated at the Hildesheim Gymnasium Josephinum, and the universities of Göttingen, Breslau, and Halle (Ph.D. 1866). From 1866 to 1871 he taught at a seminary for Jewish teachers at Hanover after which he came to America and was appointed Rabbi to the Temple Brith Kodesh in Rochester, New York. He held this position with distinction until his death in 1928. Rabbi Landsberg devoted his life to the service of both the Jewish and Gentile communities and was elected president of the New York State Conference of Charities and Correction in 1911. He was the author of numerous scholarly papers and several books including *Hymns for Jewish Worship*, 1880, and *Ritual for Jewish Worship*, 1884. His reputation as a scholar contributed to the nationwide circulation of these books.

Newton Mann, Unitarian clergyman and author, was born at Cazenovia, New York, on January 16, 1836. He began his education at the Cazenovia Seminary but the early death of his father in 1844 forced him to leave school and take up the family farming responsibilities. Despite this turn of events the boy continued to educate himself so that by the age of twenty he had learned five languages and was familiar with the best literature and philosophy of his day. After breaking with the conservative religious tradition of his family, Mann embraced Unitarianism only to find that his brand of liberalism was unacceptable even to the Unitarians. This is apparent in an incident which took place in 1859 while he was supplying the pulpit of the First Unitarian Church in Cincinnati, Ohio. He had just recently read Charles Darwin's newly published book, *The Origin of the Species*, which prompted him to preach a sermon in which he attempted to apply Darwin's theses to the traditional theological concepts of both the Old and New Testaments. The sermon caused such a furore the young preacher was forced to leave the church, whereupon he became the principal of a school in Alton, Illinois. Shortly thereafter he was appointed superintendent of the Western Sanitary Commission's soldier's home in Vicksburg. In 1865 he returned to the north and the ministry and served churches in Kenosha, Wisconsin, Troy and Rochester, New York, and Omaha, Nebraska. He died in Chicago, Illinois, on July 26, 1926. He was the author of *The Evolution of Great Literature* (1906-09), *The Import and Outlook of Socialism* (1910), and numerous poems on religious and philosophical subjects.

LEONI is the name given the tune by Thomas Olivers who heard the cantor Meyer Lyon [Meier Leon or Leoni] sing it at the Great Synagogue, Duke's Place, London. The tune and text appeared together in leaflet form c. 1770 and began appearing in hymnbooks with the Methodist, *The Pocket Hymn Book,* 1785.

Meyer Lyon (1751-1797 or 1800) was widely acclaimed as a singer by Jews and Gentiles alike. He sang for the Duke's Place Synagogue, London, for a time and then attempted to enter opera at Covent Gardens under the name "Leoni." Apparently his lack of acting skill, coupled with his refusal to sing on Friday nights or during Jewish festival days, were responsible for his unsuccessful efforts in this field. In 1787 he returned to the synagogue at a reduced salary, but later accepted his position with the Ashkenazic congregation at Kingston, Jamaica, where he remained until his death.

82   *Savior, Again to Thy Dear Name*

ELLERS 10.10.10.10.

John Ellerton, 1826-1893
Edward J. Hopkins, 1818-1901

Julian's *Dictionary of Hymnology* says this is Ellerton's "most beautiful and tender" hymn. It was written in six stanzas for the Festival of the Malpas, Middlewich, and Nantwich Choral Association in 1866, but the author revised and reduced it to the present four stanzas for the Appendix to the first edition of *Hymns Ancient and Modern,* 1868.

For a note on John Ellerton see No. 231.

ELLERS was composed for this hymn and first appeared in the 1869 edition of one Rev. E. Brown-Borthwick's compilation, *The Supplemental Hymn and Tune Book.* The present unison version with organ accompaniment is in the manner of the original version.

Edward John Hopkins was a distinguished organist, composer, and author. Born in Westminster June 30, 1818, he became a chorister at the Chapel Royal at the age of eight years. His interest in the organ became apparent early in life and he began his illustrious career at Mitcham Parish Church, Surry, in 1834. After serving several other churches he was appointed organist of Temple Church in 1843 and remained there for fifty-five years. His superb musicianship brought him many honors including membership in the Royal Society of Musicians and the Royal Academy of Musicians. The Archbishop of Canterbury awarded him the Lambeth Doctorate of Music in 1882. Another Doctorate of Music was given him by Trinity College, Toronto, in 1866. He composed a great many hymn tunes, anthems, and chants; contributed articles to *Grove's Dictionary of Music and Musicians,* and assisted in publication of other books. He died in St. Pancras, London, February 4, 1901.

83   *Let All the World in Every Corner Sing*

ALL THE WORLD 10.4.6.6.6.6.10.4.

George Herbert, 1593-1632
Robert G. McCutchan, 1877-1958

George Herbert enjoyed the favor of James I and other men of high position and counted among his close friends Sir Henry Wooton, John Donne, Lord Bacon, and Isaac Walton. He was born into an old English family at Montgomery Castle April 3, 1593, and received his education at Westminster School and Trinity College, Cambridge. After the death of James I, he took holy orders and became rector of Bemerton, Wiltshire, on April 26, 1630. His death occurred there in February of 1632.

His principal literary work was *The Temple* which was published in 1633 and from which the present hymn is derived. Herbert's poetry was not conceived or intended for public worship but as early as 1697 it began to appear in hymnbooks. It was not until the Wesleys used some forty of the poems in their *Hymns and Sacred Poetry,* 1739, that they achieved general popularity. The poem was called an antiphon and for this reason Robert Guy McCutchan suggests the congregation sing the phrase "Let all the world in every corner sing: My God and King!" and a solo voice (or choir) sing the verse with the congregation singing the final phrase.

ALL THE WORLD was composed in 1930 for this text by Robert Guy McCutchan who used the nom de plume John Porter. The present harmonization varies slightly from that which appears in the *Methodist Hymnal,* 1964, and both have lost the massive effect created by complete chords with octaves in the bass line as found in the *Methodist Hymnal,* 1935. The hymn tune is designed for unison singing.

Dr. McCutchan was born at Mount Ayr, Iowa, September 13, 1877, and was educated at Park College, Missouri, and Simpson College, Kansas. He also studied at Berlin and Paris. He taught at Baker University, Kansas, for six years during which time he organized its Conservatory of Music. In 1911 he became dean of the School of Music at DePauw University in Indiana. Dr. McCutchan was the musical editor of the *Methodist Hymnal,* 1935, author of its manual, *Our Hymnody,* 1937, and *Hymn Tune Names, Their Sources and Significance,* 1957. He died in 1958.

84   *My God, I Love Thee*

ABBEY C.M.

No me mueve, mi Dios
Attr. to St. Francis Xavier, 1506-1552
Tr. Edward Caswall, 1814-1878
Scottish Psalter, 1615

This is one of two hymns that have been ascribed to St. Francis Xavier, neither of which have been verified for a certainty. This translation is from the second of these humns which begins

O Deus ego amo te,
Nec amo te ut salves me

and is sometimes ascribed to St. Teresa of Spain. The original may have been a Spanish sonnet. Caswall's translation appeared in his *Lyra Catholica,* 1849, and has been included in many major hymnals since.

Francis Xavier was a famous Spanish missionary saint of the Roman Catholic Church. He was born at castle Xavier near Pampeluna, Spain, on April 7, 1506. After graduating from the University of Paris he taught for a while and then became acquainted with Ignatius Loyola who counted him among his first nine converts. It is said that Xavier was the most enthusiastic member of the original order of Jesuits founded at Montmartre, August 15, 1534. He traveled with Loyola to Venice where he was assigned to work in a hospital for incurables. Later he went to Rome and was selected to become Portugal's missionary to Goa, India. Arriving there on May 6, 1542, he devoted the remainder of his life to Christian work among non-Christians throughout the east as far as Japan. He died at Sancian, near Canton, China, December 22, 1552.

For a comment on Edward Caswall see No. 116.

For a note on ABBEY see No. 276.

85   *Dear Lord and Father of Mankind*

SALVATION 8.6.8.8.6.

John Greenleaf Whittier, 1807-1892

Ananias Davisson's *Kentucky Harmony,* c. 1815, adapted

This hymn is from a seventeen-stanza poem called "Brewing of the Soma." In it Whittier describes an Indian ritual of the brewing and drinking of the intoxicating liquor of the Soma plant in the belief that the deity could better communicate with them. He apparently believed that this was related to the emotionalism practiced by some religious sects in America. "Dear Lord and Father of Mankind" is taken from the final stanzas of the poem. It was first used as a hymn by W. Garrett Horder's *Worship Song, 1884.*

The Quaker poet was born in Haverhill, Massachusetts, December 17, 1807. He was a farm boy and the village shoemaker until he began writing verses. His poetic talent was discovered and cultivated while he was yet a young man. This interest led him into the field of journalism and with a limited educational background he entered the publishing field as editor of the *American Manufacturer* in 1828. He became the editor of the *New England Review* in 1830, but his love of justice and humanity led him to involvement with the antislavery movement which resulted in acceptance of the editorship of an antislavery magazine called *The Pennsylvania Freeman* in 1836.

Whittier died at Hampton Falls, New Hampshire, on September 7, 1892, one of America's best-known, best-loved, most-famous poets.

For a comment on SALVATION see No. 42.

86 Dear Lord and Father of Mankind

REST 8.6.8.8.6.

John Greenleaf Whittier, 1807-1892
Frederick C. Maker, 1844-1927

For a note on John Greenleaf Whittier and the hymn see No. 85. REST was composed for this hymn by Frederick C. Maker and first appeared in G. S. Barrett's *Congregational Hymnal,* 1887. It is also known as ELTON, MAGDALEN, PENZANCE, ALL SAINTS, and WHITTIER.

For a comment on Frederick C. Maker see No. 160.

87 Declare, O Heavens, the Lord of Space

LASST UNS ERFREUEN 8.8.4.4.8.8. with Alleluias

Robert Lansing Edwards, 1915-

Melody from *Geistliche Kirchengesäng,*
Cologne, 1623
Harm. and Arr. Ralph Vaughan Williams,
1872-1958

This space age hymn was copyrighted by the Hymn Society of America in 1962 and published in pamphlet form in *Hymns of the Twentieth Century,* 1963. All hymns published in that pamphlet were used on an ABC-TV nationwide broadcast May 5, 1963, and featured the work of the Hymn Society. Mr. Edwards says of his hymn, " . . . it gradually took shape in my mind in 1961 during a summer vacation on the beautiful waters of Lake Superior near Isle Royale in Michigan." He goes on to say, "The beauties of nature are very close and real in a place like that, and at the same time the ventures into space were beginning to gain momentum. It occurred to me that there might be use for a hymn which celebrated this latest and greatest physical adventure of man into the universe. It was also a time when some were beginning to question whether such exploration did not pretty much do away with the reality of God. I wanted, if I could, to counter that impression."

Robert Lansing Edwards, a minister of the United Church of Christ (Congregational), was born in Auburn, New York, August 5, 1915. He was educated at Princeton University (B.A., 1937), Harvard University (M.A., 1938), and Union Theological Seminary (B.D. *magna cum laude,* 1949). He was ordained on September 18, 1949, and has served churches in Litchfield and Hartford, Connecticut. He served five years in the United States Army during World War II, entering as a private and released as a captain in Intelligence. During his service he was the recipient of the Bronze Star. He has published various sermons and some devotional literature which have been circulated through his denominational publications on occasion. Three of his hymns have been published by the Hymn Society.

This tune is by an unknown composer. Conjecture has it that it may have been of folk origin. It was a popular hymn tune of the South German Catholics and appeared in a number of their early hymnbooks. It is variously known as LASST UNS ERFREUEN, VIGILES ET SANCTI, ST. FRANCIS, and EASTER ALLELUYA which gives some indication of the variety of texts to which it is sung. It is similar to tunes sung to Psalms 36, 68, and OLD 113TH in the *Genevan Psalters* and Isaac Watts' version of Psalm 117. This version comes from the *Geistliche Kirchengesäng,* Cologne, 1623, and entered the repertoire of English and American congregations through the *English Hymnal,* 1906, where it was set to "Ye Watchers and Ye Holy Ones." This present arrangement is by Ralph Vaughan Williams.

For a note on Ralph Vaughan Williams see No. 98.

88   *Creator of the Universe*

WEYMOUTH C.M.D.

J. Donald Hughes, 1932-

Theodore P. Ferris, 1908-

This hymn, from *Five New Hymns for Youth by Youth,* published by The Hymn Society of America, 1955, was written in 1954 while Dr. Hughes was a student at the University of California at Los Angeles. The author states, "It grew out of a desire to express my conviction that God is at the center of university education, and that study, properly understood, is worship of God." It is also found in *The Hymn,* Volume 6, Number 4, October, 1955, where it is given as "A Student's Hymn" set to a tune named OLD IVY by Lee Hastings

Bristol, Jr. and dedicated to the choir of Trinity Church, Princeton, New Jersey.

The hymn version consists of three stanzas of eight lines each. The second and third stanzas are as follows:

> When minds are dulled with studying,
> When words no life afford,
> When fields of knowledge seem too vast,
> Sustain us then, O Lord.
> Let not the love of easy ways
> Leave deeper truth unknown;
> Teach us that power to learn and grow
> Is found in thee alone.

> Make every desk an altar, Lord;
> Our studying a prayer;
> The classroom doors cathedral gates
> To those who enter there.
> Let science find in thee its truth;
> Technology, its goal;
> Philosophy, its noblest thought:
> Thy light makes knowledge whole!

The second stanza in the hymnal consists of the final four lines of the second and third stanzas of the original.

J. Donald Hughes, an ordained Methodist minister, was born in Santa Monica, California, June 5, 1932. He was educated in the public schools of Santa Monica, University of California at Los Angeles (Phi Beta Kappa, 1954), Boston University School of Theology (S.T.B., 1957), and Boston University (Ph.D., 1960). He also studied at Cambridge University, England, 1958-59 and did postdoctoral work at the American School of Classical Studies, Athens, Greece, 1966-67. Dr. Hughes was director of the Wesley Foundation at San Diego State College (1960-62), assistant professor of history at California Western University, San Diego (1961-66), professor of history at Pierce College, Athens, Greece (1966-67), and has been assistant professor of history at the University of Denver since 1967. Dr. Hughes has published articles and poetry in various university journals, and wrote a book for the National Park Service. Two of his hymns have been published by The Hymn Society of America.

WEYMOUTH was composed in 1941 and named for a town in Nova Scotia, the locale of the composer's summer home.

Theodore Parker Ferris was born in Port Chester, New York, December 23, 1908. He is a graduate of Harvard University and General Theological Seminary in New York City. Since his ordination as a priest in the Episcopal Church, in 1933, he has served as fellow and tutor at General Theological Seminary; assistant minister, Grace Church, New York; rector of Emmanuel Church, Baltimore; and Trinity Church, Boston.

89   *Out of the Depths I Cry to Thee*

AUS TIEFER NOT 8.7.8.7.8.8.7.

Aus tiefer Not schrei ich zu dir
Martin Luther, 1483-1546
Tr. Catherine Winkworth, 1827-1878

Martin Luther, 1483-1546
Harm. J. S. Bach, 1685-1750

Luther's version of Psalm 130 was probably written in 1523. It first appeared in *Etlich Christliche Lieder*, 1524, and again in *Eyn Enchiridion* the same year. It has been altered since Luther published it and has been translated by at least twenty-one scholars. This version is basically that of Catherine Winkworth which appeared in her *Chorale Book for England*, 1863. *"Aus tiefer Not"* was one of Luther's favorite hymns. It has been said that he and a companion sang it while he was in prison during the Diet of Augsburg and that it was sung by the "weeping multitude" attending his funeral.

For a note on Martin Luther see No. 31.

For a note on Catherine Winkworth see No. 58.

AUS TIEFER NOT is taken from the first line of Luther's version of Psalm 130. The tune sometimes appears as COBURG, the name of the castle where Luther was imprisoned during the Diet of Augsburg. The melody has been attributed to Luther. The harmonization is from J. S. Bach.

For a note on Bach see No. 193.

90   *Be Thou My Vision, O Lord of My Heart*

SLANE 10.10.10.10.

Rob tu mo bhoile, a comdi cride
Ancient Irish; tr. Mary Byrne, 1880-1931
Versified by Eleanor Henrietta Hull, 1860-1935

Traditional Irish melody
Harm. David Evans, 1874-1948

Mary Elizabeth Byrne translated this ancient Irish poem into English prose in 1905. Eleanor Henrietta Hull versified the prose version for her *Poem Book of the Gael,* 1912. Both women were brilliant scholars and ardent devotees of Irish history and literature.

Miss Byrne was born in Dublin and received her education at the Dominican Convent there. She was graduated with first-class honors in Modern Literature from the Royal University. She contributed to scholarly research in Irish literature and was a major contributor to the *Dictionary of the Irish Language.*

Miss Hull was a founder of the Irish Text Society, served on the staff of the *Literary World,* was editor of *Lives of the Celtic Saints,* served as secretary of the Royal Asiatic Society, and was a major contributor to Hastings' *Encyclopedia of Religion and Ethics.*

The melody is a traditional Irish melody found in W. Joyce's Old Irish Folk Music where it was used with "With my Love on the Road." The tune was introduced into hymnody with the present text in *The Church Hymnary Revised,* 1927. The name SLANE is the name of a hill near Tara, County Meath where St. Patrick is said to have challenged King Loigaire by lighting the Easter Eve fire.

For a note on David Evans see No. 381.

91 On This Day, the First of Days

SCHÜTZ 19, 7.7.7.7.

Die parente temporum
Breviary of Le Mans, 1748
Tr. Henry W. Baker, 1821-1877
Heinrich Schütz, 1585-1672

These words are translated from the Latin hymn beginning *"Die parente temporum."* The latin text has been found in the Carcasson Breviary, 1745, as well as the *Breviary of Le Mans,* 1748. John Mason Neale included it in his *Hymni Ecclesiae,* 1851. It was designated to be sung on Sunday mornings from Whitsuntide to Advent. The present version is made up of stanzas 1, 2, 4, and 6 of the seven stanzas which appeared in the first edition of *Hymns Ancient and Modern,* 1861.

For a note on Henry W. Baker see No. 209.

SCHÜTZ 19 is thus identified because Heinrich Schütz composed the music for the setting of Psalm 19 in Cornelius Becker's *German Psal-*

ter, 1602. Schütz's four-part settings appeared in his *Psalmen Davids,* 1628.

Heinrich Schütz has often been characterized as the "Father of German Music." Perhaps this is because he composed the first German opera *Dafne* and a ballet, *Orpheus und Eurydice.* Today, however, he is known primarily for his application of the Italian choral and dramatic-monodic style to the needs of church music and as the precursor of Bach's great passion music.

Schütz was born October 4, 1585, at Köstriz, Saxony. His early musical training was received as a choir boy in the court chapel at Cassel. He studied law at Marburg University in 1609. During that year he made his first visit to Venice to study music under Giovanni Gabrielli. He returned to Cassel in 1612 and became court organist. Shortly thereafter he was appointed kapellmeister at Dresden. Schütz traveled to Italy frequently in order to keep abreast of musical development there. During the Thirty Years' War, he made frequent visits to Copenhagen where he served as Court Conductor. He finally settled in Dresden and died there on November 6, 1672.

92   *Take Thou Our Minds*

HALL 10.10.10.10.

William Foulkes, 1877-1961
Calvin W. Laufer, 1874-1938

William Hiram Foulkes wrote this hymn in 1918 at the request of his friend, Calvin W Laufer, upon a chance meeting on the railway station platform at Stony Brook, Long Island, New York. The first three stanzas were written "almost spontaneously" on the train. Dr. Laufer had stated the need for a devotional hymn which would challenge the minds and hearts of young people. These words were the result. The fourth stanza was written several years later while Dr. Foulkes was attending a youth conference at Blairstown, New Jersey.

William Hiram Foulkes was born June 26, 1877, at Quincy, Michigan. He graduated from the College of Emporia, Kansas; Presbyterian Theological Seminary, Chicago; and McCormick Theological Seminary, after which he spent a year in graduate study at New College, Edinburgh, Scotland. During his pastorates in Presbyterian churches in Illinois, Iowa, Oregon, Ohio, New York City, and New Jersey, he was called to serve in many important positions of leadership within his denomination and became moderator of the General Assembly in 1937. He published several books, contributed articles for the *Handbook to the Presbyterian Hymnal*, 1935. He retired to Stony Brook, Long Island, in 1941. He died in 1961.

HALL was composed in 1918 with no specific text in mind and was first called STONY BROOK. After Foulkes wrote the text for this tune Dr. Laufer renamed it HALL in honor of a mutual friend, William Ralph Hall. It was first published with Dr. Foulkes' hymn in *Conference Songs*, 1918.

Calvin Weis Laufer, a distinguished Presbyterian minister, church musician, poet, hymn writer, and educator, was born in Brodheadsville, Pennsylvania, in 1874. After working his way through Franklin and Marshall College and Union Theological Seminary, he served Presbyterian churches in New York and New Jersey for fourteen years. The remainder of his life was spent in service to the church-at-large, first as the field representative of the Presbyterian Board of Publication and Sabbath School Work and finally with the Board of Christian Education of the Presbyterian Church, U.S.A. Dr. Laufer was associate editor of *The Hymnal*, 1933 (Presbyterian) as well as *The Handbook to the Hymnal*, 1936 and assisted in the publication of several excellent hymnals for church school youth. He died in 1938.

93   *Rise Up, O Men of God!*

FESTAL SONG, S.M.

William P. Merrill, 1867-1954
William H. Walter, 1825-1893

Written at the request of the editor of the Presbyterian magazine, *The Continent*, Chicago, 1911, as a contribution to the brotherhood movement, this hymn was inspired by an article entitled, "The Church of the Strong Men" by Gerald Stanley Lee. Almost immediately it began appearing in hymnals in America and Britain and now has a firm place in hymnic literature of most denominations in England and America.

William Pierson Merrill was born in Orange, New Jersey, January 10, 1867. He was educated at Rutgers College and Union Theological Seminary. After ordination to the Presbyterian ministry in 1890 he served successively as the pastor of Trinity Church, Chestnut Hill, Philadelphia, and the Sixth Presbyterian Church, Chicago, and in 1911 became pastor of Brick Presbyterian Church, New York City.

Upon retirement in 1938 he became pastor emeritus of Brick Church. A preacher and pastor of note, Dr. Merrill published more than seven books, championed many civic causes, and was the recipient of many honors from colleges and universities in America. He died in 1954.

FESTAL SONG was first published in *The Hymnal Revised and Enlarged* (Episcopal) 1894, with William Hammond's hymn, "Awake and Sing the Song." Since its first association with Dr. Merrill's text in the *Pilgrim Hymnal*, 1912, FESTAL SONG has become the favorite tune for the hymn, displacing at least twelve other tunes.

William Henry Walter was the composer of service music, hymn tunes, and anthems. For many years he was organist in Episcopal churches in Newark, New Jersey, and New York City. In 1864 Columbia University honored him with a Doctorate of Music and the following year he became organist for the university. His publications include a *Manual of Church Music*, 1860; *The Common Prayer with Ritual Song*, 1868. He was born in Newark, New Jersey, July 1, 1825 and died in New York City in 1893.

94   Take My Life, and Let It Be

PATMOS 7.7.7.7.

Frances Ridley Havergal, 1836-1879

William Henry Havergal, 1793-1870

As a hymn of self-consecration to Christ, these lines were composed at Areley House, February 4, 1874, in eleven couplets. They were published four years later in Miss Havergal's *Loyal Responses*. Subsequently, it became one of the truly popular hymns in the English language and has been translated into numerous foreign tongues. Several of the couplets have been transposed here. Her desire that the hymn be sung to her father's tune PATMOS is being fulfilled among Disciples and American Baptists for the first time in *A Hymnbook for Christian Worship*.

For a note on Miss Havergal see No. 359.

PATMOS was composed by William Henry Havergal in 1869 and was published from a dated manuscript in his *Psalmody*, 1871.

William Henry Havergal, Anglican clergyman and church musician, was born January 18, 1793, at High Wycombe in Buckinghamshire, England. After graduating from St. Edmund's Hall, Oxford, he took Holy Orders and became rector of Astley in Worcestershire, remaining there until 1842. A serious accident sustained as a result of being thrown from a carriage in 1829 interrupted his clerical activities for a time during which he turned to writing music. After returning to active ministry in 1842 he became rector of St. Nicholas, Worcester. From 1845 he was also honorary canon in Worcester Cathedral. Continued ill health caused him to abandon all parish work in 1867. He died at Leamington April 19, 1870. Although he wrote over 100 hymns, he is best known for his hymn tunes, anthems, and services.

95   Praise to God, Immortal Praise

DIX 7.7.7.7.7.7.

Anna Laetitia Barbauld, 1743-1825, alt.
Adapted from a chorale by
Conrad Kocher, 1786-1872

This harvest hymn first appeared in William Enfield's *Hymns for Public Worship,* 1772, under the title "Praise to God in Prosperity and Adversity." All nine stanzas may be found in *The Hymnal 1940 Companion* (second edition, revised). Here we use only stanzas 1, 4, 5, and 9 and all reference to "adversity" has been omitted.

Anna Laetitia Barbauld, born in Leicestershire on June 20, 1743, was the daughter of John Aikin, a dissenting minister. She married Rochemont Barbauld who was a descendent of a French Protestant family and himself a dissenting minister. Her father was a tutor at an academy at Warrington which played no small part in the development of her interest in all forms of literature and especially in hymnody. It was during this period she contributed five hymns to Enfield's *Hymns for Public Worship.* She died March 9, 1825.

For a note on the tune DIX and Conrad Kocher see No. 141

96   When Thy Heart with Joy O'erflowing

BULLINGER 8.5.8.3.

Theodore C. Williams, 1855-1915
Ethelbert W. Bullinger, 1837-1913

Written in 1891 and headed "Unity with others desired," this hymn apparently appeared for the first time in Mrs. Williams' *Hymnal Amore Dei,* 1890.

Theodore Chickering Williams was born in Brookline, Massachusetts, in 1855. After receiving his education at Harvard and Harvard Divinity School, he became a Unitarian minister and served the All Souls Church in New York from 1882 to 1896. For a number of years he was headmaster of Hackley School at Tarrytown, New York. He died in 1915.

BULLINGER, named for the composer, was written in 1874 and set to the hymn, "Jesu, Refuge of the Weary."

Ethelbert William Bullinger, English clergyman, was born at Canterbury on December 15, 1837. He was a choir boy in the famous cathedral. He graduated from King's College, London, where he studied for the ministry. He became a capable Greek and Hebrew scholar which eventually led to his being granted the Lambeth D.D. in 1881 by the Archbishop of Canterbury for his critical work in those areas. His musical interests led to serious study with John Pyke Hallah and Dr. W. H. Monk. He published several hymn tunes but this is the only survivor.

97   Rejoice, Ye Pure in Heart

MARION S.M. with Refrain

Edward H. Plumptre, 1821-1891
Arthur H. Messiter, 1834-1916

Originally written as a processional at Choral Festival in May, 1865, for the Peterborough Choral Festival, "Rejoice, Ye Pure in Heart" first appeared in eleven stanzas and was used in the Peterborough Cathedral. Novello and Company published it in the same year (1865) set to special music; without music it was included in the second edition of Plumptre's *Lazarus and Other Poems*. In 1868 it was included in the Appendix to *Hymns Ancient and Modern*. The full text may be found at 635 in the *Historical Companion to Hymns Ancient and Modern*.

Edward Hayes Plumptre, scholar, theologian, preacher, teacher, and author, was born in London August 6, 1821. He was educated at King's College, London, and University College, Oxford. After graduation in 1844 he became a Fellow of Brasenose College. He was ordained in 1846 and proceeded to become well known throughout the land for his contributions to the literary, ecclestical, university life of England. The final ten years of his distinguished career were spent as dean of Wells Cathedral. He died February 1, 1891.

MARION was composed by Arthur Henry Messiter and set to this text in the Episcopal *Hymnal*, 1893, of which he was the musical editor. The tune, named in honor of the composer's mother, has been associated with "Rejoice Ye Pure in Heart" in most major hymnals since 1893.

Born in England April 1, 1834, Messiter was educated in an English private school. He came to the United States in 1863 and began his long and distinguished musical career as a voluntary singer in the choir of New York City's Trinity Church. After several years as organist at churches in Philadelphia, he was appointed organist and choirmaster of Trinity Church, New York, where he remained for thirty-one years. He retired in 1897 and died in New York City July 2, 1916. In addition to editing the musical edition of the Episcopal *Hymnal*, 1893, Messiter edited a *Psalter*, 1889; The *Choir Office-Book*, 1891; and authored *A History of the Choir and Music of Trinity Church*, New York, 1906.

98   *As Men of Old Their First Fruits Brought*

FOREST GREEN C.M.D.

Frank von Christierson, 1900-
English melody
Arr. Ralph Vaughan Williams, 1872-1958

This hymn was first published in *Ten New Stewardship Hymns*, 1961, by The Hymn Society of America. It was one of ten selected from about one hundred and fifty submitted to be used for the Fortieth Anniversary Celebration of the Department of Stewardship and Benevolence of the National Council of Churches held at Toronto, Canada, December 12-16, 1960.

For a note on Frank von Christierson see No. 343.

FOREST GREEN is a Sussex tune to which the song "The Plowboy's Dream" was sung. Vaughan Williams arranged it for *The English Hymnal*, 1906, where it was set to Phillip Brooks' "O Little Town of Bethlehem."

Ralph Vaughan Williams was the son of a clergyman. He was born at Down Ampney, Gloucestershire, England, on October 12, 1872. He was educated at Charterhouse School, London, Trinity College, Cambridge, The Royal College of Music, London, where he studied with Parratt (organ), Parry and Stanford (composition). He studied abroad under Bruch, Berlin, and Ravel, Paris.

Vaughan Williams was one of England's great musicians. His musical interests were broad, embodying all forms of composition from the simple hymn tune to massive symphonies. He served as organist at the South Lambeth Church, London, for three years. As a member of the English Folk-Song Society he involved himself in collecting and arranging folksongs. This activity was a strong influence on his compositions. He is held in high esteem for having been responsible for the introduction of numerous folksongs into major hymnals.

Dr. Williams was the musical editor of the famous *English Hymnal*, 1906, *Songs of Praise*, 1925, and with Martin Shaw, of the *Oxford Book of Carols*, 1928.

99   Now Thank We All Our God

NUN DANKET 6.7.6.7.6.6.6.6.

Nun danket alle Gott
Martin Rinckart, 1586-1649
Tr. Catherine Winkworth, 1827-1878
Melody by Johann Crüger, 1598-1662

Written during the anguish and privation of the Thirty Years' War (1618-1648) as a table grace, this hymn continues to serve thoughtful and thankful people the world over. It has been called the German *Te Deum* and since the devastating days of the 17th century has been sung regularly at national festivals of joy and thanksgiving.

The first two stanzas seem to be a paraphrase of The Wisdom of Jesus, the Son of Sirach, or Ecclesasticus 50: 22-24 which read:

And now bless the God of all,
who in every way does great things;
who exalts our days from birth,
and deals with us according to his mercy.
May he give us gladness of heart,
and grant that peace may be in
our days in Israel,
as in the days of God.
May he entrust us to his mercy!
and let him deliver us in our days!

The third stanza is a doxology to the trinity. The hymn was first published in *Jesu-Hertz-Büchlein*, 1636. This translation appeared in Miss Winkworth's *Lyra Germanica*, second series, 1858.

Martin Rinckart was a voluminous writer of prose and poetry, an excellent musician, an outstanding preacher, and a dedicated and devoted pastor to his people. It is said that during the worst year of the pestilence he alone remained in the walled town of Eilenburg to minister to the needs of the people. During this time he conducted funeral services for forty or fifty people a day. He was born in Eilenburg, April 23, 1586, attended the Latin school there after which he became a scholar and chorister at the famous St. Thomas School in Leipzig. In 1602 he began his studies in theology at the University of Leipzig. The remainder of his life was spent in Eilenburg where he died December 8, 1649.

For a note on Miss Winkworth see No. 58.

The tune NUN DANKET takes its name from the first line of the German text and appeared with the hymn in *Praxis pietatis melica* ("musical practice of piety") 1647. The melody is believed to have been written by Johan Crüger who was the original editor of the *Praxis*. Forty editions of this work appeared and remain important as the respository of the main thrust of Lutheran hymnody of the period.

For a note on Johann Crüger see No. 162.

100   Now Thank We All Our God

GRACIAS 6.7.6.7.6.6.6.6.

> *Nun danket alle Gott*
> Martin Rinckart, 1586-1649
> Tr. Catherine Winkworth, 1827-1878
>
> Geoffrey Beaumont, 1903-

For a note on Martin Rinckart see No. 99.

For a comment on Catherine Winkworth see No. 58.

GRACIAS is the second of two Beaumont tunes to be used in *A Hymnbook for Christian Worship*. This tune was one of several Father Beaumont included in the recording of his Folk Mass after it first appeared in leaflet form in 1957. The first appearance of these tunes in a major hymnal was in the *English Baptist Hymn Book*, 1962. *A Hymnbook for Christian Worship* is the first American hymnal to include them.

For a note on Geoffrey Beaumont see No. 326.

101   Come, Ye Thankful People, Come

ST. GEORGE'S WINDSOR 7.7.7.7.D.

Henry Alford, 1810-1871
Anna L. Barbauld, 1743-1825, and others
George J. Elvey, 1816-1893

This was probably Alford's most popular hymn among congregations on both sides of the Atlantic. Contrary to popular usage, it was not a hymn particularly appropriate for the Thanksgiving festival season but an eschatological hymn, that is, one dealing with final days of the earth. In contrast to the well-known text by the same name, this is a composite drawn from Alford and other unknown authors. What portion of the text is by Mrs. Barbauld is not clear. The revision by other unknown authors was an effort to change the eschatological thrust of Alford's text so that it would be more truly appropriate for the Harvest Home Festival in England and the Thanksgiving Festival in America.

Henry Alford, one of the Church of England's leading clergymen, held many important positions in the church and became, in 1857, the dean of Canterbury Cathedral, a position he held with distinction until his death. He was born in London, October 7, 1810, and died in Canterbury, January 12, 1871. He graduated with honors from Trinity College, Cambridge in 1832.

He made a number of contributions to literature, the most important being his edition of the Greek New Testament with notes. Percy Dearmer says it "became the standard critical commentary of the nineteenth century." (*Songs of Praise Discussed*, p. 379). The principal hymonological works published by Alford were his collections: *Hymns for the Sundays and Festivals Throughout the Year*, 1836; *Psalms and Hymns*, 1844; *Year of Praise*, 1867; and *Poetical Works*, 1868.

For a note on Anna Laetitia Barbauld see No. 85.

ST. GEORGE'S WINDSOR differentiates this tune from several others having the name St. George. It designates the beautiful and historic chapel at Windsor Castle outside of London where Elvey was organist and master of the boys from 1835 until 1882.

The composer, George Job Elvey, was born at Canterbury March 27, 1816, and died at Windlesham, Surrey, December 9, 1893. He began his musical life as a chorister in Canterbury Cathedral and later studied at the Royal Academy of Music. His musical degrees were taken at Oxford. He was knighted in 1871 by Queen Victoria. Elvey's compositions include two oratorios, anthems, services, chants and a number of hymn tunes, many of which were written especially for *Hymns Ancient and Modern*. Among his instrumental music is an impromptu for organ called "Christmas Bells."

102   *We Gather Together*

KREMSER 12.11.12.11.

Wilt heden nu treden
Anonymous, 16th century
Tr. Theodore Baker, 1851-1934
Nederlandtsche Gedenckclanck, 1626
Arr. Edward Kremser, 1838-1914

In 1626 a collection of folk songs entitled *Nederlandtsche Gedenckclanck* was edited and published by one Adrian Valerius in which this hymn and tune appeared. The text is by an unknown patriot who wrote it in celebration of the Netherland's freedom from Spanish rule near the end of the sixteenth century. Its popularity was revitalized toward the end of the 19th century as a result of Edward Kremser's work for male chorus and orchestra, *Sechs Altniederländische Volkslieder* which contained material from Valerius. This translation is by Theodore Baker.

Theodore Baker, born in New York City June 3, 1851, was for many years literary editor and translator for G. Schirmer, Inc., music publishers. While employed with that firm he published his well-known *Biographical Dictionary of Musicians*, 1900, to which the present writer has referred numerous times in preparing these notes. He studied music in Leipzig, Germany, and was the author of the first significant study of the music of the American Indian. This subject was treated in his Doctor of Philosophy dissertation in 1882, *Über die Musik der nordamerikanische Wilden*. Leaving G. Schirmer in 1926, he returned to Germany where he died October 13, 1934, at Dresden.

KREMSER is the name of the arranger of the tune which appeared in Valerius' work mentioned above.

Edward (Eduard) Kremser was born in Vienna, Austria, April 10, 1838, and died there November 27, 1914. He became the director of Vienna's *Mannergesangverein* and other important musical organizations. He composed operettas, works for piano, voice, and orchestra.

His settings for the *Sechs Altniederländische Volkslieder* are his most famous compositions.

103   Creator of the Stars of Night

CONDITOR ALME L.M.

Conditor alme siderum
Ninth century
Tr. John Mason Neale, 1818-1866, alt.
Version in *The Hymnal* 1940
Sarum plainsong mode IV
Harm. J. H. Arnold, 1887-1956

For a note on this hymn see No. 104.

For a note on John Mason Neale see No. 155.

The tune known as CONDITOR ALME is the plainsong traditionally associated with this text. It has been a popular tune with both Protestants and Catholics through the centuries. There have been many alterations in its rhythm to accommodate the variety of texts to which it has been set but here we find it a beautiful example of syllabic chant which retains much of its ancient flavor. The tune name is derived from the first line of the Latin hymn with which it has been associated.

The tune appeared in America in 1848 in Mason and Webb's, *The National Psalmist,* bearing the name AMBROSE apparently because they thought it to be an advent hymn by St. Ambrose. The accompaniment was composed by John Henry Arnold, an English authority on plainsong.

104   Creator of the Stars of Night

PUER NOBIS NASCITUR L.M.

Conditor alme siderum
Tr. John Mason Neale, 1818-1866
Ninth century
Version in *The Hymnal* 1940
Adapted by Michael Praetorius, 1571-1621
Harm. George R. Woodward, 1848-1934

The hymn beginning *Conditor alme siderum* is by an unknown Latin author. According to Daniel, *Thesaurus Hymnologicus* (1841), it was found in a ninth-century manuscript in Bern.

Neale based his translation on a form found in the Sarum Breviary.

It was to be sung at vespers on the first Saturday before the first Sunday of Advent and throughout the Advent season on Sundays and weekdays except for festival days. Neale's translation appeared in the first edition of the *Hymnal Noted*, 1852, in six stanzas of four lines each.

For a note on John Mason Neale see No. 155.

The melody has been adapted by Michael Praetorius in his *Musae Sioniae*, 1609, from an earlier carol beginning *Puer nobis nascitur*, the earliest example of which was found in Cyriak Spangenberg's *Christliches Gesang-büchlein*, 1568. The Praetorius adaptation of the melody was set to the words "Geborn ist Gottes Söhnelein."

Praetorius is the latinized form of the surname Schulz. There is relatively little information concerning the life of Michael Praetorius. He was born in Thuringia in 1551, attended the University of Frankfurt an der Oder, was kapellmeister at Lüneburg, organist, kapellmeister, and secretary to the Duke of Brunswick, and Prior of Ringelheim. He died on February 15, 1621. His many choral compositions and adaptations are of high merit but his fame rests primarily on his authorship of *Syntagma Musicum,* a descriptive treatise on ancient and ecclesiastical music and musical instruments. The latter has served as an excellent resource for those interest in early German organ-building technique.

George Ratcliffe Woodward harmonized this tune for *The Cowley Carol Book,* 1901. Woodward was a graduate of Cambridge University and became a well-known scholar, musician, clergyman. He was ordained to the Anglican clergy in 1875 and during his ministry became interested in hymnody. His chief contribution to hymnody is his *Songs of Syon* (1903-1910) which contained much interesting music from plainsong melodies to Lutheran tunes, English, Scottish, and French Psalm tunes.

105   *Lift Up Your Heads, Ye Mighty Gates*

TRURO L.M.

Based on Psalm 24
Georg Weissel, 1590-1635
Tr. Catherine Winkworth, 1827-1878, alt.
Psalmodia Evangelica, 1789

Considered one of the finest German Advent hymns, "Lift Up Your Heads" is based on Psalm 24 and designated to be sung on the first Sunday in Advent. It first appeared in Part 1 of Georg Weissel's *Preussische Fest-Lieder,* 1642. This translation is from the First Series of Catherine Winkworth's *Lyra Germanica,* 1855.

Georg Weissel was one of the most important early hymn writers of Prussia. Born at Domnau in 1590, he attended the University of Königsberg from 1608 to 1611. In 1614 he was appointed rector of the school at Friedland, a position he held for three years after which he returned to the University of Königsberg to resume his study of theology. He became pastor of the Altgrossgart Church at Königsberg in 1623 and remained there until his death on August 1, 1635.

For a note on Miss Winkworth see No. 58.

TRURO is an anonymous tune first published with Isaac Watts' hymn, "Now to the Lord a Noble Song" in Thomas Williams' *Psalmodia Evangelica,* 1789. Truro is the name of the very old cathedral city in southwestern Cornwall, England.

106 Come, Thou Long-Expected Jesus

STUTTGART 8.7.8.7.

Charles Wesley, 1707-1788
Christian Friedrich Witt, 1660-1716
Psalmodia Sacra, Gotha, 1715

This hymn first appeared in a small book containing twenty-four hymns known as *Hymns for the Nativity of Our Lord,* 1744. Oddly enough it did not appear in Wesley's *Hymn Book* until the revised edition of 1875. Before that it was used in Whitefield's *Collection,* 1753, Madan's *Psalms and Hymns,* 1760, and Toplady's *Psalms and Hymns,* 1776.

For a comment on Charles Wesley see No. 180.

The tune STUTTGART is generally attributed to Christian Friedrich Witt. It first appeared in *Psalmodia Sacra,* 1715, where it was set to Christopher Titus' hymn *"Sollt es gleich besweilen scheinem."* This is an adaptation of the original tune.

The composer was born at Altenburg about 1660. He studied music at Nürnberg and became kappelmeister at Altenburg. He was the composer of cantatas, a number of hymn tunes, and instrumental works. Witt died on April 13, 1716.

107   Ah! Think Not the Lord Delayeth

ALLES IST AN GOTTES SEGEN 8.8.7.D.

Percy Dearmer, 1867-1936
Attr. to J. B. König, 1691-1758
Harmonischer Lieder-Schatz, 1738

Percy Dearmer was a distinguished English clergyman, writer, and hymnist. He was born in London in 1867 and died there in 1936. He received his education at the Westminster School and Christ Church, Oxford. After having been ordained in 1891 he served a number of small churches in London as curate. From 1901 to 1915 he was vicar of St. Mary the Virgin, Primrose Hill, London.

Dr. Dearmer served as secretary to the London branch of the Christian Social Union for a number of years and also as chairman of the League of Arts. During World War I he was a chaplain to the British Red Cross and spent most of his time in Serbia. He also served as a lecturer for the Y.M.C.A. After the war Dr. Dearmer received the appointment of professor of ecclesiastical art at Kings College, London. He held this position from 1919 until his death in 1936.

His interest in all branches of ecclesiastical art brought him in contact with two of England's finest musicians, Ralph Vaughan Williams and Martin Shaw, with whom he was to produce three outstanding hymnals. The first was The *English Hymnal,* 1906; the second, *Songs of Praise,* 1925 and 1931; and the third, *The Oxford Book of Carols,* 1931. Martin Shaw was organist at St. Mary the Virgin Church from 1908 until 1920 which means Dearmer and Shaw worked closely together and shared their concerns for music and worship of the church. Vaughan Williams served as organist at the South Lambeth Church for three years (1896-1899). This may have been the same church Dearmer served briefly in his early life. If so one can understand how these men came together and worked so closely in creating these outstanding books of music and poetry.

Oxford University honored Dr. Dearmer by conferring upon him the Doctor of Divinity degree. He was made Canon of Westminster in 1931.

Dr. Dearmer tells us in his *Songs of Praise Discussed* that the hymn "Ah! Think Not the Lord Delayeth" was written especially for a Norwegian tune both Williams and Shaw wanted to include in *Songs of Praise.* The hymn is based on scripture: stanza one is based on Matthew 24:48; 18:20; and 15:17; stanza two is based on both Matthew and Luke 13; and the final stanza on Acts 1:7.

Johann Balthasar König was born at Waltershausen in 1691 and died at Frankfurt in 1758. As a boy he was a chorister at Frankfurt-am-Main. In 1791 he was appointed choirmaster at St. Catherine's Church in Frankfurt under Georg P. Telemann and subsequently succeeded him as director of church as well as municipal music. His principal musical contribution seems to have been based on his editing the outstanding and certainly the most comprehensive choral book of eighteenth-century Germany. This book contained 1,940 tunes and included the French Calvinistic Psalm tunes. It was titled *Harmonischer Lieder-Schatz oder Allgemeines Evangelisches Choral-buch* and bore the date 1738. The name of the tune is from the first line of the original chorale.

108   O Come, O Come, Emmanuel

VENI EMMANUEL 8.8.8.8.8.8.

Veni, veni Emmanuel
Psalteriolum Cantionum Catholicarum, Cologne
1710
Sts. 1, 2: Tr. John Mason Neale 1818-1866
Sts. 3, 4: Tr. Henry Sloan Coffin 1877-1954

Adapted from plainsong phrases by
Thomas Helmore, 1811-1890

This hymn is based on the original seven great antiphons of the medieval church which were gradually introduced into the liturgy for use before and after the Magnificat during vespers in Advent. The metrical form comes from the pen of an unknown author who added the refrain in the thirteenth century. This basic form appeared in the seventh edition of the *Psalteriolum Canticarum Catholicarum* which was published in Cologne in 1710, from which John Mason Neale made his translation. It appeared in his *Mediaeval Hymns*, 1851, and in a revised form in his *Hymnal Noted*, 1854, for which Thomas Helmore provided much of the music. The present version uses two stanzas from the Neale translation.

For a note on John Mason Neale see No. 155.

The last two stanzas are the work of Henry Sloan Coffin, noted American clergyman, lecturer, and author. Dr. Coffin was born in New York City, January 5, 1877, and was educated at Yale. He also studied at New College, Edinburgh, and the University of Marburg. He was an ordained Presbyterian minister, served several churches in New York, taught practical theology at Union Theological Seminary, and served as president of that school from 1926 until 1945. He was the recipient of a number of honorary degrees from American colleges and universities in recognition of his outstanding contributions to the church and theological education. He died Nov. 25, 1954.

The tune VENI EMMANUEL derives its name from the Latin text of this hymn and is probably based on several plainsong phrases arranged especially by Thomas Helmore for Dr. Neale's translation as it appeared in the *Hymnal Noted*, 1854.

Thomas Helmore was born in Kidderminster, England, in 1811 and died in London in 1890. He was educated at Magdalen Hall, Oxford, and became an Anglican clergyman, musician, translator, author, and editor of books on church music. For a time he was vice-principal of St. Marks College, Chelsea, and master of the choristers at the Chapel Royal at St. James. His interest in the Oxford Movement led to his close association with John Mason Neale and other leaders of the movement resulting in his becoming a strong advocate of the use of Gregorian Tones in Anglican worship.

109　　*O Come, O Come, Emmanuel*

VENI EMMANUEL 8.8.8.8.8.8.

Veni, veni Emmanuel
Psalteriolum Cantionum
Catholicarum, Cologne, 1710
Sts. 1.2: Tr. John Mason Neale, 1818-1866, alt.
Sts. 3,4: Henry Sloane Coffin, 1877-1954
Plainsong Melody, Mode I
Arr. Ernest White, 1899-

For comments on this hymn see No. 108.

This arrangement of VENI EMMANUEL by Ernest White is from the *Service Book and Hymnal* (Lutheran) 1958. Note how the accompaniment preserves the flavor of the plainsong melody.

Ernest White is a native of London, Canada. He studied under Lynnwood Farnam in New York City and became director of music at the Church of St. Mary, the Virgin, on Times Square, New York City, where he remained for more than twenty-five years. For a time he taught at Butler University and Christian Theological Seminary at Indianapolis, Indiana. He established a printing business under the name of St. Mary's Press which is presently known as the Ernest White Editions and specializes in noncommercial church and organ music.

110   Comfort, Comfort Ye My People

PSALM 42 8.7.8.7.7.7.8.8.

Based on Isaiah 40:1-8
Johann Olearius, 1611-1684
Tr. Catherine Winkworth, 1827-1878, alt.
Genevan Psalter, 1551

Julian's Dictionary of Hymnology gives the author's name as Johannes, the son of Johann Olearius. Johannes was born at Halle on September 17, 1611. He was educated at the University of Wittenberg after which he first became a lecturer and then an adjunct professor on the faculty of philosophy. He was appointed the chief court preacher and chaplain at Halle and in 1680 received the same appointment at Weissenfels where he remained until his death on August 24, 1684.

Olearius was one of the most important hymn writers and compilers of hymns in seventeenth-century Germany. He published a monumental collection known as *Geistliche Singe-Kunst* in 1671 which contained 1,207 hymns, 302 of which were from his own pen. The following year the second edition contained 1,340 hymns.

This particular hymn was written St. John the Baptist's Day. Being based on Isaiah 40:1-8, a text frequently used as an Advent text, makes this hymn especially useful at that season of the year.

For a note on the translator see No. 58.

The hymn and tune have been closely associated since they first appeared together in Miss Winkworth's *Chorale Book for England,* 1863.

The history of the *Genevan Psalter* is too long and involved to be treated fully or adequately here. Suffice it to point out several aspects of its long and varied development.

Beginning with Clément Marot's translation of Psalm 6 in 1533 and John Calvin's earliest attempt to introduce congregational singing into public worship about 1539, the foundation for a long series of Psalters was laid. By 1542 Marot had published thirty translations from the Book of Psalms. Even though he had authority to make these translations, he was forced to leave France for his efforts. In 1543 we find him in Geneva where he once again published his original thirty Psalms along with twenty more. His death in 1544 brought a temporary halt to further development of the *Genevan Psalter* but Calvin requested Théodore de Bèze (1519-1605) to continue the work.

Louis Bourgeois published a musical edition of Marot's Fifty

Psalms in 1547 and it was not until 1551 that thirty-four additional Psalms translated by Beza appeared with those of Marot. Psalm 42 was one of these but it may not have been before the 1554 edition that Louis Bourgeois either adapted or composed the present tune for it. At any rate, Bourgeois was musical editor of the *Genevan Psalter* from 1545 to 1557. The *Psalter* went many editions and revisions until radical changes in language and the rise of hymnody undercut its popularity near the beginning of the nineteenth century.

111   Veiled in Darkness Judah Lay

NICHT SO TRAURIG 7.7.7.7.7.7.

Douglas LeTell Rights, 1891-1956
Johann Georg Ebeling, 1637-1676

These words were written by Douglas LeTell Rights, a Moravian divinity student, for the annual Christmas service at Harvard Divinity School in 1915.

After graduating from the University of North Carolina, Douglas LeTell Rights received his education for the ministry at the Moravian Theological Seminary, Bethlehem, Pennsylvania, and Harvard University. Except for a chaplaincy in the army during World War I, his ministry was exclusively with churches in the state of North Carolina beginning in Greensboro and ending with the Trinity Moravian Church in the city of his birth, Winston-Salem. He wrote extensively on historical and archaeological subjects, including *A Voyage Down the Yadkin-Great Peedee River* and the *American Indian in North Carolina*.

NICHT SO TRAURIG is the melody to Johann Ebeling's setting of Paul Gerhardt's hymn beginning *"Nicht so traurig, nicht so sehr,"* published in 1666. Bach composed a tune by the same name which is used widely and bears no resemblance to the present tune.

Johann Georg Ebeling, successor to Johann Crüger as director of music at St. Nicholas Church, Berlin, in 1662, was born at Lüneberg July 8, 1637. He became professor of music at College of St. Charles, or the Caroline Gymnasium at Stettin, in 1668. His chief publication was settings for many of Paul Gerhardt's hymns in his *Pauli Gerhardi Zeistliche Andachten* (1666-67). He died at Stettin in 1676.

112 Wake, Awake, for Night Is Flying

WACHET AUF 8.9.8.8.9.8.6.6.4.8.8.

> Wachet auf, ruft uns die Stimme
> Philipp Nicolai, 1556-1608
> Tr. Catherine Winkworth, 1827-1878
> and others
> Philipp Nicolai, 1556-1608
> Harm. J. S. Bach, 1685-1750

Written at the time of a great plague in 1598, this well-known text was first published in the Appendix to a series of meditations known as *Frewden-Spiegel des ewigen Lebens* (Mirror of Joy of Life Eternal), 1699. The present form is based on a translation by Catherine Winkworth which appeared in her *Lyra Germanica* second series, 1858.

For a comment on Philipp Nicolai see No. 287.

For a comment on Catherine Winkworth see No. 58.

WACHET AUF is J. S. Bach's harmonization of a tune generally attributed to Philipp Nicolai but which some scholars believe to have been borrowed from earlier material.

For a note on J. S. Bach see No. 193.

113 Hail to the Lord's Anointed

WOODBIRD 7.6.7.6.D.

> Psalm 72
> James Montgomery, 1771-1854
> Traditional German Melody

Written for and sung at a Moravian settlement, probably Fulneck, Yorkshire, where Montgomery was a member, this hymn has appeared in every major hymnal in the English-speaking world. Although first used as a Christmas ode, Montgomery added to it and printed it in the *Evangelical Magazine* in 1822 under the title, "Imitation of the 72nd Psalm (Tune Culmstock)." The additions, which are omitted here, made it a missionary hymn and as such it appeared in a number of hymnbooks. The present arrangement of stanzas provides an excellent and beautiful Advent hymn.

For a note on James Montgomery see No. 324.

WOODBIRD is the melody of the German folk song *Der Ritter zum Besuch.* A German friend informs us that school children learn this minnesong as historic poetry in German schools. *The Hymnal 1940 Companion* (Second Edition Revised) tells us it was first found in a seventeenth-century manuscript tablatur book from Memmingen. The melodic flow has a striking resemblance to LOBE DEN HERREN.

114 Let All Mortal Flesh Keep Silence

PICARDY 8.7.8.7.8.7.

Σιγησάτω πᾶσα σὰρξ βροτεία
Liturgy of St. James
Tr. Gerard Moultrie, 1829-1885
Traditional French Carol

Since about the fifth century this Prayer of the Cherubic Hymn has been sung as the sacred elements were brought into the sanctuary at the beginning of the Liturgy of the Faithful. It is from the Liturgy of St. James of Jerusalem. This metrical translation is by Gerard Moultrie and appeared in the second edition of Shipley's *Lyra Eucharistica*, 1864. A literal translation appeared in Neale and Little-dale's *Translation of the Ancient Liturgies,* 1868-1869.

Gerard Moultrie, an Anglican clergyman, was born at Rugby, England, on September 16, 1829, and died at Southleigh April 25, 1885. Educated at Rugby and Exeter College, Oxford, his life was devoted to the church, schools and colleges, and to writing. His many translations of Greek, Latin, and German hymns appeared in the *Church Times* and other publications as well as in the *Peoples Hymnal,* 1867. Included in his publications are: *Hymns and Lyrics for the Seasons and Saints' Days of the Church,* 1867, *The Espousals of St. Dorothea and Other Verses,* 1870, and *Cantica Sanctorum,* 1880.

PICARDY was the name of a province in Northern France. The tune is believed to be a 17th-century religious folk song because of its traditional association with the ballad, *"La parabole du mauvais riche"* or *"Le ballade de Jésus-Christ."* In Julien Tiersot's *Melodies,* Paris, 1887, the tune is entitled ROMANCERO. It apparently appeared for the first time as a hymn tune in the *English Hymnal,* 1906, where it was set to the present text. Its introduction to American hymnals was through the *New Hymnal* (Protestant Episcopal), 1918.

115 *On Jordan's Bank the Baptist's Cry*

ALSTONE L.M.

> *Jordanis oras prae via*
> Charles Coffin, 1676-1749
> Tr. John Chandler, 1806-1876, alt.
>
> Christopher Edwin Willing, 1830-1904

This Advent hymn is from the Latin authored by Charles Coffin, a French Latin scholar and churchman. It was first published in his *Hymni Sacri,* 1736, and was one of many of his one hundred hymns which appeared in the *Paris Breviary* the same year.

Coffin was born at Buzancy in the Ardennes in 1676. He studied at Duplessis College, University of Paris, and became successively a teacher at the College of Dormans-Beauvais, its principal, rector of the university, and again its principal. He was the greatest Latin author France has produced. His publications include a collection of Latin poems, 1727, and his *Hymni Sacri,* 1737. He died at Paris, June 20, 1749.

John Chandler, born at the Vicarage of Witley, Surrey, June 16, 1806, was educated at Corpus Christi College, Oxford, ordained in 1831, and succeeded his father as Vicar at Witley in 1837. He was an excellent translator of early Latin hymns and published several works including *The Hymns of the Primitive Church,* 1837, which included "On Jordan's Stormy Banks." He died at Putney July 1, 1876.

ALSTONE was first published in the 1868 Appendix to the first edition of *Hymns Ancient and Modern* where it was set to Cecil Frances Alexander's hymn, "We Are but Little Children Weak."

Born February 28, 1830, in Devonshire, England, Christopher Willing became one of England's important musicians. He was successively a chorister at Westminster Abbey, 1839-1845, organist of the Blackheath Park Church, 1845, assistant organist at Westminster Abbey, and from 1848 until 1879 organist at the Foundling Hospital. At various times during these years he was also organist at St. Paul's, Covent Gardens, and All Saints' in Margaret Street. In 1868 he edited *The Book of Common Praise.* Willing served for a time as chorusmaster and organist for the Sacred Harmonic Society and conducted the St. Alban's Choral Union. His death occurred December 1, 1904, at Southgate, Middlesex.

116   Hark! a Thrilling Voice Is Sounding

MERTON 8.7.8.7.

Vox clara ecce intonat Latin, c. 6th century
Tr. Edward Caswall, 1814-1878, alt.
William Henry Monk, 1823-1889

This translation is from a Latin hymn for Lauds in Advent which dates from the tenth century. From the eleventh century it appears in the Mozarabic rite for Wednesday vespers. Caswall included it in his *Lyra Catholica,* 1849, which consisted of 197 translations of Breviary hymns.

Edward Caswall was born at Yately, Hampshire, July 15, 1814, and died at Edgbaston, Birmingham, January 2, 1878. He was educated at Marlborough and Brasenose College, Oxford. After graduating with honors he took orders in the Church of England and became curate of Stratford-sub-Castle, in Wiltshire. Like many of his colleagues, he became deeply involved in the Tractarian Movement and after seven years resigned his curacy to become a Roman Catholic. Upon his wife's death in 1850, Caswall became a priest and affiliated himself with the Oratory of St. Philip Neri at Edgbaston where he worked under John Henry Newman ministering to the sick and the poor. He spent the rest of his life there, writing original hymns and translating others from Roman Breviaries. He was buried at Redwall, a few miles from Birmingham.

Caswall stands second only to John Mason Neale for the quantity and quality of translations from the Latin. His major publications include: *Lyra Catholica,* 1849; *The Masque of Mary, and Other Poems,* 1858; *Hymns and Poems,* 1863; and *A May Pageant and Other Poems,* 1865.

MERTON first appeared in *The Parish Choir,* 1850, and afterward with this text in the first edition of *Hymns Ancient and Modern.* It is named after Merton College, Oxford, which was founded by Walter de Merton before its removal to Oxford or for the parish of Merton where Merton was born and where the "seminary of learning" was founded.

For a comment on William Henry Monk see No. 47.

117   The First Nowell

THE FIRST NOWELL Irregular with Refrain

Traditional English carol
Traditional English melody

We are indebted to Davis Gilbert and William Sandys (1792-1874) for preserving this Old English Carol. The present text consists of five of the nine original stanzas. Gilbert's version appeared in his *Ancient Christmas Carols,* 1823, and is referred to as a "rougher" version than Sandys' which appeared in his *Christmas Carols, Ancient and Modern,* 1833. Despite the inaccurate reference to the biblical story in stanza two this old carol has brought joy to countless people during the Christmas season. Much of the text is better suited for Epiphany than Christmas.

THE FIRST NOWELL is the traditional tune sung to this carol. The origin of the English spelling of "Nowell" is uncertain. It is obviously derived from continental sources such as the French *"Noël,"* the Latin *"Novella"* (news), the Spanish *"Natal,"* or the Italian *"Natale."* The present harmonization is identical to that which appears in the writer's copy of *Christmas Carols, Old and New,* N.D., edited by Henry Ramsden Bramley and John Stainer (Novello, etc.). We assume it to be the work of Stainer.

118   Silent Night, Holy Night

STILLE NACHT Irregular

Stille Nacht, heilige Nacht
Joseph Mohr. 1792-1848
Tr. John F. Young, 1820-1865
Franz Gruber, 1787-1863

Since it was first sung on Christmas Eve, 1818, at Oberndorf, Austria, this Christmas hymn has become a universal favorite. It was written as a result of a change in program necessitated by the breakdown of the organ at the Oberndorf parish church. This translation, one of a dozen or more, is said to be by Bishop John Freeman Young (1820-1885), an American hymnologist and second bishop of the Episcopal Diocese of Florida.

Joseph Mohr was born at Salzburg, Austria, December 11, 1792. He was ordained a Roman Catholic priest by the Bishop of Salzburg in 1815 and spent his entire life serving churches near his birthplace. His famous hymn was written in 1818 while he was an assistant priest at Arnsdorf, near Oberndorf. He became priest of the Wagrein Church in 1837 and remained there until his death on December 4, 1848. So far as is known this is his only hymn.

STILLE NACHT was composed for this text shortly before the Christmas Eve service in 1818. Reliable sources say it was sung as a duet by Mohr and Gruber to the composer's guitar accompaniment.

Franz Gruber, a close personal friend of Joseph Mohr, was born at Hochburg, Upper Austria, November 25, 1787. As a son of a linen weaver he learned that trade but his strong musical talent led him to devote his life to music. He became the schoolmaster in a Roman Catholic school and served as organist in Arnsdorf, near Oberndorf. From 1833 until his death on June 7, 1863, Gruber was choral director at Hallein, just twelve miles from his birthplace.

119   It Came Upon the Midnight Clear

CAROL C.M.D.

Edmund H. Sears, 1810-1876, alt.
Richard S. Willis, 1819-1900

"Calm on the listening ear of night" and "It came upon the midnight clear," both by Edmund Hamilton Sears, have been called the best of their kind in the English language. Throughout his Unitarian ministry Sears held to his belief in the divinity of Christ, a belief which is duly reflected in his hymns.

Born in Sandisfield, Massachusetts, on April 6, 1810, and educated at Union College and Harvard Divinity School, Sears became in 1838 the pastor of First Unitarian Church in Wayland, Massachusetts. In 1840 he moved to Lancaster, Massachusetts, but returned to his former pastorate in 1847. After eighteen years he accepted a call to serve the church in Weston, Massachusetts, where he remained until his death on January 14, 1876.

"It came upon the midnight clear" was submitted to the editor of the *Christian Register* in December, 1849, and was published in the December issue, 1850. Since that time it has become firmly established as one of the "traditional" Christmas hymns and is sung wherever Christians gather to remember the birth of Christ.

CAROL was composed by Richard Storrs Willis. Its earliest form was as a study and was set to "See Israel's Gentle Shepherd Stand" in Willis' *Church Chorals and Choir Studies,* 1850. Willis himself adapted the tune for "While Shepherds Watched Their Flocks by Night" while he served as a vestryman in the Church of the Transfiguration in New York City.

The composer was born in Boston, Massachusetts, February 10, 1819, and was the son of the poet Nathaniel P. Willis. After graduating from Yale he spent six years in Germany studying composition with several outstanding teachers of music. Upon his return to New York, he became the music critic for several publications including the *New York Tribune*. He later became the editor of *The Musical Times* and *The Musical World*. His publications include: *Our Church Music,* 1856, *Church Chorals, Student Songs, and Waif Song,* 1876. Willis died in Detroit, Michigan, May 7, 1900.

120   O Little Town of Bethlehem

ST. LOUIS 8.6.8.6.7.6.8.6.

Phillips Brooks, 1835-1893

Lewis H. Redner, 1831-1908

During a visit to the Holy Land in 1865 Phillips Brooks spent Christmas Eve in Bethlehem where he received the inspiration for this well-known and loved Christmas hymn. It was written specifically for the children of the Sunday school at Holy Trinity Church in Philadelphia in 1868.

Phillips Brooks, one of America's great preachers, was the inspiration of millions of admirers on both sides of the Atlantic. Born in Boston, Massachusetts, December 13, 1835, he received his education in a Boston Latin School, Harvard, and the Episcopal Theological Seminary in Alexandria, Virginia. After his ordination in 1859 he was successively the rector of the Church of the Advent and Holy Trinity Church in Philadelphia, Trinity Church in Boston, and was appointed Bishop of Massachusetts in 1891. His power as a man and a preacher of the Gospel earned him invitations to preach for Queen Victoria, and in the two famous churches of London, Westminster Abbey and St. Paul's Cathedral. He died in Boston on January 23, 1893.

ST LOUIS was composed for this hymn by Lewis H. Redner, organist and Sunday school superintendent of the Holy Trinity Church in Philadelphia. William Reed Huntington gave the tune its name when he included it in a Sunday school hymnbook *The Church Porch,* 1874.

Lewis H. Redner was born and educated in Philadelphia. He was a successful real estate broker and an active layman in the church. He was organist at Holy Trinity during Dr. Brooks' tenure there and served nineteen years as the Sunday school superintendent. He composed the tune at Dr. Brooks' request and used it in the Sunday school on Christmas, 1868. He died in Atlantic City, New Jersey.

121   *O Come, All Ye Faithful*

ADESTE FIDELES Irregular

Adeste Fideles
John Francis Wade?, 1711-1786
Tr. Frederick Oakeley, 1802-1880, and others

John Francis Wade?, 1711-1786

The authorship of this famous Christmas hymn is unknown. It is attributed to John Francis Wade because of six manuscript copies of the text which carry his name. The doubt actually arises from the nature of Wade's business. He earned his living copying and selling manuscripts, and this may or may not have been an original effort. The Latin text preserved by Wade consisted of eight stanzas.

For a further comment on John Francis Wade see No. 187.

Canon Frederick Oakeley was born at Shrewsberry, England, September 5, 1802. Educated at Christ Church, Oxford, and ordained an Anglican priest, he served in various capacities at Litchfield Cathedral, Whitehall, and Margaret Chapel, London. As a result of his association with the Oxford Movement, he resigned all appointments with the Church of England in 1845 and became a Roman Catholic. He published four volumes of poetry and several prose works but is remembered primarily because of his translation of *"Adeste Fideles."* Canon Oakeley died January 29, 1880.

ADESTE FIDELES is also known as the PORTUGUESE HYMN and OPORTO. Its composer is not known for a certainty but it did appear for the first time in *Essay on the Church Plain Chant,* 1782. Vincent Novello (1781-1861), London music publisher, relates that the name PORTUGUESE HYMN was given the tune by the Duke of Leeds after he heard it sung in London's Portuguese Embassy Chapel around 1785.

122   *Joy to the World! the Lord Is Come*

ANTIOCH C.M.

Psalm 98
Isaac Watts, 1674-1748
Adapted from G. F. Handel, 1685-1759
Arr. Lowell Mason, 1792-1872

Christmas would be incomplete without the singing of this Christmas hymn which Isaac Watts derived from the final five verses of Psalm 98. The paraphrase first appeared in Watts' *Psalms of David Imitated in the Language of the New Testament,* 1719.

For a note on Watts see No. 48.

The present hymn omits the familiar stanza:

No more let sins and sorrows grow,
Nor thorns infest the ground;
He comes to make his blessings flow
Far as the curse is found.

ANTIOCH, also found under the names COMFORT, MESSIAH, HOLY TRIUMPH, JERUSALEM, and MEDIA, is of uncertain origin. Traditionally it has been ascribed to George Friedrich Handel on the grounds of its similarity to the first four notes of the chorus, "Lift Up Your Heads" from *The Messiah* and the tenor aria, "Every Valley" from the same work. Some scholars have suggested the tune is distinctively American in origin, and one has even likened it to a late eighteenth-century Methodist revival tune. Its first appearance seems to have been in Lowell Mason's *Modern Psalmist,* Boston, 1839.

George Friedrich Handel, the son of a barber and a surgeon-valet to the Prince of Saxe-Magdeburg, was born at Halle, February 23, 1685. At an early age his musical abilities were evident but were suppressed by his father who wanted the boy to become a lawyer. Handel taught himself to play the harpsichord and was eventually given the opportunity to study under Zachau, organist at the Halle Cathedral. Being made assistant to Zachau, Handel was obliged to compose a motet for each Sunday for the period of three years.

Out of deference to his father's will Handel entered the University at Halle to study law but the pull of music was too great and after one year he was employed as an instrumentalist in the German opera in Berlin. A trip through Italy gave him the opportunity to meet a number of the great Italian composers and to compose and produce a number of his first operas and oratorios.

Upon his return to Germany he became the kapellmeister to the Elector of Hanover, a position which was to become an embarrassment to him later. In 1710 Handel visited England and produced an opera. After returning to Hanover he asked for a second leave of absence, and in 1712 journeyed again to London where he produced several unsuccessful operas and the highly successful ode for the Queen's birthday, a Te Deum and Jubilate, commemorating the Peace of Utrecht. His popularity with the British helped him forget his obligations in Hanover, and he remained in England. Upon the death of Queen Ann, the Elector of Hanover became George I of England placing Handel in a precarious position with the court. He was forgiven for his unauthorized absence from Hanover and once again found himself in favor with royalty.

In 1727 Handel became a British subject where he spelled his name George Frideric Handel instead of George Friedrich Händel as it was spelled in Germany. His fame was the result of his numerous operas and instrumental compositions. Italian opera began to wane and the establishment of a rival company led to Handel's bankruptcy. In 1737 he suffered a stroke which was instrumental in his decision to give up opera. The year 1741 marks the real turning point in his career, a point at which he turned almost exclusively to the composition of oratorios. In 1742 he produced the work upon which his fame rests—*The Messiah*. This famous work was produced at Dublin on April 13.

His oratorios restored his position in musical circles and his fortune increased. Blindness struck in 1752 but did not deter his musical activity. He died in London on the Saturday between Good Friday and Easter Sunday, April 14, 1759, and was buried in the Poets' Corner of Westminster Abbey.

For a note on Lowell Mason see No. 273.

123 *Hark! the Herald Angels Sing*

MENDELSSOHN 7.7.7.7.D. with Refrain

Charles Wesley, 1707-1788, alt.
Felix Mendelssohn, 1809-1847
Arr. William H. Cummings, 1831-1915

This is another composite hymn based on an original by Charles Wesley written 1743. This version contains alterations by

Whitfield, Madan, Conyers, and DeCourney. The refrain was added in *The Supplement* to Tate's and Brady's *New Version,* 1782. The final form appeared in Kempthorne's *Select Portions,* 1810. Whitfield is responsible for the present first line which Wesley had originally written: "Hark! how all the welkin rings! Glory to the King of kings." Wesley's stanzas seven and eight, omitted here, are:

> 7) Come, Desire of nations, come,
>   Fix in us thy humble home;
>   Rise the woman's conquering seed,
>   Bruise in us the serpent's head.
> 8) Now display thy saving power,
>   Ruined nature now restore,
>   Now in mystic union join
>   Thine to ours, and ours to thine.

For a note on Charles Wesley see No. 180.

For a comment on Felix Mendelssohn see No. 328.

MENDELSSOHN, long associated with Wesley's text, is also known as ST. VINCENT, BETHLEHEM, BERLIN, and NATIVITY. The tune was adapted from the second chorus of Felix Mendelssohn's *Festegesang* for male chorus and orchestra which was composed in commemoration of the invention of printing and performed at the Gutenberg Festival in Leipzig in 1840. William H. Cummings, organist at Waltham Abbey, made the adaptation for this hymn and had it published in leaflet form in 1856. Almost immediately it was taken into hymnals and has remained the "standard" tune ever since.

William Hayman Cummings, composer, organist, conductor, tenor soloist, and musical scholar, was born in Sidbury, Devonshire, England, on August 22, 1831. As a boy he sang in the choir at St. Paul's and later at the Temple Church. He was a highly respected oratorio tenor soloist in England and America, and was particularly recognized for his performances in the Bach Passion music. Prior to full-time concertizing Mr. Cummings had been organist at Waltham Abbey (1847) (at which time he made the present setting of Mendelssohn's tune), professor of singing at the Royal Academy of Music (1879-1896), and principal of the Guildhall School of Music (1896). His musical antiquarian interests were realized in the publication of a number of books and treatises among which was a biography of Purcell, 1882, a book entitled, *God Save the King, the Origin and History of the Music and the Words,* London, 1902, and papers on a code for keyboard fingering as well as on the true composer of the music for Locke's *Macbeth.* He was one of the founders of the Purcell Society, composer of the cantata, *The Fairy Ring,* 1873, and some church music, part songs and glees. The University of Dublin conferred upon him the degree Mus. D. honoria causa. Cummings died in London on June 6, 1915.

124   Angels, from the Realms of Glory

REGENT SQUARE 8.7.8.7.8.7.

James Montgomery, 1771-1854
Henry T. Smart, 1813-1879

This hymn was written by James Montgomery for the Christmas Eve edition of his paper, *The Sheffield Iris,* in 1816. Three years later it was included in Thomas Cottrill's *Selection.* In 1825 Montgomery revised the poem and published it in his *Christian Psalmist.* It was also included as one of "three new carols" in *The Christmas Box,* 1825, published by the Tract Society of England.

The popularity of this hymn cannot be questioned. It is included in the hymnbooks of English-speaking people around the world. Originally in five stanzas the last is generally omitted. It reads:

> Sinners wrung with true repentance,
>   Doomed for guilt to endless pains,
> Justice now revokes the sentence;
>   Mercy calls you, Break your chains;
>   Come and worship,
>   Come and worship,
> Worship Christ the new-born King.

For a note on James Montgomery see No. 324.

Henry Smart, lawyer turned musician, was born into a musical family in London, October 26, 1813. His father was a violinist and his uncle, Sir George, was organist at St. George's, Windsor. He was largely self-taught but received some instruction from his father and one W. H. Kearns. He became a proficient and successful organist, composer, organ designer, and construction supervisor. He served a number of churches in London as organist, ending his career at St. Pancras, Euston Road. He became blind in 1865 but did not permit his affliction to force him into retirement. He composed several cantatas, a number of part songs, songs, organ music, and complete services. He died in London, July 6, 1879.

REGENT SQUARE was composed especially for the English Presbyterian hymnbook, *Psalms and Hymns for Divine Worship,* 1867. There the tune was used for Horatius Bonar's hymn "Glory be to God the Father." The name of the tune refers to the Regent Square Church, which was, of course, located on the famous square in an old part of London, named in honor of the Prince Regent who later became George IV. Dr. James Hamilton, pastor of the Regent Square Church, was the editor of the hymnbook.

125   Once in Royal David's City

IRBY 8.7.8.7.7.7.

Cecil Francis Alexander, 1823-1895

Henry J. Gauntlett, 1805-1876

First appearing in her *Hymns for Little Children,* 1848, this hymn is another attempt to explain or illustrate the several articles of the Apostles' Creed in language easily understood by children. The words are based on the idea of the second article, "And in Jesus Christ, His only Son, our Lord, who was conceived by the Holy Ghost, born of the Virgin Mary." These words are stanzas 1, 2, 4, and 5 of the original six-stanza text.

For a comment on Mrs. Alexander see No. 2.

IRBY was composed for this text and first appeared as a unison carol in Gauntlett's *Christmas Carols,* 1849. The four-part setting was made by the composer for *Hymns Ancient and Modern,* 1861.

Henry John Gauntlett (1805-1876) was one of England's foremost composers, as well as organist and musical historian. Felix Mendelssohn had the highest praise for his musical facility. Gauntlett was the son of a clergyman and at the age of nine he was organist at his father's church and later served as choirmaster from 1819 to 1825. Until 1844 he devoted himself primarily to the study and practice of law, but from 1844 he gave his full attention to music. The Archbishop of Canterbury conferred on him the Lambeth Musical Doctorate in 1842. He was a prolific composer of psalm and hymn tunes (some ten thousand), musical editor, and designer of new organs. He published a musical edition of Mrs. Alexander's *Hymns for Little Children* in 1858.

126   *While Shepherds Watched Their Flocks*

CHRISTMAS C.M.

Nahum Tate, 1652-1715
George Friedrich Handel, 1685-1759

"While Shepherds Watched Their Flocks by Night" appeared for the first time in the *Supplement to the New Version,* circa 1700, and has since been included in most hymnals in the English-speaking world and has been translated into several languages.

For a note on *The New Version* see No. 80.

Nahum Tate, the son of an Irish clergyman, was born in Dublin in 1652 and was educated at Trinity College, Dublin. He published a volume of poems in 1677, but wrote primarily for the stage, adapting the plays of others including Shakespeare. He collaborated with Dryden on *Absolom and Achitophel,* writing all of the second part except for about two hundred lines. Apparently he was a man of intemperate and improvident life for he died a fugitive from his creditors in a sanctuary for debtors in Southwork in 1715. His greatest achievement was his collaboration with Nicholas Brady in producing their *New Version of the Psalms of David,* 1696.

CHRISTMAS is adapted from a melody in Handel's opera *Siroe* which was premiered at His Majesty's Theatre on February 17, 1728. The arrangement here is probably by Lowell Mason. The name is mentioned in Henry L. Mason's *Hymn Tunes of Lowell Mason, A Bibliography* (p. 90), in the List Number 8, "Hymn-Tune Arrangements, Wanting" and is credited to Handel.

For a note on George Friedrich Handel see No. 122.

127   *On This Day Earth Shall Ring*

PERSONENT HODIE, 6.6.6.6.6. with Refrain

Piae Cantiones, 1582
Tr. Jane M. Joseph, *c.* 1894-1929
Piae Cantiones, 1582
Arr. by Gustav T. Holst, 1874-1934

This fourteenth-century German Latin carol was preserved in a collection of medieval music edited by a Finnish student named

Theodoric Petri. The collection was published in 1582 as *Piae Cantiones*. The *Oxford Book of Carols*, 1928 (seventh impression 1936), gives the original Latin text from which the present translation is derived. The only information available relative to Jane Marion Joseph is that she was a pupil of Gustav Holst.

PERSONENT HODIE is called THEODORIC in *Songs of Praise*, 1925, where it is set a semitone higher to the hymn, "God Is Love; His the Care," by one A.F. Both names are derived from the source of the text and music. "Personent hodie" are the opening words of the Latin carol and Theodoric is the first name of the compiler of *Piae Cantiones*.

For a note on Gustav T. Holst see No. 135.

128　*Away in a Manger*

CRADLE SONG 11.11.11.11.

Anonymous
William James Kirkpatrick, 1838-1921

For many years this hymn was attributed to Martin Luther but recent scholarship has proved otherwise. It is now believed to have been written by an anonymous American Lutheran circa 1883 for the four-hundredth anniversary of Martin Luther's birth. All evidence points to the possibility of its being written for use in a Sunday school Christmas entertainment. Richard S. Hill's interest in this hymn led him to discover forty-one different musical settings of the text.

The tune CRADLE SONG has been traced to an 1895 pamphlet which contained seven songs entitled, "Around the World with Christmas. A Christmas Exercise. Words arranged by E. E. Hewitt. Music by John R. Sweney and William J. Kirkpatrick," etc. This is among the most popular tunes used with this text and is certainly the one most frequently used in modern hymnals.

William James Kirkpatrick was born February 27, 1838, in Ireland and at an early age came to Duncannon, Pennsylvania. He was a carpenter by trade, a Methodist by profession, and a musician by interest. He and one A. S. Kenks edited *Devotional Melodies*, 1859, a collection of camp-meeting songs. Later he collaborated with J. R. Sweney in producing forty-seven books of gospel songs. His devotion to this form of music led him to produce at least forty more books by himself after Mr. Sweney's death. He died September 29, 1921, at Germantown, Pennsylvania.

129   *Angels We Have Heard on High*

GLORIA 7.7.7.7. with Refrain

French Carol
French Carol

There is little doubt that this is one of America's best-known and best-loved carols. As would be expected, there are many versions of the text and harmonizations of the melody. The exact source of many of these is obscure. Some authorities believe the carol may have dated from the eighteenth century. The first-known publication in which it appeared is believed to be *Nouveau recueil decantiques,* 1855. The tune first appeared in an English book in R. R. Chope's *Carols for use in the Church,* 1875, where it was the musical vehicle for Grantham's "When the Crimson Sun Had Set."

Armin Haeussler writing in *The Story of Our Hymns* (p. 17) shares correspondence with Earl Marlatt which indicates that Dr. Marlatt had no recollection of having had anything to do with the text, despite the fact that several books credit him with either editing or adapting the text. The complete French text may be found in *The Hymnal 1940 Companion* [Second Edition Revised] p. 33.

Other versions of this carol are:

> "Bright angels we have heard on high"
> "Bright angel hosts are heard on high"
> "Hearken all! What holy singing"
> "Shepherds in the fields abiding"

130   *Come Hither, Ye Children*

IHR KINDERLEIN KOMMET 11.11.11.11.

Christian Schmidt
Tr. Anonymous
Johann A. P. Schulz, 1747-1800

Christian Schmidt was ordained in 1791 and became headmaster of a school and school inspector in Thannhausen, Mendel. His devotion to the needs of youth made him popular and effective with them. It is said he spent every morning from four until eight o'clock writing material for them. This hymn may have been the result of this practice. The poem was first published in the second edition of *Christliche Gesänge zur öffentlichen Gotteverehrung*, Augsburg, 1811. The translator is unknown.

The tune name is derived from the first three words of the first line of Schmidt's Christmas song for children.

No information on the composer has been found.

131 Break Forth, O Beauteous Heavenly Light

ERMUNTRE DICH, MEIN SCHWACHER GEIST 8.7.8.7.8.8.7.7.

Johann Rist, 1607-1667
Tr. John Troutbeck, 1832-1899
Arthur Tozer Russell, 1806-1874

Johann Schop, c. 1590-1664
Harm. J. S. Bach, 1685-1750

The author wrote some 680 hymns in which he intended to deal with the whole of theology. They were sung by Catholics and Protestants with great enthusiasm throughout Germany. Himself a Protestant, he was ecumenical in spirit and hoped for cooperation between ecclesiastical and political elements of Germany.

Rist was born at Ottensen March 8, 1607. He received his early education at Hamburg and Bremen and then entered the University of Rinteln. While there he came under the influence of Josua Stegmann, professor of theology and hymn writer, who inspired the young Rist to undertake hymnwriting.

Upon leaving the University he became a tutor to the children of a merchant in Hamburg and while on a trip with them to Rostock he became ill with the pestilence and nearly died. After his recovery he returned to Hamburg and became the tutor to the children of a lawyer. Through this connection he met and married Elizabeth, sister of Judge Franz Stapfel. Stapfel was instrumental in having Rist appointed pastor at Wedel where he remained until his death on August 31, 1667.

This hymn is one of the stanzas of a longer Christmas hymn beginning with the words, *"Ermuntre Dich, mein schwacher Geist"* or "Bestir thyself, my feeble soul," in a modern German hymnal. The translation is from the text as used in J. S. Bach's *Christmas Oratorio*.

John Troutbeck translated several hymns from the German but his reputation as a hymnist rests on his *Manchester Psalter and Chant*

Book, 1867, his *Catholic Paragraph Psalter,* 1894, and on his compilation of the *Westminster Abbey Hymn Book,* 1883.

Troutbeck was born November 12, 1832, educated at Rugby and University College, Oxford, and was ordained in 1855. His most important positions were Chaplain and Priest in Ordinary to the Queen, Minor Canon of Westminster, and Secretary to the New Testament Revision Company. He died in 1889.

The exact dates of Johann Schop are unknown but it is generally accepted that he was born between 1590 and 1595 and died between 1665 and 1667. He was a teacher, organist, composer, and instrumental performer. He is known to have been a member of the court orchestras at Wolfenbüttel and at the Danish Court.

Schop and Rist were close friends and the former was musical editor of Rist's collection published as Erste Zehn of his *Himlische Lieder,* 1641, where this tune appeared with Rist's *"Ermuntre Dich"* under the heading, "A hymn of praise on the joyful Birth and Incarnation of our Lord and Saviour Jesus Christ."

For a note on J. S. Bach see No. 193.

For a note on Arthur Tozer Russell, see No. 138.

132   From Heaven Above to Earth I Come

VOM HIMMEL HOCH L.M.

Vom Himmel Hoch
Martin Luther, 1483-1546
Tr. Catherine Winkworth, 1827-1878
Valenin Schumann's *Geistliche Lieder,* 1539

This beautiful hymn is from a carol Martin Luther wrote for his son, Hans, for a Christmas festival. The original was written in fifteen verses and first published in Klug's *Gesangbuch,* Wittenberg, 1535, where it appeared with a popular tune. The translation is from Catherine Winkworth's *Lyra Germanica.*

For a note on Luther see No. 31.

For a note on Catherine Winkworth see No. 58.

VOM HIMMEL HOCH has often been attributed to Martin Luther but scholars are uncertain as to the composer. This tune replaced an older popular tune to which it was sung and first appeared in Valentin Schumann's *Geistliche Lieder,* Leipzig, 1539. The name is, of course, from the first words of the carol, *"Vom Himmel hoch da komm ich her."* J. S. Bach made several harmonizations for it and used it in his *Christmas Oratorio.*

133   *What Child Is This?*

GREENSLEEVES 8.7.8.7. with Refrain

William Chatterton Dix, 1837-1898
English folk song

This familiar Christmas hymn is from Dix's longer poem "The Manger Throne" which was written about 1865. He wrote a number of Christmas and Easter hymns among which is the one for Epiphany, "As with Gladness Men of Old."

For a note on William Chatterton Dix see No. 294.

GREENSLEEVES is an old English folk song probably associated with a love song. It is referred to by Shakespeare in the *Merry Wives of Windsor* which suggests the tune was probably quite familiar as well as old in Shakespeare's time. It has been associated with The Waits' Carol for the New Year, "The Old Year Now Is Fled," since about 1642. Baptists and Disciples have used it since the publication of *Christian Worship, a Hymnal,* 1941.

134   *Love Came Down at Christmas*

GARTAN 6.7.6.7.

Christina Rossetti, 1830-1894
Traditional Irish melody
Harm. David Evans, 1874-1948

This text was first published in Miss Rossetti's *Time Flies, a Reading Diary,* 1885.

For a note on Miss Rossetti see No. 135.

GARTAN is the corrected spelling of the tune often given as GARTON. It is said to be the name of a lake in the county Donegal, Ireland. It is always given as a "traditional Irish melody."

For a comment on David Evans see No. 381.

135   In the Bleak Midwinter

CRANHAM   Irregular

Christina G. Rossetti, 1830-1894, alt.

Gustav T. Holst, 1874-1934

In later editions of Miss Rossetti's poetry, this Christmas poem is noted as being written "before 1872." Its first appearance as a hymn was in *The English Hymnal,* 1906, where it was set to the present Holst tune.

Although she was, in her own time, overshadowed by her talented brother Dante Gabriel and other poets and painters with whom she associated, Christina Georgina Rossetti's poetry has secured her place in Victorian literature. She was born in London on December 5, 1830, the daughter of an Italian political refugee who taught Italian at King's College, London. Her education was acquired from her mother, through diligent reading, and from the host of Italian artists, writers, and musicians who frequented the Rossetti home. As early as 1850 seven of her poems appeared in print in a pre-Raphaelite magazine, *The Germ.* In 1862 she published the poems she had written since 1848 under the title, *Goblin Market, and Other Poems.* After suffering an illness in 1871 which left her an invalid for the remainder of her life, her poetry took on a deeply religious, devotional, and mystical aura. Her final works were published as *Sing-Song,* 1872, *Annus Domini,* 1874, *A Pageant,* 1881, *Time Flies,* 1885, and *The Face of the Deep,* 1892. Miss Rossetti died in London, December 29, 1894.

CRANHAM was probably named after Cranham Woods located near the composer's birthplace. Since its first appearance with this text in *The English Hymnal,* 1906, it has become a carol equal to many traditional Christmas carols and has been included in a number of excellent hymnals.

Born September 21, 1874, the son of the organist at All Saints' Church, young Gustav became the organist of a village church at Wyck Rissington near the Beautiful Cotswold town Burton-on-the-Water. He studied at the Royal College of Music, but difficulty with his hands forced him to give up organ playing and pursue lessons on the trombone. He spent his life teaching music and composing successfully in many musical forms. Holst was a teacher and director of music at St. Paul's Girls School, Morley College, before becoming musical director for the Army Y.M.C.A. in Salonika in 1918. After the war he returned to London and taught composition at the Royal College of Music and became director of music for Reading University. In 1923 he made a highly successful tour of the United States when he conducted at the music festival in Ann Arbor, Michigan. On his return to England, the Royal College of Music honored him by making him an honorary Fellow. The last years of his life were given entirely to composition and further establishing himself as one of England's outstanding musicians. He died May 25, 1934.

136 Infant Holy, Infant Lowly

W ZLOBIE LEZY 4.4.7.4.4.7.4.4.4.4.7.

From the Polish
Para. Edith M. G. Reed, 1885-1933
Polish carol
Harm. David Hugh Jones, 1900-

Published in *Music and Youth,* c. 1925, while Miss Reed was editor of the journal, these words are a welcome addition to the Christmas hymns included in *Hymnbook for Christian Worship.*

Edith Margaret Gellibrand Reed, born in London on March 31, 1885, is known as an exponent of music for youth and editor of journals for young people. She was an assistant to Dr. Percy Scholes in his editorial work and an associate of the Royal College of Organists. In addition to her work as editor of *Music and Youth* and *Panpipes,* she published *Story Lives of the Great Composers* in 1925. She came to America on two occasions on behalf of her *Music of Youth.* Miss Reed died in London, June 4, 1933.

W ZLOBIE LEZY is said to be an old Polish carol. Its origin is obscure. It did appear in England in *School Worship,* 1926, with a harmonization by Arthur Ewart Rusbridge. The present harmonization is by David Hugh Jones.

David Hugh Jones, Mus.D., F.A.G.O., was born on February 25, 1900, in Jackson, Ohio. In 1917 he became organist and choirmaster at the Second Presbyterian Church of Portsmouth, Ohio. From 1918 to 1925 he studied music in New York at the Guilmant Organ School, and privately with Dr. William C. Carl, Clement R. Gale, and Dr. T. Tertius Noble. During that time he held several positions as organist and choirmaster in churches and synagogues in New York. In 1921 he became an Associate of the American Guild of Organists, and in 1924, a Fellow. In 1925 he was appointed organist for the Westminster Presbyterian Church in Dayton, Ohio.

From 1926 to 1951 he was a charter member of the Faculty of the Westminster Choir College. In 1926 he married Miss Mildred Palmer. The same year he composed his first anthem, "God Is a Spirit." Walter Damrosch, Director of the New York Symphony, heard this composition in the spring of 1927 and immediately suggested a scholarship at Fontainebleau, France. Dr. Jones studied there in the summer season, 1927, as a pupil of Henri Libert, Marcel Dupré, and Andre Bloch.

He moved with Westminster Choir College to Ithaca, New York, in 1929 and to Princeton, New Jersey, in 1932. For many years he was the head of the organ and composition departments of that school. In 1934, beside his work at Westminster Choir College, he became Director of Music at Princeton Theological Seminary, Princeton, New Jersey. In 1947 he became Associate Professor of Music there and in 1951 he retired from Westminster Choir College to become Professor of Music at Princeton Theological Seminary.

He has honorary degrees of Mus.D. from Washington and Jefferson College (1941), and Beaver College (1959). He became a member of the American Society of Composers, Authors, and Publishers in 1942. He has written many anthems, tunes, arrangements. Now he devotes all of his time to choir work at Princeton Seminary and has toured extensively with his choirs through all the United States, Canada, Alaska, Cuba, Hawaii, Mexico, Guatemala, Puerto Rico, Haiti, Dominican Republic, Japan, and Korea.

Dr. Jones was the editor of *The Hymnbook,* published in 1955 by The Presbyterian Church in the United States, The Presbyterian Church in the United States of America, The United Presbyterian Church of North America and The Reformed Church in America, and The Associate Reformed Presbyterian Church. He was the musical editor for the *Armed Forces Hymnal* published in 1959.

137   Good Christian Men, Rejoice

IN DULCI JUBILO 6.6.7.7.7.8.5.5.

14th century carol
Tr. John Mason Neale, 1818-1866
14th century melody

The *Hymnal 1940 Companion* gives the full macaronic text from which John Mason Neale created this free rendering of this ancient carol. Except for the deletion of "News, News," "Peace,

Peace," and "Joy, Joy" the text given here is that which Neale published in his *Carols for Christmastide*, 1853.

For a note on John Mason Neale see No. 155.

The earliest known reference to this carol was found in the writings of a 14th-century author who said that angels sang these words to the Dominican Monk and Mystic Heinrich Suso (*d.* 1366) and that upon hearing them he was so moved that he joined in a dance with his heavenly visitors. The earliest known form of the text and tune is contained in a manuscript which is in Leipzig University, and the first publication in which it is found is Klug's *Geistliche Lieder,* 1535.

IN DULCI JUBILO literally means "in sweet jubilation." As a melody it has been popular with composers and arrangers over the years as a subject worthy of their creative experimentation. The dancelike character of the rhythm places it within the category of a true carol.

138   *Let All Together Praise Our God*

LOBT GOTT, IHR CHRISTEN C.M.

Lobt Gott, ihr Christen allzugleich
Nikolaus Herman, c. 1485-1561
Tr. Arthur Tozer Russell, 1806-1874

Nikolaus Herman, c. 1485-1561
Harm. J. S. Bach, 1685-1750

Nothing is known of the early life of Nikolaus Herman. He is believed to have been born about 1480. In 1524 he was Master of the Latin School and cantor or organist and choirmaster of the church in Joachimsthal. He was a prolific author, poet, and musician whose hymns and tunes are reckoned to be equal to the best of the Reformation era. Many of his hymns were inspired by the sermons of pastor Johann Mathesius and were written expressly for the children in the schools. This hymn was written about 1554 and first published in 1560 as the first of "Three Spiritual Christmas Songs of the new-born child Jesus, for the children in Joachimsthal." It is reputed to be one of the most popular German Christmas hymns.

Arthur Tozer Russell, the son of the Rev. Thomas Clout, who changed his name for obvious reasons, was born at Northampton, March 20, 1806. He was educated at Southwark, Merchant Taylor's School in London, Manchester College, York, and finally at St. John's College, Cambridge. He was ordained by the Bishop of Lincoln and began his clerical career as an extreme high churchman which, through the influence of the writings of St. Augustine, gradually evolved to the position of a moderate Calvinist. Like Nikolaus Herman, he too was a prolific author of prose, hymns, and chants, as well as a composer of hymn tunes of high merit. He died at Southwich on November 18, 1874.

LOBT GOTT, IHR CHRISTEN gets its name from the beginning of Herman's text. It was composed in 1554 for his own hymn which begins "Kommt her, ihr lieben Schwesterlein."

For a comment on J. S. Bach see No. 193.

139 Of the Father's Love Begotten

DIVINUM MYSTERIUM 8.7.8.7.8.7.7.

Corde natus ex Parentis
Aurelius Clemens Prudentius, 348-c. 413
Tr. John Mason Neale, 1818-1866, St. 1, alt.
and Henry W. Baker, 1821-1877, Sts. 2, 3.
13th century plainsong Mode V
Harm. C. Winfred Douglas, 1867-1944

This hymn is from a poem written by Aurelius Prudentius at the beginning of the fifth century entitled, *"Da Puer Plectrum, Choreis ut Canam Fidelibus."* From this poem the hymn, *"Corde natus ex Parentis ante mundi exordium"* was taken and our translation is of that hymn. John Mason Neale's translation first appeared in the *Hymnal Noted,* 1854. With alterations it appeared with stanzas translated by Henry W. Baker in a trial edition of *Hymns Ancient and Modern,* 1859, and the first edition of *Hymns Ancient and Modern,* 1860, carried nine stanzas from which the present hymn is taken.

For a comment on Prudentius see No. 140.

For a note on John Mason Neale see No. 155.

For a note on Henry W. Baker see No. 209.

DIVINUM MYSTERIUM is a plainsong melody found in numerous European manuscripts from the 12th to the 15th centuries set to the text "Divinum Mysterium." It was a Sanctus trope, words added to the liturgical text, and is in a sense an extension of the Sanctus. This melody was associated with Neale's text in the *Hymnal Noted,* 1854. The present harmony is by C. Winfred Douglas and was first published in *The Hymnal,* 1940.

For a note on C. Winfred Douglas see No. 252.

140 Earth Has Many a Noble City

LIEBEN IST MEIN LEBEN 8.7.8.7.

Aurelius Clemens Prudentius, c. 348-413
Tr. Edward Caswall, 1814-1878
Heil und Hülfsmittel, Dresden, 1767

Aurelius Clemens Prudentius, born into a distinguished family in Northern Spain, is considered the most prolific and finest of the early Latin Christian poets. He was a lawyer by training and profession and held several judicial posts before being appointed to a high position in the Imperial Court. At the age of fifty-seven he became a monk and devoted the remainder of his life to writing. His best hymns are those for the twelve hours of the day from the *Cathemerinon* and hymns of the saints. This hymn is from his *Hymnus Epiphaniae* and was popularized through the Roman Breviary as revised by the Council of Trent.

The translation is based on that which is found in Edward Caswall's *Lyra Catholica,* 1849. This work contains 197 translations from the Roman Breviary, Missal, and other sources. The editors of *Hymns Ancient and Modern* adapted it for worship in the Church of England.

The tune name literally means "Love is my life" and is found in the Roman Catholic *Heil und Hülfsmittel,* published in Dresden in 1767.

For a comment on Edward Caswall see No. 116.

141 As with Gladness Men of Old

DIX 7.7.7.7.7.7.

William Chatterton Dix, 1837-1898
Abridged from a chorale by Conrad Kocher, 1786-1872

Dix wrote this hymn, Epiphany, during an illness in 1860. It was first published in *Hymns of Love and Joy,* a collection for private circulation. It was included in the first edition of *Hymns Ancient and Modern.* Two slight changes were made in the second stanza in the 1875 edition of *Hymns Ancient and Modern.* These changes were as follows: the second line of stanza two originally read, "To that lowly manger bed." The fourth line read, "Him whom heaven and earth adore" and the second line of the third stanza read, "At that manger rude and bare"

The fifth stanza is omitted in many hymnals. It reads:

In the heavenly country bright
Need they no created light;
Thou its light, its joy, its crown,
Thou its sun which goes not down;
There for ever may we sing
Alleluias to our King.

For a comment on William Chatterton Dix see No. 294.

The tune DIX is adapted from the chorale *"Treuer Heiland wir sind hier"* by Conrad Kocher. It was altered somewhat in 1861 when included in *Hymns Ancient and Modern,* probably by William Monk, the music editor. Since that time the text and tune have remained together to form one of the most popular of epiphany hymns. The tune is frequently found with the hymn "For the Beauty of the Earth."

Kocher was born at Ditzingen, Württemberg, December 16, 1786. He traveled to St. Petersburg as a tutor but decided to study music while there. His interest in church music developed during a visit to Rome in 1819. Upon his return to Germany he set about to reform German church music. He founded a School of Sacred Song which helped popularize four-part singing in the German churches. He received his Ph.D. degree from Tübingen University in 1852. As a composer he produced chorales, oratorios, operas, and sonatas. He died at Stuttgart on March 12, 1872.

142   *What Star Is This, with Beams So Bright*

PUER NOBIS NASCITUR L.M.

Charles Coffin, 1676-1749
Tr. John Chandler, 1806-1876, alt.

Adapt. Michael Praetorius, 1571-1621
Harm. George R. Woodward, 1848-1934

This is a translation of Charles Coffin's Epiphany hymn beginning *Quae stella sole pulchrior.* It was included in Coffin's *Hymni*

Sacra, 1736, and again in the *Paris Breviary* the same year. The translation is from John Chandler's *Hymns of the Primitive Church,* 1837.

See No. 115 for comments on Coffin and Chandler.

PUER NOBIS NASCITUR or SPLENDOR appears in several forms. It is probably a variation of the 15th-century carol *Puer Nobis Nascitur* (Unto us a child is born). Here it is from *Musae Sioniae,* 1609, by Michael Praetorius, who adapted it to the hymn, *Geborn ist Gottes Söhnelein.* The tune's first printed form has been traced to Spangenberg's *Christliches Gesangbüchlein,* 1568.

George R. Woodward is credited with most of this harmonization.

For a comment on Woodward see No. 104.

For a note on Michael Praetorius see No. 104.

143   Our Faith Is in the Christ Who Walks

WAREHAM L.M.

Thomas Curtis Clark, 1877-1953
William Knapp, 1698?-1768

These lines are from the poem, "Our faith is not in dead saints' bones," which has appeared in several of Dr. Clark's books under the heading, "The Faith of Christ's Free Men." Originally consisting of six stanzas, stanzas one and three have been omitted here.

Thomas Curtis Clark was born in Vincennes, Indiana, January 8, 1877. He received his higher education at Indiana University and the University of Chicago. He was a member of The Christian Church, Disciples of Christ, and was a member of the editorial staff of the Christian Board of Publication from 1907 until 1911. In 1912 he began a long association with *The Christian Century* as a member of the editorial staff. For a time he was editor of the *Twentieth Century Quarterly* and associate editor of *The Pulpit.* He was a member of the Willett, Clark and Company publishing firm, the Poetry Society of America, Midland Authors, and The Hymn Society of America. Dr. Clark was a voluminous writer of verse, much of which appeared in religious journals and magazines. He published several volumes of his poetry as well as several compilations of religious verse. Clark died at Bellwood, Illinois, December 7, 1954.

For a note on WAREHAM and William Knapp see No. 364.

144   *Jesus, Friend of Thronging Pilgrims*

REGENT SQUARE 8.7.8.7.8.7.

W. Nantlais Williams, 1874-1959
Henry T. Smart, 1813-1879

This hymn was first published in pamphlet form by the Hymn Society of America in 1954. It was one of the *Five New Hymns on the City* selected by the Society for use at the Convocation on Urban Life in America, called by the Council of Bishops of the Methodist Church and held at Columbus, Ohio, February 24-26, 1954.

W. Nantlais Williams, a Welsh Presbyterian minister, was born December 30, 1874, at Gwyddgrug, Pencader, Carmarthen Shire, South Wales. He was an active and contributing member of the Hymn Society of Great Britain and the Hymn Society of the Presbyterian Church of Wales. He contributed many hymns to these groups. He published several booklets of hymns for children in the Welsh language including *Moliant Plentyn,* parts 1 and 2, and *Clychau'r Gorlan.* Thirteen of his hymns have appeared in the Methodist (Wesleyan and Calvinistic) Hymn Book. Daniel Protheroe set thirty of his songs to music for use in schools. He made significant contributions to other hymnbooks for children. He died in 1959.

For a note on REGENT SQUARE and Henry Thomas Smart see No. 124.

145   *Lord, Whose Love Through Humble Service*

IN BABILONE 8.7.8.7.D.

Albert F. Bayly, 1901-
Ouden en Nieuwe Hollantse Boerenlities, c. 1710

This hymn was written in 1961 in response to The Hymn Society of America's request for hymns on social welfare. It was selected and published by the Society in *Seven New Social Welfare Hymns,* 1961. It was selected as the conference hymn for the Second National Conference on the Churches and Social Welfare, Cleveland, Ohio, October 23-27, 1961.

Albert Frederick Bayly was born at Bexhill-on-Sussex, England, in 1901. He was educated at St. Mary Magdalen School, St. Leonards and Hastings Grammar School and took an external B.A. from London University. He decided to enter the ministry after he had been trained as a shipwright at the Royal Dockyard School at Portsmouth, England. He entered Mansfield College, Oxford, in 1925 and became a Congregational minister. He recently served as pastor of the Eccleston Congregational Church, St. Helen's, Lancashire, and is currently the pastor of the Thaxted Church. His hymns were contributed to various English periodicals and have been published by the London Missionary Society. He privately published a collection of hymns and other poems under the title, *Rejoice, O People* in 1950 and a second collection entitled, *Again I say, Rejoice* in 1967 which includes the present hymn. He is an Honorary Fellow of Westminster Choir College, Princeton, New Jersey.

For a comment on IN BABILONE see No. 175.

146   *O Love, How Deep, How Broad, How High*

DEO GRACIAS L.M.

O amor quam ecstaticus
Latin, 15th century
Tr. Benjamin Webb, 1819-1885, alt.
Arr. for *The Hymnal* 1933

From 1854, when the translation appeared in *The Hymnal Noted,* this beautiful hymn on the incarnation has appeared in numerous hymnals both in England and America. This translation is from a longer poem beginning *Apparuit benignitas* and commences at the fifth line which begins *O amour quam exstaticus.*

Benjamin Webb was born in London in 1819. He was educated at St. Paul's School and Trinity College, Cambridge. Webb was vicar of St. Andrew's, Wells Street, London, for twenty-three years. He was one of the founders of the Cambridge Camden Society, which later became known as the Ecclesiological Society, and was for many years the editor of its official organ, *The Ecclesiologist.* The objective of the Society was to promote interest in "the proper construction and operations of the church, or communion, or Society of Christians." The principal leaders of the group were John Mason Neale, Edward Jacob Boyce, and Webb. Webb collaborated with Neale in translating the most important book published by the Ecclesiologists entitled, *The Symbolism of Church and Church Ornaments: A Translation of the First Book* of the *Rationale Divinorum Officiorum, Written by William Durandus, Sometime Bishop of Mende.* Webb became one of the experts on Ecclesiology and contributed mightily to the revolution which took place in church architecture during the Victorian era.

While the Oxford Movement was primarily concerned with questions of theology and polity of the church, the Cambridge group was more concerned with the more practical aspects of church construction and renovation. Among those who were devoted to theological aspects of the movement many eventually moved from the Anglican Church to the Roman Catholic faith. Few of the Ecclesiologists found it necessary or desirable to make such a move.

DEO GRACIAS or THE AGINCOURT SONG came into being as the tune for a popular ballad extolling King Henry V's victory at Agincourt in 1415. It is said that the king forbade all public demonstrations of his victory since all praise and thanks should be given to God. Both the tune and the ballad survived the king's edict. The tune is here used appropriately with a hymn proclaiming Christ's victory over death.

147   *O Son of Man, Our Hero Strong and Tender*

CHARTERHOUSE 11.10.11.10.

Frank Fletcher, 1870-1954
David Evans, 1874-1948

Written in 1921, this hymn reflects Fletcher's commitment to the young people at Charterhouse School at Godalming, England. It was used there before it was published in *The Challenge,* a church newspaper.

Frank Fletcher was born at Atherton, Manchester, in 1870, was educated at Rossall School and went on to Balliol College, Oxford, where he achieved a brilliant academic record. He was assistant master at Rugby from 1894 to 1903, became master at Marlborough College in 1903, and finally headmaster of Charterhouse School from 1911 to 1935. He was knighted in 1937.

CHARTERHOUSE was composed for this text and was first published with it in *The Church Hymnary,* 1927. The tune was named for the school which was located at Godalming.

For a note on the composer see No. 381.

148   Jesus, with Thy Church Abide

ST. KATRINE 7.7.7.6.

Thomas B. Pollock, 1836-1896
J. Williamson, 1868-1947

Thomas Benson Pollock is remembered for his excellent litanies rather than as a hymnist. This is one of two in common use in England. It is from his *Metrical Litanies for Special Services and General Use,* 1870, and is a reprint from *The Church Hymnary,* 1898, representing stanzas 2, 5, 15, and 12 found in *Hymns Ancient and Modern,* 1875. Dr. Julian credits the litany to T. B. Pollock and others which probably means it has gone through various alterations at the hands of hymnbook compilers.

Born at Strathallan, Isle of Man, in 1836, Father Tom, as he was known in later years, intended to follow a medical career but changed his mind and entered the Church of England. He was educated at Trinity College, Dublin, B.A. and M.A., and took Holy Orders in 1861. He was successively curate of St. Luke's Church, Lee, Staffordshire; St. Thomas's Church, Stamford Hill, London; and in 1865 went to Birmingham as assistant to his brother whom he succeeded as vicar of St. Alban's in 1895. He died in Birmingham on December 15, 1896.

Except for the appearance of ST. KATRINE in *The School Hymn Book of the Methodist Church,* 1950, nothing is known of either tune or composer.

149   The Son of God, Our Christ

TOULON 10.10.10.10.

Edward M. Blumenfeld, 1927-
Abridged from *Genevan Psalter,* 1551

This hymn was the result of a request by the Hymn Society of America for hymns on the theme "Consider Your Call" for Youth Week, 1957. Mr. Blumenfeld's hymn was the "first choice hymn" for that year's observance sponsored by the United Christian Youth Movement of the National Council of Churches. This was his first hymn. It was published in pamphlet form in *Three More New Hymns for Youth by Youth* by the Hymn Society of America in 1957.

Edward M. Blumenfeld was born in Chicago, was educated in the public schools there and in Cincinnati and Milwaukee. He was graduated from Carroll College in 1949 and from Hartford Theological Seminary in 1955. He was ordained to the ministry in 1955 and has ministerial standing in the United Church of Christ. He has served churches in Vermont, Illinois, and in 1966 returned to Wisconsin where he is currently pastor of The West de Pere First Congregational Church-United Church of Christ. Mr. Blumenfeld has had two hymns published by the Hymn Society of America and informs us, "These are the only two times I have ever had material published, except for poems I wrote for high school and college newspapers and double-crostic puzzles in the *Fan books* by Simon-Schuster."

For a comment on TOULON see No. 369.

150   *Thou Didst Leave Thy Throne*

MARGARET Irregular

Emily E. S. Elliott, 1836-1897, alt.
Timothy R. Matthews, 1826-1910

Based on Luke 2:7, this hymn was written in 1864 for the children of St. Mark's Church in Brighton, England. It first appeared as a leaflet in 1864 and later in the *Church Missionary Juvenile Instructor,* 1870, and again in *Chimes of Consecration,* 1873.

Emily Elizabeth Steele Elliott, a daughter of Edward B. Elliott, English clergyman and scholar, was born in Brighton, England, July 22, 1836. She was the niece of Charlotte Elliott and, like her famous aunt, published a book of hymns for the sick and use in hospitals and infirmaries under the title, *Under the Pillow.* This book was Part II of her *Chimes of Consecration* and contained forty-eight hymns. Many of her hymns appeared in the pages of *The Church Missionary Instructor,* which she edited for six years. Miss Elliott died in London, August 3, 1897.

MARGARET, or sometimes ELLIOTT, was composed especially for this text and was published in S.P.C.K.'s *Children's Hymns and Tunes,* 1876. MARGARET is the composer's name for the tune.

Born November 4, 1826, at Colnworth Rectory, near Bedford, England, Timothy Richard Matthews received his education in the grammar school there and at Gonville and Cains College, Cambridge. For a time he was a private tutor at Windsor where he met and established a lifelong friendship with George Elvey. After his ordination in 1853 he held a curacy at Nottingham before moving to North Coates, Lincolnshire, where he remained until retirement in 1907. He was the composer of about one hundred hymn tunes, several services, and was editor of *The Village Organist.* He died at Tetney, Lincolnshire, January 5, 1910.

151   Take Up Thy Cross

DISTRESS L.M.

Charles William Everest, 1814-1877

William Walker's *Southern Harmony,* 1835

Written in 1833 and published the same year in the author's *Visions of Death and Other Poems,* "Take Up Thy Cross" soon made its way, in altered form, into important hymnals. The present text is essentially that which appeared in *Hymns Ancient and Modern,* 1861, but is here reduced from six to four stanzas. The editors of *H.A.M.* copied the altered form from an unidentified earlier source. The fourth line of stanza three originally read, "Upon the cross, on Calvary's hill." *H.A.M. Revised,* 1950, gives the same line "To save thy soul from death and hell."

Born in East Windsor, Connecticut, May 27, 1814, Charles William Everest was graduated from Trinity College, Hartford, in 1838. He was ordained an Episcopal priest in 1842 and served as rector at Hamden, Connecticut, for thirty-one years. During his ministry he conducted a school and also served as a representative of the Society of the Increase of the Ministry. He died in Waterbury, Connecticut, January 11, 1877.

DISTRESS is another of the anonymous tunes found in many nineteenth-century American songbooks. In the writer's mutilated copy of *Original Sacred Harp, revised, corrected, and enlarged,* c. 1911, the tune is given in shaped notes and three parts on page 50 with Anne Steele's hymn beginning "So fades the lovely blooming flower." In that volume the editors acknowledge their source as *Southern Harmony,* 1825. To our knowledge this is the only reference to a *Southern Harmony* of that date. George Pullen Jackson, the chief authority on this subject, has been able to trace Walker's book to circa 1835. Jackson categorizes the tune as a member of the "Kedron" family, that is to say, tunes sung to extremely solemn texts. We have not been able to discover the name of the arranger of the present version.

152 *My Master Was So Very Poor*

HERRNHUT L.M.

Harry Lee, 1875-1942
Bartholomaeus Gesius, c.1555-c.1613

Information on this hymn is elusive. It came into use as early as 1927 in the *Junior Church School Hymnal* where it was carried with Karl P. Harrington's tune, MY MASTER, composed for the text. *The Church School Hymnal for Youth,* 1928, carried both text and tune, and H. Augustine Smith's *The New Hymnal for American Youth,* 1930, used it with another tune, also called MY MASTER by George Henry Day. As far as we can ascertain, *The Hymnal,* 1933 (Presbyterian) is the only major denominational hymnal to use the hymn.

Harry Lee was born in Canton, Ohio, December 17, 1875. Educated in country schools, he later taught in them for a number of years. Apparently he left the Canton area for a while for he married Mary Davidson, a West Virginian, and brought her back to Canton where he was employed as a bookkeeper and became an assistant to the rector of an Episcopal Church. After helping found Briar Brae, a social settlement in Canton, he moved to New York City and established another settlement there under the same name. During World War I he served with the Red Cross abroad and in the United States. Lee published several literary works including *High Company,* stories of courage and comradeship of the wounded soldiers, and *The Little Poor Man,* a prize-winning poetic drama on the life of St. Francis of Assisi. Most of his poems appeared in popular magazines. He died December 19, 1942.

HERRNHUT apparently was a tune associated with a Moravian hymn. Investigation reveals a number of tunes by this name, including Nicolai's WACHET AUF and one from *The Foundery Collection,* 1742, now called SAVANNAH, none of which bears resemblance to the present tune. Zahn lists a Gesius tune that begins with this motif but the resemblance ends there.

Little is known of Bartholomäus Gesius (Gese or Göss). Born circa 1555 in Müncheberg, Germany, he studied theology before becoming cantor in Frankfurt-on-the-Oder in 1595. He composed a quantity of liturgical music for the old Lutheran Church, hymn tunes, and a setting of the *Passion according to St. John.* He is said to have died of the plague in 1613.

153   Most Wondrous Is of All on Earth

8.7.8.7.

N. F. S. Grundtvig, 1783-1872
Tr. Jean Fraser, 1951
Danish folk song

This hymn is found in *Cantate Domino,* 1951, in four languages. In all there are eight stanzas of which 1, 2, 3, 4, and 6 are used here.

For a note on N. F. S. Grundtvig see No. 349.

Jean Fraser has not been identified except as one of a "veritable army of translators" who provided translations for the *Cantate Domino,* 1951.

The tune is an unidentified and unnamed Danish Folk Song.

154   Draw Nigh to Thy Jerusalem

FARLEY CASTLE 10.10.10.10.

Jeremy Taylor, 1613-1667, alt.
Henry Lawes, 1595-1662

From a humble beginning as the son of a barber, Jeremy Taylor became an influential and important author, preacher, educator, and churchman. Throughout the period of the Commonwealth he remained a staunch Royalist and upon the Restoration was rewarded by being consecrated as Bishop of Down and Connor, appointed a member of the Irish Privy Council, then Bishop of Dromore and Vice-Chancellor of the University of Dublin—all in 1661. He died August 13, 1667.

He is remembered today for his devotional classics on *Holy Living, Holy Dying,* and *The Golden Grove,* a manual of Daily Prayers. The original version of this hymn appeared in his *Festival and Penitential Hymns* which was appended to *The Golden Grove,* 1655, and began, "Lord Come Away! Why Dost Thou Stay?" under the heading, The Second Advent; or, Christ's Coming to Jerusalem in Triumph. It consisted of twenty-one irregular lines which were altered for congregational singing for the *Leeds Hymnbook,* 1853, as "Descend to Thy

Jerusalem" and further altered for the *Sarum Hymnal,* 1868, from which this present version comes.

FARLEY CASTLE appeared as the musical setting for treble and bass to Psalm 72 in George Sandys' *Paraphrase upon the Divine Poems,* 1638. There the tunes were anonymous but in later editions they were attributed to Henry Lawes. No information can be found on the derivation of the name of the tune.

Henry Lawes, born in Wiltshire in 1595, was a composer of considerable merit who was Gentleman and Clerk of the Chapel Royal, a member of the king's private band and musician to the Earl of Bridgewater. He lost his appointments during the period of the Commonwealth and was reinstated at the Restoration. He composed songs, anthems, masques, and two- and three-part settings to the Psalms. He died in London in 1662 and is buried in Westminster Abbey.

155 *All Glory, Laud, and Honor*

ST. THEODULPH 7.6.7.6.D.

Gloria, laus, et honor
Theodulph of Orleans *c.* 770-*c.* 821
Tr. John Mason Neale 1818-1866

Melchior Teschner, 1584-1635

Through the years this has been a favorite Palm Sunday hymn. A number of translations have come and gone and this one by John Mason Neale, as altered slightly for the 1858 edition of *Hymns Ancient and Modern,* remains in common use throughout the English-speaking world.

Theodulph was born in Italy circa 770. His outstanding scholarship attracted the attention of Charlemagne who took Theodulph to France with him on his return trip and made him Bishop of Orleans. Both Charlemagne and Theodulph had enemies and, upon the former's death, these enemies arrested and imprisoned Theodulph. Bishop Theodulph is believed to have died in prison at Angers, September 18, 821.

The romantic story which grew up around the origin of this hymn has generally been discredited; however, that the hymn was written by Theodulph while he was in prison is widely accepted as fact. Neale translated the entire hymn but the following stanza has not been in common use since the seventeenth century for obvious reasons.

Be Thou, O Lord the rider,
And we the little ass,
That to God's Holy city
Together we may pass.

John Mason Neale is another of the great English translators of the nineteenth century. He was born in London, January 24, 1818, the only son of the Reverend Cornelius Neale. After a variety of educational experiences young Neale was awarded a scholarship at Trinity College, Cambridge. He was recognized as the best classical scholar of his year.

After graduating he was elected fellow of Downing College and served as chaplain and assistant tutor for a time. In 1845 Dr. Neale won the Seatonian prize for a sacred poem and the fact that he went on to repeat this accomplishment on ten subsequent occasions attests to his devotion and skill.

At Cambridge he came under the influence of the Oxford Movement. The fervor of the adherents deeply affected Neale and he accepted the High Church views and helped found the Cambridge Camden Society in 1839 which later was removed to London as the Ecclesiological Society. This activity probably accounts for his deep interest in all aspects of worship including the hymnody and devotional poetry of the medieval church.

Neale was ordained Deacon at St. Margaret's Church, Westminster, in 1841 and worked as assistant curate at St. Nicholas, Guilford, Surrey. He was ordained priest by Bishop Monk at St. Margaret's, Westminster, in 1842. He never held any high posts in the church because of his association with the Camden group but spent most of his life working to improve the lot of the poor and sick. He founded the nursing sisterhood known as St. Margaret's.

He is, of course, best known today as an author and translator of Greek and Latin Hymns. Julian says that as a translator he has no equal. He could handle twenty languages and wrote many of his hymns in Latin. A glance through any reputable hymnal will verify his great contribution to contemporary hymnody.

ST. THEODULPH was written by Melchior Teschner for Valerius Herberger's hymn *"Valet will ich dir geben."* Little is known of Teschner except that he was a schoolmaster, pastor, and musician who wrote this tune circa 1613. Moffatt and Patrick in their *Handbook to the Church Hymnary* tell us that the tune was composed "for an acrostic hymn written during a time of pestilence." Teschner was probably cantor at Fraustadt, Silesia, at the same time Herberger was serving the church as pastor [p. 518]. Melchior wrote two different settings for the hymn. Our tune is the second of these. So far as is known these are the only two tunes he ever wrote. He died at Oeberprietschen near his birthplace, December 1, 1635.

156   Ride On, Ride On in Majesty

THE KING'S MAJESTY L.M.

Henry H. Milman, 1791-1868, alt.
Graham George, 1912-

One of the most popular Palm Sunday hymns in the English language, these lines were published in Reginald Heber's *Hymns Written and Adapted to the Weekly Church Service of the year,* 1827. A number of hymnals altered the text but the present version is the restoration of the original as found in *The English Hymnal,* 1906, except for two alterations. First, "thine" in line three has been changed to "thy" and second, the present stanza four consists of the first two lines of the original stanza four and the last two lines of the original stanza five.

Henry Hart Milman was a brilliant English poet, hymnist, playwright, author, and liberal theologian, and Anglican clergyman. He was born in London, February 10, 1791. For many years, he was professor of poetry at Oxford and was appointed dean of St. Paul's in 1849. His controversial books, *History of the Jews,* and *Latin Christianity,* 1854, were landmarks in the development of liberal British theology. He wrote thirteen hymns, of which this is the most popular. His death occurred in London, September 24, 1868.

THE KING'S MAJESTY was written for this text and was first published in *The Hymnal, 1940.*

Graham George was born in Norwich, England, in 1912 and came to Canada at the age of 16. He studied under Alfred Whitehead and became a fellow of the Canadian Guild of Organists in 1936. He took his B.Mus. and D.Mus. degrees from the University of Toronto. Between periods of teaching music in the Montreal Public Schools he served in the Canadian Armed Forces overseas. Since 1946 he has taught at Queen's University. He has composed works for orchestra and a number of choral pieces, including an anthem setting of the tune, THE KING'S MAJESTY.

157 *What Wondrous Love Is This*

WONDROUS LOVE 12.9.12.9.

American folk hymn
Southern Harmony, 1835
Arr. Paul Christiansen, 1914-

This hymn is found in a number of 19th-century American songbooks, the earliest being *Southern Harmony,* 1835. The writer's copy of *Original Sacred Harp, Revised, Corrected, and Enlarged,* 1911, gives the text as "anonymous" and includes the following additional stanzas:

2. When I was sinking down, etc.
When I was sinking down
Beneath God's righteous frown
Christ laid aside his crown for my soul, etc.

3. To God and to the Lamb I will sing, etc.
To God and to the Lamb
Who is the great I am
While millions join the theme I will sing, etc.

4. And when from death I'm free, I'll sing on, etc.
And when from death I'm free
I'll sing and joyful be
And thro' eternity, I'll sing on, etc.

Like the text, the tune WONDROUS LOVE, is generally given as anonymous, although in *Southern Harmony* it is attributed to an unknown "Christopher." A wide variety of interesting arrangements of the tune appear in anthem form in the catalogues of numerous music publishers, The present arrangement is by Paul J. Christiansen.

Paul J. Christiansen is the son of F. Melius Christiansen, the well-known Norwegian immigrant who founded the famous St. Olaf Choir. From his eminent father Dr. Christiansen received his early musical training in music theory, piano, and composition. He continued his study at Oberlin Conservatory of Music and Eastman School of Music. He also studied with Dimitri Metropolis, Norman Lockwood, Howard Hanson, and Bernard Rogers. His association with the Concordia Choir, successor to the St. Olaf Choir, began at Concordia College,

Moorhead, Minnesota, in 1937. Since that time he has brought the choir to a high level of excellence. He received an honorary doctorate from Adams State College, Alamosa, Colorado, in 1966. Dr. Christiansen is a prolific composer and arranger of choral music, is in demand as a lecturer and choral clinician, and conducts choral schools each summer on college and university campuses across the nation.

158   Into the Woods My Master Went

RIDGEFIELD Irregular

Sidney Lanier, 1842-1881

Harold W. Friedell, 1905-1958

Sidney Lanier has been called the most important American poet from the end of the Civil War to the end of the century. These words were written in November, 1880, as "A Ballad of Trees and the Master" and first appeared in his posthumous *Poems,* 1901. In 1905 the poem appeared as a hymn in the *Methodist Hymnal.*

Lanier was born in Macon, Georgia, February 3, 1842. He graduated from Oglethorpe University where he was considered an excellent student and flute player. He remained at Oglethorpe for a year after graduation serving as a tutor and preparing himself to enter the University of Heidelberg. With the outbreak of the Civil War, he and his brother enlisted in the Macon Volunteers and saw action in and around Richmond, Virginia. Later, he was transferred to the signal corps and became the signal officer on a blockade runner. He was captured and imprisoned in August of 1864 during which time he became ill with tuberculosis. After his release from prison he worked wherever he could, married Mary Day, studied law and practiced with his father. Severe illness forced him to go to San Antonio, Texas, for a period of recuperation. While there, Lanier decided to give up law and devote his life to music and poetry. For a time he was first flutist with the Peabody Symphony Orchestra in Baltimore, Maryland, and lecturer in English Literature at Johns Hopkins University. Once again his health gave way, and he was forced to seek the mountains of North Carolina where he died at Lynn on September 7, 1881.

RIDGEFIELD was composed for this text by Harold W. Friedell.

For a note on the composer see No. 316.

159   Beneath the Cross of Jesus

ST. CHRISTOPHER 7.6.8.6.8.6.8.6.

Elizabeth C. Clephane, 1830-1869
Frederick C. Maker, 1844-1927

Born Elizabeth Cecilia Douglas Clephane at Edinburgh, Scotland, June 18, 1830, she was the daughter of the sheriff of Fife. She grew up in the Free Church of Scotland. Eight of her hymns were published in 1872 in *The Family Treasury,* a magazine under the editorship of a Free Church minister. These hymns appeared under the general designation, "Breathings on the Border."

Because she and her sisters gave to the poor all of their income, except that which was needed for their own meager necessities, she was affectionately known as "the Sunbeam." She died near Melrose, Scotland, on February 19, 1869.

Her fame was spread abroad by Ira David Sankey who wrote the music for her hymn, "There Were Ninety and Nine," during a meeting being conducted by Dr. Moody in Edinburgh.

For a note on the tune and composer see No. 160.

160   Before the Cross of Jesus

ST. CHRISTOPHER 7.6.8.6.7.6.8.6.

Ferdinand Q. Blanchard, 1876-1968
Frederick C. Maker, 1844-1927

The author of this hymn wrote it to be sung with this tune in the hope of bringing new relevance to worship in his church. Dr. Blanchard was a nationally recognized leader of the Congregational Christian Churches. He was for thirty-seven years minister and minister emeritus for seventeen years of the Euclid Avenue Congregational Church, Cleveland. He was a graduate of Amherst College and Yale Divinity School. He wrote other hymns and several books.

The tune ST. CHRISTOPHER was written for the hymn "Beneath the Cross of Jesus." It is named after the patron saint of travelers and first appeared in the *Bristol Tune Book,* 1881.

The composer, Frederick C. Maker, was born in Bristol, England, and spent his entire life there. He was an organist and composer of considerable distinction. He served a number of churches in Bristol before being employed by the Redland Park Congregational Church where he served for about thirty years. His contributions to the *Bristol Tune Book,* as well as to other collections, firmly established his reputation as a hymn-tune composer. He was also the composer of many anthems, several cantatas, and compositions for the piano.

161   Were You There When They Crucified My Lord?

WERE YOU THERE Irregular

Anonymous
Negro Spiritual

Both text and tune of this beloved spiritual are anonymous. George Pullen Jackson gives the earliest-known printed source as William E. Barton's *Old Plantation Hymns,* 1899, which contained material collected in Tennessee between 1880 and 1887. (See No. CVI, p. 221, *White and Negro Spirituals,* 1943.) Jackson is of the opinion that the "text theme" was popular with white Americans for a century before the Negro version was published. Tradition ascribes the song's origin to Negro slaves. Whatever its background "Were you there" is a welcomed addition to the *Hymnbook for Christian Worship.*

162   Ah, Holy Jesus, How Hast Thou Offended

HERZLIEBSTER JESU 11.11.11.5.

Herzliebster Jesu, was hast du verbrochen?
Johann Heermann, 1585-1647
Tr. Robert Seymour Bridges, 1844-1930
Johann Crüger, 1598-1662

The Thirty Years' War produced a number of outstanding hymn writers. Johann Heermann was one of them. He was a Lutheran pastor in the town of Köben in Silesia most of his life. This hymn was found in his *Devoti musica cordis* (1630). Long attributed to St. Augustine, late scholarship tells us it really comes from the writings of one Jean de Fëcamp (d. 1078) which appeared in a fifteenth-century devotional book entitled *Meditationes sanctorum patrum*. The original hymn was in fifteen stanzas.

Heermann was born in the town of Raudten, Silesia, October 11, 1585, and died at Lissa, Posen, in 1647. He has been regarded as second only to Paul Gerhardt as a hymn writer. In his hymns one senses a transition from the objectivity of the Reformation era to a more subjective tendency of later hymnists.

It has been said that Robert Seymour Bridges "added grace to our hymnody by his devotion to it" and that "his *Yattendon Hymnal* is ample evidence of his musical taste." Bridges was somewhat critical of the state of hymnody of his day and was especially critical of *Hymns Ancient and Modern* which he believed had taken much of the musical interest from many of the tunes simply by reducing both melody and harmony to the least common denominator. In an article entitled "A Practical Discourse on Some Principles of Hymn-Singing" which appeared in *The Journal of Theological Studies* (Vol. 1, October 1899, p. 40) he referred to the "inane" form of Orlando Gibbons' tune ANGELS SONG which he says is degraded. In another place he accuses *Hymns Ancient and Modern* of misstating the rhythm of Croft's setting of Psalm 148. Bridges also has little use for John Julian's well-known *Dictionary of Hymnology* which he calls "that most depressing of all books ever compiled by the groaning creature."

This hymn was a free paraphrase of the original and was created especially for his *Yattendon Hymnal* which was published in 1899 and for the Crüger tune. It is interesting to note that the *Yattendon Hymnal* was compiled by Bridges to embody his principles of hymnody which included such ideas as "The music must express the words or sense; it should not attract too much attention to itself: it should be dignified: and its reason and use is to heighten emotion." Concerning the hymn itself he goes on to point out that in the plainsong period the words were usually equal to and well matched to the music; in the Reformation period the music was superior to the poetry and the result is that there is an excellent residue of music for which the church should find appropriate words; and that the sentimentality of modern tunes should not be excused by sentimental and often poor texts.

Bridges was born October 23, 1844, received his education at Eton and Corpus Christi College, Oxford. He practiced medicine from 1874 to 1882 from which he retired in order to devote his full energy to poetry and writing. King George V appointed him Poet Laureate of England in 1913. Bridges died in 1930.

Johann Crüger was born at Grossbriesen, Prussia, April 9, 1598, and died in Berlin February 23, 1662. He was the composer of some of our finest choral tunes including this one, HERZLIEBSTER JESU, and JESU, MEINE FREUDE; JESU MEINE ZUVERSICHT; NUN DANKET ALLE GOTT. He was a pupil of Paulus Homberger at Ratisbon. The final forty years of his life were spent as organist at St. Nicholas Church in Berlin. His contributions to music were numerous and included several theoretical works, many compositions, editions, reprints, and collections too numerous to mention here. His most famous collection was *Praxis Pietatis Melica* from which many fine tunes have been drawn for use in the church. HERZLIEBSTER JESU is from his *Gesangbuch* of 1640. The name of the tune is derived from the opening words of the hymn *Herzliebster Jesu, was hast due verbrochen, das man ein solch scharf urteil hat gesprochen.*

163   O Sacred Head, Now Wounded

PASSION CHORALE 7.6.7.6.D.

Based on Latin attributed to
Bernard of Clairvaux, 1091-1153
German version Paul Gerhardt, 1607-1676
Tr. James Waddell Alexander, 1804-1859

Hans Leo Hassler, 1564-1612
Harm. J. S. Bach, 1685-1750

Perhaps the most renowned Passion hymn of all time, "O Sacred Head" was based on a medieval hymn which was itself a part of the more extensive hymn *Salve mundi Salutare,* often attributed to Bernard of Clairvaux. The hymn was primarily a meditation on the members of the body of Christ as he hung on the cross. Paul Gerhardt, one of Germany's greatest hymnists, translated Part VII of the Latin hymn into German, and it was first published in Johann Crüger's *Praxis Pietatis Melica,* 1656. The present rendering of the German is based on Dr. Alexander's translation which appeared in his *The Breaking Crucible,* 1861.

Paul Gerhardt was born March 12, 1607, near Wittenberg and died at Lübben May 27, 1676. Most of his life was spent amid the physical and psychological devastation of the Thirty Years' War. After preparing himself for the Lutheran ministry at Wittenberg he was not appointed to a pastorate until he was forty-five years of age, at which time he became pastor of the village church at Mittenwald. It was during his six years of service there that he began writing the hymns which were to make him famous. In 1657 he became a member of the clergy at St. Nicholas' Church, Berlin, and his reputation as a preacher and personality grew rapidly throughout the area. As a result of a theological controversy between the Reformed and Lutheran Churches and his uncompromising bias for the Lutheran position, he was deprived of his office for two years. In 1668 Gerhardt was reinstated and appointed Archdeacon of Lübben where he spent the remainder of his life. He has been called the "typical" Lutheran hymn writer and represents the trasition from purely objective to the subjective hymnody or from the "Confessional to the Pietist Era."

James Waddell Alexander was a distinguished Presbyterian minister and teacher. He was born at Hopewell, Virginia, in 1804, educated at New Jersey College (Princeton) and Princeton Theological Seminary, and served churches in Virginia and New Jersey before his appointment to the chair of Belles Lettres and Rhetoric at Princeton. After twelve years in that position he returned to the preaching ministry of the Duane Street Presbyterian Church, New York. He was recalled to Princeton as Professor of Ecclesiastical History and Church Government but returned to the ministry at Fifth Avenue Presbyterian Church in 1851. He was a prolific author, writing more than thirty books for the American Sunday School Union and many articles for the *Princeton Quarterly Review*. His chief contribution to hymnology was in the form of translations which were published as *The Breaking Crucible, and Other Translations*. He died at Sweetsprings, Virginia, in 1859.

PASSION CHORALE is so named because of its long association with this text. It was originally the tune for the secular song *"Mein G' müt ist mir verwirret"* found in Hassler's *Lustgarten neuer teutscher Gesäng*, 1601. As early as 1613 it was appropriated as a hymn tune and shortly thereafter began its long history with *"O Haupt voll Blut und Wunden."*

Hans Leo Hassler, the most eminent German organist of his day, was born at Nuremberg, October 25, 1564. After studying music with his father, he went to Venice and became a pupil of Andrea Gabrieli, the renowned organist at St. Mark's. From 1585 until 1600 he was the private organist to Count Octavian Fugger of Augsburg. In 1601 Hassler became the organist at Frauenkirche and director of the Nuremberg town band. After serving Emperor Rudolph II for a brief period he entered the service of Prince Christian II, Elector of Saxony at Dresden. Hassler died of tuberculosis on June 8, 1612, while attending the coronation of Emperor Mathias at Frankfurt. Hassler composed both sacred and secular music and published several volumes of choral works.

For a note on J. S. Bach see No. 193.

164 Near the Cross Her Vigil Keeping

STABAT MATER 8.8.7.8.8.7.

Latin 13th century
Tr. Louis F. Benson, 1855-1930
Mechlin Plainsong, Mode IV

Although this famous sequence came into the *Roman Missal* as late as 1727 it is known to have been used in the Breslau liturgy in 1414. It is an anonymous text sometimes ascribed to Pope Innocent III (1161-1216), as well as to Jacopone da Todi (*c.* 1228-1306), and others. Based on John 19:26-27 the Latin text begins:

> *Stabat Mater dolorosa*
> *juxta crucem lacrimosa*
> *dum pendebat filius;*
> *cujus animam gementem,*
> *contristatam et dolentem,*
> *pertransivit gladius.*

The "Stabat Mater" is one of the seven famous songs of the Medieval Church and is still used at the feast of the Seven Dolours.

For a note on Louis F. Benson see No. 309.

STABAT MATER was an anonymous tune set to the Stabat Mater text in the *Mainz Gesangbuch,* 1611. The original tune has long since disappeared.

165 'Tis Midnight, and on Olive's Brow

OLIVE'S BROW L.M.

William B. Tappan, 1794-1849, alt.
William B. Bradbury, 1816-1868

This Passiontide hymn first appeared in Tappan's *Poems,* 1822, under the title "Gethsemane."

William Bingham Tappan, a licensed Congregational minister, was born October 24, 1794, at Beverly, Massachusetts. Upon the death of his father, he was apprenticed to a clockmaker in Boston. In 1815 he moved to Philadelphia and found work as a clockmaker. In 1822 he was appointed superintendent of the American Sunday School Union, a position he held until his death on June 18, 1849. From 1840 he was a licensed Congregational minister. He conducted evangelistic campaigns in the East and West and often spoke on behalf of the Sunday school movement. His poetry appeared in about ten volumes published between 1819 and 1860. Death came suddenly when cholera struck him at West Needham, Massachusetts.

OLIVE'S BROW is derived from the first line of the hymn. It was composed for this text and was first published in an extensive work edited by George F. Root and William B. Bradbury known as *The Shawm,* 1853.

For a note on William Batchelder Bradbury see No. 45.

166   Lord, Who Throughout These Forty Days

ST. FLAVIAN, C.M.

Claudia F. Hernaman, 1838-1898

Adapt. from the *English Psalter,* 1562

This is a welcomed addition to Baptist-Disciple hymnody. Claudia Frances Hernaman, nee Ibotson, wrote about 150 hymns which were included in seven of her published books of verse, the *Church Times,* and other periodicals. A great many of her hymns were written specifically for children. There were several translations from the Latin. This hymn was first published in *The Child's Book of Praise, A Manual of Devotion in Simple Verse,* 1873, and was designated for use during Lent. Mrs. Hernaman was born at Addleston, Surrey, England, October 19, 1838, and died October 10, 1898.

ST. FLAVIAN is the first half of the tune to which Psalm 132 was set in the *English Psalter* printed by John Day and commonly known as Day's Psalter, 1562. It appeared in revised form in Ravenscroft's *Whole Booke of Psalmes,* 1621. The present form is from Richard Redhead's *Church Hymn Tunes,* 1853. In the musical edition of *Hymns Ancient* and *Modern,* 1861, the tune was called REDHEAD and was changed to ST. FLAVIAN in the revised edition of 1875.

167   *Throned Upon the Awful Tree*

ARFON 7.7.7.7.7.7.

John Ellerton, 1826-1893, alt.
Welsh hymn melody

This hymn was written in 1875 and published in the 1875 edition of *Hymns Ancient and Modern.* Julian says this is the "grandest of all his [Ellerton's] hymns."

For a note on John Ellerton see No. 231.

For a note on ARFON see No. 170.

168   *O Come and Mourn with Me Awhile*

COUTANCES L.M.

Frederick William Faber, 1814-1863
French church melody from the
Rouen Antiphoner, 1728

This Good Friday hymn was originally published in Faber's *Jesus and Mary,* 1849, in twelve stanzas of four lines. It was later revised and included in his *Hymns,* 1862. *Hymns Ancient and Modern* gave it in an abbreviated and altered form in 1861. It appears in various forms in modern hymnals.

For a note on Frederick W. Faber see No. 253.

The original source of this tune is the *Rouen Antiphoner,* 1728, where it was sung to *Jesu sacerdotum decus,* an office hymn for St. Romanus of Rouen (October 23). With slight alteration it was introduced to English worshipers through the *English Hymnal,* 1906, under the name REX GLORIOSE. In 1908 the *Oxford Hymn Book* contained the present form of the melody with the name O AMOR QUAM EXSTATICUS.

169   *Alone Thou Goest Forth, O Lord*

BANGOR C.M.

Solus ad victimam procidis, Domine
Peter Abelard, 1079-1142
Tr. F. Bland Tucker, 1895-
William Tans'ur, 1706?-1783

This beautiful Passion hymn is from the pen of the great teacher, philosopher, and theologian, Peter Abelard. His fearless attacks on and challenges to old ideas brought him much fame and misfortune, and eventually brought him to trial for heresy.

Abelard was born at Pallet, France, in 1079. In opposition to the desire of his parents, who wanted him to become a military man, he decided to give his life to the study of philosophy, theology, and teaching. His teaching attracted students from the whole of Europe including a brilliant young woman named Heloïse whom he secretly married. Her uncle, Canon Fulbert, was so angered over this development he had a group of ruffians beat and emasculate Abelard. Abelard then became a monk in the Abbey of St. Denis and his wife took the veil and entered the Abbey of the Paraclete.

His hymns were written for use at the Abbey of the Paraclete and were dedicated to Heloïse. They were not found until the middle of the nineteenth century in the Vatican and the Royal Library at Brussels.

Abelard was found guilty of heresy in 1136, at the insistence of Bernard of Clairvaux, and died in a monastery as he was traveling to Rome to defend himself. He and Heloïse are buried side by side in the Pere-la-Chaise Cemetery in Paris.

The translation of Abelard's hymn was made by F. Bland Tucker in 1938 for use in *The Hymnal 1940*. Tucker was educated at the University of Virginia and Virginia Episcopal Seminary. He has served as rector of Old Christ Church in Savannah, Georgia, and was a member of the committee which compiled *The Hymnal 1940*. He was born in 1895.

BANGOR was very popular in Scotland as a Psalm tune. Robert Burns referred to it in his poem, "The Ordination":

> Mak' haste an' turn King David ower,
> An' lilt wi' holy clangor;
> O' double verse come gie us four,
> An' skirl up the 'Bangol.'

The tune was published in William Tans'ur's *Compleat Melody: or Harmony of Sion*, 1734, which the author called "the most curiosest

Book that ever was published." The tune made its way to America and was included in the 1767 Boston edition of the Royal Melody Complete. It was originally used with Psalm 12.

The city of Bangor, Maine, is said to have been named for this tune.

William Tans'ur was the son of a laborer of German extraction whose name was Tanzer. No one is sure of the how and why of the present spelling. His year of birth is not known and is given variously from 1699, 1700, to 1706. The young man was deeply interested in music and devoted most of his life to playing the organ and teaching psalmody. Apparently he moved about considerably as he pursued his vocation. He is known to have been a bookseller at St. Neots and to have published a number of collections and books on music. He died on October 7, 1783, at St. Neots.

170   Go to Dark Gethsemane

ARFON 7.7.7.7.7.7.

James Montgomery, 1771-1854

Welsh hymn melody

This is James Montogomery's second and revised form of "Go to Dark Gethsemane" which appeared in his *Christian Psalmist,* 1825, under the heading "Christ our example in suffering." Julian gives the two versions for comparison. The fourth stanza is usually omitted. It reads:

> Early hasten to the tomb,
>   Where they laid his breathless clay;
> All is solitude and gloom,
>   Who hath taken him away?
> Christ is risen: He meets our eyes;
>   Saviour teach us so to rise.
>
> (Julian, p. 431)

For a comment on James Montgomery see No. 324.

Hugh Davis gave this arrangement of the tune ARFON for John Ellerton's hymn, "Throned Upon the Awful Tree" in *The English Hymnal,* 1906. There seems to be some question concerning the origin of the tune. Erik Routley informs us in his *Companion to Congregational Praise* that it has been found in French sources where it is set to Christmas Carols. In Guillmant's *Noëls,* 1885, Routley notes, it is given as the traditional tune to *"Joseph est bien marié."* Whether Welsh or French it is a fine tune and is quite appropriate for this text.

171 When I Survey the Wondrous Cross

HAMBURG L.M.

Isaac Watts, 1674-1748

Arr. Lowell Mason, 1782-1872

First appearing in his *Hymns and Spiritual Songs,* 1707, this has become one of Watts' most popular and widely used hymns. The second line originally read "Where the young Prince of glory dy'd" and was changed to the present rendering in the enlarged edition of the same work in 1709. Thy hymn was preceded with the scripture quotation, "Crucifixion to the World by the Cross of Christ," Gal. VI, 14. The original bracketed fourth stanza is as follows:

4. [His dying Crimson, like a Robe,
Spreads o'er his body on the Tree;
Then am I dead to all the Globe,
And all the Globe is dead to me.]

For a comment on Isaac Watts see No. 48.

HAMBURG was composed in 1824 while Mason was living in Savannah, Georgia. It was first published in the third edition of *The Boston Handel and Haydn Society Collection of Church Music,* 1824, under the name AVENTINE. The tune is said to have been based on a Gregorian Chant, tone one. Perhaps the words "inspired by" would be more fitting.

For a note on Lowell Mason see No. 273.

172 Deep Were His Wounds

MARLEE 6.6.6.6.8.8.

William Johnson, 1906-

Leland B. Sateren, 1913-

This Lenten hymn was submitted for publication in *The Lutheran Companion* in 1953. Dr. Ernest E. Ryden was the editor of the magazine at that time and was also serving on the commission for the *Service Book and Hymnal*. Struck by the poem, Dr. Ryden sent it to Dr. Leland B. Sateren for a musical setting. The hymn and tune then appeared together in the *Service Book and Hymnal*, 1958.

At the time William Johnson wrote this poem he was a bachelor farmer living near Chicago City, Minnesota. He was born in 1906 on a farm near Lindstrom, Minnesota, where he completed only eight grades of schooling. According to Dr. Sateren, Mr. Johnson married several years ago. We have been unable to locate him for further biographical information.

MARLEE was composed for this hymn at the request of Dr. Ernest E. Ryden, Executive Secretary of the *Service Book and Hymnal* Commission (Lutheran). It was first published in the *Service Book and Hymnal*, 1958. Dr. Sateren informed the present writer that "the tune name is an acrostic—composed of the first three letters of my son, Mark's, name and the three letters of the nickname (Lee) of another son (Leland B., Jr.)." He stated further that he composed the music rather quickly, it "just came" and needed very little alteration for publication.

Leland Bernhard Sateren was born in Everett, Washington, on October 13, 1913, the son of a Lutheran clergyman and educator. He was educated in the public schools of Michigan and Wisconsin and graduated from Augsburg College, Minneapolis, Minnesota (A.B., 1935) and the University of Minnesota (A.M., 1943). He is the recipient of honorary degrees from Lakeland College (Sheboygan, Wisconsin) and Gettysburg College (Gettysburg, Pennsylvania). Since 1935 Dr. Sateren has devoted himself to the cause of music education and composition. He has been teaching at Augsburg College since 1946 and has been chairman of the music department and director of the choir since 1950. Dr. Sateren has composed about three hundred choral works, a book of forty-one pieces for treble choirs, a book, *The New Song*, several monographs, and has contributed articles to professional magazines.

173   Come, Ye Faithful, Raise the Strain

ST. KEVIN 7.6.7.6.D.

Attr. to John of Damascus, c. 696-c. 754
Tr. John Mason Neale, 1818-1866
Arthur S. Sullivan, 1842-1900

John of Damascus was born about 696 and rose to fame as a theologian, hymnist, and defender of the use of icons in worship.

He was educated by an Italian monk by the name of Cosmos. He lived most of his life in a monastery called St. Sabas which was located between Jerusalem and Bethlehem overlooking the Dead Sea where he devoted himself to writing. He has been canonized by the Greek and Latin churches and is best known today for his treatise, *The Fountain of Knowledge,* and his odes on the canon of the Greek church.

For a note on the translator see No. 155.

This hymn is based on the Canon for St. Thomas' Sunday which is the Sunday after Easter and is called Low Sunday or Little Easter. Exodus 15 is the canticle from which it is derived, and is commonly called the Song of Moses. Neale's translation appeared in an article on "Greek Hymnology" in the *Christian Remembrancer,* April, 1859, and again in his *Hymns of the Eastern Church,* 1862.

ST. KEVIN was written for this hymn by Sir Arthur Seymoure Sullivan for the *Hymnary,* 1872, where it appeared unnamed. Two years later it was published in his own *Church Hymns with Tunes* bearing the name St. Kevin. In all probability he named it after St. Kevin, the Irish hermit, who lived in the Vale of Glendalough (Valley of the Two Lakes), near Dublin. It is said that he established a monastery there which became an important center of learning.

Sir Arthur Sullivan was born in London on May 13, 1842, and died there on November 22, 1900. He is buried in St. Paul's Cathedral. His superior musical talent came into evidence at an early age with the publication of an anthem by Novello when he was only fifteen years of age. From that time on he was extremely productive in all areas of musical endeavor. Sullivan's chief fame rests on his genius in light opera. The story of his success as a part of the Gilbert and Sullivan team needs no retelling here. We should remember, however, that he composed an Irish symphony and a grand opera *Ivanhoe* and numerous other theatrical works. Two oratorios came from his pen, *The Light of the World* and the *Prodigal Son,* neither of which appears to be popular today. Of particular interest to churchmen is the fact that he wrote fifty-six hymn tunes which Novello brought together in one volume in 1902. Among them, those in current use are: ST. KEVIN, FORTUNATUS, LACRYMAE, ST. GERTRUDE, ST. EDMUND, SAMUEL, ANGEL VOICES, COURAGE BROTHER, HANFORD, ST. THERESA, and HOMELAND.

The many honors he received during his life attest to the high esteem in which he was held. He was knighted by Queen Victoria, received honorary degrees from both Cambridge and Oxford, and was given the Legion of Honor by the French government.

174   Jesus Christ is Risen Today

LLANFAIR 7.7.7.7. with Alleluias

St. 1: *Surrexit Christus hodie,* 14th century
Tr. in *Lyra Davidica,* 1708
Sts. 2, 3: J. Arnold's *Compleat Psalmodist,*
1750, alt.
St. 4: Charles Wesley, 1707-1788
Robert Williams, *c.* 1781-1821
Harm. John Roberts, 1822-1877

The interesting history of this hymn is fully covered in Julian's *Dictionary of Hymnology* (pp. 596-597). Suffice it to say here that the composite hymn as given had its beginning with the 14th-century "*Surrexit Christus hodie.*" It was translated in *Lyra Davidica,* 1708, and the first stanza was recast in Arnold's *Compleat Psalmodist,* 1750, where the second and third stanzas were included but made no reference to the original Latin. The present first three stanzas and the final stanza by Charles Wesley are from the version presented in the *Supplement to Tate and Brady, c.* 1816. Wesley's stanza is from his *Hymns and Sacred Poems,* 1740.

For a note on Charles Wesley see No. 180.

LLANFAIR was called BETHEL when composed on July 14, 1817, by the blind basketweaver of Wales. It was first published in Parry's *Peroriaeth Hyfryd,* 1837, where the harmonization was attributed to John Roberts of Henllan. Robert Williams was an able musician and vocalist who enriched the Welsh church with his fine voice and original tunes.

175   Alleluia! Alleluia! Hearts to Heaven and Voices Raise

IN BABILONE 8.7.8.7.D.

Christopher Wordsworth, 1807-1885
Oude en Nieuwe Hollantse Boerenlities, c. 1710

Christopher Wordsworth was the nephew of the famous poet laureate William Wordsworth. He was born at Lambeth, October 30, 1807, received his education at Winchester and Trinity College,

Cambridge, where he took his B.A. in 1830. He was made a Fellow of Trinity that same year. From this honored position he became Public Orator for the University and Headmaster of Harrow School. In 1844 he was elevated to Canon of Westminster and after five years was engaged for one year as the Hulsean lecturer at Cambridge. Shortly thereafter he became a parish priest at Stanford-in-the-Vale-cum-Goosey, Berkshire. For nineteen years he served that parish with great distinction and was then made bishop of Lincoln, a position he held for fifteen years. He resigned his bishopric several months before his death at Harewood on March 20, 1885.

Among other things he wrote a complete commentary on the Bible and a volume of one hundred and twenty-seven hymns entitled, *The Holy Year; or Hymns for Sundays, Holy Days, and other Occasions Throughout the Year,* 1862. A few of these are still in use today. In addition to "Alleluia, Alleluia, Hearts to Heaven," we find "O Day of Rest and Gladness," "See, the Conqueror Mounts in Triumph," "O Lord of Heaven and Earth and Sea," "Father of All, from Land and Sea" in several hymnals currently in use in America.

The tune IN BABILONE was introduced to England and America through the *English Hymnal,* 1906, where it is found with the words of Wordsworth's hymn "See, the Conqueror Mounts in Triumph." The melody originally came from a collection of Dutch peasant songs and dances entitled, *Oude en Nieuwe Hollantse Boerenlities en Contradanseu,* c. 1710. Although Winfred Douglas, T. Tertius Noble, and others have made arrangements of this melody, ours is credited to Professor Julius Röntgen (1855-1932) one of Holland's great musicians, teacher, and musicologist.

176   Christ the Lord Is Risen Again

CHRIST IST ERSTANDEN 7.7.7.7.4.

Christ ist erstanden
Michael Weisse, c. 1488-1534
Tr. Catherine Winkworth, 1827-1878
Germany, 12th century

Michael Weisse was born circa 1480 at Neisse in Silesia. He became a priest and entered a monastery at Breslau. After coming under the influence of Martin Luther's writing, he and two other monks abandoned the monastery and associated themselves with the

Bohemian Brethren's House at Leutomischl, Bohemia, where he was admitted to the Brethren priesthood in 1531. Weisse and a colleague were sent to confer with Luther concerning Brethren views. His reputation rests now on his ability as the editor of the first Brethren hymnbook *Ein New Gesengbuchlen.* This book consisted of 155 translated and original hymns by the editor, the quality of which led Luther to say that Weisse was a "good poet" despite his "erroneous views of the Sacrament."

This translation appeared in Miss Winkworth's *Lyra Germanica,* second series, 1858.

For a note on Miss Winkworth see No. 58.

The tune is associated with one of Germany's earliest hymns which began *"Christ ist erstanden, wonder Marter alle."* It has been found in many variations since the twelfth century. The tune is said to have been based on a Gregorian chant for the Easter Sequence, *"Victimae paschali."*

177 *Christ Jesus Lay in Death's Strong Bands*

CHRIST LAG IN TODESBANDEN 8.7.8.7.7.8.7.4.

Christ lag in Todesbanden
Martin Luther, 1483-1546
Tr. Richard Massie, 1800-1887
Johann Walther's *Geystliche gesangk Buchleyn,* 1524
Harm. Hans Leo Hassler, 1564-1612

This hymn was first published as "The hymn, 'Christ ist erstanden,' improved" in *Eyn Enchiridion,* Erfurt, 1524. It was one of Germany's earliest and most popular hymns and apparently a favorite of Luther for he said of it, "After a time one tires of singing all other hymns, but the 'Christ ist erstanden' one can always sing again." It is doubtful if much of the original hymn appears here but this version owes its very existence to it as well as other hymnic and scriptural sources. J. S. Bach used both text and music in his moving cantata by the same name.

For a note on Luther see No. 31.

Richard Massie was born at Chester, England, June 18, 1800. In 1854 he translated Luther's *Spiritual Songs* from which our translation is derived. Massie translated many other German hymns, including a number by Spitta. Massie died March 11, 1887.

Johann Walther, born in 1496 near Cola in Thuringia, was both a hymnist and a musician. It was as a musician that he became associated with Martin Luther and spent three weeks with Luther assisting him with rearrangement of older music for the new Lutheran services. It was during this time that he published the *Geystliche gesangk Buchleyn* at Wittenberg, 1524. He was also present with Luther the following year when the newly arranged service of communion was used in the Stadtkirche at Wittenberg, October 29, 1525.

For a comment on Hans Leo Hassler see No. 163.

178   Good Christian Men Rejoice and Sing

GELOBT SEI GOTT 8.8.8. with Alleluias

Cyril A. Alington, 1872-1955

Melchior Vulpius, *c.* 1560-1616

The text was written for this tune and was first published in *Songs of Praise*, 1925. Cyril Argentine Alington was born at Ipswich in 1872, educated at Malborough and Trinity College, Cambridge. He became a Fellow of All Souls College, and was Assistant Master at Malborough and Eton. In 1908 he was appointed Head Master of Shrewsbury, and after eight years there he became Head Master at Eton. From 1933 until his retirement in 1951 he served as Dean of Durham. His published works include poetry, novels, essays, works on theology. He died in 1955.

GELOBT SEI GOTT derives its name from the hymn by Michael Weisse to which it was set in Vulpius' *Ein schön geistlich Gesangbuch*, 1609.

Melchior Vulpius, c. 1560-1616, was for many years cantor at Weimar. He composed several chorale tunes which remain popular in Germany, but he is best known for his excellent contrapuntal settings of preexisting tunes for four, five, six, seven, and eight voices. His published works consist of several collections of his contrapuntal vocal music, including the one mentioned above. In 1610 he published a new edition of Heinrich Faber's *Compendium Musicae* to which he added a chapter of his own. He also composed a setting to the Passion According to Saint Matthew. He was buried at Weimar on August 7, 1615.

179 O Sons and Daughters, Let Us Sing

O FILII ET FILIAE 8.8.8. with Alleluias

Jean Tisserand, d. 1494
Tr. John Mason Neale, 1818-1866
French melody, 15th century
Airs sur les hymnes sacres, odes et noels, 1623,
adapted

This hymn is based on a translation which appeared in Neale's *Medieval Hymns,* 1851. Scholars say it is French in origin. Neale believed it to be from the thirteenth century but Julian suggests a date not earlier than the seventeenth century. This version of Neale's translation is essentially that which appeared in *Hymns Ancient and Modern,* 1861, except for deletion of stanzas and a change of several words. Here we use only stanzas 1, 2, 3, 8, and 9. Stanza 5 (9) has been further altered from:

"To God your hearts and voices raise
In land and jubilee and praise," etc.

Jean Tisserand was a Franciscan monk and the founder of an order for penitent women. He died in Paris in 1494. He is believed to have been the author of an office commemorating the martyrdom of Franciscan monks in Morocco in 1220.

For a note on John Mason Neale see No. 155.

O FILII ET FILIAE is by an unknown composer. It is believed to be a French traditional tune. It has been traced only to *Airs sur les hymnes sacres, odes et noels,* 1623, and appears in various forms in publications from that date.

180 Christ the Lord Is Risen Today

EASTER HYMN 7.7.7.7. with Alleluias

Charles Wesley, 1707-1788, and others
From *Lyra Davidica,* 1708

"Christ the Lord Is Risen Today" first appeared in *Hymns and Sacred Poems,* 1739. It has since become one of Wesley's most popular hymns and is still a universal favorite for Easter morning. Martin Madan introduced several alterations of the hymn in his *Collection of Psalms and Hymns,* 1760, which served as a basis for subsequent versions.

The life, work, and influence of Charles Wesley are too well known to warrant an extensive biographical sketch here. A brief review should suffice.

Wesley was born at Epworth rectory December 18, 1707, the youngest son and eighteenth child of Samuel and Susanna Wesley. He was the descendant of a long line of devoted churchmen, controversial clerics, and poets. The young Wesley was educated at Westminster School and took his degree at Oxford where he became involved with the Oxford Methodist Movement.

In 1735 he crossed the Atlantic to become secretary to Governor Oglethorpe of Georgia, but became disillusioned and returned to England the following year. He came under the influence of Count Zinzendorf and Peter Böhler, leaders of the Moravian church, who probably pointed the direction he followed in his hymnological endeavors. Although he is best known as a hymn writer he was also a well-known preacher, but was eclipsed in this area by his brother, John. Charles always remained faithful to the Church of England and was often quite vocal in expressing disapproval of his brother's "ordination" practices.

Charles Wesley wrote some 6,500 hymns, thus earning the title, "Sweet singer of Methodism." Considering this tremendous output one can understand his deep involvement with every aspect of life and religion of his day, as well as the justification as "the greatest hymn writer of all time in terms of quantity and quality."

The complete title of the source of this stirring tune, also called WORGAN, is, *Lyra Davidica, or a collection of Divine Songs and Hymns, partly Newly composed, partly translated from the High German, and Latin Hymns; and set to easy and pleasant tunes, for more General use,* London, 1708. The book contained twenty-five tunes and thirty-one hymns. There was no indication of the composer's identity. The compilation has been attributed to various composers including J. W. Worgan, Henry Carey, and George Friedrich Handel. The tune was associated with the anonymous fourteenth Latin hymn beginning, *"Surrexit Christus hodie,"* "Jesus Christ Is Risen Today, Hallelujah." John Wesley included it in his *Foundry Tune Book,* 1742, with the present text.

181 Thine Is the Glory

MACCABEUS 5.5.6.5.6.5.6.5. with Refrain

Edmond L. Budry, 1854-1932
Tr. R. Birch Hoyle, 1875-1939
George Friedrich Handel, 1685-1759

In 1884 Edmond L. Budry (August 30, 1854–November 12, 1932) wrote this hymn in French which begins, "*A toi la gloire, O Ressuscité!*" It was first published in the *Y.M.C.A. Hymn Book,* Lausanne, 1904, and translated into English in 1923 by Richard Birch Hoyle (1875-1939). This hymn became popular with the Student Christian Movement when it appeared in three languages in the World's Student Christian Federation Hymnal, *Cantate Domino,* 1925. Since its enthusiastic reception by the Assembly of the World Council of Churches in Amsterdam, 1948, it has become increasingly popular and has appeared in a number of recent American hymnals.

Little is known of Edmond L. Budry except that he was pastor of the Free Church in Vevey, Switzerland, for thirty-five years.

Richard Birch Hoyle was born March 8, 1875, in Cloughfold, Lancashire. He was a Baptist clergyman and scholar who taught several years in Western Theological Seminary here in the States. He is represented in the *Encyclopedia of Religion and Ethics* by an article on the "Holy Spirit."

MACCABEUS is adapted from the chorus, "See, the conquering hero comes," from *Judas Maccabeus,* an oratorio by George Friedrich Handel.

For a note on Handel see No. 122.

182 The Strife Is O'er

VICTORY 8.8.8. with Alleluia

Finita iam sunt praelia
Latin 17th century
Tr. Francis Pott, 1832-1908, alt.

Arr. from G. P. da Palestrina, 1525-1594
William H. Monk, 1823-1889

The origin of this Latin Easter hymn is uncertain. At one time scholars were attributing it to an unknown medieval source, but recent research has not been able to trace it beyond the *Symphonia*

Sirenum, Cologne, 1695, from which Pott is said to have made his translation. Julian and others have been able to trace it only to *Hymnodia Sacra,* Muenster, 1753. Francis Pott's translation was made about 1859 and first published in his *Hymns Fitted To the Order of Common Prayer,* 1861. It was also included in *Hymns Ancient and Modern* the same year. The present version omits two alleluias originally found at the beginning of each stanza.

Francis Pott, English clergyman, was born in Southwark, December 29, 1832. Following his education at Brasenose College, Oxford, he took Holy Orders and became curate of Bishopsworth. After serving several other parishes Pott was appointed rector of Norhill in Bedfordshire. He remained there for twenty-five years until deafness forced his resignation. The final years of his life were given to the development of hymnology and the improvement of worship in the Anglican Church. He was active in the production of the first *Hymns Ancient and Modern* and made important contributions to hymnody in general through his translations from Latin and Syriac. He is best known in America for his original hymn, "Angel Voices Ever Singing."

VICTORY is an adaptation of the opening phrases of "Gloria Patri" from Palestrina's *Magnificat Tertii Toni.* William H. Monk arranged it for the first musical edition of *Hymns Ancient and Modern,* 1861.

For a note on William H. Monk see No. 47.

Giovanni Pierluigi da Palestrina (c. 1525-1594), the son of an Italian peasant, is revered by history as one of the great musical geniuses of all time and the foremost composer of the Roman Catholic Church and the Roman school. His early musical training was received as a chorister in his native town of Palestrina and later in the choir school of St. Maria Maggiore in Rome. From 1544 until about 1581 he held various important musical posts under several cardinals and popes, including Julius III, Pope Marcellus, and Pope Paul IV. The latter dismissed Palestrina from the Pontifical Choir because he was married. After this he became successively choirmaster at St. John Lateran, Santa Maria Maggiore, director of music at a new Roman seminary, and maestro of the Cappella Guilia. After the death of his two sons, his wife, and two brothers, he contemplated entering the priesthood but decided against it in favor of marrying the widow of a wealthy furrier. He was a successful businessman for many years while retaining his activity in music. During his life many abuses had found their way into sacred music. The Council of Trent was concerned with the reform of these abuses and decreed the exclusion of all lewd and profane words, and impure elements of music. Palestrina's contribution to the reform was significant if exaggerated. His technical perfection, smoothness, and beauty of sound became the model for many of his contemporaries and is still considered the example of excellence in liturgical propriety.

183 The Day of Resurrection

LANCASHIRE 7.6.7.6.D

'Αναστάσεως ἡμέρα
John of Damascus, c. 696-c. 754
Tr. John Mason Neale, 1818-1866, alt.

Henry T. Smart, 1813-1879

This is Neale's translation of the first of eight odes which comprise John of Damascus' famous *Golden Canon* composed for Easter day toward the middle of the eighth century. Identified as "Easter Canon," "King of Canons," "Queen of Canons" and "Golden Canon" it has been called "the greatest piece in Greek sacred poetry" (Julian p. 464). Neale's text appeared in his *Hymns of the Eastern Church,* 1862 and was first published for congregational use in the *Parish Hymn Book,* 1863.

John of Damascus has been looked upon as the last of the great Fathers of the Greek Church and as one of the great poet-musicians of his time.

For a further comment on John of Damascus see No. 173.

For a comment on John Mason Neale see No. 155.

For comments on LANCASHIRE see No. 214.

For a comment on Henry Smart see No. 124.

184 Crown Him with Many Crowns

DIADEMATA S.M.D.

Matthew Bridges, 1800-1894
Godfrey Thring, 1823-1903, St. 3.

George J. Elvey, 1816-1893

This hymn is based on Revelation 19:12 and originally appeared under the title *"In capite ejus diademata multa"* in Matthew Bridges' *Hymns of the Heart,* second edition, 1851. Bridges was born

July 14, 1800, at The Friars, Maldon, Essex. He was educated in the Church of England, but became involved with the Oxford Movement and adopted Roman Catholicism in 1848. He died in Quebec on October 6, 1894. The hymn was written in six stanzas of eight lines, and portions of it were revised by Godfrey Thring in his collection in 1882 in order to accommodate it to Anglican worship. One of Thring's stanzas has been used here as the third stanza. Note the names given to the Christ: The Lamb, Lord of Love, Lord of Life, Lord of Years, Redeemer, Creator. Omitted stanzas use Virgin's Son, Lord of Heaven, and Lord of Peace.

Godfrey Thring was born March 25, 1823, and died in 1903. He served several parishes until he became prebend of East Harptree in Wells Cathedral in 1876. His contributions to hymnology included several important collections and hymnals.

DIADEMATA is taken from the original title of the hymn by Bridges and refers to crowns. It was written for the 1868 Appendix to the first edition of *Hymns, Ancient and Modern,* presumably for this hymn.

For a note on the composer see No. 101.

185   *Blessing and Honor and Glory and Power*

O QUANTA QUALIA 10.10.10.10.

Horatius Bonar, 1808-1889
La Feillée's *Méthode du Plain-chant,* 1808

This hymn is taken from "The Song of the Lamb" published in the third series of *Hymns of Faith and Hope,* 1861.

Horatius Bonar comes from a family that has been connected with the clergy of the Church of Scotland for two hundred years. He was born at Edinburgh, December 19, 1808, educated at the University of Edinburgh and ordained as minister of the North Parish, Kelso. After six years Bonar decided to part company with the Church of Scotland and become the minister of the Free Church of Scotland in the same city. The University of Aberdeen honored him with a Doctor of Divinity degree in 1853. After serving a Free Church in Edinburgh for seventeen years he became the Moderator of the General Assembly of the Free Church of Scotland. His hymns remain popular with congregations in Scotland, England, and America.

This hymn is taken from "The Song of the Lamb" published in the third series of *Hymns of Faith and Hope,* 1861.

O QUANTA QUALIA is from the *Méthode du Plain-chant* and was adapted to be used with John Mason Neale's translation of "O Quanta Qualia," or "O What Their Joy and Their Glory Must Be," 1854. It is believed to have been based on a 17th- or 18th-century plainsong melody.

186 Look, Ye Saints, the Sight Is Glorious

CWM RHONDDA 8.7.8.7.8.7.

Thomas Kelly, 1769-1854
John Hughes, 1873-1932

Based on Revelation 7:9-15 this is a powerful coronation hymn for the Second Advent. It is considered to be one of the best of the 765 hymns by Thomas Kelly and equal to those of Watts and Wesley. It was first published in the author's *Hymns on Various Passages of Scripture,* third edition, 1809.

Thomas Kelly was born July 13, 1769 at Kellyville, County Queens, Ireland. He was educated at Trinity College, Dublin, where he prepared for a career in law but his deep spiritual convictions turned him to service in the church. He was ordained in 1792 but his evangelical fervor closed the doors of the Established Church to him and he withdrew and erected independent places of worship in Athy, Portarlington, and Wexford. His ministry spanned about sixty years in the city of Dublin where he died on May 14, 1854. His hymns are found in *A Collection of Psalms and Hymns,* 1800; *Hymns on Various Passages of Scripture,* 1804; and *Hymns Not Before Published,* 1815.

For a comment on the tune and composer see No. 245.

187 Lo! He Comes, with clouds Descending

ST. THOMAS (WADE) 8.7.8.7.8.7.

Charles Wesley, 1707-1788
John Francis Wade? 1711-1786

This hymn on the Second Advent serves to remind us that many of our great texts have evolved from various sources and that alterations are common. The original of this text was by John Cennick and was published in six stanzas in his *Collection of Sacred Hymns,* 1752. Wesley's version appeared next in four stanzas in his *Hymns of Intercession for All Mankind,* 1758. The third version was published by Martin Madan in six stanzas with many alterations in his *Collection of Psalms and Hymns,* 1760, and was a combination of the first two versions. From that time to the present, editors have felt free to change words, phrases, or entire lines as deemed necessary. For example compare Wesley's original first stanza with the present version:

Original

> Lo! he comes with clouds descending,
> Once for favour'd sinners slain!
> Thousand, thousand saints attending,
> Swell the triumph of his train:
> Hallelujah,
> God appears, on earth to reign!

Present

> Lo! he comes, with clouds descending,
> Once for our salvation slain;
> Thousand thousand saints attending
> Swell the triumph of his train:
> Alleluia, alleluia,
> Christ the Lord returns to reign.

A complete comparison is given in Julian, *Dictionary of Hymnology,* p. 681.

For a note on Charles Wesley see No. 180.

ST. THOMAS or WADE is probably the work of one John Francis Wade who kept manuscript copy books, one of which (c. 1740-43) contained the tunes ADESTE FIDELES and ST. THOMAS which was set to a benediction hymn, *"Tantum Ergo."* The tune was first published in *An Essay on the Church Plain Chant,* 1782.

Wade, born about 1711, was an English layman who earned his living in Douay, France, a haven for English refugees of the Jacobite rebellion of 1745. He was a devout Roman Catholic who spent his life teaching music and copying and selling plainchant and other kinds of music. He died August 16, 1786, at the age of 75.

188 Rejoice, The Lord Is King

DARWALL 148 6.6.6.6.8.8.

Charles Wesley, 1707-1788
John Darwall, 1731-1789

Originally published in John Wesley's *Moral and Sacred Poems*, 1744, the present text is a slightly altered form of the version which appeared in Charles Wesley's collection of sixteen hymns entitled, *Hymns for Our Lord's Resurrection*, 1746. Two stanzas have been omitted.

For a note on Charles Wesley see No. 180.

DARWALL 148 derives its name from the composer and the Psalm for which it was composed. Darwall composed tunes for all the psalms but this is the only survivor. It was published in Aaron Williams' *The New Universal Psalmodist* (5th edition), 1770.

John Darwall, an Anglican clergyman, a contemporary to Charles Wesley, and an avid amateur musician, was born in Hampton, Staffordshire, in 1731. He was educated at Manchester Grammar School and Brasenose College, Oxford. After graduation in 1756 he took holy orders and served as curate until he became vicar of Walsall, Staffordshire, in 1769. He died there on December 18, 1789. In addition to psalm tunes, Darwall composed a number of piano sonatas.

189 O Holy Spirit, Comforter

PONDEN COTE 8.6.8.6.6.6.6.6.

T. Ernest Holling, 1867-
Charles H. Heaton, 1928-

This hymn to the Holy Spirit continues the pattern of thought presented in many of the songs that followed the great models of the middle ages, *"Veni, Creator Spiritus"* and *"Veni, Sancte Spiritus."* "O Holy Spirit Comforter" first appeared in *The Hymnary of the United Church of Canada*, 1930, and then in *The Hymnary for Use in Baptist Churches,* 1936. It was originally given in five stanzas. Here we have omitted the final two stanzas.

We have no information on Dr. T. Ernest Holling.

PONDEN COTE was composed especially for this text and hymnal in 1965. It is the name of the composer's summer cottage at Crystal Beach Christian Assembly Grounds in Frankfort, Michigan.

For a comment on Charles H. Heaton see No. 35.

190   *O Holy Spirit, Come to Me*

ISLEWORTH 8.6.8.6.

Jacob M. Blough, 1876-
Samuel Howard, 1710-1782

The theme of this hymn is derived from the author's deep conviction that man's ministry cannot come to fruition without guidance of the Holy Spirit. The hymn appeared in *The Brethren Hymnal,* 1951.

Jacob M. Blough was born December 12, 1876, in Somerset County, Pennsylvania. He was educated at Juniata College (B.D.) and the Kennedy School of Missions (M.A.). He was a missionary to India for forty-six years (1903-1949). Upon his return to the United States he served several churches in Florida and retired to Sebring, Florida.

ISLEWORTH was set to Psalm 6 in Christopher Smart's *Translations of the Psalms of David, Attempted in the Spirit of Christianity,* 1765. ISLEWORTH is a place name.

Samuel Howard, an English composer and organist, began his musical career as a chorister of the Chapel Royal under William Croft. He also studied under Pepusch and subsequently became the organist at St. Clement Danes in the Strand and St. Bride's in Fleet Street, London. He composed songs and music for the pantomimes *Robin Goodfellow, or the Rival Sisters* and *The Amorous Goddess or Harlequin Married.* Howard graduated with a D.Mus. degree from Cambridge in 1769. He composed many songs and cantatas, frequently under the name of "The British Orpheus." He died July 13, 1782, in London.

191 Holy Spirit, Truth Divine

SONG 13 7.7.7.7.

Samuel Longfellow, 1819-1892
Adapt. Orlando Gibbons, 1583-1625

This hymn appeared in *Hymns of the Spirit,* 1864, under the heading "The Holy Spirit Desired."

Samuel Longfellow, the brother of the poet Henry Wadsworth Longfellow, was born in Portland, Maine, June 18, 1819. He was a graduate of Harvard University in arts, 1839, and in theology, 1846. After being ordained to the Unitarian ministry in 1848 he served Unitarian churches in Fall River, Massachusetts; Brooklyn, New York; and Germantown, Pennsylvania. He and Samuel Johnson edited several hymnbooks for the Unitarians which appeared as *A Book of Hymns for Public and Private Devotion,* 1846, which was revised and enlarged in 1848, and *Hymns of the Spirit,* 1864. He resigned his pastorate in 1882 and wrote a biography of his brother which was published in 1886. Samuel Longfellow died at Portland, Maine, October 3, 1892.

SONG 13 is so named because it was originally set to Song XIII which was a metrical paraphrase of part of The Song of Solomon beginning, "Oh my love, how comely now." It appeared for the first time in George Withers' *Hymnes and Songs of the Church,* 1623. It is also known as CANTERBURY, GIBBONS, NORWICH, SIMPLICITY and ST. IRENAEUS.

Orlando Gibbons was one of the outstanding organists and church musicians of the Elizabethan era. He was baptized at St. Martin's Church, Oxford, December 25, 1583. At the age of 12, he became a chorister under the leadership of his brother, Edward Gibbons, at King's College, Cambridge. In 1604 Gibbons was appointed organist for the Chapel Royal, a position he held for the remainder of his life. He took his Mus.B. degree from Cambridge in 1606. In 1619 he became chamber musician to the king and three years later received his Mus.D. from Oxford. In addition to the positions he was holding in 1623 he was given the position of organist at Westminster Abbey.

While on a trip with the king to Canterbury and Chapel Royal, where the king was to meet his new queen, Henrietta Maria of France, Gibbons suffered a stroke of apoplexy and died on June 5, 1625. He was buried in Canterbury Cathedral the following day.

His fame rests mainly on his church music compositions which included verse anthems and polyphonic music. Sixteen of his hymn tunes were included in the George Withers work mentioned above. The Gibbons madrigals are ranked with the best of the period.

192   Holy Spirit, Truth Divine

MERCY 7.7.7.7.

Samuel Longfellow, 1819-1892
Louis M. Gottschalk, 1829-1869

For a comment on the author and the hymn see No. 191.

MERCY derives its name from the sentiment of the hymn with which it was long associated, Charles Wesley's "Depth of Mercy, Can There Be." It is also called MANNA, GOTTSCHALK, and LAST HOPE. The tune was adapted from Gottschalk's romantic piano piece,"The Lost Hope," by the Dr. Edwin Parker, a Congregational minister, hymnist, and musician.

Louis Moreau Gottschalk was a famous American composer and piano virtuoso who won the plaudits of music lovers throughout Europe, Latin America, South America, and the United States. He studied with the best teachers in France at the Paris Conservatory and was ranked with the leading European virtuosi including Liszt, Thalberg, and Chopin.

He was born in New Orleans on May 8, 1829. His father was an English Jew of German descent and his French mother was the daughter of Count Antoine de Brusle. The young boy began studying violin at the age of six, but soon turned to the piano as his superb musical talent became evident. He was truly a child prodigy—and in his mature years was in great demand as a performer and conductor of his own works. He died while in Rio de Janeiro for a festival of his music on December 18, 1869.

193   Come, Holy Spirit, God and Lord

DAS NEUGEBOREN KINDELEIN L.M.

Martin Luther, 1483-1546
Tr. Catherine Winkworth, 1827-1878, alt.
Melody by Melchior Vulpius, c. 1560-1616
Harm. J. S. Bach, 1685-1750

For a note on Martin Luther see No. 31.

For a note on Catherine Winkworth see No. 58.

James Mearns writing in Julian's *Dictionary of Hymnology* classifies this hymn as one of two "Partly from the Latin, the translated stanzas being adapted from Pre-Reformation Versions." Miss Winkworth included her translation in the first series of *Lyra Germanica*, 1865. Luther's original is found in his *Geystliche Gesangk Buchleyn*, 1524.

"*Das Neugeborne Kindelein*" are the opening words of a hymn by Cyriacus Schneegass to which Melchior Vulpius supplied this tune.

For a comment on Melchior Vulpius see No. 178.

Johann Sebastian Bach, after more than two hundred years, remains the most prolific and excellent of all church musicians. He was descended from a long line of organists, cantors, or town musicians which has been traced back to Hans Bach who flourished circa 1561. For many years the name Bach was so closely associated with music that any one who played in town bands was called "the Bachs." Johann Sebastian stands at the head of this unique family as well as whole history of music and musicians of what is called the Baroque Era (c. 1600-1750).

He was born at Eisenach on March 31, 1685. This town is where Martin Luther lived as a boy and also where the German vernacular Bible came into being. Charles Sanford Terry writing in Grove's *Dictionary of Music and Musicians* (Third Edition, 1933, Vol. I, p. 156) says of the town, "Religion, music, romance, all were in the atmosphere of Eisenach to quicken the creative impulse of one in whom, in Wagner's words, 'the German spirit was born anew' . . . ."

Bach lived and worked in Arnstadt, Mühlhausen, Weimar, Cöthen, and finally settled down in Leipzig where he served as director of music in the Thomas Church and School and cantor of the famous Thomas School. His is considered by many to be the greatest name in the history of music. With the exception of opera he composed in every musical form. No one has equaled his proficiency as an organist or as a composer for that instrument.

His vocal music includes motets, masses, nearly two hundred cantatas, and two incomparable Passions, the *St. Matthew* and the *St. John*. Congregational singing has been greatly enriched and enhanced by his beautiful harmonizations of old German chorale melodies, some 370 of which have been published.

Bach died at Leipzig, July 28, 1750.

194 *Gracious Spirit, Dwell with Me*

REDHEAD NO. 76 7.7.7.7.7.7.

Thomas T. Lynch, 1818-1871

Richard Redhead, 1820-1901

W. Garrett Horder writing in Julian's *Dictionary of Hymnology* tells us, "Lynch's hymns are marked by intense individuality, gracefulness, and felicity of diction, picturesqueness, spiritual freshness, and the sadness of a powerful soul struggling with a weak and emaciated body" (p. 706). Despite these gracious words Thomas Toke Lynch was something of a controversial figure in his day. Dr. John Campbell described his hymns as "crude, disjointed, unmeaning, un-Christian, ill-rhymed rubbish." Spurgeon was critical of his "negative theology," but others applauded his hymns as a "spring of fresh and earnest piety." Lynch's true character shines through his response to his critics in these words, "The air will be clearer for this storm. We must conquer our foes by suffering them to crucify us, rather than by threatening them with crucifixion."

Lynch was born at Dunmow, Essex, July 5, 1818, and died at London, May 9, 1871. He was educated at a school in Islington and entered Highbury Independent College to prepare for the ministry, but was forced to drop out because of ill health. He became a preacher of note despite his interrupted education and ministered to small but select congregations throughout his life. While he was minister of the Mornington Chapel, he published *The Rivulet, Hymns for Heart and Voice*, 1855, in which the present hymn appeared. This collection was to be a supplement to Isaac Watts and was intended for use in his own church.

In his *Ancient Hymn Melodies and Other Church Tunes,* 1853, Richard Redhead designated his pieces by Roman numerals rather than by names. This is number 76 and has become known as PETRA (after the hymn "Rock of Ages") and GETHSEMANE (after the hymn "Go to Dark Gethsemane").

Redhead was an organist, composer, arranger, choir director, and editor of several books of music. His sympathy for the ideals of the Oxford Movement may account for his tendency to antiquarian tastes in church music. He was born at Harrow in 1820, and became a chorister at Magdalen, Oxford. From 1839 to 1864 he was the organist at Margaret Chapel, London, presently All Saints', Margaret Street. In 1864 he became organist at St. Mary Magdalene, Paddington, and remained there until his death in 1894. With his pastor, Frederick Oakeley, he edited the first *Gregorian Psalter* for use in the Anglican church. Oakeley's participation in the Oxford Movement led him to join Newman in becoming a Roman Catholic. Redhead's tunes remain popular in England and America.

195   Come, Holy Spirit, Heavenly Dove

ST. AGNES C.M.

Isaac Watts, 1674-1748
John Bacchus Dykes, 1823-1876

For a note on the author see No. 48.

This is one of the most popular of Watts' hymns. Written for Whitsuntide (Pentecost) it was first published in his *Hymns and Spiritual Songs,* 1707. The present text represents the first, third, and fifth stanzas of the original five-stanza hymn. When used, the omitted stanzas are usually altered in various ways.

ST. AGNES was originally written for use with Edward Caswall's translation of St. Bernard's *"Jesu dulcis memoria,"* or "Jesus the Very Thought of Thee." It was first found in Grey's *Hymnal for Use in the English Church,* 1866.

St. Agnes was a rich and beautiful Roman girl who was beheaded when only thirteen years of age during the persecutions of Diocletian for the "crime of being a Christian."

John B. Dykes was born in Kingston-upon-Hull, England, on March 10, 1823. By the time he had reached his tenth year he was playing the organ in his grandfather's church. He was educated at Wakefield and St. Catherine's College, Cambridge. Durham University honored him with a Doctor of Music degree in 1861. Dykes became a minor canon and precentor at Durham Cathedral in 1849 and was one of the founders and later conductor of the University Musical Society.

After 1862 he was Vicar of St. Oswald, Durham. He was by inclination a high churchman and as a result found himself in constant dispute with his low-church bishop. Being denied the assistance of two curates the burden of his large parish broke his health and he died at St. Leonard's-on-the-Sea January 22, 1876. Dykes published sermons and works on liturgics but his fame rests primarily on his productivity as a hymn-tune composer. He composed about three hundred tunes, many of which are to be found in current hymnbooks. He is also the composer of several services, music for Psalms, anthems, and part songs.

196   Spirit Divine, Attend Our Prayers

NUN DANKET ALL' (GRÄFENBERG) C.M.

Andrew Reed, 1787-1862
Johann Crüger, 1598-1662

This Whitsuntide hymn first appeared under the heading "Hymn to the Spirit. Sung on the Late Day Appointed for Solemn Prayer and Humiliation in the Eastern District of the Metropolis." It was published in the June, 1829, issue of the *Evangelical Magazine*. According to the April issue of the same publication, it was written for a day of "humiliation and prayer" called by the Board of Congregational Ministers for Good Friday, 1829. Originally in seven stanzas, the present form omits stanzas built on the metaphors "light," "dew," and "dove."

Andrew Reed was born on November 27, 1787, and died February 25, 1862. He was educated at Hackney College, London, for the Congregational ministry. He served the New Road Chapel and later Wycliffe Chapel. Although he wrote about twenty-one hymns, published a *Supple-*

ment to Watts' collection, 1817 and *The Hymn Book*, 1842, he is best known for his part in the founding of "The London Orphan Asylum," "The Asylum for Fatherless Children," "The Asylum for Idiots," "The Infant Orphan Asylum," and "The Hospital for Incurables." For these institutions, he raised some $300,000, a formidable sum in those days.

NUN DANKET ALL', also known as GRÄFENBERG and ST. MARY MAGDALENE, is a melody attributed to Johann Crüger. It first appeared in the second edition of his *Praxis pietatis melica*, 1647, with Paul Gerhardt's hymn beginning *"Nun danket all' und bringet Ehr."* Some scholars believe Crüger made a composite tune from Psalm tunes appearing in the 1562 *Genevan Psalter*.

For a note on Johann Crüger see No. 162.

197   Come, O Creator Spirit, Come

VENI CREATOR L.M.

Veni Creator Spiritus, ninth century
Tr. Robert Bridges, 1844-1930

Sarum plainsong Mode VIII
Harm. Winfred Douglas, 1867-1944

"Veni Creator Spiritus" is perhaps one of the most famous of all medieval hymns and is said to have "taken deeper hold on the Western church than any other medieval hymn, the Te Deum Laudamus alone excepted" (Julian, *Dictionary of Hymnology*, p. 1207). This hymn has been variously attributed to Charlemagne, St. Ambrose, Gregory the Great, and Rhabanus Maurus (c. 776-856) but its authorship remains uncertain. A full, interesting, and scholarly discussion relative to the problem of authorship can be found in Julian, *Dictionary of Hymnology*, pp. 1206ff.

Descriptions of the hymn's use in the medieval church indicate it was sung with great dignity amid the ringing of bells, the use of candles, incense, and the finest vestments. At the pentecostal season it was considered especially appropriate for use at Tierce, Lauds, and Vespers. It excelled as an ordination hymn and was frequently used by the priest in preparation for celebrating mass.

Julian lists fifty-three English translations taken directly from the

Latin. Robert Bridges' translation first appeared in his *Yattendon Hymnal,* 1899, and was revised for *The English Hymnal,* 1906.

For a note on Robert Bridges see No. 162.

The tune is of ancient origin, much older than the text to which it is generally associated. Erik Routley has pointed out that the tune has been traced to an association with the Ambrosian hymn, *Hic est dies verus Dei* (*Companion to Congregational Praise,* p. 116). The melody has, of course, undergone many modifications as it has been adapted to various translations and especially to those in English. Despite this the melody retains much of its original plainsong and modal flavor.

For a note on Winfred Douglas, see No. 252.

198   Lord God, the Holy Ghost

PLATTEN S.M.

James Montgomery, 1771-1854
Lee Hastings Bristol, Jr., 1923-

The original version of this "Whit-Sunday" hymn appeared in the eighth edition of Cotrill's Selection, 1819. Montgomery altered the text slightly for his *Christian Psalmist,* 1825, and *Original Hymns,* 1853. Since then the hymn has enjoyed extensive use in Great Britain and America.

For a note on James Montgomery see No. 324.

PLATTEN was composed by Dr. Lee Hastings Bristol, Jr. Dr. Bristol, who serves as vice-chairman and executive secretary of the Episcopal Church Music Commission, has had a varied career as college president, businessman, writer, composer, and as a civic and religious leader as well. Dr. Bristol, who was born April 9, 1923, served as President of Westminster Choir College from 1962 through the academic year of 1969. Before that he was associated with Bristol-Myers Company in New York, a company cofounded by his grandfather. He is a lay preacher in the Episcopal Church, a member of nine boards including the New York Philharmonic. He has edited a book on public relations published both here and in Japan, is author of a biography *Seed for a*

Song, and the composer of numerous compositions in the choral and organ field. He is a lineal descendant of Thomas Hastings, the composer of the familiar TOPLADY tune for "Rock of Ages," and is represented himself by tunes in ten hymnals. He has been a frequent contributor to such publications as *Music,* the *A.G.O. Magazine, Diapason, Christian Herald, The Journal of Church Music, Music Ministry* and many others. He is a fifth-generation alumnus of Hamilton College, holds two earned and eleven honorary degrees. He is the third American to have been made a Fellow of the Royal School of Church Music in England. He has been awarded the Outstanding Civilian Service Medal by the Department of the Army and received the 1969 Man-of-the-Year Award from the Greater Princeton (N.J.) Chamber of Commerce and Civic Council.

199   Holy Spirit, Hear Us

GLENFINLAS 6.5.6.5.

William Henry Parker, 1845-1929

Kenneth George Finlay, 1882-

The author of this hymn was the head of an insurance company in Nottingham, England, and an active layman in the Chelsea Street Baptist Church. He was born at New Basford, Nottingham, March 4, 1845. As a young man he began writing verse and his keen interest in the Sunday School Movement provided opportunity to write hymns in observance of various anniversary occasions. His hymns appeared in *The School Hymnal,* 1880, and *The Children's Book of Praise,* 1881. In 1882 he published *The Princess Alice and Other Poems.* Of his hymns the following are in common use: "Children Know but Little," "Jesus, I So Often Need Thee," and "Tell Me the Stories of Jesus." He died December 2, 1929.

GLENFINLAS was composed for the *Church and School Hymnal* (S.P.C.K.) 1926, but a delay in publication let it first appear in *Songs of Praise,* 1925, where it was set to the hymn "Summer suns are glowing." The beautifully simple tune is built on the pentatonic scale and is a favorite with children.

Kenneth George Finlay, the child of Scottish parents, was born in Aberdeen in 1882. Educated at Robert Gordon's College, Aberdeen, and Merchiston Castle School, Edinburgh, Scotland, he became a member of the Institution of Naval Architects and held a responsible position in the shipbuilding industry until 1928 when he decided to devote his life entirely to music. In preparation for this he spent a year at the Royal College of Music and another at the Jordanhill Teacher's Training College, Glasgow. He was a teacher of class singing in schools at Irvine, Ayrshire. He composed hymn tunes, part-songs, a prelude for strings based on the tune GLENFINLAS, and two church cantatas: *The Savior's Birth* and *Before the Dawn* (Passiontide).

200   Breathe on Me, Breath of God

TRENTHAM S.M.

Edwin Hatch, 1835-1889, alt.

Robert Jackson, 1840-1914

Edwin Hatch was descended from a Nonconformist family but associated himself with the Church of England. He was born at Derby on September 4, 1835, and was educated at King Edward's School, Birmingham, and Pembroke College, Oxford. For a time he taught classical languages at Trinity College, Quebec, Canada, but in 1867 returned to England to become vice-principal of St. Mary's Hall, Oxford. He has been called a historian, scholar, intellectual, and Christian gentleman. This hymn reflects the depth of his devotional life. He died November 10, 1889.

TRENTHAM is the name of the town in Staffordshire, England, where the composer was born. It was written for Henry W. Baker's hymn, "O Perfect Life of Love" which was published in *Fifty Sacred Leaflets,* 1894.

Robert Jackson was born in Oldham, Lancashire, England, in 1842. He was a teacher, conductor, composer, and organist. He studied at the Royal Academy of Music and served as organist and choirmaster at St. Mark's Church, London. He succeeded his father as organist and choirmaster at St. Peter's Church, Oldham. He died in Oldham, in 1914.

201 Spirit of God, Descend Upon My Heart

MORECAMBE 10.10.10.10.

Attr. to George Croly, 1780-1860

Frederick C. Atkinson, 1841-1897

Apparently this hymn first appeared in Charles Rogers' compilation of the best hymns of about two hundred English authors, entitled *Lyra Britannica,* 1867, under the heading of the scriptural verse: "If we live in the Spirit, let us also walk in the Spirit" (Gal. 5:25). In that book the hymn is one of four attributed to George Croly. Armin Haeussler makes a good case for Croly as being the author but cautiously concludes his remarks with the statement that it was "probably by George Croly."

George Croly was born in Dublin, Ireland, August 17, 1780. After graduation from Dublin University he took Holy Orders and ministered in Ireland until 1810 after which he moved to London and gave himself to various literary pursuits, including the writing of novels, historical and theological works, poetry, dramas, and satires. He was editor of *The Universal Review* and a contributor to several other important publications. His conservative views toward the liberal thought of his era were expressed eloquently and boldly through his preaching at St. Stephen's, Walbrook, and St. Benet Sherehog where he became rector in 1835. It was during this ministry that he published his *Psalms and Hymns for Public Worship,* 1854. He dropped dead while walking on the streets of Holborn on November 24, 1860.

MORECAMBE, originally HELLESPONT, was composed for Lyte's hymn "Abide with Me" and was first published as a leaflet in 1870. It is used extensively with the present text in American hymnals. "Morecambe" is a place name in Western England.

Frederick Cook Atkinson, English organist and choirmaster, was born at Norwich, August 21, 1841. Before going to Cambridge to study for his Mus.B. degree, he was a pupil of and assistant to Dr. Zechariah Buck. After graduation he became organist and choirmaster at St. John's and St. Paul's Anglican churches in Bradford. From 1881 to 1885 he held the same position at Norwich Cathedral and finally went to St. Mary's Church, Lewisham. He died at East Dereham in 1897.

202 Spirit, Strength of All the Weak

TON-MÂN 7.7.7.6.

Thomas Benson Pollock, 1836-1896
David Evans, 1874-1948

Although this appears under the name of Pollock, there appears to have been collaboration with Richard Frederick Littledale. Both men wrote numerous litanies, and one of Pollock's is listed in Julian as having been written with Littledale. Metrical litanies were often quite long and were easy prey for borrowing, omission, and alteration by compilers and editors. The present first stanza is probably an altered form of Littledale's eighth stanza as given in number 234 in *The Hymnal, 1940.* Another stanza, omitted here, is stanza 16 at number 524 in Charles Hutchins' *The Church Hymnal, Revised and Enlarged,* Boston, 1899. The actual authorship of our remaining stanzas is uncertain. Traditionally all metrical litanies should be sung antiphonally or responsively.

For a note on Thomas Benson Pollock see No. 148.

TON-MÂN was composed in 1912 for a hymn by one E. Rees and first appeared in a collection of Welsh hymns entitled, *Cân a Moliant,* 1917. This is the second half of Evans' original.

For a note on David Evans see No. 381.

203 God Almighty, God Eternal

GENEVA 8.7.8.7.D.

Mary Ellen Jackson Cathey, 1926-
George Henry Day, 1883-

These words were submitted to and published by The Hymn Society of America for use at the Fifth World Order Study Conference held in Cleveland, Ohio, in November, 1958, under the aegis of the Department of International Affairs of the National Council of Churches.

Mary Jackson Cathey has served as Director of Religious Education at the First Presbyterian Church, Anderson, South Carolina, and the

Bethesda Presbyterian Church, Bethesda, Maryland. She was educated at Winthrop College, Rock Hill, South Carolina (A.B. 1947) and the Assembly's Training School, Richmond, Virginia (M.R.E. 1953). She is married to Henry M. Cathey and resides in Silver Spring, Maryland. Several of her hymns have been published by The Hymn Society of America.

GENEVA is named for Geneva, New York, where George Henry Day has served as organist-choirmaster for Trinity Church (Episcopal) since 1935. It first appeared in *The Hymnal, 1940,* and again in the *Harvard University Hymnbook,* 1964.

George Henry Day was born in New York City, September 13, 1883. He studied under notable teachers and became a Fellow of the American Guild of Organists in 1910. He is a 1913 graduate of New York University and New York College of Music and was awarded a Doctor of Music degree by Lincoln and Jefferson University in 1923. Before moving to Geneva, New York, Dr. Day was organist-director in churches in the city of New York; Wilmington, Delaware; and Rochester, New York. Throughout his career he has been active in the American Guild of Organists and other professional organizations. He is the composer of a number of hymn tunes, anthems, organ pieces, and three cantatas.

204 Jesus Calls Us O'er the Tumult

REGENSBURG 8.7.8.7.

Cecil Frances Alexander, 1818-1895

Melody by Johann Crüger, 1598-1662

The original version of this hymn was submitted to the S.P.C.K. hymnal, etc., 1852. It underwent various alterations in English hymnals after its first publication but the version here is the original.

For a note on the Cecil Frances Alexander see No. 2.

REGENSBURG is the name given this tune by the editors of *The Pilgrim Hymnal* and denotes the city to which Crüger went to study with Homberger. The original tune is from Crüger's *Geistliche Kirchen-Melodien,* 1649, where it was set to Franck's hymn *"Herr, ich habe missgehandelt."* According to Ronander and Porter the present version is an abridged form of the melody and is taken from *Louange et Prière,*

1957. The present rhythmic structure bears no resemblance to that given in several German hymnbooks.

For a note on Johann Crüger see No. 162.

205 Jesus, Lover of My Soul

ABERYSTWYTH 7.7.7.7.D.

Charles Wesley, 1707-1788
Joseph Parry, 1841-1903

This is one of the most popular hymns ever written and countless attempts to improve upon the original have failed. It first appeared in Wesley's *Hymns and Sacred Poems,* 1740, under the heading "In Temptation." Authoritative sources have long since discredited many apocryphal tales associated with its writing and believe it was written shortly after Wesley's return from America. Madan and others used the hymn after 1760 but oddly it was not included in Wesleyan hymnals until 1800. Since then it has found its way into most English-language hymnals and has been translated into many other languages.

For a note on Charles Wesley see No. 180.

ABERYSTWYTH was named for the Welsh university and resort city and home of the composer. Long associated with this hymn it was first composed for the Welsh hymn "Beth sydd i mi yn y byd" and published in E. Stephen's *Tonau ac Emynau Parch,* 1879.

Joseph Parry was born in Wales on May 21, 1841. His family immigrated to America in 1854 and settled in Danville, Pennsylvania. He received his first musical training under his fellow workers in the Danville iron works, receiving his first award for composition in 1860. He went to college in Geneseo, New York, returned to Danville, and became an organist in one of the churches. In 1865 he returned to Wales for the Aberystwyth Eisteddfod and was given special honors for his work. After his return to America he gave concerts in order to earn money for further musical training. With funds contributed by his friends, he soon found himself studying at the Royal Academy of Music in London. He received his B.Music and D.Music degrees from Cambridge University. He returned to Danville in 1871 and conducted a music school for two years after which he returned to Aberystwyth as professor of music at the University College. From 1879 through 1888 he conducted private music schools in Aberystwyth and Swansea before becoming professor of music at University College, Cardiff. His death occurred at Penarth, on February 17, 1903.

Parry made many contributions to Welsh music and was the recipient of a significant financial award made by the Llandudno Eisteddfod for his service to Welsh music. His compositions include oratorios, cantatas, anthems, and about four hundred hymn tunes.

206   *More About Jesus Would I Know*

MORE ABOUT JESUS L.M. with Refrain

Eliza E. Hewitt, 1851-1920

John R. Sweney, 1837-1899

This favorite Sunday school song was written by Eliza Edmunds Hewitt and reflects her deep interest in the teaching of the young. She was a Philadelphian by birth on June 28, 1851, and lived her entire life there, dying on April 24, 1920. She was educated in the public schools and the Girls' Normal School after which she spent a number of years as a teacher. Her interest in the Sunday School Movement led her to devote much of her life to it in Philadelphia's Northern Home for Friendless Children and later in the Calvin Presbyterian Church. She suffered many years from a spinal disease but recovered sufficiently to carry on her work. Miss Hewitt's poetry came to the attention of John R. Sweney who set many of her poems to music and later collaborated with her on many other songs including "There Is Sunshine in My Soul Today" and "I Am Thinking Today of That Beautiful Land."

MORE ABOUT JESUS, OR SWENEY, was composed for this text and appeared with it in W. J. Kirkpatrick and J. R. Sweney's *Glad Hallelujahs*, 1887.

John R. Sweney was born in West Chester, Pennsylvania, December 31, 1837. At an early age he revealed his interest in musical composition and by the time he reached his twenty-second year was teaching music in Dover, Delaware. During the Civil War, Sweney was the director of the Third Delaware Regiment Band. Following the war he became Professor of Music at the Pennsylvania Military Academy, a position he held for twenty-five years. For ten years of this time he was also song leader for one of the largest Sunday schools in Philadelphia. He was much in demand as a song leader and spent his summers working in this capacity in church assemblies through the northeastern section of the country. A composer of over a thousand gospel hymn tunes, he also edited and coedited over sixty gospel hymnbooks. He died at Chester, Pennsylvania, on April 10, 1899.

207   O Christ, We Climb the Hill with Thee

WINCHESTER NEW L.M.

Kenneth Morse, 1913-

Adapted from *Musicalisch Hand-Buch,* Hamburg, 1690

These words were first published in *The Brethren Hymnal,* 1951. Mr. Morse was a member of the committee responsible for compiling and editing that work and seven of his hymns appeared in it.

For a note on Kenneth I. Morse see No. 37.

WINCHESTER NEW also appears as SWIFT GERMAN TUNE, FRANKFORT, and WINCHESTER. Zahn (2781) gives it as an anonymous melody with the hymn, *"Wer nur den lieben Gott lässt walten."* John Wesley appears to have introduced it to England in *The Foundry Tune Book,* 1742. The present form is from William H. Havergal's *Old Church Psalmody,* 1742, and was probably adapted by him. In some early American books, it is attributed to Dr. Croft.

208   In the Cross of Christ I Glory

RATHBUN 8.7.8.7.

John Bowring, 1792-1872
Ithamar Conkey, 1815-1867

The son of an English manufacturer of woolen goods, John Bowring was born in Exeter, October 17, 1792. Despite leaving school at an early age he became an outstanding scholar, author, poet, and government official. He traveled widely on behalf of his father's business but his interest in political and social reform led him to pursue a life of writing and politics. Consequently, he became editor of the *Westminster Review* in 1825, was elected to a seat in Parliament in 1835, appointed consul to Canton, China, in 1849, was knighted in 1854, and became Governor of Hong Kong the same year. It is said he knew two hundred languages and could speak one hundred. He produced more than thirty volumes on a variety of subjects. A Unitarian by religious conviction, Bowring's theology in this hymn seems oddly orthodox. It is based on Galatians 6:14 and was first published in his *Hymns,* 1825. He died in Exeter on November 23, 1872. The opening line of this hymn was inscribed on his tombstone.

RATHBUN was composed for this hymn by Ithamar Conkey in 1849 while he was organist at the Central Baptist Church in Norwich, Connecticut. He named the tune in honor of his soprano soloist, Mrs. Beriah S. Rathbun.

Conkey, a native of Shutesbury, Massachusetts, was born in 1815. In 1850 he left Norwich and went to New York City where he became well known as a bass soloist in the Grace and Calvary Churches. He was much in demand as soloist for oratorios and was for a time the director of the quartet choir in the Madison Avenue Baptist Church. He died April 30, 1867, at Elizabeth, New Jersey.

209   *Art Thou Weary, Heavy Laden?*

STEPHANOS 8.5.8.3.

John Mason Neale, 1818-1866
Based on Stephen the Sabaite, 725-794
Henry Williams Baker, 1821-1877

For note on John Mason Neale see No. 155.

The hymn was included in the Appendix to the 1868 edition of *Hymns Ancient and Modern.* This edition contained one hundred fourteen new hymns, twenty-six of which were translations of early hymns. Ten of the twenty-six translations were from hymns of the Eastern Church. Dr. Neale himself has said that some of his hymns contained so little of the Greek that they should not be called translations. (See Julian, *Dic-*

tionary of Hymnology, Article on Greek Hymnody.) Maurice Frost, writing in his *Historical Companion to Hymns Ancient and Modern,* agrees that Neale's "... debt to the Greek original is more nominal than real."

Stephen the Sabaite was placed in the monastery at Mar Saba at the age of ten years by his uncle, John of Damascus. He spent his life there. This is one of the few dialogue hymns contained in modern hymnals and lends itself nicely to antiphonal singing.

The tune STEPHANOS is named for Stephen, the Sabaite, the author of the hymn on which Neale based his text for "Art Thou Weary." Baker is said to have composed the melody which was harmonized by William H. Monk, musical editor of *Hymns Ancient and Modern.*

Henry Williams Baker was born at Lambeth, May 27, 1821. Educated at Cambridge he was ordained the year of his graduation, 1844. From 1851 until his death he was vicar of Monkland. He was one of the charter members of the committee of *Hymns Ancient and Modern* and was the first chairman. He contributed several of his own hymns and tunes to that book. He died at the Monkland vicarage, February 11, 1877.

210   O Master of the Waking World

MELITA 8.8.8.8.8.8.

Frank Mason North, 1850-1935
John B. Dykes, 1823-1876

This world service hymn was written in 1927 at the request of the editor of *The Church School Journal* and was published in that magazine in January, 1928. It was introduced into the *Methodist Hymnal* in 1935, in four stanzas, the second of which is omitted here.

Frank Mason North was one of America's outstanding Methodist ministers. Born in New York City, December 3, 1850, he spent his early years in that teeming city to which he would later minister and about which he would write. He graduated from Wesleyan University in Connecticut, was ordained minister of the Methodist Episcopal Church, and became a member of the New York Conference in 1873. He served several churches in New York and Connecticut before being appointed corresponding secretary of the New York Missionary and Church Extension Society. In 1912 he became the secretary of the Methodist

Board of Foreign Missions. For a time he served as editor of the magazine, *The Christian City*. Dr. North's interest in city and world missions is revealed in most of his hymns. Fifteen of his poems were published privately in 1931 as *Hymns and Other Poems*. He died at Madison, New Jersey, December 17, 1935.

MELITA was composed especially for William Whiting's hymn "Eternal Father Strong to Save," familiarly known in America as the Navy Hymn. It first appeared in the original *Hymns Ancient and Modern*, 1861 with those words.

For a note on John B. Dykes see No. 195.

211 Father, Long Before Creation

WINTER 8.7.8.7.4.4.7.

Chinese: Anon, c. 1952
Tr. Francis P. Jones, 1890-
Paul E. Koch, 1929-

This modern Chinese hymn was translated by Francis P. Jones and was first published in the National Council of Churches *China Bulletin*, and then later in *The Hymnbook* (Presbyterian), 1955, as well as elsewhere.

Francis Price Jones was born December 28, 1890, at Dodgeville, Wisconsin. He was educated at Northwestern University, and did graduate study at the University of Chicago, Garrett Biblical Institute, and Union Theological Seminary. He was a Methodist missionary to China from 1915 to 1950. Since his return to the States he has devoted his talents to translating Christian classics into Chinese and was associated with Drew University until his retirement in 1965. He was a member of the editorial board responsible for the publication of the interdenominational hymnbook, *Hymns of Universal Praise*, 1936.

WINTER was composed for this hymn and for *A Hymnbook for Christian Worship*, 1970. WINTER was the maiden name of the composer's wife. Mr. Koch tells us the tune "was intended to be traditional in melodic concept, yet somewhat contemporary in harmonic style, with the high point being reached at the start of the long descending scale passage with which the melody ends."

For a note on Paul E. Koch see No. 27.

212   Blessed Jesus, at Thy Word

LIEBSTER JESU 7.8.7.8.8.8.

Liebster Jesu, wir sind hier
Tobias Clausnitzer, 1619-1684
Tr. Catherine Winkworth, 1827-1878
Johann Rudolph Ahle, 1625-1673
Harm. J. S. Bach, 1750-1865

Tobias Clausnitzer was a great German preacher who was chaplain to the Swedish Army and was called upon to preach from the pulpit of St. Thomas Church, Leipzig, when Queen Christina ascended to the throne of Sweden and again for the field services at the conclusion of the Peace of Westphalia in 1648 which brought the Thirty Years' War to a conclusion. His last years were spent as pastor at Weiden. He died May 7, 1684.

This hymn was first published in *Altdorffisches Gesang-Büchlein,* 1663 and was intended to be used before the sermon.

For a note on the translator see No. 58.

The name of the tune is from the first line of Clausnitzer's hymn, *"Liebster Jesu, wir sind hier, dich und dein Wort anzuhören."* The tune first appeared with the words *"Ja, er ist's, das Heil der Welt"* in 1664 and after some alteration appeared with *"Liebster Jesu"* in 1687.

Ahle was a distinguished German composer and author whose chorale melodies are still sung in Germany. He was born at Mühlhausen December 24, 1625, and died there July 9, 1673. He was the cantor in Göttingen and organist at St. Blasius Church, Mühlausen, and served as burgomaster there for a time.

For a note on J. S. Bach see No. 193.

213   O Jesus, I Have Promised

ANGEL'S STORY 7.6.7.6.D.

John E. Bode, 1816-1874
Arthur H. Mann, 1850-1929

Originally written "O Jesus, We Have Promised," this hymn was the confirmation hymn for the author's daughter and two sons. It was first published in a leaflet by the S.P.C.K. under the title "A Hymn for the Newly Confirmed" and a year later in the Appendix to *Psalms and Hymns,* 1869.

John Ernest Bode was born in London, February 23, 1816, was educated at Eton, Charterhouse, and Christ Church, Oxford. He took Holy Orders in 1843 and became rector of Westwell in Oxfordshire in 1847. In 1860 he was rector at Castle Camps in Cambridgeshire. For a time he was tutor and classical examiner of his college. He died at Castle Camps, October 6, 1874. His publications include the *Bampton Lectures* he delivered at Oxford, *Ballads from Herodotus, Hymns from the Gospel of the Day,* and *Short Occasional Poems.*

ANGEL'S STORY was written for the hymn "I love to hear the story which angels tell" and was first published in *The Methodist Sunday-School Tune-Book* 1881.

Arthur Henry Mann, composer of anthems, hymn tunes, and organ music was born May 16, 1850, at Norwich, England. He was educated at Norwich Cathedral and New College, Oxford. He became successively the organist at St. Peter's in Wolverhampton, Tettenhall Parish Church, Beverly Minster, and King's College Chapel in Cambridge. The latter position he held for fifty-three years until his death on November 19, 1929. He was the musical editor of *The Church of England Hymnal,* 1895, and made many contributions to the world of music as an authority on Handel and conductor of boys' choirs.

214   *Go, Make of All Disciples*

LANCASHIRE 7.6.7.6.D.

Matthew 28:19-20
Leon M. Adkins, 1896-
Henry Smart, 1813-1879

This hymn was written in 1955 in keeping with the National Council of Churches' theme, based on the great commission, for Christian Education Week. In its original form it was used as a dedication hymn for church school workers in the University Methodist Church, Syracuse, New York, where Dr. Adkins was pastor. It appeared in the February, 1956, issue of *The Church School* and with the author's own minor alterations was included in *The Methodist Hymnal,* 1964-1966. Our version consists of stanzas 1, 2, and 3 of *The Methodist Hymnal* four-stanza hymn.

Leon McKinley Adkins was born in Ticonderoga, New York, on July 14, 1896. He was educated at Middlebury College (A.B., 1919 and D.D. 1945) and Boston University (S.T.B. 1925). He was ordained deacon in 1923 and elder in 1925. After serving student pastorates in Vermont and Rhode Island, Dr. Adkins served Methodist churches in Delmar (1927-1937), Schenectady (1937-1950), and Syracuse (1950-1955) New York. In 1955 he moved to Nashville, Tennessee, and served as General Secretary of the Division of the Local Church of the denomination's General Board of Education until his retirement in 1966. For the academic years of 1967-68 and 1969-70 he served as a visiting professor at Saint Paul School of Theology in Kansas City, Missouri. He has held many local and national offices in the Methodist Church, in the National Council of Churches of Christ, and has contributed articles to *Pastoral Care,* the *Upper Room,* and Christian education periodicals.

LANCASHIRE appears with a variety of texts including "Lead On, O King Eternal," "The Day of Resurrection," "Rejoice, Rejoice Believers," "O Brothers, Lift Your Voices," and "From Ocean unto Ocean." It was written especially for Heber's famous missionary hymn "From Greenland's Icy Mountains," in 1835 on the occasion of the Tercentenary Celebration of the Reformation in England held in Blackburn, Lancashire. Henry Smart was organist there at the time and named the tune after the county. The tune first appeared in *Psalms and Hymns for Divine Worship,* 1867, which was published under the aegis of the Presbyterian Church of England.

For a note on the composer see No. 124.

215   *Make Me a Captive, Lord*

LLANLLYFNI S.M.D.

George Matheson, 1842-1906

John Jones, 1797-1857
Adapt. David Jenkins, 1849-1915

Based on Ephesians 3:1, "Make Me a Captive, Lord" appeared in George Matheson's *Sacred Songs,* 1890, under the heading, "Christian Freedom."

George Matheson was born in Glasgow, Scotland, March 27, 1842. His father was a well-to-do merchant. From early boyhood Matheson was afflicted with the threat of blindness, but despite this handicap he managed to complete his education at Glasgow University with first honors in classics, logic, and philosophy. He was ordained to the ministry in the Church of Scotland in 1866 and during his career became a highly respected scholar, prolific author of books, brilliant preacher, and beloved pastor. After a brief term as assistant minister in a Glasgow church he became pastor of the Innellan Church, Argyllshire, remaining there for eighteen years. From 1886 until his retirement in 1899 he served St. Bernard's Parish Church in Edinburgh, one of Scotland's largest and most influential churches. He died at North Berwick on August 28, 1906.

According to Millar Patrick the tune LLANLLYFNI is "really by David Jenkins, who based the tune on the remarkable intonations of Mr. Jones' voice in preaching." The *Guide to the Pilgrim Hymnal* credits the tune to John Jones and the arrangement to David Jenkins. In either case the tune is excellently adapted to this text with which it appeared in *The Church Hymnary*, 1927. LLANLLYFNI first appeared in David Jenkins' *Gemau Mawl*, 1890.

John Jones (1797-1857), despite his humble background, became one of the leading Welsh Calvinistic Methodist preachers and churchmen. Without formal education, he taught himself to read at home, worked as a laborer in quarries and on roads, and became a powerful lay preacher. He was ordained in 1829 and gave the remainder of his life to preaching the gospel. He possessed natural musical gifts, including a resonant voice of remarkable range. He composed several hymn tunes which may still be heard in Welsh churches.

David Jenkins (1849-1915) began his life as an apprentice to a tailor. His interest in music led him to leave his apprenticeship and devote himself to the study of that art, at first on his own but later under Joseph Parry. He graduated from Cambridge in 1878 and apparently returned to Wales where he was appointed to the music faculty of the University College of Wales, Aberystwyth, in 1899. He eventually became head of the music department and remained in that position the remainder of his life. At the same time he served as precentor for the English Presbyterian Church at Aberystwyth for many years and established himself as a prominent figure in both national and provincial Eisteddfodau. His compositions cover a wide range of forms including anthems, part-songs, hymn tunes, cantatas, songs, and an opera.

216   Just as I Am, Without One Plea

WOODWORTH L.M.

Charlotte Elliott, 1789-1871
William B. Bradbury, 1816-1868

In his *Songs of Praise Discussed* Percy Dearmer informs us that when Miss Elliott died more than one thousand letters were found expressing thanks for this hymn. An invalid for most of her life, Charlotte Elliott possessed a brilliant and imaginative mind. It is said that she wrote this hymn after a particularly restless and painful night filled with frustration and despair over her deep feeling of uselessness. She was born on March 18, 1789, at Clapham, England, and there remained until 1823 when she moved to Brighton where she died on September 22, 1871. Her hymns appeared in her brother's edition of *Psalms and Hymns,* her own *Hours of Sorrow Cheered and Comforted,* 1836; *Hymns for a Week,* 1839; *The Invalid's Hymn Book,* 1841; and *Thoughts in Verse on Sacred Subjects,* 1869.

WOODWORTH was originally set to the hymn "The God of Love Will Sure Indulge" in Bradbury and Hastings' *Mendelssohn Collection* or *Third Book of Psalmody,* 1849. It was not associated with the present hymn until 1860 at which time it appeared in Bradbury's *Eclectic Tune Book* in long meter. Bradbury added the final "I Come" for this purpose. Since that time the tune has displaced many lesser melodies and has become wedded to the text in the American church.

For a note on William Bradbury see No. 45.

217   Just as I Am, Thine Own to Be

SAFFRON WALDEN 8.8.8.6.

Marianne Farningham, 1834-1909
A. H. Brown, 1830-1926

Farningham was the nom de plume of Marianne Hearn and was taken from the name of her birthplace in Kent, England. She lost her parents at an early age and was responsible for the care of the younger children in the family, which made it difficult to acquire a formal education. For a time she lived in Bristol and afterward taught in the primary schools of Gravesend and Northampton where she took up residence in 1865. She became active in the work of the College Street Baptist Church in Northampton and established an excellent reputation as the teacher of a large Bible class. She was a popular writer for *The Christian World* and was for a time editor of the *Sunday School Times.* Among her many publications are the following: *Lays and Lyrics of the Blessed Life,* 1861; *Poems,* 1865; *Morning and Evening Hymns for a Week,* 1870; and *Songs of Sunshine,* 1878. Miss Farningham died at Barmouth in 1909.

Saffron Walden was the site of an early settlement in Essex, England, located in a wooded valley where Saffron, a species of crocus, thrived from which food coloring and flavoring was derived. This area was apparently known and loved by the composer of the tune. SAFFRON WALDEN was first published in *The Hymnal Companion* to the *Book of Common Prayer,* 1877, where it was set to Charlotte Elliott's well-known hymn, "O Holy Savior, Friend Unseen."

Except for a few years at Romford and one other brief period Arthur Henry Brown lived in Brentwood, Essex, England, where he was born July 24, 1830, and died in 1926. He was a self-taught musician except for a few organ lessons and shortly after his tenth birthday became organist for the Brentwood parish church and remained there for nearly forty years except for the intervals mentioned above. For many years he also served as organist at Sir Anthony Browne's School in Brentwood. He was caught up in the Oxford Movement which resulted in a number of contributions to the introduction of Gregorian music into the Anglican church. He composed approximately 800 hymn and carol tunes and published an impressive list of books of hymns, carols, litanies, and psalms.

218   *O Master, Let Me Walk with Thee*

MARYTON L.M.

Washington Gladden, 1836-1918
H. Percy Smith, 1825-1898

Washington Gladden was the editor of a magazine called *Sunday Afternoon* and this hymn appeared in the March, 1879, issue under the title "Walking with God." One stanza was omitted because it was considered unsuitable for public devotions and the phrase "Tell me thy secret" was changed from "Teach me thy secret." Otherwise the text is as Dr. Gladden wrote it.

Born in Pottsgrove, Pennsylvania, February 11, 1836, and educated at Williams College, Dr. Gladden was ordained to the Congregational ministry in 1860 and became one of the most influential ministers in America. He held pastorates in Brooklyn and Morrisania, New York; North Adams, and Springfield, Massachusetts; and for thirty-two years served a church in Columbus, Ohio. He did not consider himself a hymnist but his name will remain familiar to congregations throughout the English-speaking world because of these words. He was a prolific writer, much of his work being published in periodicals. Dr. Gladden was the recipient of honorary degrees from the University of Wisconsin, Roanoke College, and is believed to be the first American Protestant minister to be so honored by the University of Notre Dame. Dr. Gladden died in Columbus, Ohio, July 2, 1918.

MARYTON first appeared in *Church Hymns with Tunes,* 1874. It was written for John Keble's well-known hymn, "Sun of My Soul." It is probably the name of a farm or manor house.

Henry Percy Smith, born in 1825, was educated at Balliol College, Oxford. He became an Anglican clergyman and began his ministry as Charles Kingsley's curate at Eversley, England. He served several other parishes before becoming a chaplain and removing to Cannes where he was associated with Christ Church. For a time he was also Canon of Gibraltar. He died in 1898.

219 *I Bind My Heart This Tide*

FEALTY 6.7.7.7.D.

Lauchlan MacLean Watt, 1867-1957

Grace Wilbur Conant, 1880-1948

The author of this hymn was educated at the University of Edinburgh and became a minister in the Church of Scotland in 1896. He served parishes in Alloa and Tullibody before going to St. Stephens, Edinburgh, and then to Glasgow Cathedral. During World War I, he was a member of the Expeditionary Forces and served as chaplain to the Forces for a year in France and Flanders. He was the author of a number of books including *In the Land of War, The Soldier's Friend,* and many devotional books such as *God's Altar Stairs, Gates of Prayer,*

Prayers for Public Worship, and *The Saviour of the World.* This hymn is in a book of poetry entitled, *The Tryst, a Book of the Soul.*

FEALTY was composed in 1927 by Grace Wilbur Conant. Our research indicates it was first published in H. Augustine Smith's *The New Hymnal for American Youth,* 1930. The composer has a second tune in the same book called AGNI set to the text "Temper My Spirit, O Lord."

220   *Savior, Like a Shepherd Lead Us*

BRADBURY 8.7.8.7.D.

Attr. to Dorothy A. Thrupp, 1779-1847
William B. Bradbury, 1816-1868

The true authorship of this hymn is uncertain although it is ascribed to Dorothy Ann Thrupp. It has been traced to Miss Thrupp's *Hymns for the Young,* fourth edition, 1836, where it appeared unsigned.

Miss Thrupp was born in London, June 20, 1779, and wrote many hymns which were particularly suited for use by children. Her hymns were published in various collections for children and a few of them were signed under the nom de plume "Iota" or simply "D.A.T." The hymns in her *Hymns for the Young* were all given anonymously. She died in London on December 14, 1847.

BRADBURY, named for the composer, was written for this text and was first published in William B. Bradbury's popular Sunday school songbook, *Oriola,* 1859.

For a note on William B. Bradbury see No. 45.

221   *O Jesus, Thou Art Standing*

ST. HILDA 7.6.7.6.D.

William W. How, 1823-1897
Justin H. Knecht, 1752-1817 and
Edward Husband, 1843-1908

Contrary to popular conjecture relative to Holman Hunt's famous picture, "The Light of the World," Bishop How wrote this hymn after reading Jean Ingelow's poem, "Brothers, and a Sermon." It was published in the Supplement to *Psalms and Hymns* edited by How and Thomas Baker Morrell, 1867.

For a note on William Walsham How see No. 279.

ST. HILDA is also known as ST. EDITH, HILDA, and BARTON. The present tune was arranged from a melody by Justin Heinrich Knecht which appeared in Johann Friedrich Christmann and Knecht's *Vollstäendige Sammlung*, 1799. Edward Husband adapted the Knecht melody in 1871.

Knecht was born in Biberach, Württemberg, September 30, 1752, where he spent most of his life as Professor of Belles Lettres and music director. For a brief period he was in Stuttgart directing the opera and court concerts but returned to Biberach to his old position. He published a number of theoretical works during his life. His musical compositions are unknown today. He died December 1, 1817.

Edward Husband, a noted English clergyman, organist, composer, and lecturer on church music was born in 1843 and died in 1908. He was vicar of St. Michael and All Angels in Folkstone for a number of years.

222　Lord Christ, When First Thou Cam'st

MIT FREUDEN ZART 8.7.8.7.8.8.7.

W. Russell Bowie, 1882-1969

Bohemian Brethren's *Kirchengesänge*, 1566

Dean Dwelly of Liverpool Cathedral invited Walter Russell Bowie to write this Advent hymn for use in *Songs of Praise*, 1931. It was written in 1928 and first published in that notable hymnal and was intended to express the "solemnity and inspiration" of Christ's "new advent" to modern man.

Dr. Bowie was born in Richmond, Virginia, October 8, 1882. His education was acquired from the Hill School, Harvard University, Virginia Theological Seminary (B.D. 1909 and D.D. 1919), and Syracuse University (S.T.D. 1933). After his ordination to the priesthood in 1909, Dr. Bowie served parishes in Greenwood, Virginia; Richmond, Virginia; and New York City. During World War I, he served as a chaplain to a hospital in France. For a number of years he was professor of practical theology and dean of students at Union Theological

Seminary. In 1950 he became a professor at Virginia Theological Seminary. Dr. Bowie held many important positions in his church, edited the *Southern Churchman*, was guest lecturer at Yale and Seabury-Western Theological Seminary, served on the Commission on Faith and Order, and on the committee for the preparation of the Revised Standard Version of the Bible. In the midst of these numerous activities he found time to author a number of books among which are *The Master, a Life of Christ*, 1928; *The Story of the Bible*, 1934; *The Children's Year*, and *The Inescapable Christ*. He died April 23, 1969.

223   *I Heard the Voice of Jesus Say*

KINGSFOLD C.M.D.

Horatius Bonar, 1808-1889

English Traditional Melody
Arr. and harm. R. Vaughan Williams, 1872-1958

Horatius Bonar wrote this hymn at Kelso and published it in his *Hymns Original and Selected*, 1846, under the heading "Christ's Invitation." It appeared again in the first series of his *Hymns of Faith and Hope* as "The Voice of Galilee." Since then the hymn has made its way into most of the hymnals in the English-speaking world.

For a note on Horatius Bonar see No. 185.

KINGSFOLD is a traditional English melody described by Covert and Laufer in their *Handbook to the Hymnal* as ". . . a joyful and quaint carol tune in a minor mode yet with a quality flexible enough to be interpretative of each of the stanzas." The same source assigns the arrangement of the melody to Miss Lucy E. Broadwood. It is, however, more likely that it is by Ralph Vaughan Williams since it appeared in the *English Hymnal*, 1906, without acknowledgment to Miss Broadwood, and also since Vaughan Williams arranged numerous other English tunes for use in that hymnal and was its musical editor. In the *Oxford Book of Carols* (No. 60) Martin Shaw has an arrangement set to a text entitled "Job" and notes that one A. J. Hipkins had previously associated the tune with the carol *Dives and Lazarus*. The tune was known in Ireland as the melody for "The Star of County Down."

For a note on Ralph Vaughan Williams see No. 98.

224 What a Friend We Have in Jesus

ERIE 8.7.8.7.D.

Joseph Medlicott Scriven, 1819-1886
Charles Crozat Converse, 1832-1918

Joseph Scriven wrote this hymn about 1855 to comfort his mother during a time when she was experiencing a great sorrow. His reply to a question concerning its authorship was "The Lord and I wrote it between us." Earlier this hymn had appeared anonymously and on occasion was attributed to Horatius Bonar. Its earliest publication date seems to have been in Hasting's *Social Hymns*, 1865.

Joseph Medlicott Scriven was born in Ireland on September 10, 1819. After being educated at Trinity College, Dublin, and Addiscombe Military College, he came to Canada. He taught school and tutored the family of a retired naval officer. His life was tragic in that the girl whom he was about to marry accidently drowned, a fate he too would suffer near Rice Lake on August 10, 1886. He gave his life in service to the poor and deprived and was held in such high esteem for his helpfulness and kindness that a monument was erected near Port Hope in his memory in 1920.

ERIE or CONVERSE was composed for this hymn by Charles Crozet Converse. It was first published in *Silver Wings*, 1870. Ira D. Sankey says he found it in a paperbacked "pamphlet of Sunday-school hymns."

Charles Crozet Converse was a lawyer by profession. Born in Warren, Massachusetts, October 7, 1832, he went to Leipzig, Germany, to study music but upon his return to America in 1859 entered law school at Albany, New York. Throughout his successful legal career in Erie, Pennsylvania, he was active in musical pursuits particularly in composition. His works include two symphonies, songs, overtures, oratorios, and many hymn tunes. After his retirement he moved to Highwood, New Jersey, where he died on October 18, 1918.

225 Father, in Thy Mysterious Presence

DONNE SECOURS 11.10.11.10.

Samuel Johnson, 1822-1882
Genevan Psalter, 1551

Samuel Johnson never affiliated with a religious denomination, but has been considered a Unitarian. He was born in Salem,

Massachusetts, October 10, 1822, and was graduated from Harvard in Arts in 1842, and in Theology in 1846. He established a Free Church at Lynn, Massachusetts, in 1853 and served as the pastor until 1870. Samuel Longfellow and Johnson jointly edited *A Book of Hymns for Public and Private Devotion,* 1846, a supplement to the same book, 1848, and *Hymns of the Spirit,* 1864. This hymn was published in *A Book of Hymns,* etc. under the heading "Divine Worship."

Johnson died on February 19, 1882, at North Andover, Massachusetts.

DONNE SECOURS is the French title for Psalm 12 with which the tune appeared in the 1551 edition of the *Genevan Psalter.* It was either composed or adapted by Louis Bourgeois and is one of the finest of the *Psalter's* surviving tunes.

For a note on the *Genevan Psalter* see No. 110.

Louis Bourgeois was born in Paris circa 1510. He was a follower of John Calvin and lived with him from 1545 to 1557 in Geneva while composing or adapting the melodies for the *Genevan Psalter.* He left Geneva in 1557 and returned to Paris where he continued his work on the *Psalter.* Besides his work on the music for the *Psalter* he claims fame for having written a treatise entitled, *Le droict chemin de musique* in which he proposed teaching music by the solfeggio method. The date of his death is not known.

226   Father, Hear

FATHER, HEAR 8.7.8.7.

Love Maria Willis, 1824-1908

Jacob Singer, 1883-1964
Adapted from the folk melody of *Eliyahu Hanavi*

This hymn of aspiration has enjoyed much popularity in England. It was an anonymous hymn in J. S. Adam's *Psalms of Life,* 1857, published in *Tiffany's Monthly,* 1859, and was included in altered form in the Unitarian hymnal, *Hymns of the Spirit,* 1864, edited by Samuel Johnson and Samuel Longfellow. Later it appeared in Horder's *Worship Song,* 1905, and the *English Hymnal,* 1906, and others.

Love Maria Willis was the wife of a physician and lived most of her life in Rochester and Glenora, New York.

FATHER HEAR, or ELIYAHU HANAVI (Elijah the prophet) was originally a song of grace after the Sabbath meal, but with a different text and slightly altered. Professor Erik Werner says, "Its dancelike rhythm is a clear indication of Slavonic elements in it."

Jacob Singer, rabbi and authority on Jewish music, was born at Kruspils (Kreutzburg), Latvia, in 1883. He was brought to America at the age of nine. His education was acquired at the University of Cincinnati, Johns Hopkins University, Peabody Conservatory of Music, and the University of Nebraska. He was ordained at Hebrew Union College. He was rabbi of congregations in Pennsylvania, Nebraska, and Illinois, and was frequently associated with faculties of colleges and universities in cities where he served congregations. His chief writings were in the area of music, and he composed liturgical music. Singer composed and arranged a number of tunes for the *Union Hymnal*, 1932. He died on August 5 or 6, 1964.

227 Have Thine Own Way, Lord!

ADELAIDE 5.4.5.4.D.

Adelaide A. Pollard, 1860-1934

George C. Stebbins, 1846-1945

This hymn is believed to have been written following a prayer meeting during a time when Miss Pollard was suffering "great distress of soul." She was born at Bloomfield, Iowa, November 27, 1860, and was given the name Sarah Addison Pollard. Her distaste for the name Sarah caused her to adopt the name Adelaide. Miss Pollard was educated at Denmark Academy, Denmark, Iowa, a school at Valparaiso, Indiana, and Boston School of Oratory. She was always interested in mission work and for a time taught at a Missionary Training School at Nyack-on-the-Hudson. Before World War I began, she spent several months in Africa but upon the outbreak of hostilities was transferred to Scotland. After the war she returned to America and worked for her religious causes in New England.

Her religious zeal seemed to draw her into various unorthodox Christian sects and for a time she worked with Alexander Dowie in his faith-healing services. She was the author of a number of hymns, but "Have Thine Own Way" is the only one in common use.

ADELAIDE or POLLARD was written for this text by George Coles Stebbins and appeared in his *Northfield Hymnal* and *Alexander's Supplement*, 1907. In the same year, Sankey used it in his *Hallowed Hymns New and Old*. It also appeared in Sankey and Clement's *Best Endeavor Hymns*, 1907.

For a note on George Coles Stebbins see No. 230.

228   *Lord Jesus Christ, Be Present Now*

HERR JESU CHRIST L.M.

J. Niedling's *Lutherisch Handbüchlein*
Second Edition, 1638
Tr. Catherine Winkworth, 1827-1878, alt.

Pensum Sacrum, 1648
Harm. from *Cantionale Sacrum,* 1651

The authorship of this hymn is uncertain despite its being sometimes attributed to Wilhelm II, Duke of Saxe-Weimar, 1598-1662. Conflicting dates for its first appearance are common. Its appearance in J. Niedling's *Lutherische Handbüchlein*, 1638, is conjectural. Julian says it was included in the second edition of Part I of the *Cantionale Sacrum*, 1651, as *"Herr Jesu Christ, dich zu uns wend."* Ronander and Porter in their *Guide to the Pilgrim Hymnal* set its first appearance as in the second edition of the *Lutherische Handbüchlein*, 1648, while Julian gives the fourth edition, 1655, as its first appearance in Niedling's work. Whatever its origin it is a worthy hymn designed to be sung before the sermon.

The translation is by Catherine Winkworth and was included in her *Chorale Book for England,* 1863.

For a note on Miss Winkworth see No. 58.

For a comment on HERR JESU CHRIST and *Pensum Sacrum* see No. 394.

229   Father Almighty, Bless Us with Thy Blessing

FLEMMING 11.11.11.5.

> Berwick Hymnal, 1886
> Friedrich F. Flemming, 1778-1813

This anonymous prayer hymn is taken from A. W. Oxford's *Berwick Hymnal*, 1886. Oxford was vicar of St. Luke's Church on Berwick Street, London.

FLEMMING was composed in 1811 as the setting for Horace's ode beginning *"Integer vitae scelerisque purus"* and became very popular with students in Germany and England. It was written for male voices. The tune is also known as INTEGER VITAE, ST. THERESA, and NACHT- LIED. Dr. Erik Routley informs us that it first appeared as a hymn tune in the 1875 edition of the *Congregational Psalmist* and again a year later in the *Bristol Tune Book,* 1876.

Friedrich Ferdinand Flemming was born at Neuhausen, Saxony, on February 28, 1778, and died at Berlin on May 27, 1813. Little is known of his life except that he became a successful physician after studying medicine at Wittenberg, Jena, Vienna, and Trieste. He established his practice in Berlin where he participated in the musical life of the city. He composed numerous part songs for the famous men's singing group known as the "Liedertafel" which had been founded in 1808 by Carl F. Zelter. He is listed in Grove's *Dictionary* solely because of this one tune.

230   Take Time to Be Holy

HOLINESS 6.5.6.5.D.

> William Dunn Longstaff, 1822-1894
> George Coles Stebbins, 1846-1945

Three accounts of the origin of this hymn exist. The first is that given by Ira D. Sankey which says Longstaff was inspired by a sermon he heard in Brighton, England, on the theme of 1 Peter 1:16b, "Ye shall be holy; for I am holy." The second states that Longstaff heard a speaker at Keswick, England, quote these words of the missionary to China, Griffith John, "Take time and be holy." The third version relates that Dr. Griffith John himself made the statement at the meeting in Keswick. Whatever the case, Longstaff is reported to have written the hymn that same evening. According to McCutchan it was first published in Sankey's *Gospel Hymns* No. 6 and in *Sacred Songs and Solos,* both issued in 1891.

William Dunn Longstaff, born January 22, 1822, was a wealthy land and ship owner who devoted his time, talents, and means to many philanthropic causes. He was long associated with Bethesda Free Chapel at Sunderland after leaving the Church of England. Through his work with the Free Church he became a close friend to such notables as Dwight L. Moody, Ira D. Sankey, and General William Booth of the Salvation Army. He died at Sunderland, the place of his birth on April 2, 1894.

HOLINESS (LONGSTAFF) was composed for these words late in 1890 while George C. Stebbins was assisting with evangelistic and conference work in India. It first appeared in Ira David Sankey's *Winnowed Songs for Sunday School,* 1890.

Born in East Carlton, Orleans County, New York, on February 26, 1846, George Coles Stebbins lived to become one of America's outstanding composers of gospel hymn tunes. Before becoming the song leader for the Moody and Sankey revival team he studied music privately, clerked in the Chicago music store of Lyon and Healy, directed music at the First Baptist Church in Chicago and in Boston's Tremont Temple. His association with Drs. Moody and Sankey took him on tours through England, India, Egypt, Palestine, and America. His many songs are considered to stand among the best of their type. He assisted in editing numerous gospel song collections in which many of his songs appeared. His death occurred on October 6, 1945, at Catskill, New York.

231   *Behold Us, Lord, a Little Space*

WINCHESTER OLD C.M.

John Ellerton, 1826-1893

Thomas Este's *Whole Book of Psalms,* 1592

This hymn was written in 1870 for a midday service in a city church and was published the following year in *Church Hymns.*

John Ellerton was born in London, December 16, 1826, and died at Torquay, June 15, 1893. He was a prolific hymn writer, translator, editor, and author. He has been called a hymnologist of the first order. Seventy-six of his original and translated hymns were published in 1888. Canon Ellerton served many churches throughout England but never identified himself with any party within its ranks. In addition to compiling several hymnbooks he was consultant to others and was a contributor to *Hymns Ancient and Modern*.

The tune WINCHESTER OLD is of ancient origin. The tune predated its name by more than twenty-nine years. It was first published in Thomas Este's *Whole Book of Psalms* in 1592 where it was nameless and used with the eighty-fourth Psalm. It was not until 1621 when Ravencroft published his *Whole Book of Psalms* that it was designated simply as WINCHESTER. Even so it is one of the first hymn tunes to receive a name. When the tune WINCHESTER NEW appeared about 1690 the OLD was added to avoid confusion. It was probably named for the city of Winchester in Hampshire, England.

232   Mid All the Traffic of the Ways

ST. AGNES C.M.

John Oxenham, 1852-1941
John B. Dykes, 1823-1876

Written during World War I this text is from a book of Oxenham's verse entitled, *The Vision of Splendor,* 1917.

For a comment on John Oxenham see No. 269.

For a note on ST. AGNES and John B. Dykes see No. 195.

233   Talk with Us, Lord

NUN DANKET ALL' (GRÄFENBERG) C.M.

Charles Wesley, 1707-1788
Johann Crüger, 1598-1662

First appearing as "Saviour, who ready art to hear" in *Hymns and Sacred Poems,* 1740, under the heading "On a Journey," this hymn was slightly altered and the first stanza omitted when it appeared in Wesley's *Collection of Hymns,* 1780. The second stanza as given here suggests Eve's words to Adam in Milton's *Paradise Lost,* IV, 639:

> With thee conversing, I forget all time,
> All seasons and their change; all please alike.

For a note on Charles Wesley see No. 180.
For a note on NUN DANKET ALL' see No. 196.
For a note on Johann Crüger see No. 162.

234 Have Faith in God

SOUTHWELL S.M.

Bryn A. Rees, 1911-
Adapted from Damon's *Psalmes,* 1579

"Have Faith in God" was first published in *Congregational Praise,* 1951. The author, Bryn Austin Rees, is the son of a Congregational minister. Born in Chelsea in 1911, he was trained for the ministry at Hackney and New College, London. Mr. Rees has held pastorates at Sawbridgeworth, Ipswich, Felixstowe, Muswell Hill, London, and in 1962 began serving the Woodford Green United Free Church, Essex. Other works published by Novello & Co. (with music by Dr. Lloyd Webber) include "The Savior," "The Good Samaritan," "Meeting Place," and various anthems.

SOUTHWELL first appeared in Damon's *Psalmes* in 1579 where it was set to Psalm 45. The original harmonization by Martin Peirson can be found in the *Historical Companion to Hymns Ancient and Modern,* 1962. The name was given it in Ravencroft's Psalter, 1621, where it is set to Psalms 50, 70, and 134 and is listed as one of the "Northerne Tunes."

235 Father of Heaven

ANGLORUM APOSTOLUS L.M.

Edward Cooper, 1770-1833
A. Gregory Murray, O.S.B., 1905-

This hymn to the Holy Trinity is based on the Litany and was contributed to one of the Staffordshire hymnbooks which were published at the beginning of the nineteenth century known as the *Uttoxeter Selection*, 1805. The author published several volumes of his sermons and edited a small collection of hymns. He was educated at Queen's College and for a time was a Fellow of All Soul's College, Oxford. He spent his life as rector of Hamstall-Ridware and of Yoxall, Staffordshire.

ANGLORUM APOSTOLUS was written in 1935 for the Latin hymn beginning with these words which honor St. Gregory, apostle of the English. It was first published in *The Westminster Hymnal*, 1940.

For a comment on A. Gregory Murray see No. 356.

236   *Hope of the World*

DONNE SECOURS 11.10.11.10.

Georgia Harkness, 1891-

Genevan Psalter, 1551

For many years Georgia Harkness has been interested in the Ecumenical Movement and has been officially involved in the conferences at Oxford, Madras, Amsterdam, Lund, and Evanston. The present hymn was inspired by this great movement and was one of the prize-winning hymns submitted to a competition under the aegis of The Hymn Society of America. It was written in 1953 and published in The Hymn Society's *Eleven Ecumenical Hymns*, 1954.

Born in Harkness, New York, in 1891, she received her education at Cornell University, A.B. 1912, and Boston University, M.A., M.R.E. 1920 and Ph.D. 1923. Dr. Harkness also studied at Harvard, Yale, and Union Theological Seminary. For a time (1922-1939) she was on the faculty of Religion and Philosophy at Elmira and Mount Holyoke Colleges. From 1940-1950 she was professor of applied theology at Garrett Biblical Institute, Evanston, Illinois. She was ordained to the Methodist ministry in 1926. For a number of years, 1950-1961, she taught applied theology at the Pacific School of Religion, Berkeley, California, from which she is now professor emeritus. Dr. Harkness is the author of more than thirty books dealing with various aspects of religion, of which several are: *The Sources of Western Morality*, 1954, *Christian Ethics*, 1957, and *The Providence of God*, 1960. The most recent are *The Fellowship of the Holy Spirit,* 1966, *Stability and change,* 1969, and *Grace Abounding: A Devotional Autobiography,* 1969.

For a note on DONNA SECOURS see No. 225.

For a comment on the *Genevan Psalter* see No. 110.

237　　*O Lord, We Do Adore Thee*

PEARSALL 7.6.7.6.D.

Edgerton Grant, 1931-1969

Robert L. Pearsall, 1795-1856

These lines are the second and third stanzas of the hymn, "O Lord, We See Thy Glory" by Edgerton Grant. The entire hymn was published by The Hymn Society of America in the pamphlet *Four More New Hymns for Youth by Youth,* 1958, for use during National Youth Week of that year. It appeared with the tune BLAIRGOWRIE with a suggested alternate tune GREENLAND.

Edgerton Grant was a native of New York City, and lived in Scotch Plains and Watchung, New Jersey. He was a member of the Congregational church, and the Wilson Memorial Union Church, attended the Holderness School, an Episcopal preparatory school, was a graduate of the Quaker Institution, Haverford College, and for a brief period was a student at Princeton Theological Seminary. He has had several hymns published by The Hymn Society of America. Mr. Grant died November 1, 1969.

PEARSALL receives its name from the composer. It is from Oehler's *Katholisches Gesangbuch,* 1863, in which Pearsall assisted as musical editor. The tune was written for the words *"Singt heilig, heilig, heilig, ist unser Herr und Gott."*

Robert Lucas de Pearsall was born at Clifton, England, on March 14, 1795. Educated for the bar, he practiced four years and then went to Mainz to study music under Joseph Panny. Upon his return to England he settled at Carlsruhe but soon liquidated his inherited property and returned to Europe where he bought Wartensee Castle on Lake Constance. He remained there until his death on August 5, 1856. He composed music for both the Anglican and Roman Catholic churches but is better known for his madrigals, glees, and other part songs. The prefix "de" was added to his name on the occasion of being received into the Roman Catholic Church under the Bishop of St. Gall.

238 Jesus, My Lord, My God, My All

ST. CHRYSOSTOM 8.8.8.8.8.8.

Henry Collins, 1827-1919
Joseph Barnby, 1838-1896

"Jesus, My Lord, My God, My All" is one of two hymns Henry Collins contributed to *Hymns for Schools and Missions,* 1854. He was born in Barningham, Darlington, in 1827, educated at Oxford, and ordained in 1853. He became a Roman Catholic in 1857, entering the Trappist Order Monastery at St. Bernard's Abbey, Coalville, North Leicester. He was chaplain to the Cistercian Order of nuns at Staplehill, Wimborne, Dorset, from 1882 to 1913. He died at St. Bernard's Abbey in 1919.

ST. CHRYSOSTOM was composed for this hymn by Joseph Barnby. It first appeared in the supplement to the *Musical Times,* December, 1871, and was included in the *Hymnary,* 1872.

For a note on Joseph Barnby see No. 375.

239 I Look to Thee in Every Need

O JESU 8.6.8.6.8.8.

Samuel Longfellow, 1819-1892, alt.
Melody from *Hirschberg Gesangbuch,* 1741

First published in *Hymns of the Spirit,* 1864, which was jointly edited by Longfellow and Samuel Johnson, this hymn was largely ignored in America until after its appearance in *The English Hymnal,*

1906, and Horder's *Worship Song*, 1905. The hymn did appear in *The Christian Hymnbook*, a compilation of psalms, hymns, and spiritual songs original and collected by Alexander Campbell and others, 1871, under the heading: They looked to him, etc. with the scriptural reference which reads, "Look to him, and be radiant; so your faces shall never be ashamed." Psalm 34:5 It has a wonderful message for all who would face the vicissitudes of life with a courageous faith in the love of God.

For a note on Samuel Longfellow see No. 191.

O JESU is from the first line of the hymn, *"Jesu, warum legst du mir"* to which the tune is found in J. B. Reimann's *Hirschberg Gesangbuch* entitled *Sammlung alter und neuer Melodien Evangel. Lieder,* 1747. Reimann (1702-1749) was the cantor and organist in the town of Hirschberg. The fame of J. S. Bach led him to make a journey to Leipzig to meet and hear the master. He was well received and greatly influenced by the unique experience. The present harmonization is that which appeared in *The English Hymnal*, 1906.

240   *I Need Thee Every Hour*

NEED 6.4.6.4. with Refrain

Annie S. Hawks, 1835-1918

Robert Lowry, 1826-1899

This hymn was first sung for the meeting of the National Baptist Sunday School Association in Cincinnati, Ohio, in November, 1872. It was published the following year in Robert Lowrey's *Royal Diadem*.

Annie Sherwood Hawks was a native of Hoosick, New York, where she was born May 28, 1835. She lived for a number of years in Brooklyn, New York, where she was an active member of the Hanson Place Baptist Church. She married Charles H. Hawks in 1859 and after his death in 1888 she returned to Bennington, Vermont, where she spent the remainder of her life living with her daughter and son-in-law, Dr. and Mrs. W. E. Putnam.

She authored some four hundred hymns but this is the only one to survive. It was during her years in Brooklyn that the pastor, Robert Lowry, encouraged her with her hymnic endeavors.

The tune NEED or I NEED THEE was written for this hymn by Mrs. Hawks' pastor. He added the refrain.

Robert Lowry was born in Philadelphia on March 12, 1826. He was a graduate of Bucknell University, and for a time was professor of rhetoric there. After serving pastorates in West Chester, Pennsylvania; New York City and Brooklyn, New York; and Lewisburg, Pennsylvania, he moved to the Park Avenue Baptist Church in Plainfiield, New Jersey, where he died on November 25, 1899. Bucknell University honored him with a Doctor of Divinity degree in 1875, the year he moved to Plainfield.

Although Dr. Lowry had little formal musical training he composed many tunes and edited a great number of gospel songbooks, working with some of the outstanding tune composers of the gospel song movement.

241 And Can It Be

SAGINA 8.8.8.8.8.8.

Charles Wesley, 1707-1788
Thomas Campbell, 1825-1876

This hymn was written in May, 1738, along with another which begins "Where Shall My Wandering Soul Begin." It first appeared in John Wesley's *Psalms and Hymns* which was published the same year. It was included in his *Hymns and Sacred Poems* in 1739.

It is said that it was written at Little Britain, London, during a time of "great spiritual change." The Wesleys published at least fifty books and tracts of hymns. The first collection of *Psalms and Hymns* was published in America while John Wesley was a missionary in Georgia. He revised the work after he returned to England and published it under the original name. George John Stevenson, writing in Julian's *Dictionary of Hymnology* (p. 726), says, "This work was the first collection of hymns published for use in the Church of England."

The original hymn was written in six stanzas of six lines each under the heading "Thanksgiving for Salvation." Some authorities believe this to be the actual conversion hymn inspired by his experience of "finding peace with God." Here we are using only the first three stanzas of the original.

For a note on Charles Wesley see No. 180.

Little is known of the composer of the tune SAGINA. He is believed to have been a native of Sheffield, England, and to have had something to do with the Methodist movement. The tune was included in a collection of twenty-three original tunes entitled *The Bouquet,* 1825. Botanical terms were used as names for all of the tunes. "Sagina" is a genus of aquatic herbs native to temperate and cool regions. So far as is known this is the only one of these tunes extant. Although contemporaries, Thomas Campbell, the composer, is probably not related in any way to Alexander Campbell's father.

242 *Jesus, Still Lead On*

ROCHELLE 5.5.8.8.5.5.

Jesu, geh' voran
Nicolaus L. von Zinzendorf, 1700-1760
Tr. Jane L. Borthwick, 1813-1897

Adam Drese, 1620-1701

Count Nicolaus Ludwig von Zinzendorf was the greatest and most prolific of the Moravian hymnists. In all he wrote 2,000 hymns which are characterized by a "deep and earnest personal devotion to and fellowship with the crucified Saviour" [Julian, p. 1302]. He was born in Dresden, May 26, 1700, educated at Halle and the University of Wittenberg where he studied law, and, after three years of travel in Europe, settled at his estate in Saxony. In an attempt to put the pietistic ideas of Spener into practice he built for a group of refugee Moravians a village which was named Herrnhut. Under his visionary leadership the Moravian Church was reestablished, and he became its bishop in 1737. He was banished from Saxony and spent many years as a missionary, traveling to America and England. The influence of his American visit resulted in the establishment of the Moravian communities of Bethlehem, Nazareth, Lancaster, Hebron, and York, all in Pennsylvania. He was permitted to return to Saxony in 1748 where he carried on his work at Herrnhut. He died there on May 9, 1760.

This translation is by Jane Borthwick and appeared in her *Hymns from the Land of Luther,* first series, 1853. It first appeared in the *Free Church Magazine,* 1846.

For a note on Miss Borthwick see No. 338.

ROCHELLE is also known as SPIRE, ARNSTADT, and SEELENBRÄUTIGAM. It is a later form of a melody by Adam Drese, 1620-1701, which is first found in the *Geistreiches Gesang-buch*, 1798, set to one of his own hymns.

Adam Drese studied music in Warsaw under the aegis of Duke Wilhelm of Weimar. He was the kapellmeister at Darmstadt and at Jena, becoming the mayor of Jena in 1672. His interest in the Pietist Movement led him to open his home for their meetings. His final years were spent in Arnstadt where he died on February 15, 1701.

243   We Walk by Faith, and Not by Sight

AZMON C.M.

> Henry Alford, 1810-1871
> Carl G. Gläser, 1784-1829
> Mason's *Modern Psalmist,* 1839

This text appeared in Alford's *Psalms and Hymns, etc.,* 1844, under the heading "St. Thomas."

For a comment on Henry Alford see No. 101.

For a comment on AZMON and Carl G. Gläser see No. 72.

244   My Faith Looks Up to Thee

OLIVET 6.6.4.6.6.6.4.

> Ray Palmer, 1808-1887
> Lowell Mason, 1792-1872

This hymn was not written for or intended to be used in Christian worship, but rather as a deeply personal and private exercise of the author's own Christian faith. Dr. Palmer wrote the words during moments of reflection and meditation shortly after graduating from Yale and while he was teaching in a select school for girls in New York City. While visiting Boston he met Lowell Mason on the street and was invited to contribute several hymns to a new collection of hymns and tunes which Mason and Thomas Hastings were in the process of compiling. The two gentlemen stepped into a store and Dr. Palmer copied these words from his notebook and gave them to Mason. Several days later Mason and Palmer chanced to meet again and the famous musician predicted that Palmer would go down in history as the author of this beautiful text.

For a note on Ray Palmer see No. 320.

OLIVET was composed especially for this hymn. The words and music were first published in *Spiritual Songs for Social Worship*, 1831, edited by Lowell Mason and Thomas Hastings and have remained happily together ever since.

For a comment on Lowell Mason see No. 273.

245   God of Grace and God of Glory

CWM RHONDDA 8.7.8.7.8.7.7.

Harry Emerson Fosdick, 1878-1969
John Hughes, 1873-1932

Dr. Fosdick wrote this hymn for the dedication of the Riverside Church where it was first sung on October 5, 1930, and again for the dedication service on February 8, 1931.

Dr. Fosdick was born on May 24, 1878, at Buffalo, New York. He was ordained as a Baptist minister in 1903. He was educated at Colgate University (A.B. 1900), Union Theological Seminary (B.D. 1904), and Columbia University (M.A. 1908). *Who's Who in America* lists twelve honorary degrees bestowed upon him by universities in America and Scotland. From 1908 until 1915 he was pastor of the First Baptist Church in Montclair, New Jersey. For about seven years, Dr. Fosdick was associate pastor of the First Presbyterian Church in New York but his liberal views led to a forced resignation. In 1926 he became the pastor of Park Avenue Baptist Church which later became the Riverside Church. Dr. Fosdick remained there until 1946. He died at Bronxville, New York, on October 5, 1969, at the age of 91.

Harry Emerson Fosdick, one of America's great preachers, distinguished himself from the pulpit at Riverside Church in New York City, as a teacher of homiletics (1908-1915) and professor of practical theology, from 1915 until his retirement, at Union Theological Seminary, and as author of numerous books.

Several of his later publications are *A Faith for Tough Times,*

1952; *The Living of These Days: An Autobiography,* 1956; *River-side Sermons,* 1957; and *Dear Mr. Brown,* 1961.

It may come as a surprise when the hymn is sung to CWM RHONDDA since *Christian Worship, a Hymnal* used REGENT SQUARE, the tune Fosdick had in mind when he wrote the hymn. Both are excellent tunes which are used with a variety of texts. CWM RHONDDA was composed by John Hughes in 1907 for anniversary services in the Capel Rhondda, Pontypridd, Wales. According to the composer's wife, inspiration for the tune came as he attended worship at Salem Chapel, in the village of Llantwit Fardre, where he had been a lifelong member and where he succeeded his father as deacon and precentor. Since then the tune has been sung far and wide on both sides of the Atlantic, usually with the hymn "Guide Me, O Thou Great Jehovah." CWM RHONDDA, literally means the low valley of the Rhondda, a river in South Wales.

John Hughes was born at Dowlais, Wales, 1873. As a boy he was employed as a doorboy at the Glyn Colliery. As a young man he became associated with the Great Western Railway and rose to a responsible position in the traffic department. He remained with the company until his death on May 14, 1932.

Although Hughes composed anthems, hymn tunes, and Sunday school marches, CWM RHONDDA is his musical monument.

246   *Lead On, O King Eternal*

LANCASHIRE 7.6.7.6.D.

Ernest W. Shurtleff, 1862-1917

Henry Smart, 1813-1879

Written at the request of fellow students for graduation events at Andover Theological Seminary in 1877 this hymn has found its way into many American hymnals.

Ernest W. Shurtleff was born in Boston, Massachusetts, April 4, 1862. He was educated at Boston Latin School, Harvard, and Andover Theological Seminary. As an ordained Congregational minister he served churches in California, Massachusetts, and Minnesota before taking up residence in Germany and France where he organized the American Church in Frankfurt in 1905 and ministered to American students at the Academy Vitti in Paris, 1906. During World War I, he and his wife devoted themselves to relief work. It is said that he was a musician of some ability, but his real forte was poetry of which he wrote several volumes. He died in France on August 24, 1917.

For a note on LANCASHIRE see No. 214.

For a comment on Henry Smart see No. 124.

247   Once to Every Man and Nation

EBENEZER 8.7.8.7.D.

James Russell Lowell, 1819-1891
Adapt. W. Garrett Horder, 1814-1922
Thomas John Williams, 1869-1944

W. Garrett Horder selected and edited these lines from Lowell's ninety-line poem, "The Present Crisis," in which the poet made a strong protest against the war with Mexico. Horder published the present text in his *Hymns, Supplemental to existing collections,* 1896, and again in his *Worship Songs,* 1905.

James Russell Lowell, a descendant of a distinguished New England family who were prominent as lawyers and clergymen, was born at Cambridge, Massachusetts, February 22, 1819. He was educated at Harvard where he failed to distinguish himself as a scholar and from which he was suspended for neglect of certain duties. After reinstatement he did graduate in 1838 and continued as a student of law. Afterward he opened offices in Boston, but for want of clients he devoted himself to reading and writing. In 1855 he succeeded Longfellow at Harvard as professor of modern languages and literature. Lowell was active in the antislavery movement and for a time was editor of the *Pennsylvania Freeman* and a frequent contributor to the *National Anti-Slavery Standard.* During his illustrious literary career he also edited *The Atlantic Monthly* and *The North American Review.* He was appointed Minister to Spain in 1877 and was transferred to London as Ambassador to Great Britain in 1880. He died at Cambridge, Massachusetts, August 12, 1891.

William Garrett Horder, an English Congregational minister, was born at Salisbury on October 6, 1841. He was educated at the City of London School and prepared for the ministry at Cheshunt College. After his ordination he held pastorates successively in St. Helen's, Lancashire; Torquay; Wood Green, London; College Chapel, Bradford; and finally in London. He is known as an outstanding compiler of hymnbooks such as, *Congregational Hymns, A Hymnal for Free Churches,* 1884, *Hymns, Supplemental to Existing Collections,* 1896, and *Worship Song with Accompanying Tunes,* 1905. He was awarded an honorary Doctor of Divinity degree by Howard University, Washington, D. C., for his outstanding work in hymnology. He died at Ealing, London, on December 19, 1922.

EBENEZER or TON-Y-BOTEL is from the anthem "Goleu yn y Glyn" or "Light in the Valley" by Thomas John Williams. It was published as a hymn tune in the Welsh hymnal *Llwalyfr Moliant,* 1890, where it was named EBENEZER. The story of the second name is romantic and fictional. Before the tune's publication, it had achieved great popularity and a young English singer is credited with the legend of the "tune-in-a-bottle" which had been washed ashore on the coast of Eleyn.

Thomas John Williams (1869-1944) was a native of Ynysmeudwy, Swansea Valley, Glamorganshire. He studied with Dr. David Evans of Cardiff and became a well-known Welsh organist, choirmaster, and composer of hymn tunes. He died in 1944 at Llanelly.

248   Christian, Dost Thou See Them

KING'S WESTON 6.5.6.5.D.

Attr. to St. Andrew of Crete, c. 660-c. 732
Tr. John Mason Neale, 1818-1866, alt.
Ralph Vaughan Williams, 1872-1958

Andrew of Crete was born circa 660 at Damascus. After entering the monastic life at Jerusalem he rose to important positions of leadership within the church. He was deputized by Theodore, Patriarch of Jerusalem, and sent to the Sixth General Council at Constantinople in 680 and was ordained deacon there. Andrew was elevated to the Archepiscopate of Crete during the reign of Philippus Bardesanes. Except for a brief period during which he followed the Monothelite heresy, Andrew remained an adherent to the orthodox faith throughout his life. He died on the Island of Hierissus, circa 732.

For a note on John Mason Neale see No. 155.

For a note on KING'S WESTON see No. 291.

For a note on Ralph Vaughan Williams see No. 98.

249   *That Cause Can Neither Be Lost nor Stayed*

OSTERGAARD 9.9.10.10.

Kristian Ostergaard, 1885-1931
Tr. Jens C. Aaberg, 1877-
Danish Folk Tune
Arr. Ellwood S. Wolf, 1903-

Pastor Aaberg translated this text in 1928. It appeared in *The World of Song,* 1941 and 1958. *The World of Song* was a general song book, containing some hymns, published by the Danish Young People's League. The hymn obviously reflects Ostergaard's concern with the tensions created by the Americanization of the Danish Church and the unification of various Lutheran groups which was gaining momentum as early as his arrival in America in 1878.

Kristian Ostergaard, Danish Lutheran pastor, educator, author, and poet, was born in Denmark in 1855. He immigrated to America in 1878 and began teaching in the newly established Elk Horn Folk High School when it opened on November 1, 1878. Seven years later he returned to Denmark for a time but was back in America serving as Pastor in Marquette, Nebraska by 1892. Subsequently, he served congregations in Ringsted, Iowa; Hetland, South Dakota; and Sheffield, Illinois. He wrote more than twenty books in the Danish language, including novels, history, and poetry, as well as numerous articles dealing with the problems of Danish immigrants and the Danish Church in America. He died in 1931.

Jens Christian Aaberg, Danish Lutheran pastor, was born in Denmark in 1877. He immigrated to America in 1900 and assumed positions of leadership in the Danish Church in addition to serving as pastor of churches in Marinette, Wisconsin; Dwight and Gardner, Michigan; and Minneapolis, Minnesota. His larger ministry included service on the committee on missions, member of The Lutheran Intersynodical Hymnal Committee, secretary to the general board, and member of the Council on Elementary Religious Education. He is best known as a translator of Danish hymns and through his numerous contributions to several Lutheran hymnals. He edited *Favored Hymns and Songs,* 1961, and authored *Danish Hymns and Hymn writers,* 1945. He contributed articles on hymns and hymnbooks to various Lutheran periodicals.

OSTERGAARD is a Danish folk tune. It was popular with Danish-Americans and has also appeared in several non-Lutheran hymnals including

Christian Worship, a Hymnal, 1941; *The Hymnal for Youth,* 1944; and *Hymns and Songs of the Spirit,* 1966. Mr. Wolf's arrangement of OSTERGAARD first appeared in *Hymns and Songs of the Spirit,* 1966.

Ellwood Shermer Wolf was born in Philadelphia, Pennsylvania, April 1, 1903, the son of Maurice S. and Louisa E. Wolf. He married Sarah Thomas in 1926. He was educated in the public schools of Philadelphia, studied engineering at Drexel Institute of Technology (now Drexel University) and was for seven years a civil engineer specializing in structural detail and design. He received a Bachelor of Science degree from Rutgers University in secondary education and his Master of Arts degree in Musicology from New York University. Mr. Wolf was attracted to the Christian ministry and became pastor of the North Baptist Church, Jersey City, New Jersey, and enrolled for theological study at the National Bible Institute (no longer in existence) in New York City. Following his ordination in 1934 he served pastorates at the Leonardo, N.J., Baptist Church and Lower Dublin (Old Pennepack) Baptist Church in Philadelphia. After twenty-six years in the pastoral ministry Mr. Wolf was appointed Assistant Editorial Director of Judson Press at Valley Forge, Pennsylvania, in 1957, where he served the American Baptist Board of Education and Publication for ten years. He also served three terms on the Board of Managers of the American Baptist Historical Society and was for a time secretary to the Society.

As a specialist in church music he has directed choral groups including the United Choral Society of New Jersey, served several terms as president of the Philadelphia Chapter of The Hymn Society of America, composed numerous short musical selections, and made a number of arrangements, including orchestrations. Mr. Wolf retired from his position with Judson Press on April 30, 1968, and is living in Oreland, Pennsylvania.

250 *God Is My Strong Salvation*

WEDLOCK 7.6.7.6.D.

James Montgomery, 1711-1854

Melody *The Sacred Harp,* 1844
Harm. C. H. Heaton, 1928-

These words are based on Psalm 27 and were first published in Montgomery's *Songs of Zion,* 1822.

For a note on James Montgomery see No. 324.

WEDLOCK is another interesting melody from *The Sacred Harp*, 1844. It is remarkably similar to, and probably a variation of, the tune WONDROUS LOVE. In his *Down-East Spirituals and Others*, George Pullen Jackson refers to another close relative of the tune used for the Irish captain chanty, "The Banks of New Foundland." WEDLOCK was frequently sung to "When Adam was created He dwell'd in Eden's shade," a song once attributed to Abraham Lincoln, but later traced to English sources.

For a comment on Charles Huddleston Heaton see No. 35.

251   *Guide Me, O Thou Great Jehovah*

CWM RHONDDA 8.7.8.7.8.7.7.

> Arglwydd, arwain trwy's anialwch
> William Williams, 1717-1791
> Tr. Peter Williams, 1727-1796
> John Hughes, 1873-1932

William Williams has been called the "Sweet Singer of Wales" by some and the "Watts of Wales" by others. In the *Baptist Hymn Book Companion* (London, 1962), Elvet Lewis is quoted as saying: "What Paul Gerhardt has been to Germany, what Isaac Watts has been to England, that and more William Williams of Pantycelyn has been to the little Principality of Wales."

Williams was born at Cefn-y-Coed in 1717. He began his training for the medical profession but upon hearing the preaching of one Howell Harris in 1738 he decided to enter the ministry. He was refused priest's orders in the Church of England because of his evangelical views. As a result he withdrew from the established church and became an itinerant preacher for churches in Llanllian, Caio, and Llansawel. For thirty-five years he continued serving these churches on a once-a-month basis. He was held in high esteem as a preacher and traveled throughout Wales conducting revival meetings.

Williams published several books of hymns in the Welsh language and two in English. The present hymn appeared in Welsh and was translated into English by Peter Williams, a Methodist minister, in

1771 and William Williams himself or his son, John, in 1771 or 1772. The author died at Pantycelyn January 11, 1791.

For a comment on CWM RHONDDA and John Hughes see No. 245.

252 *He Who Would Valiant Be*

ST. DUNSTAN'S 6.5.6.5.6.6.6.5.

John Bunyan, 1628-1688, alt.
Adapt. Percy Dearmer, 1867-1936
C. Winfred Douglas, 1867-1944

This poem followed a conversation between Mr. Great-Heart and Valiant-for-Truth in Bunyan's *Pilgrim's Progress*, Part II. It was not intended to be used as a hymn but rather as a summation of the main thrust of Bunyan's story. The poem was adapted for use as a hymn by Percy Dearmer and others for use in the *English Hymnal*, 1906.

John Bunyan's life was filled with trials and tribulations. Born at Elstow in 1628, the son of a tinker or mender of pots and pans, he was called into the Parliamentary Army at the age of sixteen and after three years' service was mustered out in 1674. After suffering a series of spiritual crises he became a member of the Baptist church and began preaching in 1653. He is said to have been a powerful preacher who drew large audiences and the ire of the government as well. He was a fearless prophet in the pulpit which led to conflicts with civil authorities and resulted in his imprisonment for a term of three months. When he refused to terminate his preaching as a condition for his release, his term was extended to twelve years. It was during this time that he wrote his autobiography, *Grace Abounding to the Chief of Sinners*, 1666.

In 1672 he was released under the Declaration of Indulgence and immediately began his preaching but three years later the Declaration was revoked and Bunyan went to prison again. During this second term of imprisonment he wrote his *Pilgrim's Progress*. Part I appeared in 1678 and Part II in 1684. He was finally released and resumed his preaching in and around London. He died of complications resulting from a cold contracted while on a mission of mercy to one of his friends. He was buried in Bunhill Fields.

For a comment on Percy Dearmer see No. 107.

ST. DUSTAN'S is the name of a cottage where Charles Winfred Douglas and his family lived at St. Mary's School in Peekskill. At the time Canon Douglas was choirmaster to the Community of St. Mary's and a lecturer at a seminary in New York. It was while returning home from New York by train that he wrote this tune for Bunyan's text.

An excellent biography of Canon Douglas appears in the Papers of the Hymn Society of America, Number XXIII, 1958, under the title, "To Praise God, the Life and Work of Charles Winfred Douglas, by Leonard Ellinwood and Anne Woodward Douglas." Space here will limit us to the barest outline of his life.

Born in Oswego, New York, February 15, 1867, he was educated at Syracuse University and St. Andrew's Divinity School, Syracuse. He was ordained priest August 6, 1899. His scholarly interests were many and led him to the study of the theory and practice of plainsong with the Benedictines of Solesmes, the music and folklore of the American Indian, exploration of the West, linguistics, liturgy, and musicology. He was in great demand as a lecturer on a variety of subjects. He has been called "a great pastor, leader, and visionary, [and] a truly ecumenical Christian."

Canon Douglas' deep interest in and knowledge of hymnology were responsible for his being chosen musical editor of the *New Hymnal*, 1916 and its successor, *The Hymnal*, 1940. He was the editor of several other hymnals and published other works relating to church music. He died January 18, 1944.

253 *Faith of Our Fathers! Living Still*

ST. CATHERINE 8.8.8.8.8.8.

Frederick W. Faber, 1814-1863, alt.
Henri F. Hemy, 1818-1888
Adapt. James G. Walton, 1821-1905

This hymn first appeared in the author's *Jesus and Mary; or, Catholic Hymns, for singing and reading,* 1849.

Two versions of this hymn were written by Faber, one for England and the other for Ireland. This version is from the English hymn and has been altered somewhat to fit Protestant worship. For example one of the stanzas originally began:

> Faith of our Fathers! Mary's prayers
> Shall win our country back to thee.

Frederick W. Faber was born in Yorkshire, England, June 28, 1814. Graduating from Balliol College, Oxford, and taking Holy Orders in 1837 in the Church of England he was led to accept the Roman Catholic faith in 1846. Faber went to London in 1849 and founded "Priests of the Congregation of Saint Philip Neri." He published a number of prose and poetical works before becoming a Roman Catholic, but his hymns all came afterwards. He admired the works of Wesley and of Cowper and Newton's Olney Hymns and used them as a model for his own. In all Faber wrote 150 hymns, all of which appeared in his *Hymns,* 1862. He died at Brompton on September 26, 1863.

ST. CATHERINE is also known as TYNEMOUTH and was originally set to a hymn beginning "Sweet Saint Catherine, maid most pure, Teach us to meditate and pray."

Henri F. Hemy, born November 12, 1818, at Newcastle-on-Tyne, was organist at St. Andrew's Roman Catholic Church in that city. For a time he was professor of music at Ushaw Catholic College, near Durham. He died at Hartlepool in 1888. This tune appeared in the second part of a two-volume work entitled, *Crown of Jesus Music,* 1864.

James G. Walton is responsible for the final eight measures which he added to the original for his *Plainsong Music for the Holy Communion Office,* 1874.

254 *Soldiers of Christ, Arise*

SILVER STREET 6.6.8.6.

Charles Wesley, 1707-1788

Isaac Smith, 1725-1800

The original heading for this hymn, "The Whole Armour of God," or "Confirmation," suggests Ephesians 6:10-20 as the scriptural inspiration. When first published in the Wesley's *Hymns and Sacred Poems,* 1749, it contained sixteen stanzas of eight lines each.

For a note on Charles Wesley see No. 180.

SILVER STREET was found in Isaac Smith's *A Collection of Psalm Tunes in Three Parts,* c. 1770. The tune is known as FALCON STREET in English hymnals.

Isaac Smith (c. 1725 London—c. 1800 London) is said to have been the first salaried precentor among the Dissenting Churches of England. His salary was in the amount of £20 a year (about $48.00) during his service to the Alie Street Meeting House in London. He later abandoned this profession in favor of one with more respectability as a linen-draper. He maintained enough interest in music to publish his *Collection of Psalm Tunes* circa 1770 and to become one of the early advocates of weekly congregational rehearsals for the purpose of improving hymn singing during services.

255 *Lord Jesus, Think on Me*

SOUTHWELL S.M.

Synesius of Cyrene, c. 375-430
Tr. Allen W. Chatfield, 1808-1896, alt.

Adapted from Damon's *Psalmes* 1579

Synesius wrote ten odes at various times in his life. This free paraphrase of the last one is the only one which has come into common use, the others have been considered borderline Christian verse and unsuitable for Christian worship.

It is said that Synesius' illustrious lineage could be traced back seventeen centuries to Spartan kings. A native of Cyrene, born circa 375, he devoted much of his life in the study of philosophy and became an ardent Neoplatonist. He became a Christian in 401 and was elected Bishop of Ptolemais in 409 or 410. He has been characterized as a man of great eloquence, a distinguished statesman, patriot, and churchman, and a man devoted to books and the chase. He died in 430.

Chatfield's translation apparently first appeared in *Hymns Ancient and Modern*, 1875, and again, in extended form, in his own *Songs and Hymns of Earliest Greek Christian Poets, Bishops, and Others translated into English Verse*, 1876. Allen William Chatfield was a distinguished Cambridge scholar and Anglican clergyman. He was born at Chatteris, October 2, 1808, educated at Charterhouse School, and Trinity College, Cambridge, where he graduated First Class in Classical Honors in 1831. After taking Holy Orders in 1832 he became vicar of Stotfold, Bedfordshire, and in 1847 Vicar of Much-Marcle, Herefordshire. He published sermons from time to time, a prayer book in Greek verse, and the previously mentioned *Songs and Hymns*. He died January 10, 1896.

For a comment on the tune SOUTHWELL see No. 234.

256 *Fight the Good Fight*

DEUS TUORUM MILITUM L.M.

John Samuel Bewley Monsell, 1811-1875, alt.
Grenoble Antiphoner, 1753

Born at Londonderry on March 2, 1811, and educated at Trinity College, Dublin, Monsell took Holy Orders in 1834. His life was spent in parish work of all kinds including assisting in the repair and upkeep of the buildings. Monsell was killed on April 9, 1875, when he fell from the roof of his church which was being rebuilt. He was the author of several prose works and eleven volumes of poetical works which were published between 1837 and his death. The latter include some three hundred hymns. This hymn entitled "Fight of Faith" appeared in his *Hymns of Love and Praise for the Church's Year,* 1863.

The tune is from the *Grenoble Antiphoner,* 1753. The tune lacks the plainsong quality one would normally expect from such a work. This is accounted for by a development which was taking place in some of the cathedrals and churches of France during the sixteenth and seventeenth centuries. During that time certain measured tunes were being adopted to replace some of the unmeasured plainsong melodies. Many of these were based on plainsong, but others were secular melodies or popular airs which, of course, had their origin outside the church. This tune may well have been one of the latter.

257 *Now in the Days of Youth*

DIADEMATA S.M.D.

Walter John Mathams, 1853-1932
George J. Elvey, 1816-1893

This hymn reflects the author's interest in the Sunday School and Christian Endeavor Movements. It was first published in *Worship in Song,* 1913.

Walter John Mathams was born in London, October 30, 1853. When but a young man he became a seaman, traveling widely, and ultimately adventured into the Alaskan Gold Fields. By 1871 he returned to London and began study in preparation for the Baptist ministry at Regent Park Baptist College. Poor health led him to spend about four years in Australia after which he returned to England and served churches at Falkirk, Scotland, and Birmingham, England. In 1900 he left the Baptist church and affiliated with the Church of Scotland. For three years he served as chaplain to the forces in Egypt. Upon his return from the service he ministered to churches at Stronsay, Orkney, and Mallaig, retiring in 1919. He was the author of several popular books and numerous hymns including "Christ of the Upward Way," and "Jesus, Friend of Little Children."

For a note on George J. Elvey see No. 101.

For a note on DIADEMATA see No. 184.

258 Lord, as to Thy Dear Cross We Flee

ST. COLUMBA 8.7.8.7.

John H. Gurney, 1802-1862

Ancient Irish Melody

After graduating from Trinity College, Cambridge, B.A., 1824, M.A. 1827, John Hampden Gurney became curate of Lutterworth, Leicester, remaining there until 1844. In 1847 he was appointed rector of Marylebone, London and in 1857 prebendary of St. Paul's Cathedral. He was born at Serjeants' Inn, Fleet Street, London, August 15, 1802, and died in the same city March 8, 1862. This hymn was first published in his Lutterworth Collection of Hymns in 1838.

ST. COLUMBA is named for the famous Irish Saint, 521-597, whose work as founder of monasteries led him to the Island of Iona from which the Christianization of Scotland began. He was highly revered in Northern Ireland as a warrior, statesman, as well as an ecclesiastic. Although the tune was used earlier in the English church, the present version appeared in Charles V. Stanford's *Complete Collection of*

Irish Music as noted by George Petrie, 1902, where it was called an "Irish Hymn Sung on the dedication of a Chapel—County Londonderry."

259   Give to the Winds Thy Fears

ST. BRIDE S.M.

Paul Gerhardt, 1607-1676
Tr. John Wesley, 1703-1791, alt.

Samuel Howard, 1710-1782
Harm. David Evans, 1874-1948

This hymn of trust in God was an acrostic on the initial words of Luther's version of Psalm 37:5 which began *"Befiehl du deine Wege."* It was first published in Johann Crüger's *Praxis pietatis melica,* 1656. In 1739 John Wesley published his free and shortened translation in his *Hymns and Sacred Poems.* Wesley's version began "Commit thou all thy griefs" and is here presented in altered form.

For a comment on Paul Gerhardt see No. 163.

John Wesley, the founder of Methodism, was born at Epworth Rectory, June 17, 1703. Like other members of his family he received his early education from his mother. Subsequently he studied at Charterhouse and Christ Church, Oxford. He was ordained priest in 1728, served as curate to his father from 1727 to 1729, returning to Oxford as a tutor in 1729 where he became the leader of a group who called themselves the "Oxford Methodists." He experienced an unsuccessful sojourn in Georgia as a missionary in 1735 and upon returning to England came under further influence of the Moravians, especially Peter Böhler, and experienced his personal conversion at Aldersgate, May 24, 1738. The remainder of his life was given entirely to spreading the gospel. It is said that he traveled more miles, preached more sermons, published more books, and made more converts than any man before or since. He died March 2, 1791. John Wesley is known in hymnody primarily for his translations from German, French, and Spanish sources.

ST. BRIDE is from William Riley's *Parochial Harmony . . . A Collection of Psalm Tunes in Three and Four Parts, Etc.,* 1762. It was set to the new version of Psalm 130 and called ST. BRIDGET.

For a note on Samuel Howard see No. 190.

For a note on David Evans see No. 381.

260 Savior, Thy Dying Love

SOMETHING FOR JESUS 6.4.6.4.6.6.6.4.

Sylvanus Dryden Phelps, 1816-1895

Robert Lowry, 1826-1899

The author published this hymn in the Baptist journal, *The Watchman and Reflector,* in 1862. Phelps was at that time editor of the publication. Robert Lowry requested Phelps to submit hymns for a book he was preparing for publication and "Savior, thy Dying Love" was among those submitted. The collection was published under the title *Pure Gold* in 1871. More than a million copies of the book were sold which may, in part, account for the popularity of both tune and text.

Sylvanus Dryden Phelps was the father of the distinguished author, lay minister, and professor of literature at Yale, William Lyons Phelps. The elder Phelps, a Baptist minister, was born in Suffield, Connecticut, on May 15, 1816. He was a graduate of Brown University, and two years after graduating from Yale Divinity School, he became pastor of the First Baptist Church, New Haven, Connecticut, where he remained for twenty-eight years. Besides his editorial work Dr. Phelps published three volumes of poetry and authored several prose works, one of which, the *Holy Land,* passed through nine editions in twenty-five years. He died at New Haven, November 23, 1895.

SOMETHING FOR JESUS was composed for the present text, while Lowry was professor of literature at Bucknell University and pastor of a Baptist congregation in Lewisburg, Pennsylvania.

For a note on Robert Lowry see No. 240.

261 *We Give Thee But Thine Own*

SCHUMANN, S.M.

William Walsham How, 1823-1897

Mason and Webb's *Cantica Laudis,* Boston, 1850

This offertory hymn was written about 1858 and first published in Morell and How's *Psalms and Hymns,* 1864, in six stanzas. It is considered one of Bishop How's finest hymns.

For a comment on William Walsham How see No. 279.

SCHUMANN has been ascribed to the famous composer Robert Schumann (1810-1856). Competent scholarship has failed to discover this theme in any of Schumann's compositions. The tune is said to have appeared in Mason and Webb's *Cantica Laudis,* 1850. A study of Henry L. Mason's *Hymn Tunes of Lowell Mason* reveals that the only tune arranged from Robert Schumann is called ALLAN and that appeared in Mason's *The Hymnist,* 1850.

For a note on Lowell Mason see No. 273.

262 All Things Are Thine; No Gift Have We

GERMANY L.M.

John Greenleaf Whittier, 1807-1892

Gardiner's *Sacred Melodies,* 1815

For a comment on John Greenleaf Whittier see No. 85.

The tune GERMANY first appeared in William Gardiner's *Sacred Melodies,* 1815. This book consisted of tunes adapted from Haydn, Mozart, and Beethoven to which poems of English poets were set. This tune was indicated as being based on a subject by Beethoven. Scholars have not been able to trace its origin to any known Beethoven compositions. Frank J. Metcalf, in his *Stories of Hymn Tunes* [The Abingdon Press, 1928, p. 79], believes we should accept Gardiner's word as well as that of others who were living at the time of Beethoven's productivity. It should be said that Gardiner himself was not sure of the specific composition but that it was "somewhere" in Beethoven's works.

GERMANY is also known as WALTON, FULDA and MELCHISEDEC. Many Disciples congregations will remember this tune through its long association with John Mason North's "Where Cross the Crowded Ways of Life."

For a comment on William Gardiner see No. 317.

263 The Wise May Bring Their Learning

FOREST GREEN C.M.D.

Anonymous
From *The Book of Praise for Children, 1881*

English Traditional Melody
Arr. R. Vaughan Williams, 1872-1958

This anonymous hymn appeared in *The Book of Praise for Children,* 1881, and again in the *Congregational Church Hymnal,* 1887, under the heading "Childhood for Christ." A third stanza is omitted here. It read:

> We'll bring the little duties
> We'll have to do each day;
> We'll try our best to please Him,
> At home, at school, at play;
> And better are these treasures
> To offer to our King
> Than richest gifts without them;
> Yet these a child may bring.

The 7.6.7.6.D. meter fits the C.M.D. (8.6.8.6.D.) tune nicely.

For a note on FOREST GREEN and Ralph Vaughan Williams, see No. 98.

264 O Brother Man, Fold to Thy Heart

WELWYN 11.10.11.10.

John Greenleaf Whittier, 1807-1892
Alfred Scott-Gatty, 1847-1918

These lines are from the last stanzas of a fifteen-stanza poem entitled "Worship" which Whittier wrote in 1848 and published in his *Labor and Other Poems,* 1850.

For a note on John Greenleaf Whittier see No. 85.

WELWYN was first published in Part IV of a collection of Roman Catholic hymns known as the *Arundel Hymns,* 1900. The present form of the tune is from *The English Hymnal,* 1906, and varies slightly in rhythm from the original. This seems to be the composer's only hymn tune.

Alfred Scott-Gatty was born in Yorkshire, England, April 26, 1847. He became subdean of York cathedral and was interested in both heraldry and music. He was knighted and became Knight Commander of the (Royal) Victorian Order and held other important positions in the College of Heralds including the Garter Principal King-of-Arms. His forte in the pursuit of music was in the light popular idiom, which included songs and musical plays for children. He died in London, December 18, 1918.

265   Father Eternal, Ruler of Creation

LANGHAM 11.10.11.10.10.

Laurence Housman, 1865-1959

Geoffrey Shaw, 1879-1943

This hymn was written in 1919 at the request of H. R. L. Sheppard, rector of St. Martin's-in-the-Fields on Trafalgar Square, London, for a meeting of the newly formed Life and Liberty Movement. It was included in *Songs of Praise,* 1925.

Laurence Housman, English art critic, dramatist, poet, illustrator, and novelist, was born at Bromsgrove, Worcestershire, July 18, 1865. Educated at Bromsgrove and South Kensington, Housman became one of the most controversial figures in English literary circles. His *An English-Woman's Love Letters,* 1900, and play *Victoria Regina,* 1934, were highly controversial and the latter was banned from the London stage only to enjoy a successful season on Broadway in 1935 with Helen Hayes as leading lady. Housman left the Anglican Church to become a Roman Catholic but later associated himself with the Society of Friends because of his pacifist views. He wrote more than eighty books and plays. He died at Glastonbury, Somersetshire, on February 20, 1959.

LANGHAM was composed for this text for a meeting of the Life and Liberty Movement held in Queen's Hall, London, 1921. It appeared with this text in *Songs of Praise,* 1925.

The composer was the brother of Martin Shaw and both were very much involved in the musical life of London during their lives. Geoffrey was born in London, November 14, 1879, and began his musical career as a chorister in St. Paul's Cathedral. He became a student of organ under Charles Stanford and Charles Wood at Caius College, Cambridge. He succeeded his brother as organist as St. Mary's, Primrose Hill, and for a time was the Inspector of Music for the London Board of Education. His compositions include a number of anthems, organ works, and hymn tunes. He died April 14, 1943.

266   O Day of God, Draw Nigh

SAINT MICHAEL S.M.

R. B. Y. Scott, 1899-, alt.

Adapted from *Genevan Psalter,* 1551

This hymn first appeared in 1937 on a hymn sheet for use by the Fellowship for a Christian Social Order over which the author presided for four years. Two years later it was included in *Hymns for Worship* and subsequently in *The Hymnal,* 1949, and *Pilgrim Hymnal,* 1958. The hymn is probably based on inspiration from Isaiah 26:9.

Robert Balgarnie Young Scott was born in Toronto, Ontario, Canada, July 16, 1899, and was educated at the University of Toronto and Knox College. After his ordination to the ministry in the United Church of Canada in 1926 he served in the pastorate for two years, and subsequently in theological seminaries of the United Church of Vancouver and Montreal, as Professor of Old Testament studies. In 1955 he came to the United States to be Professor of Religion in Princeton University. He has written extensively in the fields of Old Testament and biblical archaeology. One or more of his hymns have appeared in more than twenty hymnbooks in Canada, the United States, and Great Britain.

ST. MICHAEL began its long history in the *Geneva Psalter,* 1551, where it was either composed or adapted by Louis Bourgeois for Marot's version of Psalm 101. Ten years later it appeared in England as the setting for Psalm 134 in *Four Score and Seven Psalmes.* At the turn of the century it was either forgotten or ignored and was not in common use until William Crotch rescued it, renamed it ST. MICHAEL, and arranged it for his *Psalm Tunes,* 1836.

For a note on Louis Bourgeois see No. 225.

For a note on William Crotch see No. 438.

267   The Savior's Wondrous Love

KOREA S.M.

Korean
Tr. William Scott and Yung Oon Kim, 1959

Tai Jun Park, 1900-

In a letter dated December 9, 1969, Dr. Park says of this hymn and tune, "In 1949, one of the students of Yonsei University asked me to write a hymn when he attended an international young people's meeting in India. And I wrote this hymn for him. The young man evidently made this hymn known at the conference. Moreover, I did ask neither Dr. William Scott nor Miss Yung Oon Kim to translate it into English. When I visited America for the second time in 1951, I was surprised to find that this hymn was included in *Cantate Domino* (No. 50) translated into English. I wrote both the words and the tune of the hymn." The hymn was slightly revised when it appeared in a 1967 Korean hymnal where it is found at No. 473 with the English subtitle "Precious Love of the Lord."

Dr. William Scott was for many years a Canadian missionary to Korea. He retired about ten years ago and returned to Canada.

Miss Yung Oon Kim was a professor at Ewha Woman's University, Seoul, Korea, about twenty years ago. Dr. Park believes she is now in America connected with some sort of mission work. We have not been able to trace her.

Tai Jun Park was born in Korea, November 22, 1900. He was educated at Union Christian College, Pyeng Yang, Korea, 1921; Tusculum College, Greenville, Tennessee, 1933; Westminster Choir College, Princeton, New Jersey, 1935, B.M., and 1936 M.M. He received a Music Doctorate from Wooster College, Wooster, Ohio, in 1952. Dr. Park was Professor of Music at Union Christian College, 1936-38. In 1948 he became a professor at Yousei University and was dean of the College of Music, 1964-65. He has served as president of the Federation of Church Music and the Music Association of Korea.

GERMANY L.M.

Frank Mason North, 1850-1935
Gardiner's *Sacred Melodies,* 1815

Caleb T. Winchester, a professor at Wesleyan University in Middletown, Connecticut, and a member of the commission charged with the responsibility for the preparation of *The Methodist Hymnal,* 1905, invited Frank Mason North to write a missionary hymn for the book. "Where Cross the Crowded Ways of Life" was the result. The hymn was based on Matthew 22:9, a text which North was using in the preparation of a sermon. The hymn was first published in *The Christian City,* June, 1903, of which North was then editor. It appeared in *The Methodist Hymnal,* 1905, and has since been included in most hymnals in use in America.

For a note on Frank Mason North see No. 210.

For a note on GERMANY see No. 262.

For a note on Gardiner's *Sacred Melodies,* see No. 317.

269   In Christ There Is No East or West

ST. PETER C.M.

John Oxenham, 1852-1941
Alexander R. Reinagle, 1799-1877

This familiar hymn is from Oxenham's first book of verse, *Bees in Amber,* 1913. Born William Arthur Dunkerley, November 12, 1852, he adopted John Oxenham as his pseudonym after leaving the world of business to devote his life to writing. He was educated at Old Trafford School and Victoria University in Manchester, England, the city of his birth. His father was an active Congregationalist churchman in Manchester. Oxenham himself was a businessman whose work provided opportunity to travel extensively in Europe, Canada, and America. For a time he was the publisher of the London edition of the *Detroit Free Press.* He began his writing as an avocation but enormous success led him to devote full time to his literary efforts. Oxenham wrote some forty novels and a number of books of poetry and other prose. He taught a Bible class at the Ealing Congregational Church, London, where he also served as a deacon. Oxenham died January 24, 1941.

For a note on ST. PETER and Alexander R. Reinagle see No. 343.

270 From Thee All Skill and Science Flow

ST. MARIA C.M.D.

Charles Kingsley, 1819-1875
William Gawler, c. 1750-1809

This hymn was written for the laying of the foundation stone for the workingmen's block of Queen's Hospital, Birmingham, England, at which time it was sung by a thousand-voice children's choir. These stanzas are from a longer text which began with the stanza:

Accept this building, gracious Lord,
No temple though it be;
We raise it for our suffering kin,
And so, good Lord, for thee.

The text reflects the spirit of a man who was deeply concerned with the spiritual and physical welfare of his fellowmen. His social idealism led Kingsley to join forces with F. D. Maurice and J. M. Ludlow and form a Christian Socialist group which was concerned with and committed to open conflict "with the unsocial Christians and the unChristian Socialists."

Kingsley was born at the Holne Vicarage, Devonshire, on June 12, 1819. He was educated at Magdalen College, Oxford, after which he became rector of Eversley, canon of Chester, canon of Westminster, and Professor of Modern History, Cambridge. As a strong leader of the church he held other important positions of leadership. He was an exceptionally productive writer and is remembered today chiefly for his novels.

ST. MARIA is from William Gawler's *Hymns and Psalms,* 1789. It is also called ST. MICHEL'S (Michael), BEULAH, GOSHEN, HINTON, and PALESTINE.

William Gawler was an English organist, composer, compiler, and music publisher. Born at Lambeth circa 1750 little is known of his early life until 1785 when he was organist for the Asylum of Refuge for Female Orphans, Lambeth. He published a book of *Psalms and Hymns* in 1786 which was followed by a *Supplement.* As a publisher he produced a *Harmonia Sacra, Dr. Watts' Divine Songs, Voluntaries for the Organ, Lessons for the Harpsichord,* and a variety of sheet and other music.

271 The Voice of God Is Calling

MEIRIONYDD 7.6.7.6.D.

John Haynes Holmes, 1879-1964

Welsh Hymn Melody
Attr. to William Lloyd, 1786-1852

This hymn is based on Isaiah 6:8 and was written as the author was returning to the United States aboard the S. S. *Laconia* after spending the summer in Europe in 1913. Holmes had been asked to write the hymn by the Young People's Religious Union (Unitarian) for their convention which was to be held that fall. It was published in the *Christian Register* and then in the *New Hymn and Tune Book,* 1914.

John Haynes Holmes was a brilliant preacher, hymnist, author, lecturer, and social reformer. Born in Philadelphia November 29, 1879, he was educated at Harvard, graduating summa cum laude and Phi Beta Kappa in 1902. In 1904 he received the Bachelor of Sacred Theology from the same university. Shortly after his ordination as a Unitarian minister, Holmes accepted a call to serve the Church of the Messiah (Unitarian) in New York City where he remained for forty-two years. In 1919 both Holmes and the church severed their relationship with the Unitarians and became independent and nonsectarian, at which time the church was renamed the Community Church of New York. He was the recipient of many honorary degrees from American colleges and universities and was noted for his work in the area of pacificism and race relations. He classified himself as a casual hymn writer, but published a volume entitled, *Collected Hymns* in 1964. Dr. Holmes died in 1964.

MEIRIONYDD is the name of a county in Wales south of Carnarvon where Lloyd lived. It is uncertain whether this tune was of his composition or merely arranged by him. The present version of the piece is from *Caniadau Seion*, 1840.

William Lloyd was a self-taught musician-singer who apparently earned his living as a farmer and cattle dealer. He is said to have possessed a singing voice of good quality and considerable talent for conducting singing societies. His interest in congregational singing led him to avail himself of every opportunity to hear the singing in English churches during frequent excursions to that country. Lloyd was born in Rhos Goch, Llaniestyn, Carnarvon, Wales, in 1786 and died there in 1852.

272 Where Restless Crowds Are Thronging

MEIRIONYDD 7.6.7.6.D.

Thomas Curtis Clark, 1877-1953
William Lloyd, 1796-1852

This is one of the five new hymns selected by the Hymn Society of America for use at the Convocation on Urban Life, called by the Council of Bishops of The Methodist Church, held at Columbus, Ohio, February 24-26, 1954. This and the other four hymns were published in pamphlet form by the Hymn Society in 1954.

For a note on Thomas Curtis Clark see No. 143.

For a comment on MEIRIONYDD and William Lloyd see No. 271.

273 Blest Be the Tie That Binds

DENNIS S.M.

John Fawcett, 1740-1817
Johann G. Nägeli, 1768-1836
Arr. Lowell Mason, 1792-1872

This hymn is said to have been written on the occasion of the author's resignation and attempted departure from his parish at Wainsgate, Yorkshire. After having packed his belongings, and, as he was saying his farewells, he found himself unable to leave and remained with his people. John Fawcett was converted by George Whitfield but after three years as a Methodist he joined the Baptists and was ordained a Baptist minister in 1765 at Wainsgate, Yorkshire. After having decided against going to Carter's Lane Church in London, he also declined the offer to become president of the Bristol Baptist Academy. Fawcett published a number of books on practical theology.

This hymn is from his *Hymns Adapted to the Circumstances of Public Worship and Private Devotion,* 1782.

The tune DENNIS was first published in Mason and Webb's *The Psaltry,* 1845.

Johann G. Nägeli was a Swiss composer and publisher who is known to musicians for having added four bars of music to Beethoven's Sonata Opus 31 No. 1. He was born on May 26, 1773, at Wetzikon, near Zürich; he died the day after Christmas, 1836.

Lowell Mason was born at Medfield, Massachusetts, January 8, 1792. He was an important American musician who spent his life for the cause of music in the public schools. Except for a brief time when he was working in a bank in Savannah, Georgia, he devoted himself to teaching, composing, and arranging music. He and F. L. Abel compiled a book of choral music based on William Gardiner's *Sacred Melodies* which was published in 1822 under the title *Boston Handel and Haydn Society Collection of Church Music.* Mason founded the Boston Academy of Music and was the first person to receive a Doctor of Music degree from New York University. He began music classes for children which eventually led to music education being included in the school curriculum and was the founder of the Musical (Singing) Conventions.

While on a trip to Germany to study the teaching methods of Pestalozzi, he became acquainted with Nägeli who also was an admirer of Pestalozzi. The influence of these men helped shape the course of public school music in America. He died on August 11, 1872.

274   O Lord, May Church and Home

LAND OF REST C.M.

Carlton Buck, 1907-
Traditional American Melody
Harm. Annabel Morris Buchanan, 1888-

This hymn first appeared in The Hymn Society of America's *Thirteen New Marriage and Family Life Hymns,* 1961, as "Bless Thou Our Christian Homes, O Lord."

Carlton C. Buck was born August 31, 1907, at Salina, Kansas. He moved to Santa Ana, California, with his family while in his teens and graduated from high school there. He has a Bachelor of Sacred Music Degree from Los Angeles Bible Seminary (now Talbot) and a Certificate in Church Music from California Christian College (now Chapman), took summer work at Whittier College and has a Master of Arts and an honorary D.D. from San Gabriel College. He served Christian Churches in Southern California for more than twenty-five years including pastorates at Arlington, 1934-39; Holtville, 1939-43; Orange, 1943-46; and Fullerton, 1946-60. In July, 1960, he became pastor of the First Christian Church in Eugene, Oregon.

He has served as chairman of Commission of Christian Churches for Chapman College, as member of the State Board of Christian Churches of both Southern California and Oregon, as president of Oregon Christian Convention; director of All-Church Evangelism and the National Association of Evangelism. He is author and composer of numerous sacred songs, and a member of the American Society of Composers, Authors, and Publishers; The Hymn Society of America; and United Commercial Travelers. He is a regular contributor to *The Christian* and other religious periodicals. Publications include: *At the Lord's Table*, 1956, *At the Lord's Treasury*, 1959 (both Bethany Press); *Quiet Time Verse*, 1965; a religious drama, *The Tragedy of Procrastination*, 1957; a sermon, "Journey into Resurrection Faith" in *Preaching on New Testament Themes*, 1964; a sermon, "God Speaks" in *The Vital Pulpit of the Christian Church*, 1969.

LAND OF REST is a traditional American melody Mrs. Buchanan learned from her grandmother. It carried the words of the hymn "O land of rest, for thee I sigh." Mrs. Buchanan believed the tune to have originated in Northern England or Scotland. It has appeared in various forms with sacred and secular texts. It was published as given here in Mrs. Buchanan's *Folk Hymns of America*, 1938.

Annabel Morris Buchanan, distinguished folklorist and student of hymns and songs of the Southern Appalachian Mountains, was born at Groesbeck, Texas, on October 22, 1888. Her musical education was acquired from the Landon Conservatory of Music, Dallas, the Guilmant Organ School, New York, and privately with such teachers as John Powell, Emil Liebling, and William C. Carl. She taught music in Texas, Oklahoma, and Virginia before her marriage to John Preston Buchanan in 1912. She was one of the founders of the Virginia State Choral Festival, the White Top Music Festival and Conference, was president of the Virginia Federation of Music Clubs and vice-president of the National League of Pen Women.

275   Our Father, by Whose Name

RHOSYMEDRE 6.6.6.6.8.8.8.

F. Bland Tucker, 1895-
John D. Edwards, 1806-1885

Written in 1939 this hymn first appeared in *The Hymnal*
1940.

For a note on F. Bland Tucker see No. 169.

RHOSYMEDRE was named LOVELY when it first appeared in Edward's
Original Sacred Music, 1840 (?) and concluded with an extended Hal-
leluia.

John David Edwards was born in 1806. He was graduated from
Jesus College, Oxford, after which he was ordained deacon (1832)
and priest (1833). After 1843 he was vicar of Rhosymedre, Ruabon,
North Wales, for a number of years. He composed much church music
which appeared in his two-volume work, *Original Sacred Music* 1840?/
1843. He is remembered primarily for this tune. He died at Lland-
doget, Denbighshire, November 24, 1885.

276   Blest Is the Home When God Is There

ABBEY C.M.

Henry Ware, 1794-1843
Scottish Psalter, 1615

This hymn is one of the many written by Henry Ware.

Henry Ware, born at Hingham, Massachusetts, April 21, 1794, was
the son of a Unitarian minister. He graduated from Harvard College
with high honors in 1812 and taught at Exeter Academy for two years.
He received his license to preach in 1815 and was ordained in 1817 as
minister of the Second Unitarian Church of Boston. Twelve years
later his health failed and Ralph Waldo Emerson was appointed his
copastor. In 1830 he became Professor of Pulpit Eloquence and Pastoral Care at the Cambridge Theological School. He remained there for

twelve years. Ware died at Framingham, Massachusetts, September 25, 1843. His hymns are considered to be of high merit and have been widely used by the Unitarians in America.

The tune ABBEY is one of the twelve Common Tunes in the *Scottish Psalter*, 1615. The origin of the tune is not known.

277 O God, Who to a Loyal Home

KINGSFOLD C.M.D.

Harry Emerson Fosdick, 1878-1969
Traditional English Melody
Arr. R. Vaughan Williams, 1872-1958

First published in pamphlet form by The Hymn Society of America in 1956, this hymn was a feature of the observance of National Family Week, May 6-13, 1956, under the aegis of the Division of Christian Education of the National Council of Churches in the U.S.A.

For a note on Harry Emerson Fosdick see No. 245.

For a comment on the tune KINGSFOLD see No. 223.

For a comment on R. Vaughan Williams see No. 98.

278 O Happy Home, Where Thou Art Loved

WELWYN 11.10.11.10.

O selig Haus
Karl Johann Philipp Spitta, 1801-1859
Tr. Sarah Borthwick Findlater, 1823-1907
Alfred Scott-Gatty, 1847-1918

This is a free translation of K. J. P. Spitta's hymn *"O selig Haus, wo man dich aufgenommen"* written in 1826 and first published in his *Psalter und Harfe*, 1833. Mrs. Findlater made her translation for the third series of *Hymns from the Land of Luther*, 1858.

Karl Johann Philipp Spitta, a Lutheran pastor and superintendent, was born August 1, 1801, at Hanover, Germany. After a severe illness when he was only eleven years of age his family gave up the idea of preparing him for a professional career and apprenticed him to a watchmaker. He was unhappy in this work and when his younger brother died, Karl was given the opportunity to study for the ministry. He entered the Gymnasium at Hanover in 1818 and then the University of Göttingen in 1821. After graduation in 1824 he served as tutor in the family of Judge Jochmus at Lüne until his ordination on December 10, 1828. The remainder of his life was spent in serving the Lutheran Church in and around Hanover. Spitta died on September 28, 1859. He wrote many hymns which reflect the period of the revival of evangelical theology, piety, and hymnody in which he lived. This probably accounts for his being called the most popular hymnist of nineteenth-century Germany.

Sarah Borthwick Findlater was the youngest daughter of James Borthwick and the sister of Jane Borthwick. Both of the sisters will long be remembered for their many translations from the German language. Sarah married Eric John Findlater, a minister of the Free Church of Scotland, and this hymn reflects the happiness of her devoted Christian homelife just as the original reflected that of Spitta.

For a comment on WELWYN and Alfred Scott-Gatty see No. 264.

279 For All the Saints

SINE NOMINE 10.10.10.4.

William Walsham How, 1823-1897
Ralph Vaughan Williams, 1872-1958

The original first line of this hymn read, "For all thy saints," but was changed by permission of the author to its present reading. It was first published in Lord Nelson's *Hymns for Saints' Days, and Other Hymns*, 1864, and since that time has appeared in practically all of the major hymnbooks published on both sides of the Atlantic.

Bishop How began his illustrious career as a churchman as curate of St. George's, Kidderminster. After serving several other parishes he became suffragan bishop of East London with the title of Bishop of

Bedford. In 1888 he became Bishop of Wakefield. He was the author of many prose works, including a *Commentary on the Four Gospels, Lectures on Pastoral Work,* and four series entitled *Plain Words.* In addition, Bishop How was compiler and joint editor of several hymnals to which he contributed his own work. His name will remain with us as the author of such favorites as, "O Jesus, Thou Art Standing," "We Give Thee but Thine Own," "O Word of God Incarnate," and especially, "For All the Saints."

Bishop How was born December 13, 1823, and died August 10, 1897.

SINE NOMINE means "without a name" and was assigned to this tune by the composer, Ralph Vaughan Williams when he composed it for this text for the *English Hymnal,* 1906. This is one of the three original tunes he composed for that collection. Erik Routley tells us it was "condemned . . . by Bernard Manning . . . as 'jazz music' " (*Companion to Congregational Praise,* No. 363). It is, however, now considered to be one of the best tunes of the century.

For a note on Ralph Vaughan Williams see No. 98.

280   What Joy to Think of That Vast Host

LOBT GOTT IHR CHRISTEN C.M.

W. A. Wexels, 1796-1866
Tr. R. Birch Hoyle, 1875-1939
Melody by Nikolaus Herman, c. 1485-1561

This hymn appeared in *Cantate Domino,* 1924, as *"otaenk når engang samles skal"* and subsequent editions with R. Birch Hoyle's translation (1923).

Wilhelm Andreas Wexels appears to be an obscure Norwegian cleric and teacher. He is known to have been a member of the staff of the Oslo Cathedral and to have lectured for several years at the University of Oslo.

For a note on R. Birch Hoyle see No. 181.

For a note on LOBT GOTT IHR CHRISTEN see No. 138.

For a note on Nikolaus Herman see No. 138.

281   *Softly Now the Light of Day*

SEYMOUR 7.7.7.7.

George W. Doane, 1799-1859

Arr. from Carl M. von Weber, 1786-1826

Bishop Doane published this hymn in his *Songs by the Way,* 1824. It is based on the words of Psalm 141:2, "Let my prayer be set forth as incense, and the lifting up of my hands as the evening sacrifice." George Washington Doane was born in Trenton, New Jersey, May 27, 1799. After graduating from Union College, Schenectady, New York, he studied law for a time and then entered General Theological Seminary in New York. He was ordained deacon in 1821 and priest in 1823. Subsequently, he served as an assistant at Trinity Church, New York; professor at Trinity College, Hartford, Connecticut; assistant minister and then rector of Boston's Trinity Church. At the youthful age of thirty-three Doane became the Bishop of New Jersey and established his cathedral in the city of Burlington. He was the founder of St. Mary's Hall, a school for girls, and Burlington College for men. Julian says of him, [his] "exceptional talents, learning, and force of character, made him one of the great prelates of his time" (p. 303). He died April 27, 1859.

SEYMOUR is also known by the following names: WEBER, SHORE, HOLSTEIN, CHATHAM, and VESPERS. The tune is from the opening chorus of Carl Maria von Weber's opera, *Oberon* and was arranged by Henry W. Greatorex, organist of the Center Church, Hartford, Connecticut. In this instance it was named in honor of one Mr. Seymour who sang bass in the church choir.

For a comment on H. W. Greatorex see No. 414.

Carl Maria von Weber was born December 18, 1786. From earliest childhood he seemed destined to become one of Germany's great composers. He grew up in the theater under the aegis of his father. His serious musical training was with Michael Haydn, and Abt Vogler. Through Vogler's influence he was appointed kapellmeister of the Breslau Municipal Theatre. Weber became the outstanding German opera composer and is said to have paved the way for Richard Wagner. His influence was felt in all areas of musical activity of his day, including the composition of short pieces for piano, symphonies, and songs for men's choral societies. He wrote several pieces for the church but his fame rests almost entirely on his reputation as the "father" of German Romantic opera. He died of tuberculosis in London on June 4, 1826.

282 Jesus, the Very Thought of Thee

ST. AGNES C.M.

Jesu dulcis memoria
Latin: 12th century
Tr. Edward Caswall, 1814-1878
John B. Dykes, 1823-1876

Nothing is known of the origin of this poem other than that the basic work was found in an eleventh-century manuscript and apparently other verses were added later. It is a rather long work beginning with the words *"Jesu dulcis memoria."* The present translation is by Edward Caswall and was included in his *Masque of Mary,* 1858.

For a comment on Caswall see No. 116.

ST. AGNES was composed for this text by John B. Dykes and first appeared in the Reverend J. Grey's *A Hymnal for Use in the English Church* 1866.

For a note on ST. AGNES and John B. Dykes see No. 195.

283 O Splendor of God's Glory Bright

SOLEMNIS HAEC FESTIVITAS L.M.

Splendor paternae gloriae
St. Ambrose, 338?-397
Tr. Compilers of Hymns Ancient and Modern,
1904
Paris Gradual, 1689

This translation of St. Ambrose's morning hymn, *"Splendor paternae gloriae"* was made by the Compilers of the 1904 edition of *Hymns Ancient and Modern.* Here stanzas 1, 2, 3, and a doxology are given.

Ambrosius or St. Ambrose (338/40-397) began his illustrious career as a lawyer and statesman. His appointment as Consular of Liguria and Aemilia in 374 necessitated his living in Milan. Shortly afterward Bishop Aexentius, a convert to the Arian party, died and Ambrosius was elected by public acclamation to succeed him despite the fact that he was still only a catechumen. After his baptism Ambrosuis was consecrated Bishop of Milan on December 7, 374. He became the defender of the faith, working diligently to bring order to the church. He died April 4, 397. Although he is known as a great scholar, theologian, statesman, and organizer, we are concerned here with his unique talents as a musician and poet. He has been called "the father of church song" primarily because he is said to have introduced congregational and antiphonal chanting into the Western church and to have begun the task of systematizing church music which was completed under the leadership of St. Gregory. Many of the hymns attributed to him were set to simple metrical tunes.

SOLEMNIS HAEC FESTIVITAS is one of the "measured" tunes frequently found in sixteenth- and seventeenth-century French antiphoners and graduals. These metrical forms replaced the traditional unmeasured plainsong melodies but were often free adaptations of the chant. The present tune is from a *Paris Gradual,* 1689.

284   *All Hail the Power of Jesus' Name*

CORONATION C.M.

Edward Perronet, 1726-1792
Alt. John Rippon, 1751-1836

Oliver Holden, 1765-1844

"All Hail the Power of Jesus' Name" was written some time during the year of 1779 and the first stanza was published in the *Gospel Magazine* in November of that year with a new tune by William Shrubsole. That tune was given the name "Miles Lane" at a later date. It was not until the April issue of the *Gospel Magazine,* 1780, that the remaining stanzas of the hymn were published.

As his name suggests, Edward Perronet was of French extraction. His father, a Church of England vicar at Shoreham, Kent, was a friend of John and Charles Wesley. Edward himself came under the influence of the Wesleys and eventually became an itinerant preacher on behalf of their cause. This relationship was not destined to last, however. By 1771 Perronet broke his ties with the Wesleys and became associated with the Countess of Huntingdon Connexion. His radical views of the established church brought even this association to a halt and he spent the remainder of his life as the pastor of a small independent church at Canterbury.

It is interesting to note that Perronet's break with the Wesleys began after the publication of a satire in *The Mitre* (1757) in which he attacked certain abuses of the church. Apparently he did not hesitate to argue with the Wesleys concerning the matter of complete separation from the church and particularly their position on matters relating to the licensing of itinerant preachers so that they could administer the sacraments.

Someone has suggested that this man's poetic talent and devotional spirit suffered because of his frequent displays of violent and uncontrollable temper. So far as we know this is the one and only hymn to come from his pen. Even so, John Julian, in his *Dictionary of Hymnology*, ranks it as one of the first ten in the English language.

John Rippon altered several words and added the final stanza to the hymn as we have it. He was a Baptist minister and has been called "one of the most distinguished and influential Nonconformist ministers of his time" [*Songs of Praise Discussed*, p. 491]. He was an excellent hymnologist and published several collections of hymns and tunes. *The Comprehensive Edition* of his work, published after his death, remained for a number of years the standard collection of Baptist hymnody. Rippon was born at Tiverton, Devonshire, England, on April 29, 1751. He became a Baptist at the age of 16, prepared for the ministry at the Bristol Baptist College, began serving the Carter Lane Church, London, at the age of twenty-one, and remained there for sixty-three years. He died in London, December 17, 1836.

CORONATION is perhaps the only early American hymn tune in general use in churches of all denominations today. It was composed for this text in 1792 and was first published in Holden's compilation known as *The Union Harmony*, Boston, 1793.

Oliver Holden was a man of many talents and interests. He was born at Shirley, Massachusetts, on September 18, 1765. He went to Charlestown, Massachusetts, when twenty years of age, where he assisted in rebuilding the city which had been burned by the British during the famed battle of Bunker Hill. Through his carpentry work he became interested in building and real estate which proved to be a highly rewarding enterprise. About 1790 he opened a general store in which he sold music in addition to the usual merchandise. His prosperity made it possible for him to give land for the construction of a Baptist church after which he built the Puritan church and served as its pastor from 1818 to 1833. For several years Holden was also a member of the Massachusetts House of Representatives. He is remembered today primarily for his musical endeavors and especially for the tune CORONATION. His publications were numerous and included, in addition to *The Union Harmony, The American Harmony*, 1792; *Sacred Dirges, Hymns, and Anthems*, 1800; *The Modern Collection of Sacred Music*, 1800; and *The Charlestown Collection of Sacred Songs*, 1803. He has been called one of the most popular and important of the early American composers. The organ which he used for his work may still be seen in the Old State House in Boston. Holden died on September 4, 1744, in Charlestown.

285 *Christ, Whose Glory Fills the Skies*

LUX PRIMA 7.7.7.7.7.7.

Charles Wesley, 1707-1788
Charles F. Gounod, 1818-1893

This morning hymn first appeared in John and Charles Wesley's *Hymns and Sacred Poems*, 1740. For many years after its appearance in Toplady's *Psalms and Hymns*, 1776, he was believed to have written it but Montgomery restored it to the Wesleys in his *Christian Psalmist*, 1825. The hymn has enjoyed wide popularity in England and America.

For a note on Charles Wesley see No. 180.

LUX PRIMA means first light and is so called because of the spirit of this text to which it is widely sung.

Charles Francois Gounod is one of the famous Romantic composers of the nineteenth century. A man of deep religious convictions, he contemplated becoming a priest and despite the fact he never did, he was known affectionately as Abbé Gounod. He was born June 17, 1818, in Paris and died there October 17, 1893. After entering the Paris conservatory in 1836 he won the Grand Prix de Rome which enabled him to journey to that city to study for a time. He rose to the heights of the musical world as a composer of operas, symphonies, songs and other vocal music, and many pieces for the church including masses, a cantata *Gallia*, an oratorio, *The Redemption* and *Mors e Vita*, and a *Stabat*

Mater. American evangelical churches will remember him for his hymn tunes, the anthem, *Send Out Thy Light,* and the song, "Nazareth."

286 Fairest Lord Jesus

ST. ELIZABETH 5.6.8.5.5.8.

Anonymous in *Münster Gesangbuch,* 1677
Silesian Melody

This is one of the favorite hymns of American churches. Unfortunately, its origin has been beclouded by a considerable amount of fiction. The story that it was a Crusader's hymn has long since been discredited. The earliest known form of this hymn appeared in the *Münster Gesangbuch,* 1677, where the authorship is unidentified.

The tune is variously known as SCHÖNSTER HERR JESU, from the first line of the original; CRUSADER'S MELODY, from the nineteenth-century idea that it was sung by German Crusaders. ASCALON was a variation on the CRUSADER'S MELODY by Dr. Gauntlett. The meaning of "Ascalon" is not known.

We owe a debt of gratitude to August Heinrich Hoffman von Fallersleben (1798-1874) and Ernst Fredrich Richter (1808-1879) for giving the church this tune. Their interest in hymnody and folk songs led them to discover this Silesian melody and to incorporate it in their compilation bearing the title *Schlesische Volkslieder* published in Leipzig, 1842. Interested readers will find the text and tune as they appeared in that book in Armin Haeussler's *The Story of Our Hymns* (p. 234).

St. Elizabeth was the mother of John the Baptist. The name as applied to this tune was taken from *The Legend of St. Elizabeth,* an oratorio by Franz Liszt, in which he used the melody for a theme in Crusader's March.

"Fairest Lord Jesus" was first published in America in Richard Storrs Willis' *Church Carols and Choir Studies* in 1850. Willis informed James Mearns, assistant editor of Julian's *Dictionary of Hymnology* (p. 1016), that the translator was unknown.

The setting appearing in the hymnbook should be sung in unison. The arrangement of the accompaniment is by Charles H. Heaton, editor of *Hymnbook for Christian Worship.*

287 How Brightly Beams the Morning Star

WIE SCHÖN LEUCHTET
DER MORGENSTERN 8.8.7.8.8.7.4.8.4.8.

Philipp Nicolai, 1556-1608
Philipp Nicolai, 1556-1608
Harm. J. S. Bach, 1685-1750

Philipp Nicolai, the son of a Lutheran pastor, was born at Mengeringhausen, Waldeck, August 10, 1556. Following his education at the University of Erfurt and Wittenberg he was ordained and served churches at Dortmund and Cologne. For a time he was the court preacher to the Countess of Waldeck before becoming pastor at Unna, Westphalia. During his Unna pastorate the plague struck and amid the devastation his contemplation of his Christian faith led him to write his *Frewden Spiegel des ewigen Lebens* (literally, "Joyful Mirror of Everlasting Life"). This work included two texts and tunes which have become famous in the churches of Germany and to which J. S. Bach composed two of his finest cantatas, *Wachet Auf* and *Wie schön leuchtet der Morgenstern.*

From 1601 Nicolai was pastor of the church of St. Katherine, Hamburg, until his death on October 26, 1608.

Since Nicolai was also a musician, he is often given credit for the present melody. Recent scholarship, however, believes he based his work in the preexisting melody found in the 1538 Strassburg Psalter set to a metrical version of Psalm 100, *"Jauchzet dem Herren, alle Land."* The present name of the tune represents the first words of Nicolai's text. There are several versions of the text, this being the Hymnal Version, 1955.

For a comment on J. S. Bach see No. 193.

288 Jesus Shall Reign Where'er the Sun

DUKE STREET L.M.

Isaac Watts, 1674-1748
John Hatton, ?-1793

This hymn has been called the "first lyric call to the Great Commission." It first appeared in Watts' *Psalms of David,* 1719, under the title, "Christ's Kingdom among the Gentiles." It is part two of his version of Psalm 72. It was not used extensively until after 1800 but since then it is found in almost every important collection including the early collections of Alexander Campbell. An often omitted stanza follows:

> Where he displays his healing power,
> Death and curse are known no more,
> In him the tribes of Adam boast
> More blessings than their father lost.

For a comment on Isaac Watts see No. 48.

DUKE STREET is one of our most durable tunes. Composed by John Hatton, it first appeared in Henry Boyd's *A Select Collection of Psalm and Hymn Tunes,* 1793, where both tune and composer were nameless. These were added for the first time in William Dixon's *Euphonia,* 1805. Duke Street is where Hatton lived in St. Helen's, Windle, Lancashire, England. Nothing is known of his life. He was buried in the Presbyterian Chapel at St. Helen's in 1793. The tune is believed to have arrived in America around 1820 in a publication of the Boston Handel and Haydn Society.

289   Jesu, Priceless Treasure

JESU, MEINE FREUDE 6.6.5.6.6.5.7.8.6.

Jesu, Meine Freude
Johann Franck, 1618-1677
Tr. Catherine Winkworth, 1827-1878

German Traditional Melody Adapt. and harm.
Johann Crüger, 1598-1662

The one hundred and ten hymns of Johann Franck mark a transition from an objective to a subjective spirit of worship and praise and in their own day were criticized as being inappropriate for public worship. Despite criticism several of the hymns lived and continued to enhance Christian worship. This one was first published in Peter's *Andachts Zymbeln,* 1655.

For a comment on Johann Franck see No. 310.

The translation given here is that of Catherine Winkworth and appeared in her *Chorale Book for England,* 1863.

For a note on Miss Winkworth see No. 58.

JESU MEINE FREUDE are the opening words of the original German text. The tune has been associated with these words since appearing in Johann Crüger's *Praxis Pietatis Melica,* 1656. It is uncertain whether or not this tune is a German Traditional Melody or the work of Crüger. More often than not it is attributed to Crüger. It was a popular tune which Bach used in several cantatas and as the principal thematic material for his superb motet by the same name.

For a note on Johann Crüger see No. 162.

290   *The Church's One Foundation*

AURELIA 7.6.7.6.D.

Samuel John Stone, 1839-1900

Samuel Sebastian Wesley, 1810-1876

Born of a bitter doctrinal and constitutional dispute which raged between Bishop Gray and Bishop Colenso of South Africa and which involved the whole of the Church of England, these words first appeared in Stone's *Lyra Fidelium,* 1866. The book consisted of twelve hymns based on the articles of the Apostles' Creed, this being the hymn based on the ninth article: "The holy Catholic Church; the Communion of Saints." These hymns were in defense of Bishop Gray and represented an attempt to discredit the radical and revolutionary point of view of Bishop Colenso. The controversy began when Bishop Colenso published *St. Paul's Epistle to the Romans; newly translated, and explained from a missionary point of view,* 1861, and came to a head upon the publication several years later of his *The Pentateuch and the Book of Joshua Critically Explained.* This battle between conservative fundamentalism and liberal higher criticism shook the foundations of the established church which may indeed be felt in many segments of the church today. A full account of this dispute may be found in Peter Hinchliff's *The Anglican Church in South Africa,* 1963.

Samuel John Stone, an English clergyman, was born April 25, 1839. After being educated at Charterhouse and Pembroke Colleges, he was ordained and became curate of Windsor (1862), St. Paul's, Haggerston (1870), and succeeded his father as vicar there (1874), and finally became rector of All Hallows on the Wall, London, in 1890. He died at Charterhouse, November 19, 1900.

For a note on AURELIA see No. 359.

For a note on Samuel Sebastian Wesley see No. 359.

291 At the Name of Jesus

KING'S WESTON 6.5.6.5.D.

Caroline Maria Noel, 1817-1877
Ralph Vaughan Williams, 1872-1958

The hymn was used in the revised edition of *Hymns Ancient and Modern*, 1875. We use only 1, 2, 3, and 6 of the original seven-stanza hymn.

Miss Noel was born in London, April 10, 1817, and died there December 7, 1877. She wrote her first hymns at the age of seventeen, but did not continue her poetic efforts until about twenty years later. By that time she had become ill and was getting progressively worse to the point of being an invalid. In 1870 she published a volume of hymns and verses entitled, *The Name of Jesus and Other Verses for the Sick and Lonely*. This hymn appeared in that collection.

KING'S WESTON was composed especially for this text for *Songs of Praise*, 1925. It is named for a country house situated on the River Avon, near Bristol, England.

See No. 98 for a note on Ralph Vaughan Williams.

292 O Gladsome Light

NUNC DIMITTIS 6.6.7.6.6.7.

Greek: Φῶς ἱλαρόν, 3rd century?
Tr. Robert S. Bridges, 1844-1930

Attr. to Louis Bourgeois, c. 1510-c. 1561
Harm. adapted from Claude Goudimel, c. 1505-1572

Excepting the Ter Sanctus and other canticles of the New Testament "The Candlelighting Hymn" is perhaps one of the oldest in existence. It is of unknown authorship and date but is sometimes attributed to Sophronius in Greek liturgical books. The hymn probably came into existence sometime during the second century when Christians gathered at dawn and dusk to sing hymns to Christ. The present translation is by Robert S. Bridges and was made for his *Yattendon Hymnal,* 1899.

For a note on Robert Bridges see No. 162.

NUNC DIMITTIS is a historic tune which was composed or adapted by Louis Bourgeois for the Genevan Psalter, 1549, where it was set to the Song of Simeon (Luke 2:29-32).

For a comment on Louis Bourgeois see No. 225.

The harmony is adapted from Claude Goudimel's four-part settings of the Psalter, 1551. He was born in Besançon, France, circa 1505 and lived to become a celebrated theorist and composer who will be long remembered for his sacred and secular songs, masses, motets, and settings to the psalms. He holds the distinction of being the first to set the complete Psalter to music under the title *Les Pseaumes mis en rime franc. par Clément Marot et Th. de Bèze, mis en mus. à quatre parties par Cl. G.,* published by Le Roy and Ballard, 1565. He had been converted to the Protestant faith and was killed during the St. Bartholomew massacre at Lyons August 28-31, 1572.

293 *Master of Eager Youth*

ST. DUNSTAN'S 6.5.6.5.6.6.6.5

St. Clement of Alexandria, c. 170-220
Para. Francis Bland Tucker, 1895-
Winfred Douglas, 1867-1944

This is the earliest extant Christian hymn. It was found appended to Titus Flavius Clemens' *The Tutor,* three books describing the Tutor (the Word), the students (Christians), and the manner and mode of living the Christian life.

St. Clement of Alexandria is said to have been a Stoic and Eclectic who sought truth from every source, including the Greeks, Assyrians, Egyptians, and Jews. While he followed his quest in the city of Alexandria, he embraced Christianity and succeeded his teacher, Pantaenus, as master of the Alexandrian Catechetical School. During the persecutions of Severus (202-203) he was forced to leave the city for unknown destinations. Nothing more is known of his life and work except for a letter dated 211 (or sometimes 220).

For a note on Francis Bland Tucker see No. 169.

ST. DUNSTAN'S and Canon Winfred Douglas are discussed under No. 252.

294   *Alleluia! Sing to Jesus*

HYFRYDOL 8.7.8.7.D.

William Chatterdon Dix, 1837-1898

Rowland Hugh Prichard, 1811-1887

This hymn reflects the words of Revelation 5:9, "Thou hast redeemed us to God by thy blood out of every nation." The product of a dedicated layman who was educated for the business world "Alleluia, Sing to Jesus" is but one of numerous hymns William Chatterdon Dix contributed to the church. Despite his position in the world of business, where at one time he was the manager of Glasgow Marine Insurance Company, Dix was a first-rate scholar and hymn writer.

He published many hymns in his *Hymns of Love and Joy* (1861), *Altar Songs, Verses on the Holy Eucharist* (1867), *A Vision of All Saints* (1871), and *Seekers of a City* (1878). Many more, however, were contributed directly to contemporary hymnbooks including *Hymns Ancient and Modern; St. Raphael's Hymn Book*, 1861; *Lyra Eucharistica*, 1863; *The Hymnary*, 1872; and *Church Hymns*, 1871. Dix wrote many Christmas and Easter carols.

Dix is probably best known for such hymns as "As with Gladness Men of Old," "What Child Is This?" and "Come Unto Me, Ye Weary."

He was born June 14, 1837, at Bristol and he died at Clifton, September 9, 1898.

The tune HYFRYDOL literally means "good cheer."

For a comment on Rowland H. Prichard see No. 79.

295 Come, Christians, Join to Sing

MADRID 6.6.6.6.D.

Christian Henry Bateman, 1813-1889
Source Unknown
Harm. David Evans, 1874-1948

Christian Henry Bateman was born at Wyke, near Halifax, on August 9, 1813. He began his role as clergyman as a Moravian minister then became the pastor of a Congregational church and finally was ordained priest in the Church of England.

In 1843 he edited *Sacred Melodies for Sabbath Schools and Families* which had sales of millions and was used regularly in the Sunday schools of Scotland. This hymn appeared in that collection as "Come, Children, Join to Sing," under the heading, "Praise to Christ."

The source of the tune MADRID is unknown. According to James Moffatt its earliest use as a hymn tune was in a publication with the unwieldy title, *The Spanish Hymn, arranged and composed for the Concerts of the Musical Fund Society of Philadelphia, by Benjamin Carr. The Air from an ancient Spanish melody. Printed from the condensed score of the Society and presented to the composer as a tribute of respect and regard by some of the members, his friends, Philadelphia, 1826.* December 29, 1824, is given as the date of performance. Moffatt informs us further that the tune appeared in *A Collection of Metrical Versions, etc. by M. Burgoyne* (London, 1827) with the title SPANISH CHANT (*Handbook to the Church Hymnary*, Revised edition with supplement, Moffatt and Patrick).

For a note on David Evans see No. 381.

296 When Morning Gilds the Skies

LAUDES DOMINI 6.6.6.6.6.6.

Beim frühen Morgenlicht
German: anon., 1828
Tr. Edward Caswall, 1814-1878, alt.

Joseph Barnby, 1838-1896

Edward Caswall's translation of the anonymous German hymn beginning, *"Beim frühen Morgenlicht"* from Pörtner's *Katho-*

lisches Gesangbuch, 1828, was first published in Formby's *Catholic Hymns,* 1854. Here we use only four of the original fourteen stanzas.

For a comment on Edward Caswall see No. 116.

LAUDES DOMINI was composed for this text for the Appendix to the first edition of *Hymns Ancient and Modern,* 1868.

For a note on Joseph Barnby see No. 375.

297   Love Divine, All Loves Excelling

BEECHER 8.7.8.7.D.

Charles Wesley, 1707-1788, alt.

John Zundel, 1815-1882

In terms of popular usage this well-known hymn can be considered one of Charles Wesley's finest hymns. It was first published in *Hymns for those that seek and those that have Redemption,* 1747.

For a comment on Charles Wesley see No. 180.

The composer of the tune BEECHER was associated with the famous Henry Ward Beecher as organist for the Plymouth Church in Brooklyn, New York. John Zundel was born in Germany, December 12, 1815. As a young man he spent seven years in Russia as organist and bandmaster in St. Petersburg. In 1847 he journeyed to America where he lived for thirty years in New York City and Brooklyn except for several months he spent in Detroit. In 1851 he assisted Darius E. Jones in compiling *Temple Melodies* and four years later, he, Dr. Beecher, and Dr. Beecher's brother Charles compiled the now famous *Plymouth Collection of Hymns and Tunes.* While living in America Zundel edited and published a monthly choir and organ journal. He died in July, 1882.

298   Jesus, Our Lord and King

POTSDAM S.M.

Anonymous

Church Psalter and Hymn Book, 1854

This anonymous hymn was added to the hymnal to augment the section on Baptism. It was found as number 191 in *Christian*

Hymns, 1945, where it was set to OLD 134TH and adapted from the *Genevan Psalter,* 1551.

POTSDAM appears to be an adaptation of the theme of Johann Sebastian Bach's Fugue in E Major and is taken from Mercer's *Church Psalter and Hymn Book,* 1854. The arrangement and harmonization is thought to be by a Mr. Phillips, organist at St. George's, Sheffield. The tune name recalls J. S. Bach's famous visit to his son, Karl Philip Emanuel in May of 1847. While there he played for Frederick the Great.

299   Master, We Thy Footsteps Follow

STEPHANOS 8.5.8.3.

F. A. Jackson, 1867-1942

H. W. Baker, 1821-1877

This is a newcomer to the Baptist and Disciple hymnbook. It was written by Frederick Arthur Jackson and was first published in *British Baptist Church Hymnal Revised,* 1933. The author, a nephew of C. H. Spurgeon, was educated at Spurgeon College for the Baptist ministry, and held several pastorates before going to Campden, Gloucestershire, and finally to Brington in Northamptonshire. A number of his hymns appear in various English Sunday school collections. He published a volume of poems, *Just Beyond,* and contributed to various religious journals.

For a comment on STEPHANOS and Henry W. Baker see No. 209.

300   Come, Holy Spirit, Dove Divine

WILTON L.M.

Adoniram Judson, 1788-1850

Samuel Stanley, 1767-1822

Adoniram Judson, son of a Baptist minister, was born August 9, 1788, at Malden, Massachusetts. He received his education at Brown University, Providence, Rhode Island. In 1815 he and his first wife became missionaries to India but difficulties with the East India Company led them to establish their mission in Burma. Judson

263

was held prisoner by the Burmese when the British took possession in 1824 and remained in prison until 1826 at which time the Burmese capitulated to the British.

After his wife's death on October 24, 1826, he continued his work and on April 12, 1834, married Sarah, the widow of a Rev. George D. Boardman, a friend and colleague. She was a hymn writer in her own right, having written the missionary hymn "Proclaim the lofty praise." She died September 1, 1845. Judson died and was buried at sea April 12, 1850.

In addition to writing three hymns, Judson translated the Bible into Burmese. A Burmese-English dictionary was compiled from his papers after his death.

The present hymn is his third hymn and is made up of stanzas seven, five, and six of his second, entitled "Our Saviour bowed beneath the wave." It was found in Winchell's *Collection*, 1832.

Although the tune name WILTON is that of a small town near Salisbury, England, it is believed to be an arbitrary selection by the composer, Samuel Stanley.

Born in 1767, Samuel Stanley was one of the well-known church musicians in Birmingham, England. He was a concert performer on the violoncello and played throughout the English Midlands as well as at the Vauxhall Gardens in London and three Birmingham Festivals. For a time he operated the Crown Tavern in Great Charles Street, Birmingham, while serving as leader of singing at the Carr's Lane meetinghouse. Later he became musical director at the Ebenezer Chapel in Steelhouse Lane where he developed highly acclaimed musical services. During and after his death he was often quoted as an authority on the concert performance of George Friedrich Handel.

He published two sets of hymn tunes during his lifetime and his wife published the third after his death. WILTON is taken from one of these entitled *Twenty-four Tunes in Four Parts,* composed chiefly to Dr. Watts' *Psalms and Hymns* (c. 1796). He died October 29, 1822.

301 *Dear Master, in Thy Way*

ST. AUGUSTINE S.M.

John Thomas, 1859-1944
J. S. Bach's *Choralegesänge*, 1769

John Thomas was educated at Pontypool and Bangor University College. For a number of years he was a Baptist minister at

Huddersfield, Liverpool, and Sutton. This hymn was in the original *Baptist Church Hymnal.*

The tune is from J. S. Bach's *Choralegesänge,* 1769, which was the second part of an earlier collection entitled *Vierstimmige Choralegesänge, gesammelt von C. Ph. E. Bach,* 1765. The melody has been traced to Michael Weisse's *Ein Neu Gesengbuchlen,* 1531, the first hymnbook of the Bohemian Brethren. It is probably a pre-Reformation melody.

For a note on Johann Sebastian Bach see No. 193.

302 A Parting Hymn We Sing

FRANCONIA S.M.

Aaron Roberts Wolfe, 1821-1902

Melody by J. B. König, 1691-1758
William H. Havergal 1793-1870

Aaron Roberts Wolfe was born at Mendham, New Jersey, September 6, 1821. He was a graduate of Williams College, class of 1844 and of Union Seminary in 1851. The New York Presbytery licensed him in 1851. From 1852 until his retirement in 1872 he worked with schools for women in Florida and New Jersey.

This is one of the nine hymns Mr. Wolfe contributed to Dr. Thomas Hastings' *Church Melodies* which was published in 1858. In it the author, by his own confession, wrote to fill a specific need in the corporate worship of God rather than out of pure inspiration. The hymn is intended to be sung at the conclusion of the communion service as the worshiper prepares to return to the workaday world.

Our hymnal omits the original third stanza which reads,

The purchase of Thy blood—
By sin no longer led—
The path our dear Redeemer trod
May we rejoicing tread.

FRANCONIA is W. H. Havergal's adaptation of a melody found in Johann Balthaser König's *Harmonischer Liederschatz* which was published in 1738 at Frankfurt-am-Main which was a part of old Franconia. Since its origin is uncertain, it has been assumed that König wrote the tune.

For a comment on W. H. Havergal see No. 94.

For a note on J. B. König see No. 107.

303 *Bread of the World, in Mercy Broken*

RENDEZ À DIEU 9.8.9.8.D.

Reginald Heber, 1783-1826
Genevan Psalter, 1543

This communion hymn was first published in Heber's post-humous collection entitled *Hymns Written and Adapted to the Weekly Service of the Church Year,* 1827, under the heading "Before the Sacrament."

For a note on Reginald Heber see No. 304.

RENDEZ À DIEU was adapted or composed by Louis Bourgeois for Marot's version of Psalm 118 for the *Genevan Psalter,* 1543.

For a note on the *Genevan Psalter* see No. 110.

For a note on Louis Bourgeois see No. 225.

304 *Bread of the World, in Mercy Broken*

EUCHARISTIC HYMN 9.8.9.8.

Reginald Heber, 1783-1826
John S. B. Hodges, 1830-1915

For a note on this hymn see No. 303.

Reginald Heber was born at Malpas, Cheshire, April 21, 1783, and after completing his education at Brasenose College, Oxford, became Vicar of Hodnet, Shropshire, where all of his hymns were written. From 1811 through 1816 some hymns appeared in the *Christian Observer* but fifty-seven were published after his death in a book entitled *Hymns written and adapted to the Weekly Church Service of the Year,* 1827. Heber was made Bishop of Calcutta in 1823 where he made a great contribution to the people and the church during his short term of office. He died at his home following a confirmation service at Trichinopoly, India, on April 3, 1826.

The name was given this tune by the editor of *The Hymnal, 1869,* of the Protestant Episcopal Church.

John Sebastian Bach Hodges was born in Bristol, England, in 1830. His father was an organist who came to America to practice his art in 1838. The children were brought to America in 1845. Young Hodges was educated at Columbia University and General Theological Seminary in New York. During his career he earned an outstanding reputation for himself as a leader in the Protestant Episcopal Church. He compiled the *Book of Common Praise* in 1868 and participated in the revision of *The Hymnal, 1869.* Hodges died at Baltimore, May 1, 1915.

305 Come, Risen Lord, and Deign to Be Our Guest

HOLBORN 10.10.10.10.

George Wallace Briggs, 1875-1959
Eric Harding Thiman, 1900-

This communion hymn was written by George Wallace Briggs for *Songs of Praise,* 1931. Percy Dearmer is responsible for the change in text in the last line of the first stanza. The original read "In thine own sacrament" rather than "In this our sacrament."

Briggs, an outstanding preacher, scholar, writer, and editor, was born December 14, 1875, in Nottingham. His influence on and interest in education was significant. Educated at Emmanuel College, Cambridge, Briggs served successively as chaplain in the Royal Navy, vicar of St. Andrews, Norwich, rector of Loughborough College, canon of Leicester Cathedral, and shortly thereafter as canon of Worcester Cathedral. In addition he held the position as select preacher at Cambridge, Proctor in Convocation of Canterbury, and served on many important committees for the church. He wrote sixteen original hymns and seven tunes which are included in *Songs of Praise,* 1931. The present hymn is based on Luke 24:28ff.

It was Briggs himself who, in 1948, suggested that Eric Harding Thiman compose a tune for this hymn and it appeared for the first time in *Congregational Praise,* 1953.

Thiman was born at Ashford, Kent, and received his education at the Caterham School and Guild Hall School of Music. He became a Fellow of the Royal College of Organists in 1921, and a professor of harmony at the Royal Academy of Music, 1930. In 1927 he received his Doctor of Music degree from the University of London.

From 1927 to 1958 he was organist at the Park Congregational Church, Crouch End, London, and then became organist at the City Temple. He was appointed Dean of the Faculty of Music at University of London in 1956. Thiman is the composer of many anthems, hymn tunes, cantatas, and organ works.

306   Come, Risen Lord, and Deign to Be Our Guest

BIRMINGHAM 10.10.10.10.

George W. Briggs, 1875-1959

From F. Cunningham's *A Selection of Psalm Tunes,* 1834

For a comment on this hymn and author see No. 305.

BIRMINGHAM is the name of the great industrial city in the English Midlands. The tune is from Francis Cunningham's *A Selection of Psalm Tunes,* second edition, 1834, where it appears with the hymn "Come, Gracious Spirit, Heavenly Dove."

Francis Cunningham is known only for two collections of Psalm tunes published in 1826 and 1834.

307   Here at Thy Table, Lord

BREAD OF LIFE 6.4.6.4.D.

May P. Hoyt

William F. Sherwin, 1826-1888

This is one of the favorite communion hymns of the Disciples of Christ. No information has been found on the author.

For a note on the tune and composer see No. 327.

308   *Jesus, to Thy Table Led*

TYHOLLAND 7.7.7.

Robert Hall Baynes, 1831-1895, alt.

German Carol Melody
Adapt. D. F. R. Wilson, 1871-1957

In 1864 this hymn appeared in Robert Hall Baynes' *The Canterbury Hymnal.* He was the author of the hymn and editor of the hymnal. The text given here represents stanzas 1, 2, and 5 from a six-stanza text from the *Canadian Baptist Hymnal.*

Robert Hall Baynes, the son of a Church of England minister, was born at Wellington, March 10, 1831. He was educated at St. Edmund's Hall, Oxford, ordained in the Church of England in 1855, and served churches in London, Maidstone, and Coventry. For a time he was honorary canon of Worcester Cathedral before becoming vicar of Holy Trinity at Folkstone. He died March 12, 1895. He compiled and edited a number of volumes of religious poetry and several hymn-books.

TYHOLLAND was named after the birthplace of the composer. The melody is believed to have been a fourteenth-century German carol melody although it has been traced only to Spangenberg's *Gesangbuch,* Eisleben, 1568. This adaptation is found in *The Irish Hymnal* which was edited by Wilson.

David Frederick Rudell Wilson, born in Tyholland, 1871, was ordained into the Episcopal Church of Ireland in 1895 and apparently spent his life in Dublin where he served in St. Patrick's Cathedral successively as Master of the Choir School, Canon and Precentor, and finally as Dean. He was the editor of *The Irish Hymnal* and *Irish Chant Book.*

309   *For the Bread, Which Thou Hast Broken*

KINGDOM 8.7.8.7.

Louis F. Benson, 1855-1930

V. Earle Copes, 1921-

This communion hymn was first published in Dr. Benson's *Hymns: Original and Translated,* 1925, a book containing thirty-eight original and sixteen translations from Latin hymns. It has been called a postcommunion hymn.

Louis Fitzgerald Benson is America's claim to greatness in hymnological studies. He was a Philadelphian by birth, studied law at the University of Pennsylvania and practiced law for seven years before entering Princeton Theological Seminary to prepare for the Christian ministry. He was ordained in 1886 and held a pastorate for six years, but his great love of music led him to resign in order to devote his life to research, writing, editing, and poetry. Among his books, the following would be excellent additions to either the church's or the minister's library: *The Hymnology of the Christian Church; The English Hymn: Its Development and Use in Worship.*

His personal library has been called "one of the world's most valuable private hymnological libraries" and may be found in the library of Princeton Theological Seminary.

KINGDOM was composed expressly for this hymn by V. Earle Copes for use in a national convocation of Methodist youth held the summer of 1959. It was first published in the program booklet for the convocation and was included in the *Methodist Hymnal,* 1966.

V. Earle Copes was born August 12, 1921, at Norfolk, Virginia. He received his education in the public schools of Norfolk, Davidson College, School of Sacred Music of Union Theological Seminary (M.S.M., 1944), Union Theological Seminary (B.D. 1945), and further graduate study at the University of Texas (1952-53). He has been Minister of Music in McAllen and Dallas, Texas; Associate Professor of Music (organ and choral) at Hendrix College, Conway, Arkansas; and the same at Cornell College, Mt. Vernon, Iowa. For nine years he was music editor for the Methodist General Board of Education in Nashville, Tennessee. Since 1967 he has been head of the Department of Organ and Church Music at Birmingham Southern College and Minister of Music at Canterbury Methodist Church in Birmingham. He has published twenty-two anthems, numerous articles in professional journals, founded and edited *Music Ministry,* and has been in demand as a recitalist, lecturer, and workshop leader.

310   Deck Thyself, My Soul, with Gladness

SCHMÜCKE DICH 8.8.8.8.D.

Schmücke dich, O liebe Seele
Johann Franck, 1618-1677
Tr. Catherine Winkworth, 1827-1878
Johann Crüger, 1598-1662

The hymn is sung as a communion hymn in German churches. It was written about 1649 and the first stanza appeared in Crüger's

Geistliche kirchen Melodien the same year. The entire hymn in full was included in Crüger's *Praxis Pietatis Melica* from 1653 onward.

Johann Franck was born at Guben, Brandenburg, June 1, 1618, the year the Thirty Years' War began. He was raised by an uncle, educated at the University of Königsberg, and became a practicing lawyer. He was successively a burgess, councillor, burgomaster, and deputy from Guben to the Landtag of Lower Lusatia. He died June 18, 1677, at Guben.

As a hymn writer he is compared favorably to Paul Gerhardt but tends to be more personal and subjective. His hymns appeared primarily in collections made by his friends Weichman, Crüger, and Peter. He published his *Geistliches Sion* in 1674 which contained one hundred and ten of his hymns, approximately half of which were versions of Psalms.

The translation was first published in Miss Winkworth's *Lyra Germanica*, second series, 1858. In 1863 she had recast it in its original meter for this tune in her *Chorale Book for England*.

For a note on the translator see No. 58.

The name of the tune is, of course, taken from the first line of Franck's hymn, *"Schmücke dich, O liebe Seele."*

For a note on Johann Crüger see No. 162.

311   Be Known to Us in Breaking Bread

DUNFERMLINE C.M.

James Montgomery, 1771-1854

Scottish Psalter, 1615

This hymn was first published in the author's *Christian Psalmist,* 1825, under the title "The Family Table" and republished in his *Original Hymns,* 1853. It is based on Luke 24:30-31.

For a note on James Montgomery see No. 324.

The composer of the tune is unknown. Dunfermline was at one time the capital of Scotland. The tune first appeared in the *CL Psalmes of David & C,* Andro Hart, Edinburgh, 1615. In his *Whole Book of Psalms,* 1621, Ravencroft classified it as a Scottish tune and called it by its present name. It was originally one of the twelve COMMON TUNES in the Scottish Psalter. These common tunes were those which were not assigned to be sung with specific Psalms.

312 O Lord and Savior, as We Kneel Before Thee

DONNE SECOURS 11.10.11.10.

George MacLaren Brydon, 1875-
Genevan Psalter, 1551

Written for the Second Assembly of the World Council of Churches, Evanston, Illinois, August, 1954, this hymn was first published by The Hymn Society of America in pamphlet form in *Eleven Ecumenical Hymns,* 1954, where it was set to the tune WELWYN.

George MacLaren Brydon, an active Episcopal clergyman, was born in Danville, Virginia, June 27, 1875. He was educated at Roanoke College where he received his B.A. degree in 1896. After graduating from the Protestant Episcopal Seminary in 1899 he served a number of parishes in Virginia, Maryland, and West Virginia. He was the secretary and treasurer of the Diocese of Virginia from 1919 until 1940. For a number of years he was also the historiographer of the same Diocese. In addition to his interest in the hymnody of the church he published many historical articles and a two-volume work entitled *Virginia's Mother Church and the Political Conditions under Which It Grew.* Roanoke College honored him by bestowing upon him the Doctor of Divinity degree in 1928.

For a note on the tune DONNE SECOURS see No. 225.

For a note on the *Genevan Psalter* see No. 110.

313 From Every Race, from Every Clime

BLACKBOURNE C.M.

Thomas B. McDormand, 1904-
Harrison's Sacred Harmony, 1784

Dr. McDormand says of the writing of this hymn, "On an air trip one day I was thinking of World Communion Sunday, and of the missionary movement which had made this worldwide Christian fellowship in prayer possible and I took out my pen and jotted down the hymn. . . . It reflects my thought as to the solidarity of all mankind, and the conviction that Jesus Christ alone has the answer to human need, in whatever country or culture man may be found." (From a letter dated November 3, 1969.)

Thomas Bruce McDormand was born March 15, 1904, in Bear River, Nova Scotia. He was educated at Edmonton (Alberta) Normal School; Acadia University, Wolfville, Nova Scotia, 1929; St. Stephen's College, Edmonton, Alberta (B.D. 1935); and Victoria University, Toronto, Ontario (Th.D. 1950). He received honorary degrees from McMaster University (D.D. 1951) and Judson College (LL.D. 1964). After his ordination in 1929 Dr. McDormand served churches in Alberta and Nova Scotia. Since 1938 he has held various important positions of leadership on the local and national level of the work of the Canadian Baptists, including General Secretary of the Baptist Convention of Ontario and Quebec, and General Secretary of the Baptist Federation of Canada, 1955. In 1959 he became Executive Vice-President of Acadia University where he served until his appointment in 1961 as President of the Eastern Baptist Theological Seminary, Philadelphia, and Eastern Baptist College, St. Davids. In October of 1969 Dr. McDormand left Philadelphia to accept the preretirement position of General Secretary of the United Baptist Convention of the Atlantic Provinces, Canada. He has published several books, the latest being *The Christian Must Have an Answer,* 1959, and the *Judson Concordance to Hymns* with F. S. Crossman, 1965. He has been a member of the joint committee charged with the production of *Hymnbook for Christian Worship,* 1970.

The tune BLACKBOURNE is also found as BLACKBURN. The composer is not known for a certainty, but the tune has been ascribed to a John Fish of Blackburn and also to a William Defesch. Defesch was a Dutch organist who wrote the oratorios, *Joseph* and *Judith,* a mass, and some instrumental music. It has been suggested that the tune may be found in a search through his compositions.

Ralph Harrison, born at Chinley, Derbyshire, September 10, 1748, and died at Manchester, November 4, 1810, was a Presbyterian minister who found time to establish a school in which he gained a reputation as a teacher of ancient languages. When the Manchester Academy was established in 1786 he was appointed the classical tutor. His publications included *Institutions of English Grammar* and several other educational manuals in addition to the two volumes of ancient and modern psalm tunes entitled *Sacred Harmony,* 1784 and 1791. The tune BLACKBOURNE is from the first of these volumes.

314   This Is the Hour of Banquet and of Song

CANTICUM REFECTIONIS 10.10.10.10.

Horatius Bonar, 1808-1889
David McKinley Williams, 1887-

These are additional stanzas to Bonar's communion hymn, "Here, O My Lord, I See Thee Face to Face," discussed at No. 323. Other stanzas omitted here, but appearing in other hymnals are:

> I have no wisdom, save in him who is
> My Wisdom and my Teacher, both in One;
> No wisdom can I lack while thou art wise,
> No teaching do I crave save thine alone.

> I have no help but thine, nor do I need
> Another arm save thine to lean upon.
> It is enough, my Lord, enough indeed;
> My strength is in thy might, thy might alone.

For a note on Horatius Bonar see No. 185.

CANTICUM REFECTIONIS was composed for this hymn in 1941 for use in *The Hymnal 1940.*

David McKinley Williams was born in Carnarvonshire, Wales, February 20, 1887. His parents came to America when he was only three months old and settled in Denver, Colorado, where he grew up. As a youth he studied music under Henry Houseley, sang in the choir at the Cathedral of St. John in the Wilderness, and was appointed organist-choirmaster of St. Peter's Church, Denver, at the age of 13. When he became twenty-one years of age, he became the organist at Grace Church Chapel in New York City and a pupil of Clement Gale. From 1911 to 1914 he studied abroad under such masters as Vierne, Widor, and D'Indy. Upon his return to America he became organist at the Church of the Holy Communion in New York City. In 1916 he saw service abroad with the Canadian Artillery and upon his return to the States he assumed his former position with the Church of the Holy Communion, but six months later accepted a position of organist-choirmaster of St. Bartholomew's Church where he remained until his retirement in 1947. He was a distinguished teacher at the School of Sacred Music of Union Theological Seminary and Juilliard School of

Music and served on the Joint Commission on Revision of the Hymnal (Episcopal) and Joint Commission on Church Music.

315 Let Us Break Bread Together

LET US BREAK BREAD 7.3.7.3. with Refrain

Negro Spiritual
Negro Melody

This hymn is typical of a true folk song in that neither author nor composer is known. These songs simply came into existence out of a deep response to religion and life. One cannot help but feel and respond to the highly reverent spirit of this hymn and the moving strains of the music.

The text points up the corporateness of our worship and especially our unity in celebrating the Lord's Supper. The last line of the refrain reminds us of our deepest need as we struggle with our successes and failures with God and our fellowmen.

316 Draw Us in the Spirit's Tether

UNION SEMINARY 8.7.8.7.4.4.7.

Percy Dearmer, 1867-1936

Harold Friedell, 1905-1958
Adapt. Jet Turner, 1928-

This hymn is found in *Songs of Praise, Enlarged Edition,* 1931, where it is listed as a communion hymn and is sung to the tune AD PERENNIS VITAE FONTEM. Percy Dearmer, editor of *Songs of Praise,* acknowledges a number of copyright hymns under initials and this is credited to one B. R. The relationship B. R. has to Percy Dearmer is uncertain.

For a comment on Percy Dearmer see No. 107.

The tune was given the name UNION SEMINARY by Jet Turner, who adapted it to congregational singing from an anthem by Harold Friedell which makes use of this text. Both Turner and Friedell were closely connected with the School of Sacred Music of Union Theological Seminary. The former is a graduate and the latter was a professor of theory and composition.

Harold Friedell, born in Jamaica, New York, has served as organist to Calvary Episcopal Church (1928-31) in New York City, St. John's Episcopal Church (1931-39), Jersey City, New Jersey; and St. Bartholomew's Church (1946-58), New York City. He taught theory and composition at the Guilmant Organ School, Juilliard School of Music, and School of Sacred Music of Union Theological Seminary. Dr. Friedell was a Fellow of the American Guild of Organists and of Trinity College, London, and served as a delegate to the International Congress of Organists which met in London in 1957. Missouri Valley College awarded him an honorary Doctor of Music degree. He was the composer of a number of anthems, hymn tunes, carols, and service music. He was stricken with a fatal heart attack on February 17, 1958, as he was walking through heavy snow from his home at Hastings-on-Hudson to the railroad station.

Jet E. Turner is a native of California, born in Monrovia, March 3, 1928. He took his B.A. degree from Pomona College in 1949 and has done graduate work in education, philosophy and political science at the Claremont Graduate School and holds the B.D. degree from Andover Newton Theological School and the M.S.M. degree from Union Theological Seminary where he has also done advanced work in theology. He has served the First Baptist Church, Westfield, New Jersey (1956-1961), the First Baptist Church, Keene, New Hampshire (1961-1964), and is currently minister of education and music at the First Baptist Church, Peoria, Illinois. He is also a member of the faculty at Bradley University.

Mr. Turner is the founder and current chairman of the Fellowship of American Baptist Musicians, the editor of the bimonthly "Newsletter" published by that group in cooperation with the Board of Education and Publication of the American Baptist Convention, and the Dean of the Conference for Church musicians which is held each summer at the American Baptist Assembly, Green Lake, Wisconsin. In addition he has served as a leader for numerous music and education workshops, has appeared as an organ recitalist, and is the author of articles which have appeared in such magazines as the *Baptist Leader, Today, Clavier,* and the *International Journal of Religious Education.*

As a member of the Baptist-Disciples Hymnbook Committee, Mr.

Turner served as chairman of the Tunes and Service Music Subcommittee.

317   *Beneath the Forms of Outward Rite*

BELMONT C.M.

James A. Blaisdell, 1867-1957

William Gardiner's *Sacred Melodies,* 1815

The exact date of writing and publication of this hymn is not known. Dr. Blaisdell wrote many hymns and several of them have been included in student hymnals. This hymn appeared in *The Student Hymnary,* 1937.

James Arnold Blaisdell was born in Beloit, Wisconsin, December 15, 1867. He was educated at Beloit College (A.B. 1889, M.A. 1892) and Hartford Theological Seminary. Ordained as a Congregational minister in 1892, he served pastorates in Waukesha, Wisconsin, and Olivet, Michigan, before becoming professor of biblical literature and librarian at Beloit College and pastor of the Second Congregational Church there. He was the recipient of six honorary degrees during a lifetime devoted to the church, education, and various civic and educational organizations. For many years he served as president of Pomona College and helped found a cooperating group of colleges at Claremont, California, serving as its president from 1926 to 1936. As a member of the Commission of the American Board of Missions, Dr. Blaisdell traveled extensively in Japan visiting churches and educational institutions. He died January 29, 1957.

William Gardiner's *Sacred Melodies* was a collection of melodies from the master composers to which English hymns had been set. The purpose of the collection was to introduce new and vital music to the churches in the hope that they would replace or hasten the demise of the old Sternhold and Hopkins and Tate and Brady styles.

Gardiner was a devotee of Beethoven and is credited with the introduction of the master's work to the English public. His *Sacred Melodies* appeared in six volumes in 1812. BELMONT appeared therein unnamed but credited to Beethoven. The tune has also been called BERNARD, ENTREATYM and VIGILS.

William Gardiner was born in Leicester, England, March 15, 1770, and died there on November 11, 1853. As a stocking manufacturer he traveled throughout Europe. His natural curiosity about music and musicians made it possible for him to meet many of the great composers and performers and to hear their music as he visited the principal cities on business ventures. On one occasion he was in Bonn for the unveiling of a statue of Beethoven. When he was spotted in the crowd, he was invited to come to the podium and sign his name to parchment under the signatures of Queen Victoria and Prince Albert. The parchment was placed in the base of the statue.

318   Beneath the Forms of Outward Rite

PERRY C.M.

James A. Blaisdell, 1867-1957
Leo Sowerby, 1895-1968

For a note on this hymn, see No. 317.

For a note on James A. Blaisdell, see No. 317.

PERRY was first published in *The Methodist Hymnal*, 1964, where it appeared with the present text.

Leo Sowerby was born in Grand Rapids, Michigan, May 1, 1895. He began musical study in that city and in 1918 completed his work at the American Conservatory of Music, Chicago (M. Mus.) His teachers included Calvin Lampert, Arthur Olaf Anderson, and Percy Grainger. During World War I he saw service as a bandmaster in England and France. In 1921 he was the first recipient of the Rome Prize, granted by the American Academy in Rome, which provided for three year's study in Italy. After returning to America he became the head of the composition and theory department of the American Conservatory and also served as organist-choirmaster of St. John's Episcopal Cathedral, Chicago. He was awarded an honorary D. Mus. degree by Eastman School of Music, Rochester, New York, in 1936. His oratorio, *Canticle of the Sun*, for mixed chorus and orchestra, won the Pulitzer Prize in 1946. Dr. Sowerby was devoted to the development of music for the church, and his contributions in this area have been significant and numerous. He served on the Joint Commission on the Revision of the Hymnal and was a member of the Tunes Committee for the *Hymnal, 1940*. He became director of the College of Church Musicians at the National Cathedral (Episcopal), Washington, D. C. in 1962. Dr. Sowerby died of a heart attack at Port Clinton, Ohio, July 7, 1968.

319 *Humbly I Adore Thee*

ADORO TE DEVOTE 11.11.11.11.

Thomas Aquinas, c. 1227-1274
Tr. J. R. Woodford, 1810-1885
Plainsong Melody
Solesmes version; adapted

This is a part of a hymn believed to have been written by Thomas of Aquino while he was in Paris writing on the communion circa 1260. His hymns have never been included in the public services of the Roman church but have, since their composition, been incorporated in various Missals for private devotions. There have been numerous translations and alterations during its long history. This version is basically that of James Russell Woodford with minor alterations by others. It first appeared in his hymns in 1852.

Thomas of Aquino was born about 1227. He was a most precocious child who received his early education at a Benedictine Monastery at Monte Cassino. He was there for seven years before returning to his family. He came under the influence of the Dominicans when he went to Naples to study at the university. The young Thomas decided to become a member of the order, a decision which was violently opposed by his family, especially his mother, who caused her son to be arrested and imprisoned for two years. Intervention by the Pope and the highest civil authorities led to his release and he returned once again to Naples. From this point onward he became one of the great teachers and preachers and authors of the thirteenth century. He was offered a number of high offices in the Roman church but each time declined the honors. Thomas did serve as a member of Louis LX's Council of State but his first love was his teaching, writing, and preaching. He died as he was traveling to the Second Council of Lyons on March 7, 1274.

James Russell Woodford was born April 30, 1820. Educated at Merchant Taylors School and Pembroke College, Cambridge, he was ordained in 1843 and became second Master at Bishop's College, Bristol, and curate of St. John the Baptist in the same city. After that he served as vicar of Kempsford, Leeds. Woodford was for a time honorary chaplain to the Queen and, on a number of occasions, Select Preacher at Cambridge. He was consecrated Bishop of Ely at Westminster Abbey in 1873. He was the publisher of sermons and lectures and the editor of several hymnbooks. His death occurred at Ely on October 24, 1885.

The tune name is from the first line of the hymn. ADORO TE DEVOTE is the tune generally associated with this text. It is a harmonized version of a plainchant that has been traced to the late seventeenth century. The *Historical Companion to Hymns Ancient and Modern* gives its source as the *Paris Processional*, 1697.

320   *Jesus, Thou Joy of Loving Hearts*

HESPERUS L.M.

Anonymous Latin, 12th century
Tr. and arr. Ray Palmer, 1808-1887
Henry Baker, 1835-1910

Another cento from *"Jesu dulcis memoria"* (see also "Jesus, the Very Thought of Thee," No. 282), this is a favorite hymn on both sides of the Atlantic. The translation was made especially for Park and Phelps' *Sabbath Hymn Book*, 1858.

Born in Little Compton, Rhode Island, on November 12, 1808, Ray Palmer grew up in Boston where he worked in a drygoods store and became a member of the Park Street Congregational Church. After attending Phillips Academy and Yale College, he entered the ministry and served churches in Bath, Maine, and then Albany, New York. In 1865 he became corresponding secretary to the American Congregational Union. He retired to Newark, New Jersey, in 1878 and died there on March 29, 1887.

Dr. Palmer wrote about thirty-eight hymns including a number of free translations from the Latin. He is held in high esteem by hymnologists and churchmen alike for his thoughtfulness, poetic flow, and deep Christian devotion.

HESPERUS is also called QUEBEC, ELIM, and WHITBURN. It was composed by Henry Baker while he was an undergraduate student at Exeter College, Oxford, in 1854. The tune did not appear in a hymnal until 1866 when it was used in *Hymnal for Use in the English Church* with the text "Sun of my Soul."

The composer was born in Nuneham, Oxfordshire, in 1835. He was the son of a clergyman and was educated at Winchester, and Cooper's Hill, where he studied civil engineering. For many years he followed his engineering career with the railway system of India. On his return to England, John B. Dykes encouraged him to pursue the study of music, which he did at Exeter College, Oxford, where he received his music degree in 1867. He died at Wimbledon in 1910.

321   Jesus Christ, Our Blessed Savior

JESUS CHRISTUS, UNSER HEILAND 8.8.9.8.

Jesus Christus nostra salus
? Jan Hus, 1369?-1415
German version, Martin Luther, 1483-1546
Tr. from Hymnal for Colleges and Schools, 1956

Enchiridion Erfurt, 1524
Harm. from Songs of Syon, 1904

The authorship of this hymn is uncertain although it has been attributed to Jan Hus, the Czech reformer who died at the stake at the Council of Constance. The present translation is from Martin Luther's German version which appeared as "The Hymn of St. John Hus Improved" in Eyn Enchiridion, Erfurt, 1524, and the Wittenberg Geystliche gesank Buchleyn, 1524, and is taken from the Hymnal for Colleges and Schools, New Haven, 1956.

For a note on Martin Luther see No. 31.

The tune has been associated with Luther's version of the Latin text of the present hymn since it appeared in Klug's Geistliche Lieder, Wittenberg, 1535. It is said to have been based on an earlier medieval tune REGINA COELI. The version presented here is from Songs of Syon, 1904, which was edited by George Ratcliffe Woodward.

322   Father, We Thank Thee Who Hast Planted

WEISSE 9.8.9.8.

From the Didache, c. 110
Versified by F. Bland Tucker, 1895-

Source unknown
Harm. J. S. Bach, 1685-1750

This hymn represents a versification of prayers from an early document known as the Didache or "The Teaching of the Twelve Apostles." The author is unknown but scholars believe it was written in the second century and that the author might have used material in common usage during the last part of the first century. Its contents deal with instructions relating to the proper way of observing the Lord's Supper and other aspects of Christian worship. This version was written in 1939 and was included in *The Hymnal 1940*.

For a note on F. Bland Tucker see No. 169.

The source of the tune is unknown. The tune name, however, might suggest that Michael Weisse, 1480-1534, used it for one of his Bohemian Brethren hymns. The present harmonization is by J. S. Bach and was taken from the second edition of his *Choralgesänge*, 1769, where it was set to Christian Weise's *"Gottlob es geht mehr zum ende."* This is a funeral hymn which Henry Drinker translates "Thanks be to God my end is near me."

For a note on J. S. Bach see No. 193.

323 *Here, O My Lord, I See Thee Face to Face*

HOLBORN 10.10.10.10.

Horatius Bonar, 1808-1889

Eric H. Thiman, 1900-

This communion hymn is ranked with the best of Bonar's work. His brother, John J. Bonar, made a practice of making a memorandum of each of his services to which he appended an appropriate hymn. He requested his poet brother to write one for the communion service observed on the first Sunday of October, 1855. This is a portion of the hymn submitted. It was first published in *Hymns of Faith and Hope,* 1857, in ten stanzas of four lines.

For a comment on Horatius Bonar see No. 185.

For a note on HOLBORN and Eric H. Thiman see No. 305.

324 *According to Thy Gracious Word*

DUNDEE C.M.

James Montgomery, 1771-1854

Scottish Psalter 1615

This hymn first appeared in the *Christian Psalmist*, 1825, and has since become one of the most beloved communion hymns of evangelical churches. The text is based on Luke 22:19 and is a beautiful example of the Christian's resolve to obey the eucharistic command of Jesus, "Do this in remembrance of me."

In the *Handbook to the Church Hymnary*, Moffatt and Patrick quote Canon Ellerton as saying Montgomery was "our first hymnologist: the first Englishman who collected and criticized hymns, and who made people who had lost all recollection of ancient models understand something of what a hymn meant, and what it ought to be" (p. 437).

The third stanza of the original has been omitted:

> Gethsemane can I forget,
> Or there thy conflict see,
> Thine agony and bloody sweat,
> And not remember thee?

The son of a Moravian minister and missionary, James Montgomery was born in Irvine, Ayrshire, Scotland, November 4, 1771. Both of his parents died in the West Indies while serving their church as missionaries to those islands.

He was sent to the Moravian seminary at Fulneck, Yorkshire, in the hope that he would follow in his father's steps. He was not interested in pursuing this course and spent more time writing poetry than in preparing for his classes. He withdrew from seminary in favor of seeking his fortune in the business world. After several years of wandering from job to job and city to city he settled down in Sheffield and began working as an assistant to one Robert Gales who was a bookseller and journalist with the *Sheffield Register*.

When Gales was forced to leave England because of his liberal political stance, Montgomery, at the age of twenty-three, stepped into the publishing field. He changed the name of the paper to the *Sheffield Iris* and managed it for thirty-one years, from 1794 to 1825. During his early years as the editor he was twice imprisoned for his liberal political views. The first was a result of his writing concerning the abolition of slavery in the West Indies, and the second was a result of his reporting a riot which took place in Sheffield.

Montgomery was a prolific writer of hymns. He gave the church more than four hundred altogether, many of which first appeared in the columns of his paper. He is ranked as one of England's outstanding nonconformist hymn writers. He died April 30, 1854.

The tune DUNDEE first appeared in the *Scottish Psalter*, 1615. It was called FRENCH TUNE but Ravenscroft changed it to DUNDY in his *Whole Book of Psalms*, 1621, and classified it as a Scottish tune. It may be conjectured that the original reference to it as a French tune gives some credence to the notion that it was probably a product of Protestant Europe.

Strangely, the tune has apparently been confused with the English tune WINDSOR or COLESHILL. This may be because in Scotland WINDSOR is called DUNDEE.

325   The Heavens Declare Thy Glory, Lord

UXBRIDGE L.M.

Based on Psalm 19
Isaac Watts, 1674-1748
Lowell Mason, 1792-1872

Appearing under the title, "The Book of Nature and of Scripture Compared" this hymn was first published as Psalm 19 in Watts' *Psalms of David Imitated in the Language of the New Testament,* 1719.

For a comment on Isaac Watts see No. 48.

UXBRIDGE is named for a town in Massachusetts, the significance of which is unknown. The tune first appeared in the *Boston Handel and Haydn Society Collection of Church Music,* 1831, and was set to Watts' text in *The Modern Psalmist,* 1839. It is said to be one of Mason's original tunes.

For a note on Lowell Mason see No. 273.

326   Lord, Thy Word Abideth

CHESTERTON 6.6.6.6.D.

H. W. Baker, 1821-1877
Geoffrey Beaumont, 1903-

Under the heading Holy Scripture this hymn was written especially for and published in *Hymns Ancient and Modern,* 1861.

It has gained wide use throughout the English-speaking world and has been translated into several languages.

For a comment on H. W. Baker see No. 209.

CHESTERTON is one of several hymn tunes composed by Geoffrey Beaumont who gained notice through his *Twentieth-Century Folk Mass*, 1956. His interest in the youth of Britain motivated his experimentation with the popular musical idiom as a basis of material for use in public worship. This tune was first broadcast from the Martock parish church in Somerset in October of 1955 before it was incorporated in the recording of the *Folk Mass*. It was published in leaflet form in 1957 and first appeared in an English hymnal in the *Baptist Hymn Book*, 1962. This is the tune's first appearance in a major American hymnbook. Erik Routley gives an excellent analysis and evaluation of the Twentieth Century Church Light Music Group in his *Twentieth Century Church Music*, Oxford University Press, 1964.

Geoffrey Beaumont was educated at a school in Cheltenham, Cambridge University, and Ely Theological College. He was ordained Anglican priest in 1932 and immediately became curate of a mission church in the south of London. After going to St. John's Church, Waterloo Road, he saw service as a chaplain during World War II. In 1947 he became Chaplain to Trinity College, Cambridge, a post he held for five years and during which he began to compose music for London musical reviews, hymn tunes in the light music idiom, and incidental music for plays. From 1952 he spent five years as chaplain to the British Embassy in Madrid, Spain. For two years he was vicar of St. George's, Camberwell, but resigned his post in 1959 and entered the Community of the Resurrection in Mirfield.

327 *Break Thou the Bread of Life*

BREAD OF LIFE 6.4.6.4.D.

Mary A. Lathbury, 1841-1913
William F. Sherwin, 1826-1888

Miss Lathbury wrote seven hymns for use at Chautauqua, New York. This and "Day Is Dying in the West" are the two best known and loved. It was written at the request of Bishop John H. Vincent, one of the founders of the institution, for use at vesper services.

The author was born August 10, 1841, in Manchester, New York, the daughter of a Methodist minister. She was a teacher of art, writer, and poet. She is often called the poet laureate of Chautauqua because of her long and unique relationship to the institution. She was the editor and author of many articles for children and young people and was the founder of a youth-oriented group known as the "Look-Up Legion" whose motto was:

> Look up, and not down;
> Look forward, and not back;
> Look out, and not in;
> And lend a hand.

She died at East Orange, New Jersey, on September 30, 1913.

The tune name is derived from the first line of the hymn. It was composed for this hymn in 1877 by William Fisk Sherwin who was the director of music at Chautauqua from 1874 until his death in 1888. Born at Buckland, Massachusetts, he studied music under Lowell Mason and George Webb and after holding various teaching and church music positions, he taught vocal and choral music at the New England Conservatory of Music. He was especially well known as an outstanding conductor of amateur choral organizations.

328   O Word of God Incarnate

MUNICH 7.6.7.6.D.

William W. How, 1823-1897

Neu-vermehrtes Gesangbuch, Meiningen, 1693
Harm. Felix Mendelssohn, 1809-1847

This hymn first appeared in the supplement to *Psalms and Hymns,* 1867, which was edited by Bishop How and one Thomas Baker Morrell. It is based on Psalm 119:105.

For a comment on William Walsham How see No. 279.

For a note on MUNICH see No. 9.

Felix Mendelssohn, the son of a Jewish banker and grandson of the philosopher Moses Mendelssohn, was born February 3, 1809, at Hamburg. When his family settled in Berlin in 1812, they were baptized into the Lutheran Church and the "Bartholdy" was added to their name. Mendelssohn was a child prodigy who composed and played the piano at the age of ten years. By 1826 his reputation was firmly established as a composer with the performance of a *Midsummer Night's Dream.* In 1829 the young musician gathered together sixteen voices and produced J. S. Bach's *St. Matthew Passion,* the first performance since the master's death in 1750. He traveled widely and was much in demand as a performer and conductor. Several visits to England to produce his *Elijah* enhanced his reputation. In 1833 he was appointed director of the Düsseldorf concerts at which time he introduced a new musical form which he called "Songs Without Words." From 1835 to 1843 he was director of the Gewandhaus concerts in Leipzig and in 1843 went to Berlin to become the royal kapellmeister and director of music for the Academy of Arts. Two years later he returned to Berlin to resume his old post with the Gewandhaus and to establish the Conservatorium.

Mendelssohn conducted his *Elijah* at the Birmingham Festival in 1846 and the following year returned to London to conduct the same work. While there he received news of the death of his sister, which, combined with his own physical fatigue, hastened his death at Leipzig on November 4, 1847.

329   Book of Books, Our People's Strength

LIEBSTER JESU 7.8.7.8.8.8.

Percy Dearmer, 1867-1936
Melody by Johann R. Ahle, 1625-1673

According to Dr. Dearmer this hymn was written for *Songs of Praise,* 1925, to give an up-to-date appreciation of the Bible.

For a note on Percy Dearmer see No. 107.

For a note on the composer and tune see No. 212.

330   O Zion, Haste, Thy Mission High Fulfilling

TIDINGS 11.10.11.10. with Refrain

Mary A. Thomson, 1834-1923
James Walch, 1837-1901

Mrs. Thomson began this hymn one night in 1868 as she sat up with one of her children who was ill with typhoid fever. For lack of a suitable refrain she left it unfinished for three years at which time she added the present refrain to complete the work. It was introduced into hymnals through the Episcopal *Hymnal, 1892.*

Mary Ann Thomson (nee Faulkner) was born in London, December 5, 1834. She came to America and married John Thomson who was librarian for the Free Library of Philadelphia. Both were active members of the Church of the Annunciation in Philadelphia where Mr. Thomson served as the accounting warden of the church. More than forty of her hymns and poems appeared in *The Churchman,* New York, and *The Living Church,* Chicago. She died in Philadelphia on March 11, 1923.

TIDINGS, also known as ANGEL SONG and PROCLAMATION, was composed for Frederick Faber's hymn, "Hark, Hark, my Soul, Angelic Songs Are Dwelling." It apparently became associated with Mrs. Thomson's hymn when they appeared together in the Episcopal *Hymnal, 1892.*

James Walch, an English organist, composer, and music dealer, was born June 21, 1837. After studying music with his father and Henry Smart he was organist at several churches until about 1870. From 1870 until 1874, he was the conductor of the Bolton Philharmonic Society. He became a dealer in music at Barrow-in-Furness in 1877. He composed hymn tunes and other church music but is known today only for this tune. He died at Barrow-in-Furness in 1901.

331   Let There Be Light, Lord God of Hosts

ELTON L.M.

William Merrill Vories, 1880-1964
Lowell Mason, 1792-1872

This hymn might be classed as a World War I protest song. It was written in 1908 as a personal protest to the sabre rattling and the rising German militarism prior to the outbreak of the war. It was first published in the organ of the American Peace Society, the *Advocate of Peace,* in February, 1909.

Born in Leavenworth, Kansas, October 28, 1880, Dr. Vories went to Japan under the auspices of the International Y.M.C.A. as a young man and founded the Omi Mission which later became the Omi Brotherhood. This organization became a powerful and effective religious, social, economic, educational, medical, and architectural force in that country. In 1919 he married the daughter of a Japanese nobleman and about 1940 became a citizen of Japan assuming his wife's family name. He is known now as Merrill Vories-Hititsuyanagi. This hymn is expressive of the motivation that led him to devote his life to lay missionary endeavors.

ELTON is from *The Hallelujah*, 1854, and is the second of Mason's tunes having the same name. The first was in short meter.

For a comment on Lowell Mason see No. 273.

332   *Draw Thou My Soul, O Christ*

ST. EDMUND 6.4.6.4.6.6.6.4.

Lucy Larcom, 1826-1893
Arthur S. Sullivan, 1842-1900

This hymn is from Miss Larcom's book of poems, *At the Beautiful Gate*, 1892. The author was born at Beverly Farms, Massachusetts, March 5, 1824 or 1826. As a young girl, she was employed by a mill in Lowell, Massachusetts, where she became active in the first factory woman's club known as the Improvement Circle. Her poems were first published in the club's official organ, the *Lowell Offering*. This was a magazine written entirely by women and through it her poetry attracted the attention of John Greenleaf Whittier, and resulted in a lifelong friendship.

At the age of twenty years, Miss Larcom went to Illinois as a rural schoolteacher and while there she taught, studied, and graduated from Monticello Female Seminary at Alton. Upon her return to Massachusetts she continued her teaching and found time to attend Wheaton Seminary at Norton. Her final years were devoted to editorial work and writing. She and Whittier jointly edited several collections of poetry. She died on April 17, 1893.

The tune ST. EDMUND is so called in honor of an ancient English king who was captured and slain by the invading Danes. The tune is also known as FATHERLAND and PILGRIMAGE because of the nature of the hymn to which it was originally set, "We Are but Strangers Here," by T. R. Taylor. It first appeared in *The Hymnary*, 1872.

For a note on Arthur Sullivan see No. 173.

333 Not Always on the Mount

DANIEL L.M.

Frederick Lucian Hosmer, 1840-1928
Irish Traditional Melody

This transfiguration hymn was written in 1882, first published in the *Chicago Unity,* 1884, revised by the author and published again in *The Thought of God in Hymns and Poems,* first series 1885, by Hosmer and W. C. Gannett. Since then it has found its way into a number of American hymnals.

The author was born in Farmington, Massachusetts, October 16, 1840. Educated at Harvard University he was ordained a Unitarian minister in 1872. For a time he was lecturer in hymnology at Harvard. Dr. Hosmer held pastorates in Quincy, Illinois; Cleveland, Ohio; St. Louis, Missouri; and Berkeley, California. He was the author of a compilation of prayers and responsive services for use in Sunday schools entitled *The Way of Life.* John Julian calls him a "powerful and original" Unitarian hymnist. He died June 7, 1929, in Berkeley.

DANIEL is a traditional Irish melody and was first arranged for the text "To God who makes all lovely things" by Martin Shaw for *Songs of Praise for Boys and Girls,* 1930.

For a comment on Martin Shaw see No. 2.

334 God of the Prophets! Bless the Prophets' Sons

TOULON 10.10.10.10.

Denis Wortman, 1835-1922
Genevan Psalter, 1551

This hymn was written for the observance of the centennial year of New Brunswick Theological Seminary in October, 1884. Dr. Wortman's message accompanying his hymn is quoted from William Cobert and Calvin Laufer, *Handbook to The Hymnal* (p. 491): "May I take the liberty of sending you the enclosed verses; a very humble attempt to express the prayer that our Class of 1860, and indeed all loyal sons of New Brunswick Seminary, lift to God at this unusual anniversary, for His blessing upon her and all who go forth from her instructions." The "Prayer for Young Ministers" originally consisted of seven stanzas of which we use four.

Denis Wortman, D.D., L.H.D., was born at Hopewell, New York, April 30, 1835. He was a graduate of Amherst College and the New Brunswick Theological Seminary. In 1860 he was ordained a minister of the Reformed Church in America. He served Reformed Churches in Brooklyn, Philadelphia, and Schenectady and was secretary of his church's Ministerial Relief Program for seventeen years and was in 1901 president of its General Synod. He died August 28, 1822, at East Orange, New Jersey.

For a note on TOULON see No. 369.

For a note on the *Genevan Psalter* see No. 110.

335 *Renew Thy Church, Her Ministries Restore*

ALL IS WELL 10.6.10.6.8.8.8.6.

Kenneth L. Cober, 1902-
Old English Melody

This hymn was written for the Baptist Jubilee Advance, a five-year national denominational program. Dr. Cober tells us he wrote it specifically for the second-year program, the theme of which was "The Renewal of the Church: Imperative to Evangelism." It was first sung at the American Baptist Convention in May, 1960. The author says he wrote the hymn "while riding across the country on trains and planes."

Kenneth L. Cober, son of missionary parents, spent his boyhood in Puerto Rico. He was educated at Bucknell University and Colgate Rochester Divinity School. He received the Doctor of Divinity degree from Bucknell in 1950. Dr. Cober recently retired as Executive Director of the Division of Christian Education, American Baptist Convention, a position he held for sixteen years. He is presently Interim Executive Secretary of the Connecticut Convention of American Baptist

Churches. He has also served as Director of Christian Education for the New York State Convention and Executive Secretary of the Rhode Island Baptist State Convention. Dr. Cober has written many books and articles in the area of Christian education. His latest book is *The Church's Teaching Ministry,* Judson Press, 1964. Dr. Cober was a member of the joint committee for the *Hymnbook for Christian Worship.*

ALL IS WELL may well be an American rather than an English tune. Alexander Schreiner, organist at the Mormon Tabernacle, Salt Lake City, Utah, informs us that he and a librarian searched through several thousand songbooks in The Bodlian Library, Oxford, and could not locate the tune. Our researches reveal that the tune appeared as early as 1844 in the *Sacred Harp* with the text "What's this that steals upon my frame? Is it death?" In our copy of *Original Sacred Harp, Revised, Corrected and Enlarged,* 1911, both tune and text are attributed to one J. T. White, nephew of B. F. White, compiler of *Sacred Harp,* 1844. It further states that "The tune has been published before it was printed in the *Sacred Harp,*" and that the tune was named by White for the SACRED HARP. As early as 1866, the text appears anonymously in *The Christian Hymnbook* by Alexander Campbell and others with ALL IS WELL as the suggested tune. The following year A. D. Fillmore and Robert Skene give the tune in six-eight meter to this text in *Fillmore's Christian Psaltery.* See also Jackson's *Spiritual Folksongs of Early America,* number 58.

336   Mid Blackness of the City's Night

ST. PETERSBURG 8.8.8.8.8.8.

Sarah E. Taylor, 1883-1954

Arr. Dmitri S. Bortniansky, 1751-1825

This is another of The Hymn Society of America's *Five New Hymns on the City,* published in leaflet form in 1954 where it was entitled "We See Thee in the Starry Height." See comment on No. 144. Here the first and second stanzas have been transposed.

Miss Taylor was born in England, the daughter of a Primitive Methodist minister. She came to America at nine years of age, was educated at Woman's College, Brown University (1904 and 1910).

She spent her life as a teacher including six years in mission schools at Talladega, Alabama, and Richmond, Virginia. She retired in 1949, lived at Central Falls, Rhode Island, for a time, and died at Pawtucket, Rhode Island, October 5, 1954. Miss Taylor was the author of a number of sacred poems, a prize song for the state of Rhode Island, and has had several hymns published by The Hymn Society of America.

ST. PETERSBURG, known also as WELLS, WELLSPRING, and SHANGANA, entered Western church hymnals via Tscherlitsky's CHORALBUCH, Leipzig, 1825, where it was set to Gerhard Tersteegen's hymn *"Ich bete an die Macht der Liebe."* Some sources say the tune is from one of the composer's masses, others doubt he even wrote any masses, and still others suggest its origin is from Russian folk music. Whatever its source it is a fine tune and is used in modern hymnals set to a variety of texts.

Dmitri Stepanovitch Bortniansky was born in Gluckoff, Ukraine, in 1751. He studied music in Moscow, St. Petersburg, Venice, Rome, Bologna, and Naples. During his stay in Italy he produced several operas and upon his return to St. Petersburg in 1779 became the director of Empress Catherine's Church Choir which later was known as the Imperial Chapel Choir. It is said he brought this organization to a high degree of perfection and composed many choral pieces for it. Tchaikovsky edited his works which were published in ten volumes in St. Petersburg. A number of his anthems are still heard in churches today. He died October 7, 1825, in St. Petersburg.

337   Give Me the Eyes to See This Child

SALVATION 8.6.8.8.6.

Miriam Dewey Ross, 1927-
Ananias Davisson's *Kentucky Harmony,*
c. 1815, adapted

Mrs. Ross wrote this hymn while serving as superintendent of the primary department of a church school in Hanover, New Hampshire. It was first published by The Hymn Society of America in *Fifteen New Christian Education Hymns,* 1959.

Miriam Dewey Ross, the fourth daughter of a Congregational minister, was born in Cleveland, Ohio, in 1927. After graduating from Doane College in 1949, she married James F. Ross. Dr. Ross' teaching career has taken the family to Hanover, New Hampshire (Dartmouth

College), Madison, New Jersey (Drew Theological School), and Alexandria, Virginia (Virginia Theological Seminary). Mrs. Ross has been an active church woman throughout her life and is presently a member and deacon of The First Congregational Church, Washington, D. C.

For a comment on Salvation and Ananias Davisson see No. 42.

338   Come, Labor On

ORA LABORA 4.10.10.10.4.

Jane Laurie Borthwick, 1813-1897, alt.

T. Tertius Noble, 1867-1953

The author of this hymn was the daughter of the manager of the North British Insurance Office in Edinburgh, Scotland. She was born there on April 9, 1813. Miss Borthwick published works in both prose and verse and is remembered chiefly as a translator of German hymns which appeared in series from 1854 to 1862 under the title *Hymns from the Land of Luther*. She was assisted in her project by her sister Sarah Findlater who contributed fifty-three translations. "Come, Labor On" is one of her original hymns and appeared in her *Thoughts for Thoughtful Hours*, 1859. She died on September 7, 1897.

Nothing is known of the tune ORA LABORA other than that it was written for this text by Thomas Tertius Noble and appeared in the *New Hymnal*, 1918. The composer was born in Bath, England, on May 5, 1867, and became one of the best-known organists in both England and America. He studied under Parratt, Bridge, and Stanford at the Royal College of Music for five years before devoting his life to composition, playing the organ, directing choirs, and teaching.

He served All Saints' Church, Colchester (1881-89), as assistant to Charles V. Stanford at Trinity College, Cambridge (1890-92), Ely Cathedral (1892-98), York Minster (1898-1913), where he also founded the York Symphony Orchestra and revived the York Music Festival which had been defunct for seventy-five years. In 1913 he came to America to succeed Will C. Macfarlane as organist-choirmaster of St. Thomas' Episcopal Church, New York, a position he held until his retirement in 1943. In his busy life he found time to make recital tours through Eastern United States and Canada, teach privately, and, as a member of the faculty at Union School of Sacred Music, to serve on the Joint Committee on The Hymnal, 1916 and the Joint Commission on Church Music until 1943. Dr. Noble composed many popular anthems including *Fierce Was the Wild Billow,* and *Souls of the Righteous,* and numerous services and hymn tunes as well as organ works. He retired to his home in Rockport, Massachusetts, in 1943 and died there in 1953.

339 Turn Back, O Man, Forswear Thy Foolish Ways

OLD 124TH 10.10.10.10.10.

Clifford Bax, 1886-1962
Genevan Psalter, 1551

Clifford Bax wrote this hymn at the request of the composer Gustav Holst in 1916. It was written especially for the tune OLD 124TH. Holst later used both words and music in a setting for chorus and orchestra.

Clifford Bax (1886-1962) was an English playwright, essayist, and poet who wrote numerous popular works on a wide variety of subjects. Among his plays are *The Poetasters of Ispahan,* 1912, *The Rose without a Thorn,* 1932, *The House of Borgia,* 1935. Other works include *Midsummer Madness,* 1924, *Pretty Witty Nell,* 1932, and *Ideas and People,* 1936. Martin Shaw set two of his works to music, *Mr. Pepys,* 1926, and *Waterloo Leaves,* 1928. His brother, Arnold Bax, a well-known composer, wrote two songs using his texts.

OLD 124TH was the tune set to Théodore de Bèze's paraphrase of Psalm 124 in the *Genevan Psalter,* 1551. It was adopted by German, English, and Scottish Psalters and was used with other psalms.

See also the comment on TOULON, No. 369.

340 Word of Life, Most Pure, Most Strong

PLEYEL'S HYMN 7.7.7.7.

Jonathan F. Bahnmaier, 1774-1841
Tr. Catherine Winkworth, 1827-1878
Ignace Pleyel, 1757-1831

This is Catherine Winkworth's translation of Jonathan Friedrich Bahnmaier's "Missions" hymn, *"Walte, fürder, nah und fern"* published separately in 1827 and subsequently, with minor alterations, in many hymnbooks. Miss Winkworth published a full translation in her *Lyra Germanica*, second series, 1858. This hymn, beginning with the fifth stanza, as here, is found in Longfellow and Johnson's *Hymns of the Spirit*, 1864.

Jonathan Friedrich Bahnmaier was born in Oberstenfeld, near Bottwar, Württemberg, on July 12, 1774. He was educated at Tübingen and for several years afterward was assistant to his father who was the Town Preacher at Oberstenfeld. After serving as diaconus in several towns and head of a girls' school he was, in 1815, appointed professor of education and homiletics at Tübingen. From 1819 until 1841 he served as Town Preacher at Kirchheim-unter-Teck. He died on August 18, 1841, after suffering paralysis which struck him while inspecting a school in a nearby village.

For a comment on Catherine Winkworth see No. 58.

PLEYEL'S HYMN is named for the composer and is the theme from the slow movement of his String Quartet No. 7, opus 4. Its first use as a hymn tune seems to have been in a Long Meter setting to Joseph Addison's hymn, "The Spacious Firmament on High" in Arnold and Callcott's *Psalms of David for Use in Parish Churches*, 1791.

Ignace Josef Pleyel, born June 1, 1757, at Ruppertsthal, Austria, was a prolific composer of instrumental works and the founder of the famous Pleyel Piano Manufacturing Company. He studied and lived with Haydn for five years and for a time studied also in Rome. He was first kapellmeister at the Strasbourg Cathedral, but the revolution forced him to leave Strasbourg and go to London where he conducted concerts in competition with Solomon, manager of Haydn's London concerts. He returned to his house near Strasbourg, but revolutionary harassment forced him to sell his property and move to Paris. It was at this time Pleyel entered the music-selling business and established his piano company in 1807. He died in Paris on November 14, 1831.

341   *Teach Me, My God and King*

MORNINGTON S.M.

George Herbert, 1593-1632
Adapt. John Wesley, 1703-1791
Garrett Wellesley, 1735-1781

Herbert's original hymn appeared in his *Temple*, 1633, under the title "The Elixir." John Wesley published his adaptation of the poem in his collection of *Psalms and Hymns*, 1738. Here we have Wesley's version of stanzas 1, 2, 4, and 5 of the original six stanzas with minor alterations of several words in stanza four.

For a comment on George Herbert see No. 83.

For a comment on John Wesley see No. 259.

MORNINGTON was composed as a chant circa 1760 by Garrett Wellesley, the first Earl of Mornington.

Garrett Wellesley, or Wesley, a distant relative of John and Charles Wesley and the son of John Colley Wesley, was born July 19, 1735. Educated at Trinity College, Dublin, he served in the Irish House of Commons and on the death of his father in 1758 became a member of the House of Lords. He was the father of the Duke of Wellington. Lord Wellesley is known chiefly as a musician, having become the first professor of music at Dublin University, and the composer of a quantity of secular and sacred music. Trinity College conferred upon him the Doctor of Music degree in 1764. The Wesley family name was changed to Wellesley around 1790.

The history of hymnody and Methodism might have been different had Charles Wesley consented to adoption by the Duke of Wellington's grandfather. When he declined the offer, Richard Colley was chosen in his stead and succeeded to the Wesley estates and titles. Garrett Wellesley died at Kensington, London, on May 22, 1781.

342   *We Are Living, We Are Dwelling*

EBENEZER 8.7.8.7.D.

Arthur C. Coxe, 1818-1896, alt.

Thomas J. Williams, 1869-1944

This hymn was written in 1840 when Coxe was only twenty-two years old. He was keenly aware of the great changes taking place around him which prompted James Russell Lowell to write "The Present Crisis" and the hymn, "Once to Every Man and Nation" (See 247).

Arthur Cleveland Coxe, born May 10, 1818, at Mendham, New Jersey, was the son of the eminent Presbyterian minister, Samuel Hanson Cox. The son changed the spelling of the sir name. After graduating from the University of New York City (1838) and General Theological Seminary (1841) he was ordained and served successively as rector at St. John's, Hartford, Connecticut; Grace Church, Baltimore, Maryland; and Calvary Church, New York City. After declining his election as bishop of Texas, he accepted and was ordained bishop of the Western Diocese of New York. He wrote at least seventeen hymns, but refused permission for them to appear in the Episcopalian hymnal until after his death. He authored a treatise on the history of the Church of England and contributed to editing *The Ante-Nicene Fathers* and published *Christian Ballads,* 1840, which went through many editions here and in England. Coxe died July 20, 1896, in Buffalo, New York.

For a note on EBENEZER and Thomas J. Williams see No. 247.

343 *Break Forth, O Living Light of God*

ST. PETER C.M.

Frank von Christierson, 1900-
Alexander R. Reinagle, 1799-1877

Mr. Christierson has this to say of the hymn. "When I was a student at the Seminary, I learned one day that Elder John Robinson of the Plymouth Congregation once said, 'There is yet more light to break forth from the Word of God.' This impressed me greatly at the time. Years afterward, when the Revised Standard Version of the Bible was about to be issued, and The Hymn Society of America called for new hymns to celebrate this event, those words of Elder Robinson returned to me and I wrote

> Break forth, O living light of God,
> Upon the world's dark hour!"

It was first published in *Ten New Hymns on the Bible,* 1952, by The Hymn Society of America.

Frank von Christierson was born in the village of Lovisa, about thirty-five miles east of Helsinki, Finland, on December 25, 1900, in a house previously owned by Jean Sibelius and where he composed some of his glorious music. Christierson's father was a customs officer, judge, and at one time a member of the Finnish Parliament.

As a boy of four, he was brought to America by his parents. The family settled in California and have remained there. Christierson was educated at Stanford University and San Francisco Theological Seminary. He served as pastor of Calvary Presbyterian Church, Berkeley; and as organizer and pastor of Trinity Presbyterian Church, North Hollywood, and of Celtic Cross Presbyterian Church, Citrus Heights, near Sacramento. He was elected moderator of the San Francisco Presbytery and of Los Angeles Presbytery and for three years was chairman of the radio and television activities of the Sacramento Council of Churches. Since his retirement he has served a number of Northern California churches ad interim.

He wrote the prize-winning hymn for the Golden Gate Exposition in 1939 and also a hymn which was used for the 150th anniversary observance of the American Bible Society. The Hymn Society of America has published six of his hymns including the present text.

ST. PETER is named for the church, St. Peter's-in-the East, Oxford, where the composer was organist for many years.

Alexander Robert Reinagle was born at Brighton, England, August 21, 1799. His father, Joseph, was of Austrian extraction and a celebrated violincellist who for a while was leader of the orchestra for the Edinburgh Theatre. Reinagle himself was a teacher of violin and violincello and wrote and compiled several books of instructions for those instruments. In addition to other instrumental music, Reinagle published two books of hymn tunes and chants. He died on April 6, 1877, at Kidlington, near Oxford.

344   Lord, Speak to Me, that I May Speak

HOLLEY L.M.

Frances R. Havergal, 1836-1879

George Hews, 1806-1873

Based on Romans 14:7 and headed "A Worker's Prayer," this hymn was written at Winterdyne on April 28, 1872.

For a note on Miss Havergal see No. 359.

HOLLEY first appeared in Lowell Mason's *Boston Academy's Collection*, 1835, and is the composer's best-known tune.

George Hews was born January 6, 1806, at Weston, Massachusetts. He manufactured pianos in Boston and was a professional musician of some note. Little is known of him except that he was an organist, tenor soloist, teacher of music, and active in the Boston Handel and Haydn Society. He died in Boston on July 6, 1873.

345   O Son of Might, O Son of Light

INDONESIAN FOLK TUNE

Ross Coggins, 1927-

Arr. James Bigelow, 1956

Both the text and music of this hymn appeared as an anthem in *The Church Musician*, Vol. 8, No. 8, August, 1957. This magazine is published by the Sunday School Board of the Southern Baptist Convention in Nashville, Tennessee. Under the title "Send Me, O Lord, Send Me" the text was given in three stanzas, the third of which is omitted here. Mr. Coggins informs us he wrote the hymn while serving as a Southern Baptist missionary to Indonesia in 1956.

Ross Coggins was born on November 23, 1927, at Wichita Falls, Texas. He is a graduate of Baylor University and Southwestern Baptist Theological Seminary. After serving as a missionary to Indonesia he became Director of Communications of the Christian Life Commission of the Southern Baptist Convention. Mr. Coggins is the author of *To Change the World*, Broadman Press. He is currently associated with Translinear, Inc., and lives in Austin, Texas.

James Bigelow is the pseudonym of a Southern Baptist composer who, we are told, wants to remain anonymous. A number of his arrangements have appeared under this name in *The Church Musician*.

346   O Church of God in Every Land

WINDHAM L.M.

Wilbur C. Christians, 1912-

Daniel Read, 1757-1836

These lines were written in 1965 to fill what Dr. Christians considered a need for a "specific World-Wide Communion Hymn." In a letter dated January 6, 1970, Dr. Christians says, "We [his organist, G. Leland Ralph] presented the hymn in its original form in 1965, and we continued to revise it during the coming year. In 1966 it was entered in the Religious Arts Festival of Sacramento . . . and it won Special Honors. Mary Beth Fulton, of Riverside Church in New York City, asked me about it, and I sent a copy to her. That's how it got into the light." The hymn was used in a citywide worship service that concluded the Festival of Religious Art in 1966.

Wilbur Carl Christians is the senior minister of the two-thousand-member First Baptist Church, Sacramento, California, a position he has held with distinction for nineteen years. He is a graduate of Denison University (A.B.) and Colgate Rochester Divinity School (B.D.). He has studied at the University of Rochester, the University of Chicago, the University of California, and the American School of Oriental Research in Jerusalem. The Berkeley Baptist Divinity School awarded him the Doctor of Divinity degree. Dr. Christians is in demand as a public speaker and lecturer, appears regularly on radio and television, and is active in community affairs. He is a member of the board of the

American Red Cross, and was recently appointed to the California Division of the National Council on Crime and Delinquency. He has traveled extensively, preaching, speaking, and conducting Spiritual Life Retreats at home and abroad. He recently returned from a round-the-world tour under the aegis of the United States Air Force.

WINDHAM was composed by Daniel Read, one of America's most important, and neglected, composers and compilers. This tune was first published in his *American Singing Book*, 1785. WINDHAM is found in a number of early American songbooks and is frequently set to Isaac Watt's hymn, "Broad Is the Road that Leads to Death."

Daniel Read was born in Attleboro, Massachusetts, November 16, 1757, and died in New Haven, Connecticut, December 4, 1836. Like many musicians of his time, he did not earn his living composing or publishing music, but rather as a proprietor of a general store. He was well known as a composer and compiler of such landmarks as *The American Song Book*, 1785, which saw six editions and *The American Musical Magazine*, 1786-1787, with several editions up to 1810. Irving Lowens devotes a full chapter to Read and his Letter-books in *Music and Musicians in Early America* (see Chapter 8).

347   Lord Christ, the Father's Mighty Son

HAMPTON POYLE 8.8.5.8.6.

Brian A. Wren, 1936-

Peter Warwick Cutts, 1937-

This hymn was written in 1962 and, after being used in two ecumenical student conferences, was published in *Dunblane Praises I* (Scottish Churches Music Consultation). Since then it has been quoted in David Cairns' book on the Lord's Supper, *In Remembrance of Me*, 1967, and has appeared in the *Contemporary Loose-Leaf Hymn-book*, 1968. It will be in the *New Catholic Hymnal* (Faber). The Lutheran Church of America is using it in a new collection entitled *Sing*, and it is under consideration for use in a publication by the Episcopal Church. Dr. Wren says this is his first successful attempt at hymn writing and that it came out of an "ecumenical student experience in the Student Christian Movement at Oxford, where I first felt the scandal of disunity."

Brian A. Wren was born at Romford, Essex, England, in 1936, was reared there and in London during World War II. He was baptized and received into membership at Upminster Congregational Church, Essex, on Whitsun, 1955, after which he served two years in the army. He took his degrees from New College, 1960 (in modern languages) and Mansfield College, Oxford 1962 (in theology). After doing research in Old Testament he left Mansfield College in 1965 to become the minister of the Hockley and Hawkwell Congregational Church, Essex, where he still serves (1970). In 1968 he received his D.Phil. degree at Oxford on the language of eschatology in the Old Testament prophets. In addition to writing several hymns Dr. Wren was a contributor to *Contemporary Prayers for Public Worship*, S.C.M. 1967.

HAMPTON POYLE appeared with this text in a hymnal entitled *Dunblane Praises I*. It was composed in 1962 and named after a small village near Oxford, England.

Peter Warwick Cutts, an honor graduate in music from Cambridge University, has been active in the Student Christian Movement. With Ian Mackensie he organized the Quadrennial Congress of the Student Christian Movement held at Bristol, England, in January, 1963, and introduced several new hymns and tunes to the conferees. Erik Routley says it was the first time music became a "subject of study in one of the study commissions." Cutts has composed several interesting hymn tunes in a style quite different from those of members of England's Light Music Group. His tunes have appeared in *Dunblane Praises I and II; New Songs for the Church I; A Hundred Hymns for Today*, 1969; *Hymns and Songs*, 1969; *The Methodist Hymnal* (U.S.A.) 1964; and in a booklet by the U.S.A. Lutheran Board of Publications. Mr. Cutts presently serves as Warden and Lecturer in Music and is in charge of college chapel music at Bretton Hall College of Education, West Bretton, Wakefield, Yorkshire.

348   I Love Thy Kingdom, Lord

ST. THOMAS S.M.

Timothy Dwight, 1752-1817
Williams' *New Universal Psalmodist*, 1770

Timothy Dwight is often referred to as the first American hymnist. This is probably due to his famous revision of Isaac Watts' *The Psalms of David* which hymnologists call "Dwight's Watts." Before this book was published in 1800 Psalm singing was considered the only proper congregational song in the American churches. Dwight, however, changed this by adding to the Watts' book thirty-three of his own paraphrases and hymns. The present hymn was one of these and authorities say it is not a paraphrase of Psalm 137, but was inspired by it. The addition of "hymns of human composure" to the songs of the church was a point of bitter debate in those days and Dwight's book may well have been the turning point which opened the way for the demise of exclusive use of the Psalms in worship and the birth of hymnody in America.

Timothy Dwight was born in Northampton, Massachusetts, May 14, 1752. He graduated from Yale in 1769 and was a tutor there from 1771 to 1777. For a time he was a chaplain in the Revolutionary Army and for his service and patriotism he won the attention and admiration of George Washington. He was a Congregational minister in Connecticut and in 1795 was appointed to the presidency of Yale. He died in Philadelphia, January 11, 1817, highly esteemed as an educator, teacher, preacher, and author.

ST. THOMAS has served American churches well for a hundred and fifty years or more. It was probably composed by Aaron Williams for Charles Wesley's hymn "Soldiers of Christ, Arise" to which it was set in Williams' *The Universal Psalmist*, 1763. There it was called HOLBORN and was of greater length. The present "shortened" form first appeared in *The New Universal Psalmist*, 1770. ST. THOMAS was a suggested tune for several hymns in the early Alexander Campbell hymnbooks and has been in continuous use by many denominations since its introduction to America.

Aaron Williams was born in London in 1731, and died there in 1776. He was the compiler and publisher of Psalm tune collections, a music engraver, a teacher of music and psalmody. American and English churches drew heavily from his books for some of their best tunes.

349 Built on the Rock the Church Doth Stand

KIRKEN DEN ER ET 8.8.8.8.8.8.8.

Nicolai F. S. Grundtvig, 1783-1872
Tr. Carl Doving, 1867-1937
Revised, Fred C. M. Hansen, 1888-

Ludvig M. Lindeman, 1812-1887

Nicolai Frederik Severin Grundtvig published this hymn in his *Sang-Värk til den Danske Kirke* in 1837. He was born at Udby, Seeland, in 1783, the son of a Lutheran pastor. After graduating from the University of Copenhagen he became a teacher of history and an assistant to his father. In 1811 he was ordained and became a controversial figure in church affairs which led to his suspension for thirteen years. He was finally permitted to resume preaching for the afternoon services at a German church in Christianhavn. In 1839 he was fully reinstated and appointed chaplain to the hospital Vartou where he remained until his death on September 2, 1872. He was given the honorary title of Bishop in 1863 by Fredrik VII. Grundtvig has been called the most important hymn writer of the nineteenth century. Julian adds that he was the "Great Danish reformer of hymnology and theology" (p. 1001). Five volumes of his poems and hymns were published after his death with the title, *Hymns and Spiritual Songs*.

Carl Doving, noted Norwegian hymnologist, was a member of a committee appointed by three Norwegian synods to prepare an English hymnal. This was published as the *Lutheran Hymnary, 1913*, in which this translation was given to America.

Fred C. M. Hansen was born June 25, 1888 at Vejle, Denmark. His parents, Peder and Marie (Mortensen), immigrated to America in 1890. He was educated at Dana College, the University of Nebraska, and Trinity Seminary after which he was ordained pastor of the United Evangelical Lutheran Church (1914). He served churches in Davenport, Iowa (1914-18), Audubon, Iowa (1918-28), Milwaukee, Wisconsin (1928-36), Council Bluffs, Iowa (1936-43) and Chicago, Illinois (1943-58). From 1959 until 1961 Pastor Hansen served various interim pastorates. He served terms as president of the Iowa District and Illinois District of his church and was for ten years a member of the Board of Charities. He was one of the translators for the *Hymnal for Church and Home*, 1927. He died at Blair, Nebraska, April 4, 1965.

The tune was written for this text by Ludvig Mathias Lindeman and first appeared in W. A. Wexel's *Christelige Psalmer*. Born at Trondheim, Sweden, November 28, 1812, his first academic interests were in theology, but by 1840 he had decided to become a musician. He was appointed organist of Our Saviour's Church at Christiania and teacher of singing at the theological seminary. With the help of his son, he established a school of music which later became the Oslo Conservatory of Music. Lindeman was an avid collector and publisher of Norwegian Folk Music which may account for the folk character of this tune.

350 Forgive, O Lord, Our Severing Ways

EISENACH L.M.

John Greenleaf Whittier, 1807-1892, and others
Johann Hermann Schein, 1586-1630
Harm. J. S. Bach, 1685-1750

It has been established that the first stanza of this hymn is not by Whittier. Its source is unknown but it does reflect the spirit of the Quaker poet in his call for a truly ecumenical church. The second stanza is from Whittier's hymn, "Amidst These Glorious Works of Thine" which he wrote for the dedication of the Unitarian House of Worship in San Francisco, 1864. Omitted stanzas are as follow:

2) Thy grace impart; in time to be
Shall one great temple rise to Thee—
One Church for all humanity.

3) White flowers of love its wall shall climb,
Soft bells of peace shall ring its chime,
Its day shall all be holy time.

5) That song shall swell from shore to shore,
One hope, one faith, one love restore
The seamless robe that Jesus wore.

For a note on John Greenleaf Whittier see No. 85.

This tune appears in a variety of forms and with a variety of names such as MACH'S MIT MIR GOTT, LEIPSIC, and STUTTGART. This is actually a later form of the melody by Schein.

The composer was born January 29, 1586, at Grünhain, Saxony, and died at Leipzig, November 19, 1630. He was the son of a Lutheran pastor. He began his education as a chorister in the Dresden Court Chapel and continued at the Gymnasium of Schulpforta and the University of Leipzig. For a short time he was kapellmeister at Weimar and then became cantor of Thomasschule at Leipzig where he remained until his death. It is interesting that he was born almost a century before Bach and worked in the same places. Schein is renowned for his collection of old and new chorale melodies which were arranged for congregational use. The collection was published in 1627 under the title *Cantional oder Gesangbuch Augsburgischer Confession*; a second edition appeared in 1645. This book is said to have contained over two hundred chorale melodies of which eighty were from his own pen. He was not only a composer, but was also represented in that collection as a poet and harmonizer.

For a note on J. S. Bach see No. 193.

351   Our Father, Thou Almighty God

ALL SAINTS NEW C.M.D.

Russell F. Harrison, 1918-
Henry S. Cutler, 1824-1902

Under the title "God's Power Redeems the World" this hymn was written in 1961 and was first published on the inside cover of the Christian Board of Publication bulletin for the Easter Week of Prayer Services, 1962. Dr. Harrison states that the inspiration for the hymn came from his thought on the approaching Third Assembly of the World Council of Churches to be held at New Delhi, India, under the theme "Jesus Christ . . . the Light of the World." He says further that he was challenged to action by the leader of a chapel service at the Missions Building in Indianapolis, who emphasized the fact that few worthy hymns were being written today and raised the question, Why? Viewing this as a challenge, Dr. Harrison returned to his desk and wrote the words to this tune at one sitting, making practically no revisions in his second and final draft.

Russell F. Harrison was born December 28, 1918, at DuQuoin, Illinois. He was educated in the public schools of Granite City, attended Brown's Business College in East St. Louis, was graduated from Southern Illinois University, B.Ed.; and Lexington Theological Seminary, B.D. He was ordained to the Christian ministry by Dr. A. W. Fortune and Dr. Stephen J. Corey at Central Christian Church, Lexington, Kentucky, in 1945. After serving on the staff of the Kentucky Christian Missionary Society, he became director of youth program in the Department of Christian Education of The United Christian Missionary Society of the Christian Church (Disciples of Christ). For several years he served as chairman of youth work in the National Council of Churches. Dr. Harrison has written three books in the field of youth work and contributed many articles to *World Call, The Christian,* and other church publications. He has also edited a number of books.

Dr. Harrison resigned his post in 1955 to become associate general secretary of the ecumenical body known as the World Council of Christian Education, traveling extensively throughout the world. In 1959 he returned to the Christian Church, serving as executive secretary in the World Outreach Education Department until June 30, 1969.

Since 1969 Dr. Harrison has been executive coordinator of Planning and Research for the Christian Church, serving in the offices of the Division of Church Life and Work of The United Christian Missionary Society.

ALL SAINTS NEW first appeared in J. Ireland Tucker's *Hymnal with Tunes Old and New,* 1872. It was composed for Reginald Heber's hymn, "The Son of God Goes Forth to War."

Henry Stephen Cutler, a controversial American church musician, was born in Boston, Massachusetts, October 13, 1824, and holds the distinction of having introduced robed choirs to American churches. After basic musical training in Boston he went to Frankfurt, Germany, for further study. As a result of extensive travel in England where he came under the influence of the Oxford Movement, his interest in cathedral services was aroused to such an extent that upon his return to America in 1846 he instituted a robed choir of men and boys in Boston's Church of the Advent. He removed to New York City's Trinity Church in 1858 and remained there until he was "fired" on June 30, 1865, for going on a concert tour and being "absent without leave."

After serving churches in Brooklyn, Providence, Philadelphia, and Troy, Cutler retired in 1885 and made his home in Boston where he died December 5, 1902. Cutler composed anthems, service music, hymn tunes and published the *Trinity Psalter,* 1864, and *Trinity Anthems,* 1865.

352   *Lord, We Thank Thee for Our Brothers*

AUSTRIAN HYMN 8.7.8.7.D.

Roger K. Powell, 1914-

Franz Joseph Haydn, 1732-1809

Roger K. Powell wrote this hymn when he was the minister of the Baptist church in Camillus, New York, for a union Thanksgiving service in 1948.

The hymn was introduced at the organization meetings of the National Council of Churches in 1950 and has appeared in several hymnals, both Catholic and Protestant. Several tunes have been used with it, but it was written for Haydn's *Austria* and hence it is this musical theme which is becoming wed to the words.

Roger Kingsley Powell was born August 4, 1914, at Kingston, New York. He was educated at Syracuse University (B.A.), Colgate Rochester Divinity School (B.D.) and the University of Rochester (M.A.). After ordination as an American Baptist minister Mr. Powell held pastorates in New Berlin, New York and Camillus, New York. In 1952 he was appointed Registrar and Instructor in Speech at Colgate Rochester Divinity School, Rochester, New York, where he remained until February, 1970. He is currently Assistant Director of Extended Services in the College of Continuing Education at Rochester Institute of Technology.

For a note on the AUSTRIAN HYMN and Franz Joseph Haydn see No. 354.

353   O Church of God, Divided

BLOMSTERTID 7.6.7.6.D.

Marion Franklin Ham, 1867-1956

Swedish *Koralbok,* 1697

Although a number of Marion Ham's hymns have appeared in various hymnals, "O Church of God, Divided" seems to have been published only in *Christian Worship, a Hymnal,* 1943, where it was given at No. 433 with permission of the Beacon Press which suggests it was probably first published in a book of his poems.

Marion Franklin Ham, an American Methodist Unitarian, was born at Harveysburg, Ohio, on February 18, 1867. For a time he was a newspaper reporter and bank clerk in Chattanooga, Tennessee. He was ordained to the ministry in 1898 and began his ministry in Chattanooga. In 1904 he moved to Dallas, Texas, and served a church there for five years. From 1909 he served the Community Church in Reading, Massachusetts. He wrote three slight volumes of poetry under the titles, *The Golden Shuttle,* 1896, *Songs of the Spirit,* 1932, and *Songs of Faith and Hope,* 1940. He died in 1956.

BLOMSTERTID is from the Swedish *Koralbok,* 1697. So far as we have been able to ascertain, the tune appears here for the second time in an American hymnal, the first being at No. 449 in the *Lutheran Service Book and Hymnal,* 1958.

354 *Glorious Things of Thee Are Spoken*

AUSTRIAN HYMN 8.7.8.7.D.

John Newton, 1725-1807

Franz Joseph Haydn, 1732-1809

This hymn appeared in the *Olney Hymns, Book One,* 1779, with the title "Zion, or the City of God." It has been called the "only joyful hymn in the collection." These hymns were written for use in the church and at prayer meetings at the Great House at Olney.

John Newton summarized his life when he composed his own epitaph, which reads:

> John Newton, Clerk,
> Once an infidel and libertine,
> A servant of slaves in Africa,
> Was by the rich mercy of our Lord and Saviour, Jesus Christ,
> Preserved, restored, pardoned,
> And appointed to preach the Faith
> He had long laboured to destroy.

Newton was born in London, July 24, 1725, and died there December 21, 1807. At the age of eleven he went to sea and became an "abandoned and godless sailor" who deserted the navy, lived in total degradation with a slave trader in Africa. At the age of twenty-three he became the commander of his own slave ship. Earlier, he had read Thomas a Kempis and the insights he gained from that eventually led him to abandon the slave trade and begin studies in Hebrew and Greek as a follower of Whitfield, Wesley, and other nonconformists.

After nine years of study, Newton applied for ordination to the Archbishop of York but was refused. Afterward the Bishop of Lincoln ordained him and sent him to the curacy of Olney where he became an intimate friend to William Cowper. Cowper and Newton collaborated in producing the famous *Olney Hymns* in which 280 were by Newton and 68 were by Cowper.

Newton's final years were spent in the heart of the Evangelical movement as rector of St. Mary, Woolnoth, London (1780-1807).

AUSTRIAN HYMN is believed to be based on a Croatian folk tune. Franz Joseph Haydn composed it for the nationalistic hymn "Gott, erhalte Franz, den Kaiser" by Haschka. It was first performed for the

Emperor's birthday on February 12, 1797. Haydn also used the theme in his famous "Emperor" *String Quartet Number 77.* Edward Miller introduced it into English collections in his *Sacred Music, etc.,* 1802 and since that time it has found its way into major hymnals of the English-speaking world.

Franz Joseph Haydn was born at Rohrau, Austria, March 31, 1732. He began his musical career as a student of a cousin whose influence remained with him throughout his life. As a chorister at St. Stephen's in Vienna he developed his singing voice and developed his ability at playing the clavier and violin. Unfortunately, he was not taught harmony or composition and was thus forced to learn this art through his own dedication and effort.

After a brief stint as music director to Count Ferdinand Maximilian Morizin he received an appointment as kapellmeister to Prince Paul Anton Esterhazy, remaining in the service of the family until his death on May 31, 1809. In this position he was associated with the best musicians, had an excellent band at his disposal, and was given utmost freedom for composition and experimentation. By 1766 his music was known throughout the major cities of western Europe and London.

Haydn made two trips to England where he received the deepest affection, praise, and attention of the realm. He composed prodigiously, conducted his works and earned great respect and many honors, one of which was an honorary Doctor of Music degree from Oxford. His most excellent compositions at that time were the London or Soloman Symphonies which firmly established the form of that genre of musical composition.

Haydn produced a phenomenal number of compositions representing all forms, but his symphonies and string quartets remain the best known of all. His church music includes such favorites as "The Creation," "The Seven Words on the Cross" (originally instrumental), fourteen masses, a number of offertories, two Te Deums, and four motets.

355 Christ Is the King!

SOUTH GORE 8.8.8.8.8.8.

George Kennedy Allen Bell, 1883-1958
Ronald Arnatt, 1930-

This hymn was written especially for the enlarged *Hymns of Praise,* 1931, where it appears with the tune LLANGOEDMOR. Originally, it was in four stanzas. Here we use the composite altered version of the first and second stanzas as given in *The Hymnal, 1940,* and the original third and fourth stanzas. The alteration makes use of the opening phrase, "Christ is the King! O friends . . ." and then continues with the word "upraise" proceeding with the remainder of the second stanza.

Born on Hayling Island in 1883 George Kennedy Allen Bell was interested in the ecumenical movement and for a time served as president of the World Council of Churches. He was educated at Westminster and Christ Church, Oxford, won the Newdigate Prize for English verse, and became a Fellow of his college. After serving as curate at Leeds for several years he became chaplain to the Archbishop of Canterbury, dean of Canterbury, and bishop of Chichester from 1929 until his death in 1958. He wrote both poetry and prose; the latter dealing mainly with social and religious problems.

SOUTH GORE was composed for this text and the *Hymnbook for Christian Worship.* South Gore is the name of the street in Webster Groves, Missouri, on which Dr. Arnatt lives.

Ronald Arnatt, an American concert organist, composer, and conductor, was born in London on January 16, 1930. He attended Westminster Abbey Choir School; King's College Choir School, Cambridge; Trent College, Derbyshire; Trinity College of Music, London; and Durham University. He is a Fellow of Trinity College, London, and of the American Guild of Organists and is a D.Mus. of Westminster Choir College, Princeton, New Jersey. After migrating to the United States in 1947 he held positions in Washington, D. C., and founded the Washington Cantata Chorus. In 1954 he was appointed director of music and organist at Christ Church Cathedral, St. Louis. From 1954 to 1968 he was director of music at Mary Institute, St. Louis. In 1968 he was appointed associate professor of music at the University of Missouri in St. Louis.

Dr. Arnatt founded and is music director and conductor of the St. Louis Chamber Orchestra and Chorus.

356 *Thy Hand, O God, Has Guided*

REX SUMMAE MAJESTATIS 7.6.7.6.D.

E. H. Plumptre, 1821-1891

A. Gregory Murray, 1905-

Edward Hayes Plumptre's hymn was included in *Supplemental Hymns to Hymns Ancient and Modern,* 1889. These lines are stanzas 1, 2, 4, and 6, of the six stanzas given in the *Historical Companion to Hymns Ancient and Modern.*

For a comment on Edward Hayes Plumptre see No. 97.

REX SUMMAE MAJESTATIS was written for the composer's own translation of a low mass offertory hymn beginning with these words. It is given as "O King of might and splendor" in the *People's Mass Book*, 1964.

Anthony Gregory Murray, an English Roman Catholic priest, was born in 1905. He was educated at Westminster Cathedral Choir School (London) where he was a choir boy and pupil-assistant to organist Richard Terry. When he was only seventeen years of age, he earned his diploma as a Fellow of the Royal College of Organists. For ten years (1930-1940) he served as director of music and organist at Downside Abbey and School after his graduation from Christ's College, Cambridge. He did parochial work for twelve years and then returned to Downside where he continued his work (1952). He made valuable contributions to the *Westminster Hymnal*, 1940, in the form of harmonizations and original hymn tunes. As an authority on Gregorian Chant, Dom Gregory recently published the important book, *Gregorian Chant According to the Manuscripts*, 1963.

357   *Father, Let Me Dedicate*

DEDICATION 7.5.7.5.D.

Lawrence Tuttiett, 1825-1897

George A. Macfarren, 1813-1887

This New Year's hymn was included in Tuttiett's *Germs of Thought on the Sunday Special Service,* 1864, and was written to fill the need for more hymns related to the New Year.

Lawrence Tuttiett, a son of a Royal Navy surgeon, was born at Cloyton, Devonshire, 1825. He was educated at Christ's Hospital, where he fully intended to follow in his father's footsteps, and then at King's College, London.

Having decided to devote his life to the church rather than to medicine, he took Holy Orders in 1848 and began a long career which concluded as prebendary in St. Ninian's Cathedral, Perth, Scotland. He authored several manuals of prayers, a number of prose works and several books of hymns. He died May 21, 1897.

George Alexander Macfarren was indeed a remarkable person. He was born in London on March 3, 1813, and began his study of music at the Royal Academy of Music at the age of fourteen. His major interest was in composition and the trombone. His talent was such that he was made a faculty member when he was only twenty-two years of age, a position he retained until his death on October 31, 1887. He succeeded Sternhold Bennett both as principal of the Royal Academy and as professor of music at Cambridge University. Total blindness did not deter his activities as a composer and teacher, and despite this tragedy he continued his work by dictating his compositions. Arthur Sullivan, George Grove, and Macfarren received their knighthood the same year, 1883.

His compositions included all forms of music, both vocal and instrumental. An interesting article on his life and work appears in Grove's *Dictionary of Music and Musicians.*

358 *God Is Working His Purpose Out*

PURPOSE Irregular

Arthur Campbell Ainger, 1841-1919

Martin Shaw, 1876-1958

"For the earth shall be filled with the knowledge of the glory of the Lord, as the waters cover the sea," Habakkuk 2:14, was the inspiration for this hymn. It was written at Eton in 1894, dedicated to Archbishop Benson, and first published in leaflet form.

The author was born at Blackheath, July 4, 1841. He was educated at Eton and Trinity College, Cambridge. After graduation with honors he returned to Eton and remained there as an assistant master until his retirement in 1901. It is said that he was "one of the most distinguished and useful of Eton masters, a man with a clear head, controlling character, wide accomplishments, a fine and habile scholar of the old school, with a remarkable memory, an incisive speaker, a good critic, fertile in suggestion, complete in execution . . ." (Quoted by Moffatt and Patrick in their *Handbook to the Church Hymnary,* Revised Edition, p. 248). Ainger died at Eton on May 26, 1919.

PURPOSE was especially written for this hymn and first appeared in the *Enlarged Songs of Praise,* 1931. Martin Shaw and Ralph Vaughan Williams were coeditors of the musical portions of the book.

For a comment on Martin Shaw see No. 2.

359   *Another Year Is Dawning*

AURELIA 7.6.7.6.D.

Frances Ridley Havergal, 1836-1879

Samuel Sebastian Wesley, 1810-1876

"Another Year Is Dawning" was written in 1874 as the text for a New Year's greeting card which Miss Havergal distributed to her friends. It was entitled, "A Happy New Year! Ever Such May It Be."

Miss Havergal, the youngest daughter of William Henry Havergal, was born at Astley, England, December 14, 1836. She was a precocious child and was reading at the age of three and writing verses by her seventh year. She delighted in learning languages, mastering French, Latin, German, Greek, Italian, and Hebrew. Educated in English and German boarding schools Miss Havergal was a product of a highly cultured environment and her home life contributed to her deeply devotional nature. She authored many hymns and several hymn tunes, one of which is HERMAS. Miss Havergal died at Caswell Bay near Swansea, Wales, on June 3, 1879.

AURELIA was composed especially for "The Voice that Breathed O'er Eden," a wedding hymn by John Keble. Before it was used with that hymn, however, Wesley had been asked to be the musical editor for Charles Kemble's *Selection of Psalms and Hymns.* The composer used his tune for three sections of St. Bernard's hymn, the last of which was "Jerusalem, the Golden." The name can be traced to the Latin word, *aurum* (gold) to Aurelius (glorious, brilliant), ultimately to the feminine form "Aurelia."

Samuel Sebastian Wesley was one of England's great church musicians. A descendent of Charles Wesley, Samuel Sebastian was born in London, August 14, 1810. At the age of ten he was playing the organ for church services. From that time on he held organist positions in such places as Hereford Cathedral, Exeter Cathedral, Leeds Parish

Church, Winchester Cathedral, and Gloucester Cathedral. He composed numerous anthems, several sacred services, and many organ pieces and exercises. He died at Gloucester, April 19, 1876.

360   Lord, Thou Hast Set an Open Door

PARIS 8.10.10.10.

Roger K. Powell, 1914-

William Billings, 1746-1800

Mr. Powell tells us he wrote this hymn in the mid 1950's at the request of a minister who had been searching in vain for a new and fresh hymn dealing with the New Year theme.

For a note on Roger K. Powell see No. 352.

PARIS was composed by William Billings, one of the earliest American musicians whose hymn tunes, anthems, fuguing tunes, and collections of his works are considered to be landmarks in the history of American music. A tanner by trade, Billings was an uneducated enthusiast of choral music. He was born in Boston on October 7, 1746, lived through the tumult of the Revolutionary War and died in Boston, September 29, 1800. His pioneering spirit on behalf of good church music in America led him to leave the tanner's trade and devote his full time and energy to promoting choral singing through singing schools. His lusty primitivism was often criticized by his more highly educated contemporaries but his music enjoyed wide popularity throughout the colonies. His CHESTER was one of the hit tunes of the Revolutionary War and might be classed with "Over There" or "God Bless America" in popularity.

His famous fuguing tunes introduced points of imitation in musical composition to the Puritan culture of New England which hitherto had sung only the austere Psalm tunes. It goes without saying that the boldness of this man came under criticism by the establishment. It is said that he also was the first American to use the pitch pipe and the cello in church choirs. Students of Americana should be proud of the following Billings publications: *The New England Psalm Singer,* 1770; *The Singing Master's Assistant,* 1776; *Music in Miniature,* 1779; *The Psalm Singer's Amusement,* 1781; *The Suffolk Harmony,* 1786; and *The Continental Harmony,* 1794.

361 Sing to the Great Jehovah's Praise

LOBT GOTT IHR CHRISTEN C.M.

Charles Wesley, 1707-1788

Melody by Nikolaus Herman,
c. 1485-1561

In 1750 the Wesleys published two hymn tracts; one was *Hymns for New Year's Day*, the other *Hymns Occasioned by the Earthquake, March 8th.* The former contained seven new hymns for New Year's Day. The present hymn was number seven in the eleven-page pamphlet. Our version consists of stanza one and the first half of stanza two. The repetition of the last line as given here does not appear in the original which was in three stanzas of eight lines each. Alterations include "Inspires" for Wesley's "Demands" in stanza one; "His" for "Whose" in stanza two; and "and thy continued" for "Thy still-continued" in the final stanza.

For a note on Charles Wesley see No. 180.

For a note on the tune and composer see No. 138.

362 Praise to God, Your Praises Bring

SAVANNAH 7.7.7.7.

William C. Gannett, 1840-1923, alt.

The Foundery Collection, 1742

From the gifted Unitarian hymnwriter and poet comes this hymn for the changing seasons. It was written for a harvest festival in St. Paul, Minnesota, in 1872 and appeared in a compilation he jointly edited with Frederick Lucian Hosmer entitled, *The Thought of God in Hymns and Poems*, 1885. The original began "Praise to God and thanksgiving" and ended "Praise and love and thanksgiving." Here we have omitted the original fourth stanza.

William Channing Gannett, who was born in Boston, 1840, and died in New York, 1923, was educated at Harvard and then at the Harvard Divinity School. He became a Unitarian minister in 1868. From 1889 until 1908 he served the First Unitarian Church in Rochester, New

York. In addition to the works mentioned above, his publications included *A Year of Miracle,* 1882, *The Childhood of Jesus,* 1890, and *Frances David,* 1914.

SAVANNAH also appears under the names HERRNHUT, IRENE, SUMMER EDYFIELD, and LATROBE. The original source is unknown but it is believed to have come from Germany. Its first appearance in England seems to have been in the famous *Foundery Collection,* the first Methodist tune book, compiled by John Wesley for use in the Foundery Chapel. It has been conjectured that Wesley may have heard the tune sung by Moravians aboard ship during his voyage to Savannah, Georgia, in 1735. HERRNHUT was the Moravian haven built on the estate of Count von Zinzendorf in Saxony and IRENE was the name of the ship on which Wesley traveled to America.

363 Ring Out the Old, Ring In the New

DEUS TUORUM MILITUM L.M.

Alfred Tennyson, 1809-1892
Grenoble Antiphoner, 1868

This hymn is from Tennyson's *In Memoriam,* 1850, section 106, stanzas 2, 4, 7, and 8.

For a further comment on *In Memoriam* and Alfred Tennyson see No. 15.

DEUS TUORUM MILITUM is the tune used for these words in *Songs of Praise,* 1926.

For a further comment on this tune see No. 256.

364 Great God, We Sing That Mighty Hand

WAREHAM L.M.

Philip Doddridge, 1702-1751
William Knapp, 1698-1768

Job Orton, a close friend of Philip Doddridge, gathered the hitherto unpublished hymns of the poet and published them as *Hymns founded on Various Texts in the Holy Scriptures* in 1755. This hymn is from that collection and was specified for the New Year.

Philip Doddridge, the youngest of twenty children, was born to a London merchant on June 26, 1702. The Duchess of Bedford offered to provide him with a university education in order for him to be ordained into the Anglican ministry but he refused and entered a nonconformist seminary at Kibworth instead. He began his preaching career in 1723 at Kibworth. In 1729 he began a twenty-two-year ministry at Castle Hill Meeting, Northampton, where he also trained two hundred young men from Scotland, Holland, and England for the dissenting ministry and other professions. His great learning was recognized throughout the land. The University of Aberdeen honored him with a Doctor of Divinity Degree, and his close friends included such personages as Isaac Watts, and John and Charles Wesley. Doddridge died of tuberculosis in Lisbon, Portugal, October 26, 1751, where he had gone for rest and a possible cure for the disease.

WAREHAM is named after the birthplace of the composer. The town came into existence in England's pre-Roman days, was the scene of much bloodshed during the Danish invasions, and was once destroyed by Canute. The tune is also called ALL SAINTS and BLANFORD TUNE. It first appeared in Knapp's *Sett of New Psalm Tunes,* 1738, where it was set to Psalm 38 in three meter. In his *New Church Melody,* 1754, Knapp cast it in four meter for Psalm 139. WAREHAM has been called one of the best congregational tunes ever written.

William Knapp was born at Wareham in 1698 and died there in 1768. It is believed that he was an organist at Wareham before becoming the parish clerk at St. James in Poole, Dorset, a position he retained for thirty-nine years. He and the sexton, George Savage, must have established some sort of reputation for themselves through their work if we can trust this little poem which was published in the London Magazine, 1742:

> From pounce and paper, ink and pen,
>   Save me, O Lord, I pray;
> From Pope and Swift and such-like men,
>   And Cibber's annual lay;
> From doctor's bills and lawyer's fees,
>   From ague, gout, and trap;
> And what is ten times worse than these,
>   George Savage and Will Knapp.[1]

---

[1] By a fellow townsman, H. Price, and quoted by K. L. Parry and Erik Routley in *Companion to Congregational Praise,* London, 1953, p. 442.

365 Lord of the Church, We Humbly Pray

CORNWALL 8.8.6.D.

Charles Wesley, 1707-1788
Edward Osler, 1798-1863
Samuel Sebastian Wesley, 1810-1876

In his *Hymns and Sacred Poems*, 1749, Charles Wesley published the hymn, "O Thou Who at Thy Creature's Bar" from which he used a cento for another hymn, "Thou Jesu, Thou My Breast Inspire" which was published in the *Wesleyan Hymn Book*, 1780. From the latter hymn Edward Osler created the present hymn and published it in Hall's *Mitre Hymn Book*, 1836, and in a slightly altered form the following year is his own *Church and King*. The present text is appropriate for use with mission themes and services of ordination and installation. An omitted stanza reads:

> So may they live to thee alone,
> Then hear the welcome word, "Well done,"
> And take their crown above;
> Enter into their Master's joy,
> And all eternity employ
> In praise and bliss and love.

For a note on Charles Wesley see No. 180.

For a comment on Edward Osler see No. 79.

CORNWALL is one of 131 original hymn tunes published in Samuel Sebastian Wesley's anthology, *The European Psalmist*, 1872, where it was set to the words "O love divine, how sweet thou art." Cornwall is a place name in southwest England.

For a note on Samuel Sebastian Wesley see No. 359.

366 In This House by Men Constructed

PLEADING SAVIOR 8.7.8.7.D.

Herbert E. Hinton, 1890-
Joshua Leavitt's *Christian Lyre*, 1830

Dr. Hinton wrote this hymn for the dedication of the First Baptist Church and Sunday school building in West Hartford, Connecticut, in 1938. It was written specifically for the tune AUTUMN. He informs us that "copies were pasted in their hymnal and sung each anniversary for several years." Subsequently the hymn was used for the dedication of the new church school building of the First Baptist Church in Santa Ana, California, where it was sung to the AUSTRIAN tune on January 8, 1958, and again for the dedication of the new building of the First Baptist Church at Demarest, New Jersey, on the first Sunday in May of 1967, sung to the author's preferred tune AUTUMN. This is his only published hymn.

The original arrangement of the text as submitted to the publishers is as follows:

Dedication of a New Church Building

God of man, Thou great Creator,
    Thou the Architect Divine,
By thy law, perfected, ordered,
    All the universe is thine.
In this house by men constructed
    Wilt thou here thy children meet,
Hear our prayers, accept our worship,
    Grant communion pure and sweet?

Come we here with supplications,
    Come the lame, the lone, the sad;
Come we all to thee, our Father,
    Smile Thou on us, make us glad.
Open here the gate of heaven,
    Let this house thy threshold be;
May all hearts in need of comfort
    Here find life and peace in thee.

Just as thou didst lead our fathers
    Ever onward to the Light;
Lead thou us in faithful living,
    In thy love and in thy might.
Send us forth till all creation
    Sing thy praises, own thy sway;
Guide our hearts in loving service,
    By thy Light, thy Truth, thy Way. Amen

Herbert Ernest Hinton was born at Littleton, Massachusetts, on March 31, 1890, to English immigrant parents. He was the only one of nine children to graduate from high school. After grammar school he left home and worked his way through preparatory school, college, seminary, and postgraduate schools in preparation for the Baptist ministry. He was ordained on May 8, 1917. He is an alumnus of Bates College (B.A. 1917), Andover-Newton Theological Seminary (B.D. 1919), and the University of Cincinnati (M.A. 1927) and has also studied at Teacher's College of Columbia University and at Harvard. Bates College elected him to Phi Beta Kappa and conferred on him the Doctor of Divinity degree. Dr. Hinton has been a pastor, high school administrator, college teacher, denominational administrator and writer, and served twelve years as a Baptist missionary to Burma. He has deep interest in music and has enjoyed private study in voice, church music appreciation, and choir directing. In a letter to the writer, dated April 20, 1970, Dr. Hinton says, "As you will see I am now 80 years of age, but I was told by some kindly souls that my tenor solo last Sunday in Vespers was pleasing and hoped I'd do it again. I know my weakness, however, and choose easy ones these days. I love to sing."

PLEADING SAVIOR is apparently an early American hymn tune. William Jensen Reynolds, in his *A Survey of Christian Hymnody,* 1963, gives its source as *The Christian Lyre,* 1831, a collection of popular evangelical hymns intended for use in meetings conducted by evangelist Charles G. Finney. The tune appeared in *The Methodist Hymn Book of England,* 1933, under the name SALTASH and was credited to the *Plymouth Collection* (U.S.A.) 1855 with the suggestion that John Zundel may have composed it. (See Lightwood, *The Music of The Methodist Hymnbook,* No. 261.) Our copy of the *Original Sacred Harp,* 1911, notes that the tune was composed by William Walker about 1866. In that book it is set to an anonymous text which begins "Now see the Savior stands pleading." It has recently appeared with various texts in such hymnbooks as *Christian Hymns,* 1947; *The Brethren Hymnal,* 1951; and *The Hymnbook,* 1955. The first two of these give credit to *The Plymouth Collection,* 1855, while the latter recognizes the *Christian Lyre,* with permission of Oxford University Press.

367   *O Thou, Whose Own Vast Temple Stands*

DUNDEE C.M.

William Cullen Bryant, 1794-1878
Scottish Psalter, 1615

One of the first of America's great poets, William Cullen Bryant, wrote this hymn in 1835 for the dedication of a chapel in New

York City. It found its way into English hymnals two years later and since has appeared in a number of hymnals in America and England.

William Cullen Bryant, a native of Cunnington, Massachusetts, was born November 3, 1794. He was educated for law at Williams College. He began to practice law at Great Barrington in 1815 but retired ten years later to take up residence in New York City where he launched his literary career. He wrote about twenty-five hymns, most of which were printed privately in 1869. Bryant was the founder of the *New York Review* and for a time edited the *New York Evening Post.* He died June 12, 1878.

For a note on DUNDEE see No. 324.

368 *Jesus Friend, So Kind and Gentle*

DULCE CARMEN 8.7.8.7.8.7.

Philip E. Gregory, 1886-
"An Essay on the Church Plain
Chant," 1782

This hymn was written in order to afford the participation of the congregation in the baptism or dedication of infants. The first two stanzas may be used as a processional as the parents bring the child to the chancel, and the last stanza as a recessional.

Philip E. Gregory was born in London, England, in 1886. He came to the United States and was ordained as a Congregational minister in 1909. He studied at the University of Chicago and the Chicago Theological Seminary. He also studied philosophy in the Graduate School of the University of Minnesota. He served Congregational Churches in South Dakota, Wisconsin, Minnesota, and Illinois. In 1946 he became pastor of the Neighborhood Congregational Church of Laguna Beach, California, and served it until his retirement in 1956.

DULCE CARMEN is also known as ALLELUIA; CORINTH; WEBBE; ST. WERBERGH'S; GLORIA PATRI; LEBANON; WALPOLE; TANTUM ERGO; and ORIEL. Its earliest publication date has been traced to *An Essay on the Church Plain Chant*, 1782. This was a Roman Catholic collection of anthems, litanies, proses, and hymns used in public chapels in London. The setting was in two parts and no composer or source is given. It appeared again in 1792 in Webbe's *Collection of Motetts or Antiphons,* still anonymous but in modern notation. The present harmonization is essentially the same as that found in Monk's *Hymns Ancient and Modern,* 1861, and is identical to that found in the *English Hymnal,* 1933, and *The Hymnal,* 1940.

369   God of the Nations, Who from Dawn of Days

TOULON 10.10.10.10.

W. Russell Bowie, 1882-1969

Abridged from *Genevan Psalter,* 1551

For a comment on Walter Russell Bowie, see No. 222.

This hymn was originally published in *The Survey,* January, 1914, and first included in the hymnal, *Social Hymns of Brotherhood and Aspiration,* published the same year. The *Pilgrim Hymnal* was the first major denominational hymnal to use it.

TOULON is a shortened version of the grand old tune so long associated with Psalm 124 in the Genevan, Scottish, and German Psalters. The original tune contained four additional measures between the second and third lines as presented here.

It is sometimes attributed to Claude Goudimel, the famous French composer and theoritician, but most scholars say it was "composed or arranged by Louis Bourgeois" for the *Genevan Psalter,* 1551. It was introduced to England through Day's *Whole Booke of Psalmes,* 1563, and was used for several Psalms in the *Ainsworth Psalter* which was brought to America by the Pilgrims.

370   Eternal Father, Strong to Save

MELITA 8.8.8.8.8.8.

William Whiting, 1825-1878

John B. Dykes, 1823-1876

This is known as the United States Navy Hymn and was sung at the funeral of Franklin Delano Roosevelt in 1945 and played at the services for John F. Kennedy in 1963. William Whiting wrote other hymns but his fame rests entirely on this beautiful hymn which lifts up all those who go down to the sea in ships.

The author was born in London, November 1, 1825. He was for several years master of Winchester College Choristers' School. The hymn was written in 1860 and was included in a revised form in *Hymns Ancient and Modern,* 1861.

In all John B. Dykes submitted seven tunes to be included in *Hymns Ancient and Modern,* 1861. MELITA was composed for this text and appeared with it in *Hymns Ancient and Modern,* 1861. The name is an ancient form of the island Malta, the refuge of Paul after the shipwreck as related in Acts 28:1.

For a comment on John Bacchus Dykes see No. 195.

371   My Country, 'Tis of Thee

AMERICA 6.6.4.6.6.6.4.

Samuel F. Smith, 1808-1895

Anonymous in *Thesaurus Musicus,* 1744

This well-known and beloved patriotic hymn was written by Samuel F. Smith while he was a student at Andover Theological Seminary. The author gave 1832 as the year he wrote the poem. However, William Jenson Reynolds tells us in his *Hymns of Our Faith* that a copy of the text appeared on a program celebrating American Independence, July 4, 1831, held in the Park Street Congregational Church, Boston, and was designated to be sung by the juvenile choir under the direction of Lowell Mason. The hymn was first published in Lowell Mason's *The Choir, or Union Collection of Church Music,* 1832.

Samuel F. Smith was born in Boston, Massachusetts, October 21, 1808. He was educated at Harvard and Andover Theological Seminary and became one of the outstanding Baptist ministers of his era. For a time he edited the *Baptist Missionary Magazine.* While he was pastor of a church in Waterville, Maine, he also taught modern languages at Colby College (Waterville, Maine). He became pastor of the Baptist Church at Newton Center, Massachusetts, in 1842. He wrote about a hundred hymns and with Baron Stow compiled the popular Baptist hymnal, *The Psalmist,* 1843. He resigned this pastorate in 1854 in order to devote his energies to the American Baptist Missionary Union. His work gave him the opportunity to visit Baptist missions in Asia and Europe in 1880, and resulted in the publication of his *Rambles in Mission Fields,* 1884. He died at Newton Center, Massachusetts, November 16, 1895.

AMERICA is of uncertain origin. It has long been used as the British National Anthem and has generally been assumed to have originated there but its popularity in Europe casts doubt on that theory. The tune has been variously ascribed to John Bull, Henry Purcell, James Oswald, Henry Carey, Lully, and Handel and has been used in major musical compositions by Beethoven, Von Weber, Brahms, and others. It has been reasonably established that it was brought to America by William C. Woodbridge who brought a number of hymnals and tune books with him from a visit to Germany and gave them to Lowell Mason. Mason, unable to read German, showed the books to Samuel F. Smith who found the tune in one of them and apparently wrote his text for it. It appears to have been always associated with nationalistic or patriotic texts.

372   *Thou Judge by Whom Each Empire Fell*

NUN FREUT EUCH 8.7.8.7.8.8.7.

Percy Dearmer, 1867-1936

Klug's *Geistliche Lieder,* Wittenberg, 1535

This hymn was first published in *Songs of Praise,* 1925. Dr. Dearmer, we read, wrote it out of a sense of need for more hymns to fit a number of good tunes cast in this particular meter as well as a need for more hymns dealing with the judgment of God.

For a note on Percy Dearmer see No. 107.

NUN FREUT EUCH, also LUTHER'S HYMN, derives its name from the first line of Martin Luther's hymn which begins *"Nun freut euch, lieben Christen gmein."* The text and music appeared together in Joseph Klug's *Geistliche Lieder,* 1535.

373 O God of Earth and Altar

LLANGLOFFAN 7.6.7.6.D.

Gilbert K. Chesterton, 1874-1936
Traditional Welsh Melody

First published in Henry Scott Holland's magazine the *Commonwealth,* this hymn was included in the *English Hymnal,* 1906.

Gilbert Keith Chesterton was one of England's great twentieth-century authors. He began his career by writing criticisms and reviews for London periodicals and became the prolific and controversial author of studies, short stories, poetry, and biography. He was born May 29, 1874, in Kensington, London, and received his education at St. Paul's School, London, and Slade School of Art. His work is sometimes categorized as impressionistic and symbolic which, according to one writer, made it easy for him to embrace the Roman Catholic faith in 1922. He died on June 14, 1936.

LLANGLOFFAN is a traditional Welsh melody of unknown origin. It seems to have made its first appearance in a hymnbook in D. Evans' *Hymnau a Thonau,* 1865. Here the tune is in the minor mode, which is typical of many Welsh tunes, but in some books it is cast in the major mode under the name LLANFYLLIN. (See the Canadian *Book of Common Praise,* 1938 and *The Hymnal 1940.*)

374 O Beautiful For Spacious Skies

MATERNA C.M.D.

Katharine Lee Bates, 1859-1929
Samuel A. Ward, 1847-1903

Written after a visit to the Columbian Exposition in Chicago, Illinois, then a visit to Colorado Springs, Colorado, and a trip to the summit of Pike's Peak in 1893, this patriotic song will enshrine the name Katharine Lee Bates in the hearts of Americans for years to come, the paradoxical nature of the text notwithstanding.

Miss Bates, the grand-daughter and daughter of Congregational ministers, was born in Falmouth, Massachusetts, August 12, 1859, and died in Wellesley, Massachusetts, March 28, 1929. She was educated at Wellesley College and, except for several years as a high school teacher, spent her life teaching English there. Miss Bates was the author of a *History of American Literature*, 1908, a collection of verse entitled *America the Beautiful*, 1911, *Fairy Gold*, 1916, and *Pilgrim Ship*, 1926. She received honoris causa degrees from Middlebury, Oberlin, and Wellesley Colleges.

MATERNA was composed for the hymn "O Mother Dear, Jerusalem," circa 1882. It first appeared in *The Parish Choir*, VIII No. 378 and then in a hymnal in 1894. In 1912 Miss Bates' text became associated with MATERNA through the efforts of the president of the Massachusetts Agricultural College.

Samuel Augustus Ward, a native of Newark, New Jersey, was born December 28, 1847. He was active in the musical life of the city as the operator of a music store, organist of Grace Episcopal Church, and founder-director of the Orpheus Club. In 1934 he was honored by the Schoolmen's Club and the children of the Newark Public Schools when a plaque was placed on the exterior wall of the parish hall of Grace Church. He died in Newark, September 28, 1903.

375   Before Thee, Lord, We Join Our Hearts

ROSEATE HUES C.M.D.

Mildred Harner Foltz, 1910-
Joseph Barnby, 1838-1896

These words were written in response to a request for new marriage and family life hymns which The Hymn Society of America made through *The Christian*. Mrs. Foltz writes, "I saw the request for submissions . . . , and having a few ideas and some strong feelings about what such a hymn should contain I jotted them down and worked on them until I was satisfied." The hymn first published in *Thirteen New Marriage and Family Life Hymns*, The Hymn Society of America, 1961.

Mildred Harner Foltz (Mrs. Ralph A.) was born in Phoenixville, Pennsylvania, August 16, 1910. She graduated from Chatham College, Pittsburgh, Pa., B.A., 1931. Mr. and Mrs. Foltz are active members of the East Dallas Christian Church where she was part-time secretary from 1952 until becoming a full-time staff member in 1957. Since 1964 she has been employed in the Accounting Department of Southern Methodist University. Mrs. Foltz tells us she has been writing poetry since her "talent" was discovered by an eighth-grade teacher. She won the Omega prize for poetry in her Junior year at Chatham College, and has since had poems published in *Bethany Guide* and *The Christian*.

ROSEATE HUES was composed in 1892 for Cecil F. Alexander's hymn, "The Roseate Hues of Early Dawn." The only instance we have found of its use with Mrs. Alexander's hymn is in *The Church Hymnal, revised and enlarged, Edition B,* 1899 (Episcopal) edited by Charles L. Hutchins. The tune appears to have had limited use in major denominational hymnals.

Joseph Barnby was a prolific hymn-tune writer. He was born in York, England, August 12, 1838, and died in London, January 28, 1896. His life was devoted to music. At the age of seven he began as a chorister at York Minster; at the age of twelve he was already appointed as organist; and was the music master at a school at the age of fifteen. He studied at the Royal Academy of Music, London, and was church organist in a number of churches. His reputation as a choral conductor was great. He conducted the Royal Choral Society, Cardiff Festival, South Wales Festival, London Music Society, and was appointed precentor and director of music at Eton. He was knighted in 1892. Barnby holds the distinction of being the first to conduct a performance of Bach's *St. Matthew Passion* in an English church. This he did at Westminster Abbey in 1871.

Barnby, the musical editor of *The Hymnary,* 1872, composed some two hundred and forty-six hymn tunes, as well as numerous other compositions for voices, organ, and piano.

376   O Love Divine and Golden

BLAIRGOWRIE (DYKES) 13.13.13.13.

John Samuel Bewley Monsell, 1811-1875
John B. Dykes, 1823-1876

The source of this hymn is difficult to trace. Julian gives the source as Monsell's *Spiritual Songs, etc.,* 1857, but later apologetically corrects himself and gives *Hymns of Love and Praise,* 1866. MacCutchan tells us the source is the *Spiritual Songs, etc.,* 1857, and leaves the matter there while Covert and Laufer say it is from *Hymns and Miscellaneous Poems,* 1837. To compound the problem for future compilers the present form of the text appears for the first time in this book. It consists of the first half of the first and third stanzas and omits the second stanza as given in *The Hymnbook,* 1955, *The Hymnal,* 1933 (both Presbyterian), and *The Methodist Hymnal,* 1939. The metrical indication is normally given as 7.6.7.6.D. Despite the problems involved in researching the source and text, the hymn is a welcomed addition to the hymnbook and helps fill a much-needed wedding or holy matrimony category.

For a note on John Monsell see No. 256.

BLAIRGOWRIE was composed by John B. Dykes in 1872 for the hymn, "The Voice that Breathed O'er Eden." (Dykes) simply distinguished it from another tune by the same name by Robert Thompson. BLAIRGOWRIE is the name of a town situated on an island to the northwest of Dundee, Scotland.

For a note on John B. Dykes see No. 195.

377   O Thou Whose Favor Hallows All Occasions

THOMAS CIRCLE 11.10.11.10.11.10.

Miriam Drury, 1900-
Lawrence D. Schreiber, 1933-

These words were written in 1960 and first published in pamphlet form in *Thirteen New Marriage and Family Life Hymns* by the Hymn Society of America, 1961. The hymns were used at the North American Conference on Church and Family held April 30 to May 5, 1961, at Cleveland, Ohio.

Miriam Drury (Mrs. Clifford Merrill Drury) is a native Californian and has lived there most of her life. She has written many hymns (words and music), anthems, and poems for both children and adults. A number of her hymns have been published by The Hymn Society of America and her stories, poems, and songs for children have appeared in Sunday school and grade school books. She is a past award winner of The Hymn Society of America.

THOMAS CIRCLE was composed in 1965 for this hymn and the *Hymnbook for Christian Worship.* The name designates the location of The

National City Christian Church in Washington, D.C., where Lawrence P. Schreiber is Minister of Music. The name was also chosen for the symbolic significance of the circle or ring in the wedding ceremony. For a note on Lawrence Schreiber see No. 59.

378   O Perfect Love

O PERFECT LOVE 11.10.11.10.

Dorothy F. Gurney, 1858-1932

Joseph Barnby, 1838-1896

"O Perfect Love" was written in 1883 for use at the wedding of Mrs. Gurney's sister. Six years later it became almost inseparably associated with this tune.

Dorothy Frances Blomfield was born in London in 1858. Her father and grandfather were Anglican clergymen and she married Gerald Gurney, himself ordained in the Church of England, and a son of an Anglican clergyman and hymn writer. Both Mrs. Gurney and her husband became Roman Catholics in 1919.

O PERFECT LOVE is arranged from the anthem Joseph Barnby composed in 1889 for the wedding of the Duke of Fife and Princess Louise of Wales. The hymn and tune have enjoyed wide popularity as a wedding hymn and have appeared in nearly all of the major denominational hymnals in America.

For a comment on Joseph Barnby see No. 375.

379   O Perfect Love

ZU MEINEM HERRN 11.10.11.10.

Dorothy F. Gurney, 1858-1932

Johann G. Schicht, 1753-1823

Harm. David Evans, 1874-1948

For a note on this hymn and author see No. 378.

ZU MEINEM HERRN was set to a German metrical version of Psalm 110 in the *Allgemeines Choralbuch* (Leipzig, 1819), edited by Johann G. Schicht and containing 306 of his own tunes.

Johann G. Schicht was born in Reichenau, Saxony, September 29, 1753. He is remembered today as a composer of chorales, an avid collector of J. S. Bach's manuscripts, and the first publisher of Bach's motets. Schicht received early training as an organist and pianist but entered the university at Leipzig to study law which he gave up after he was appointed pianist for Johann Adam Hiller's "Liebhaber-Konzerte" which became the famous Gewandhaus concerts in 1781. In 1785 Schicht succeeded Hiller as conductor of the concerto, a post he held until 1810 when he became cantor at Thomaskirche where J. S. Bach had served from 1723 to 1750. Schicht died in Leipzig on February 16, 1823. He composed oratorios, Te Deums, masses, motets, and published the edited works of Pleyel and Clementi, as well as the *Allgemeines Choralbuch* which contained 1,285 melodies, 306 of which were original.

For a note on David Evans see No. 381.

380   *As We Before Thine Altar Bow*

EMMANUEL L.M.

Franklin P. Frye, 1903-
Carl C. N. Balle, 1806-1855

This text was written in response to The Hymn Society of America's request for new hymns on marriage and family life. It was selected to be published in *Thirteen New Marriage and Family Life Hymns,* 1961, for use at the North America Conference on Church and Family Life at Cleveland, Ohio, 1961. Mr. Frye writes that, "It is the authors' hope that it may be used not only in the marriage service but as a prayer and guide for daily married life."

Born in 1903 at Tansworth, New Hampshire, Franklin Pierce Frye was educated at Wesleyan University, Middletown, Connecticut, and Boston University School of Theology. After serving as a supply pastor of Methodist churches in Connecticut he was ordained deacon (1925) and elder (1927) in The Methodist Church (now The United Methodist Church). He retired in 1965 after serving Methodist churches for forty years in New Hampshire and Massachusetts and is presently active as a free-lance preacher and writer. He is a member of The

Hymn Society of America; of World Federalists, USA; and a frequent contributor the *The Upper Room.*

The writer has been unable to find information on Carl C. N. Balle, the composer of the tune EMMANUEL. The tune is reported to have appeared in a number of Lutheran Hymnals in America during the early nineteen hundreds. It appears as Number 28 in the *Service Book and Hymnal,* Augsburg, 1958, and as Number 23 in the *Common Service Book of the Lutheran Church* [United Lutheran Church in America, 1917]. It was written in 1850 and has been commonly associated with Nicolai F. S. Grundveg's Christmas Hymn *"Det Kimer nu til Julefest."* Lester Hostetler writing in his *Handbook to the Mennonite Hymnody,* 1949, gives the composer's name as C. Belle.

381   O Father, All Creating

NYLAND 7.6.7.6.D.

John Ellerton, 1826-1893
Finnish Melody
Adapt. David Evans, 1874-1948; arranged

This wedding hymn was written at the request of the Duke of Westminster especially for the marriage of his daughter to the Marquess of Ormonde. It was written on January 29, 1876, and appears to have been first published in Thring's *Collection* in 1880.

For a comment on John Ellerton see No. 231.

NYLAND is a Finnish folk song which had its origin near the village of Kourtane and was named after the province of Nyland. It first appeared as a hymn tune in the 1909 edition of the Finnish Evangelical Lutheran Church hymnbook, *Susmen Evankelis Luteraisen Kirken Koraalikirja.* The Finnish Lutheran Church adapted and used twentynine folk tunes derived primarily from the research of Pastor O. Immanuel Colliander in this book. It was introduced to England through *The Church Hymnary Revised,* 1927, and given the name NYLAND by Millar Patrick, one of the members of the Revision committee. The tune is most familiar to American congregations as the setting to Anna Laetitia Waring's hymn, "In Heavenly Love Abiding."

David Evans was one of the great musicians of Wales. Born at Resolven, Glamorganshire, in 1874 and educated at Arnold College, Swansea; University College, Cardiff; and Oxford, Dr. Evans became a leading figure in Welsh music education and church music. After serving as organist and choirmaster at the Jewin Street Welsh Presbyterian Church in London he became Professor of Music at University College, Cardiff, and then Professor at the University of Wales. He served as chairman of the subcommittee on musical editorship for the Joint Revision committee of *The Church Hymnary,* 1927.

382   *Come, Bless the Lord*

Psalm 134:2

Austin C. Lovelace, 1919-

Psalm 134:2 provides the text for Austin C. Lovelace's setting for this introit. It was written for the chancel choir of the First Methodist Church, Evanston, Illinois, in 1955 and was first published in W. L. Jenkins' *Service Music for the Adult Choir,* 1956.

Austin C. Lovelace, a native of North Carolina, is a graduate of High Point College (A.B., 1939) and the School of Sacred Music, Union Theological Seminary (M.S.M. 1941; D.S.M. 1950). He was awarded an honorary Doctorate of Music by High Point College in 1963. He has held organist-director positions in churches in Nebraska, North Carolina, Illinois, New York, and Colorado and taught at the University of Nebraska; Queens College, Charlotte, North Carolina; Garrett Theological Seminary, Evanston, Illinois; Union Theological Seminary, New York; Iliff School of Theology, and Temple Buell College, both in Denver, Colorado. He is an active member of National Fellowship of Methodist Musicians, The Hymn Society of America, The American Guild of Organists, and the Choristers Guild. Dr. Lovelace has published articles in numerous religious and professional journals and is the author of four books, *Music and Worship in the Church; The Organist and Hymn Playing; The Youth Choir;* and *The Anatomy of Hymnody;* and coauthor of the *Companion to the Hymnal* (Methodist), 1970.

383 Enrich, Lord, Heart, Mouth, Hands in Me

WULFRUN 8.8.8.

George Herbert, 1593-1633, alt.

George W. Briggs, 1875-1959

These words are from Herbert's poem "Trinitie Sunday" which was included in his *The Temple,* 1633. The poem is in three stanzas, the first two of which follow.:

> Lord, who hast form'd me out of mud,
> And hast redeemed me through thy bloud,
> And sanctifi'd me to do good;

> Purge all my sinnes done heretofore:
> For I confesse my heavie score,
> And I will strive to sinne no more.

For a note on George Herbert see No. 83.

WULFRUN was composed for this text and appeared in *Hymns for Little Children.*

For a note on George W. Briggs see No. 305.

384 I Was Glad

Psalm 122:1

Austin C. Lovelace, 1919-

Written in 1955 for the chancel choir of First Methodist Church, Evanston, Illinois, this response was first published in W. L. Jenkins' *Service Music for the Adult Choir,* 1956.

For a note on Dr. Lovelace see No. 382.

385   Glory to Thee, O God Most High

MAINZER L.M.

Philip Gell's *Psalms and Hymns,* 1815
Joseph Mainzer, 1801-1851
Alt. and Harm. Austin C. Lovelace, 1919-

An anonymous version of the first part of the Te Deum, beginning "We Praise, We Worship Thee, O God" appeared in Philip Gell's *Psalms and Hymns,* 1815. Julian says this doxology was added to the hymn at a later date.

MAINZER was altered and harmonized by Austin C. Lovelace for *The Methodist Hymnal,* 1964, where it appears with Charles Wesley's hymn, "Author of Faith, Eternal Word." Routley informs us the tune was set to a version of Psalm 107 in Joseph Mainzer's *Choruses,* 1841. Dr. Lovelace tells us he based his arrangement on a version found in the *British Methodist Hymnal* and that his main alteration was in the rhythm.

Joseph Mainzer was born at Trier November 10, 1801, and died at Manchester, England, November 10, 1851. He was a musician, teacher, and publisher. Exiled from Poland during a revolution, he lived successively in Brussels, Paris, London, and Manchester, establishing successful singing schools and writing books on music pedagogy.

For a note on Dr. Lovelace see No. 382.

386   Praise to the Holiest in the Height

ST. MARY C.M.

John H. Newman, 1801-1890
Melody, *Prys' Psalter,* 1621

This hymn is from Newman's *The Dream of Gerontius,* 1865. It was first published in his *Verses on Various Occasions,* 1868, and in the same year it was included in the Appendix to *Hymns Ancient and Modern.*

For a note on John Henry Newman see No. 46.

ST. MARY has been a popular tune in English and American hymnody for many years. It was the tune for Psalm 2 in a Welsh psalter by Archdeacon Edmund Prys entitled *Llyfryy Psalmau*, 1621.

Edmund Prys (1541-1624), Welsh cleric, served several churches and chapels before becoming archdeacon of Merioneth and chaplain to the Lord President of Wales, Sir Henry Sidney, in 1576. He was appointed canon of St. Asaph's in 1602. His chief literary work was in translating the psalms into the Welsh language.

387 Lord, for the Mercies of the Night

FARRANT C.M.

John Mason, c. 1645-1694

Attr. to Richard Farrant, c. 1530-1580

This text is from John Mason's *Spiritual Songs, or Songs of Praise to Almighty God upon Several Occasions*, 1683, where it was given as a "morning" hymn.

John Mason, the son of a dissenting minister, was educated at Strixton School, Northhamptonshire, and Clare Hall, Cambridge. He remained faithful to the Church of England throughout his ministry despite close friendships with men of nonconformist bent. His hymns were probably used in public worship and may well have been among the earliest hymns so used by the Established Church. Shortly before his death he had a vision of Christ and preached a sermon he called "The Midnight Cry," proclaiming the approach of the Second Advent which brought people from far and wide to the site of the vision, Water-Stratford. We are told that "most extraordinary scenes occurred, singing and leaping and dancing." He continued to testify to his vision and exhort Christians to "trim their lamp" until his death on May 22, 1694.

FARRANT is adapted from the anthem, "Lord, for Thy Tender Mercies' Sake" which has been attributed to Richard Farrant. Edmund H. Fellowes writing in Grove's *Dictionary of Music and Musicians* points out that the anthem was by John Hilton (d. 1608) who was a lay clerk at Lincoln Cathedral (1584), and organist at Trinity College, Cambridge (1594). This harmonization of the melody is from William H. Havergal's *Old Church Psalmody*, 1847, and is credited to Dr. Edward

Hodges who left England to become organist-choirmaster at Trinity Church in New York City from 1846 to 1863.

Richard Farrant was an important sixteenth-century English composer. He became Gentleman of the Chapel Royal under Edward VI and later organist, master of the choristers, and lay clerk at St. George's, Windsor, holding this position until his death.

388   Bless the Lord, O My Soul

M. Ippolitof-Ivanoff, 1859-1935

This text is an adaptation of three verses of the *"Benedicite, omnia opera Domini"* with a musical response from Psalm 134:1. The "Benedicite" is derived from the "Song of the Three Hebrew Children" of the Apocrypha. It is a liturgical hymn of praise and is found in numerous medieval manuscripts for use at Lauds on Sunday.

The music is adapted from Ippolitof-Ivanoff's setting of a part of the Russian liturgy with the English text adapted by N. Lindsay Norden.

Mikhail Mikhailovich Ippolitof-Ivanoff (1859-1935) was a Russian conductor, composer, and teacher. He began his musical career as a child, playing the violin and singing in the choir of the Issaky Cathedral. He studied at the Moscow conservatory where he did his work in composition under Rimsky-Korsakov. His work as a professor and later director at the conservatory had great influence on Russian music. He composed an impressive list of compositions for the stage, orchestra, chamber groups, the church, as well as for individual instruments and vocal solos and duets.

389   Glory Be to God the Father

REX GLORIAE 8.7.8.7.D.

Christopher Wordsworth, 1807-1885, alt.

Henry Smart, 1813-1879

This is stanza eight of Wordsworth's hymn, "See the Conqueror Mounts in Triumph," which first appeared in his *Holy Year,* or *Hymns for Sundays and Holy Days,* 1862. The entire hymn is given in *The Hymnal, 1940* at 103.

For a note on Christopher Wordsworth see No. 175.

REX GLORIAE was first published with another version of this hymn in the Appendix to *Hymns Ancient and Modern,* 1868.

For a note on Henry Smart see No. 124.

390   This Is the Day the Lord Hath Made

TWENTY-FOURTH C.M.

Isaac Watts, 1674-1748

Probably by Lucius Chapin, 1760-1842

This is Dr. Watts' free paraphrase of Psalm 118:24-26 which appeared in his *Psalms of David,* 1719.

For a note on Isaac Watts see No. 48.

TWENTY-FOURTH also appears as PRIMROSE in a number of early American hymnbooks and is often set to Isaac Watts' "Salvation, O the Joyful Sound." In several of these old books the tune is given as a "folk tune," in others it is attributed to one Amzi Chapin (c. 1768) and still others to Lucius Chapin. We assume this is the same person. In George Pullen Jackson's *White Spirituals in the Southern Uplands,* 1933, the tune is given as one of the most popular in the Southern tradition. Nothing is known of Chapin other than that he was an excellent musician and a composer of much sacred music.

391   Jesus Stand Among Us

GLENFINLAS 6.5.6.5.

William Pennefather, 1816-1873

Kenneth G. Finlay, 1882-

Written for the "conferences" Pennefather instituted at Barnet and continued at Mildmay, this hymn was published posthumously in his *Original Hymns and Thoughts in Verse,* 1873.

William Pennefather was born in Dublin, Ireland, on February, 5, 1816. He attended Wesbury College near Bristol and entered Trinity

College, Dublin in 1832. After graduation in 1840 he served several churches in Ireland before going to England in 1848. His greatest work was with the religious and charitable organizations he instituted. He died April 30, 1873.

For a note on GLENFINLAS and Kenneth G. Finlay see No. 199.

392 Open Now Thy Gates of Beauty

UNSER HERRSCHER 8.7.8.7.7.7.

Benjamin Schmolck, 1672-1737
Tr. Catherine Winkworth, 1827-1878
Melody by Joachim Neander, 1650-1680

"*Thut mir auf die schöne Pforte*" is the hymn from which Miss Winkworth made her translation. The original appeared in Schmolck's *Kirchen-Gefährte*, 1732, and all except a third stanza appeared in Miss Winkworth's *Chorale Book for England*, 1863.

Benjamin Schmolck is considered the most popular hymn writer of his day. He was born December 21, 1672, at Brauchitzchdorf. After graduating from Leipzig University he was ordained in 1701 as his father's assistant. A year later he became a deacon of the Friedenskirche at Schweidnitz, Silesia, and remained there the rest of his life achieving various promotions until he was made first pastor and inspector in 1714. He worked long and hard for his parishioners and still found time to write voluminously. From 1730 he suffered a series of strokes which eventually claimed his life on February 12, 1737.

For a note on Catherine Winkworth see No. 58.

For a note on UNSER HERRSCHER and Joachim Neander see No. 20.

393 The Sacrifices of God

Psalm 51:17
Tonus Regius

The text is the King James Version of Psalm 51:17.

TONUS REGIUS (Royal tone) is probably a modern adaptation of Tone VI of the eight Gregorian tones. Here it is set in a typical Anglican chant style. The harmony is from the United Lutheran Church in America's *Common Service Book with Hymnal,* 1917.

394　All Things Are Thine

HERR JESU CHRIST L.M.

John Greenleaf Whittier, 1807-1892
Pensum Sacrum, Gorlitz, 1648
Arr. Johann Sebastian Bach, 1685-1750

For a note on this text and John Greenleaf Whittier see No. 85.

HERR JESU CHRIST is a German chorale melody used with the chorale, *"Herr Jesu Christ, dich zu uns wend."* When it first appeared in the *Pensum Sacrum,* published at Gorlitz in 1648, it was given in the appendix with eight other melodies without texts. It became associated with *"Herr Jesu Christ"* in the *Cantionale Sacrum, Gotha,* 1651, and maintains this relationship in German hymnals of today. J. S. Bach used the tune freely for several of his organ works.

For a note on Bach see No. 193.

395　Bless Thou the Gifts

CANONBURY L.M.

Samuel Longfellow, 1819-1892
Robert Schumann, 1810-1856

This is the final stanza of a dedicatory hymn Longfellow wrote about 1886. It was first published in his *Hymns and Verses,* 1894, which was edited by his niece, Alice M. Longfellow.

For a note on Samuel Longfellow see No. 191.

CANONBURY is adapted from Robert Schumann's piano nocturnes entitled *Nachtstücke,* Opus 23, 1839. It appears in many American hymnbooks with Havergal's hymn, "Lord, Speak to Me, That I May Speak."

Robert Schumann (1810-1856) was one of the leaders of the German "Romantic School" of composition. His promising career as a virtuoso pianist was destroyed when he injured his hands with a contraption he used to strengthen his fingers, after which he devoted his talents to composition and journalism. His criticism and essays played an important role in shaping the course of music in the nineteenth century. He was one of the founders of the periodical, *Die Neue Zeitschrift für Musik,* and was its editor for ten years. His compositions included four symphonies, numerous piano pieces, vocal solos, choruses, a quantity of chamber music, as well as organ pieces.

396   *Bless Thou the Gifts*

EAST DALLAS L.M.

Samuel Longfellow, 1819-1892

A. Eugene Ellsworth, 1910-

For comments on this text see No. 395.

For a comment on Samuel Longfellow see No. 191.

EAST DALLAS was composed by A. Eugene Ellsworth. Dr. Ellsworth was Minister of Music at the East Dallas Christian Church in Texas for a number of years.

Allen Eugene Ellsworth was born in Grand Island, Nebraska, October 2, 1910. He was educated at the University of Nebraska (B.A.), Northwestern University (M.M.), and the Union Theological Seminary School of Sacred Music (D.S.M.). For a time he directed bands and orchestras in the public schools of Kansas, was supervisor of high school music in Minden, Nebraska, taught at the Nebraska School of Agriculture and was organist at the First Methodist Church, Curtis, Nebraska. Since 1949 Dr. Ellsworth has been professor of Theory and Sacred Music at Southern Methodist University in Dallas, Texas.

397   *Bless Thou the Gifts*

BRESLAU L.M.

Samuel Longfellow, 1819-1892

Melody, Leipzig, 1625

For a comment on this text see No. 395.

For a comment on Samuel Longfellow see No. 191.

is a modern version of a melody published in *As Hymnodus Sacer,* Leipizig, 1625, where it appeared with the hymn *"Herr Jesu Christ, mein Lebens Licht."*

398   O King of Kings, Before Whose Throne

LEICESTER 8.8.8.8.8.8.

John Quarles, 1624-1665
Alt. Thomas Darling, 1816-1893
John Bishop, c. 1665-1737

Thomas Darling adapted John Quarles' poem beginning "Great God, whose sceptre rules the earth" for use in his *Hymns for the Church of England,* 1887. The original poem was published in Quarles' *Divine Meditations,* etc., 1655.

John Quarles, born at Essex in 1624, was educated at Exeter College, Oxford, and as a supporter of the crown (Charles I), took part in the defense of Oxford against the Parlimentary Army. After the defeat of the king, Quarles retired to London and devoted the remainder of his life to literary pursuits. He died there during the Great Plague of 1665.

Thomas Darling, born in London in 1816, was educated at Charterhouse and St. John's College, Cambridge. After taking Holy Orders in 1839 he served churches in Thanington, near Canterbury, and then in London. He included about twenty original hymns in the 1887 edition of *Hymns for the Church of England.* He is said to have excelled in "adapting" hymns from other writers. He died in 1893 in London.

LEICESTER became associated with the present text in the *Oxford Hymn Book,* 1908. It originally appeared with Psalm 112 in John Bishop's, *A Set of New Psalm Tunes,* c. 1711.

Little is known of John Bishop except for a few scattered facts. He was temporarily employed as the organist-choirmaster of King's College, Cambridge, in 1688 and was organist at Winchester College in 1695, becoming the lay vicar of Winchester Cathedral in 1696, and finally the organist and master of the choristers there in 1729. He died in Winchester in 1737.

399   *All Things Come of Thee*

1 Chronicles 29:14

Ludwig van Beethoven, 1770-1827

The text is adapted from the King James Version of 1 Chronicles 29:14.

Although attributed to Beethoven this tune has not been identified in any of his works. It is written in the style of Anglican Chant and may have been harmonized by one E. J. Hopkins in whose *The Temple Choral Service Book*, 1867, it is said to have first appeared.

For a note on Beethoven see No. 1.

400   *We Give Thee But Thine Own*

ST. ANDREW S.M.

William Walsham How, 1823-1897

Joseph Barnby, 1838-1896

This response is the first stanza of a six-stanza hymn written in 1858. It was first published in How and Marrell's *Psalms and Hymns*, 1864.

For a note on William Walsham How see No. 279.

ST. ANDREW was composed by Barnby while he was organist at St. Andrew's Church, London. It was written for Monsell's hymn, "Sweet Is Thy Mercy, Lord" and first appeared in the composer's *Hymn Tunes*, 1869, where it was unnamed. The name appeared with the tune in the posthumous *Hymn Tunes*, 1897.

For a note on Joseph Barnby see No. 375.

401   Thy Word Have I Hid

CHESHIRE TUNE 8.8.8.5.

Psalm 119:11-12
Este's Psalter, 1592

Psalm 119:11-12 is given "I have laid up thy word . . . " in the Revised Standard Version and "Thy word have I laid up . . . " in the King James Version.

CHESHIRE TUNE originally appeared as CHESSHIRE TUNE in Thomas Este's *Whole Book of Psalmes with Their Wonted Tunes as They are Sung in Churches,* 1592, set to Psalm 146.

Thomas Este (also spelled Est, Easte, or East) was a music printer in Aldersgate, London, during the reign of Elizabeth I. His craftmanship was hailed with the publication of William Byrd's *Psalms, Sonets, and Songs of Sadness and Pietie,* 1587. His *Whole Book of Psalmes,* 1582, is important not only for the music it contained but also as the earliest publication where identifying names are given to several of the tunes. There were three such names given. CHESSHIRE TUNE was one of them.

402   Divine Instructor, Gracious Lord

TALLIS' ORDINAL C.M.

Anne Steele, 1716-1778
Thomas Tallis, c. 1505-1585

This is a stanza of a longer poem which appeared in her *Poems on Subjects chiefly devotional,* 1760. The stanza is generally included in her hymn, "Father of Mercies, in Thy Word," which is taken from the same source.

Anne Steele, born in 1716, was one of the most important Baptist hymn writers of her day. She was the daughter of a tinker merchant and lay pastor of the Baptist Church in Broughton, Hampshire, England. She used the *nom de plume* "Theodosia" in her first publication, *Poems on Subjects chiefly devotional*. She died November 11, 1778.

For a note on TALLIS' ORDINAL see No. 55.

For a note on Thomas Tallis see No. 68.

403 Teach Me, O Lord

Psalm 119:33
William Henry Hewlett, 1873-

This response is based on Psalm 119:33.

The music was composed for this text and was first published in *The Hymnary* in Canada, 1930.

English born, William Henry Hewlett has spent his life in Canada where he studied piano, organ, and theory. For a time he also studied in Berlin, and London. He was active in the Canadian College of Musicians, serving as its president at one time. He served as principal of the Hamilton Conservatory of Music and director of the Elgar Choir in addition to participating on the Hymnbook Committee of Methodist Churches of Canada and subsequently on the Hymnal Committee of the United Church.

404 O Lord, Open Thou Our Eyes

Psalm 119:18
John Camidge, 1735-1893

Psalm 119:18 provides this versicle and respones.

John Camidge, the first of a famous Yorkshire family of musicians who served York Minster from 1756 to 1858, was born in York, England, in 1735 and died there in 1803. He studied under Maurice Green (1695-1755) and, for a time, George Friedrich Handel (1685-1759) before his appointment as organist of York Minster in 1756. He held this post until his death on November 11, 1799.

405   Thanks Be to Thee

Thomas Tallis, c. 1505-1585

For a note on Thomas Tallis see No. 68.

406   Praise Be to Thee

John Playford, 1674-1730

This is the *Laus tibi* which is normally sung in old Protestant communions after the reading of the Gospel for the day.

We have been unable to find information on this John Playford. His dates indicate he is not the famous seventeenth-century English publisher of music.

407   Glory Be to Thee

Thomas Tallis, c. 1505-1585

The *Gloria tibi* is from the Sarum Missal. It is traditionally sung before the reading of the Gospel.

For a note on Tallis see No. 68.

408   Glory Be to Thee

Thomas Tallis, c. 1505-1585

This is another setting of the *Gloria tibi*.
For a note on Tallis see No. 68.

409   Lord, Have Mercy Upon Us

John Merbecke, 1523-c. 1585

This is an English version of the ancient *Kyrie eleison* in its common three-part formula.

John Merbecke, or Marbeck, was an eminent English composer, church musician, and author. Grove's *Dictionary* gives his dates as c. 1510-c. 1585. Merbecke apparently lived and died at Windsor in the service of English monarchs. He was listed in record books as organist in St. George's Chapel for a time, a music copier, and clerk. His chief claim to fame was his great work in the *Booke of Common Praier Noted*, 1550, which was the first musical setting of the English liturgy as authorized by the Act of Uniformity, 1549. His other work was a *Concordance* of the entire Bible published also in 1550.

410 Lord, Have Mercy Upon Us

KYRIE

From a Lutheran Service of 1528

A very old Kyrie from the formative period of the Lutheran service.

411 Write These Words

Ancient Chant

No information has been found on this response. The setting is from *The Methodist Hymnal*, 1964.

412 Praise God, from Whom All Blessings Flow

OLD HUNDREDTH L.M.

Thomas Ken, 1637-1711
Attr. to Louis Bourgeois, c. 1510-1561
Genevan Psalter, 1551

This doxology is the closing stanza of Bishop Ken's morning and evening hymns (see No. 68). It is so popular in American Protestant worship that it has been called our "Te Deum."

For a note on Thomas Ken see No. 68.

OLD HUNDREDTH is given here with the original rhythm.

Percy Dearmer and Archibald Jacobs in their *Songs of Praise Discussed* say that OLD HUNDREDTH "is probably the most famous of all psalm-tunes, whether early or late" [p. 238]. There has been some question about the authorship of the tune but late authorities agree that in all probability the tune was composed (and some add "or adapted") by Louis Bourgeois for the *Genevan Psalter* of 1551. There it was used for Psalm 134. It appeared with Kethe's *Psalm One Hundred* in the *Four Score and Seven Psalms of David*, Geneva, 1561, and also in Day's *Whole Book of Psalms* which was published in the same year.

For a comment on Louis Bourgeois see No. 225.

413   Praise God from Whom All Blessings Flow

OLD HUNDREDTH L.M.

Thomas Ken, 1637-1711

Attr. to Louis Bourgeois, c. 1510-1561

Genevan Psalter, 1551

OLD HUNDREDTH is given here in the rhythm adopted by most American congregations.

For note on this doxology see No. 412.

For a note on Thomas Ken see No. 68.

For a note on Old Hundredth see No. 412

For a note on Louis Bourgeois see No. 225.

414   Gloria Patri

Henry W. Greatorex, 1813-1858

This ancient canticle is known as the Lesser Doxology in contrast to the Greater Doxology or *Gloria in excelsis*. Both of these ascriptions of praise were probably among the earliest forms of Christian worship. The first part of the "Gloria Patri" is probably based on the great commission found in Matthew 28:19. The second half is of later origin and may have been added during the fourth-century Arian heresy. It is traditionally sung after the reading or singing of the Psalms.

Henry Wellington Greatorex (1813-1858) was born at Burton-upon-Trent, England, the son of Thomas Greatorex who was a well-known teacher, composer, and organist and who served as organist at Carlisle Cathedral and at Westminster Abbey during King George IV's reign. Born on December 24, 1813, young Henry began his musical training under his father. He migrated to the United States in 1839 and began a career as organist in Hartford, Connecticut. In 1846 he went to New York City where he became organist at St. Paul's Chapel and afterwards at Calvary Episcopal Church. He left New York in 1853 to become organist at an Episcopal church in Charleston, South Carolina. He died there of yellow fever September 18, 1858.

415   Gloria Patri

Charles Meineke, 1782-1850

For a note on this text see No. 414.

This tune is from Charles Meineke's "Evening Prayer" in his *Music for the Church* . . . etc., a collection he composed for use in St. Paul's Church, Baltimore, Maryland, in 1844.

Charles Meineke was a German organist and pianist who came to the United States about 1822 after having lived for a time in England. It is said he left Germany in 1810 and his first known residence in America was at Baltimore in 1822. Apparently nothing more is known of his activities. We assume he remained the organist of St. Paul's Church until his death in 1850.

416   Gloria Patri

Old Scottish Chant

For a note on this text see No. 414.

This setting of the Gloria Patri is of unknown origin. It appears here as given as No. 511 in the *Pilgrim Hymnal*, 1958, which in turn took it from the *Pilgrim Hymnal*, 1931.

417   Holy, Holy, Holy

Peter C. Lutkin, 1858-1931

Variously known as the "Trisagion," "Tersanctus," or simply the "Sanctus," this text is based on an ancient synagogue doxology which was in turn based on Isaiah 6:3.

Peter Christian Lutkin was born March 27, 1858, in Thompsonville, Wisconsin, and grew up in Chicago. The early and sudden death of both parents left the boy to fend for himself but despite difficulties he attended school and developed his musical skill. He was appointed organist of St. James' Church, Chicago, and remained there for nine years. Fortune smiled on him, and he was able to study music in Europe for three years under the best teachers. Upon his return to Chicago in 1884 he held important positions as teacher, organist, and conductor. He became the first dean of the School of Music at Northwestern University in 1896 and under his leadership the school achieved nationwide recognition in the field of music education, church music, and choral music. Dr. Lutkin was one of the founders of the American Guild of Organists, instituted the Chicago North Shore Music Festivals, and was twice president of the Music Teachers' National Association. This "Sanctus" and the "Benediction" are but two of his widely known compositions. He died December 27, 1931.

418   Holy, Holy, Holy

Communion Service in E Minor

Phillip R. Dietterich, 1931-

For a comment on the text see No. 417.

The music is from the Communion Service in E Minor as given in *The Methodist Hymnal,* 1964, 1966. This is the Sanctus for the service which includes the Gloria in Excelsis, Kyrie Eleison, Sarsum Corda, Sanctus, and Agnus Dei.

Philip Richard Dietterich was born in Buffalo, New York, on September 17, 1931. He was graduated from Ohio Wesleyan University, Mus.B. 1955, and Boston University, S.T.B. 1958. He was ordained deacon in 1956 and elder in 1958 and has since made valuable contributions to the musical life of the Methodist Church. Mr. Dietterich has served as minister of music for Centre Methodist Church, Malden, Massachusetts (1956-62), and First Methodist Church, Westfield, New Jersey (1962-). He served on the Commission on Worship (1961-62), was consultant to the Hymnal Committee (Methodist), and was chairman of the North East Ohio Conference Chapter of the National Fellowship of Methodist Musicians (1961). Mr. Dietterich is a prolific composer and arranger of anthems and service music. He has collected and arranged a considerable amount of folk music and is considered to be an authority in this field of endeavor.

419   Holy, Holy, Holy

John Merbecke, 1523-c. 1585

For a note on the text see No. 417.

For a note on John Merbecke see No. 409.

420   The Lord Be with You

Thomas Tallis, c.1505-1585

An ancient biblical greeting taken over by the church for use in the liturgy, these words are adapted from *The Book of Common Prayer*, 1549.

For a note on Thomas Tallis see No. 68.

This setting is from *The Cathedral Prayer Book*, 1891, used at St. Paul's in London and is based on the John Goss arrangement.

421   The Lord Be with You

Traditional

For a note on the text see No. 420.

The present setting is from Tallis' *Festal Responses*, c. 1564, and the arrangement is credited to Joseph Barnby.

For a comment on Joseph Barnby see No. 375.

422   *Hear Our Prayer*

Psalm 143:1
George Whelpton, 1847-1930

Long a popular response to prayer, "Hear Our Prayer" was probably written in the 1890's and first published in leaflet form in H. Augustine Smith's *Hymns for American Youth*, 1924.

Born in Redbourne, England, on May 17, 1847, Whelpton came to the United States with his family in 1851. He served in the Union Army during the Civil War and afterward studied music under one H. R. Palmer and then privately in Boston. For twenty years he was a choir director in Buffalo, New York, when he retired in 1925. He became an editor of various publications. He died on November 25, 1930, at Oxford, Ohio.

423   *Our Father Who Art in Heaven*

Anonymous
Harold W. Friedell, 1905-1958

For a note on Harold W. Friedell see No. 316.

424   *Day By Day, Dear Lord*

St. Richard of Chichester, 1197-1253
Harold W. Friedell, 1905-1958

This brief prayer is from enlarged *Songs of Praise*, 1931, where it is set to the tune STONETHWAITE by Arthur Somerville and designated as a "grace." Dr. Dearmer in *Songs of Praise Discussed*, 1933, indicates the text was received by the British Museum on March, 18, 1915, printed on a card and described as "Partly—at least" written by St. Richard of Chichester.

St. Richard of Chichester, born Richard Wycke at Droitwich, Worcester, England, was educated at Oxford and Paris. Historians say he spent seven years in Bologna studying Canon Law. He held important positions in the church, becoming successively chancellor of Oxford University (1235), chancellor of Canterbury (1237), and after several years of further study, at Orléans, was consecrated Bishop of Chichester by the Pope at Lyons (1245). King Henry III, miffed because his personal candidate failed to receive the appointment, refused to recognize the new bishop and made every effort to bar his entry into the city. The following year, however, Henry received Richard's homage and the remainder of the Bishop's life was given to notable diocesan work and reform. Richard was canonized by Pope Urban IV at Viterbo in 1262.

For a note on Harold W. Friedell see No. 316.

425   Father of All Grace

Arden D. Keen, 1930-

This response was written for use by the choirs of the First Christian Church, Eureka, Illinois.

Arden D. Keen, born September 3, 1930, at Libertyville, Illinois, was educated at Illinois State University (B.S. 1952, M.S. 1964). He studied at the Navy School of Music in Washington, D. C. while serving in the Army band from 1952 to 1953. In addition to teaching instrumental music for the past fifteen years, Mr. Keen has been working with junior and senior church choirs. From 1957 to 1967 he was choirmaster at the First Christian Church, Eureka, Illinois. At the present he is conducting a bell choir at the First Christian Church in Canton, Illinois. Mr. Keen is a member of the American Band Directors Association, National Band Association, the Illinois Music Educators Association, the Illinois Education Association, and is the current president of the West Central Illinois Band Directors Association.

426   Lead Me, Lord

Based on Psalms 5:8 and 4:8
Samuel S. Wesley, 1810-1876

Both words and music are from an anthem by S. S. Wesley. The text is based on selected phrases from Psalms 5:8 and 4:8. The response is from the first half of the anthem.

For a note on Samuel S. Wesley see No. 359.

427   May the Words of Our Mouths

Psalm 19:14, alt.
Alan Walker, 1927-

The verse from Psalm 19 has been adapted to corporate worship needs by substituting "May" for "Let," "Mouths" for "Mouth" and the collective for the personal pronouns.

The response was composed for use with the choir of Howard Memorial Presbyterian Church, Tarboro, North Carolina, during the composer's tenure as organist-choir director from 1953-1956. It was first published in *The Pilgrim Hymnal,* 1958.

Alan Walker received his Bachelor of Music degree from Boston University, 1951, and his Master of Sacred Music from Union Theological Seminary, 1953, where he studied organ under Dr. Hugh Porter. After serving churches in Massachusetts, New Jersey, and North Carolina, Mr. Walker returned to Worcester, Massachusetts, to serve as director of music at Central Church from 1956 to 1966. While there he also directed the glee club at Becker Junior College and served as dean of the local chapter of the American Guild of Organists (1960-62). From 1966 to 1969 he was the director of music at Central Union Church in Honolulu, Hawaii. Mr. Walker is currently organist at Calvary Lutheran Church in that city, is employed as a hotel desk clerk during the week, and is pursuing an evening course in Computer Programming, expecting to enter that field of work when qualified.

428   O Thou Who Hearest Prayer

Unknown

Welsh Melody

The words and music of this prayer response were submitted anonymously to the committee engaged in compiling *The Pilgrim Hymnal*, 1968. No source was indicated for either. Extensive search has failed to throw any light on this material.

429   Almighty Father, Hear Our Prayer

Arr. from Felix Mendelssohn, 1809-1847

The source of this text is unknown. The response has appeared in a number of American hymnals since the early 1930's.

The music is adapted from Mendelssohn's well-known oratorio *Elijah*. There it represents the people's repetition of Elijah's prayer to God for relief from the great drought.

For a note on Felix Mendelssohn see No. 328.

430   To My Humble Supplication

MON DIEU, PRÊTE-MOI L'ORIELLE 8.8.7.7.

Joseph Bryan, c. 1610, alt. 1955

Genevan Psalter, 1543

Based on Psalm 86 this prayer reponse is part of a cento from a poem by Joseph Bryan. Percy Deamer prepared the text for *The English Hymnal*, 1906, from a British museum manuscript, c. 1620. Here we use the first and fourth stanzas of the hymn that appeared in *Songs of Praise with Music*, 1931, with a slight alteration in the third line.

Except for the museum manuscript containing some metrical Psalms, nothing is known of Joseph Bryan.

MON DIEU, PRÊTE-MOI L'OREILLE is the Genevan Psalter (1543) setting for Clément Marot's version of Psalm 86. It was composed or adapted by Louis Bourgeois. This response makes use of the first half of the tune.

For a note on Bourgeois see No. 225.

431 Spirit of Truth, of Life

MENDON L.M.

Horace Westwood, 1884-
German Melody
Arr. Samuel Dyer, 1785-1835

We have not found information on the author of the text of this response. Its earliest appearance seems to be in *Christian Hymns,* published by the Christian Foundation, Columbus, Indiana, 1945.

MENDON first appeared in the *Supplement of Samuel Dyer's Third Edition of Sacred Music,* 1824. The original tune is said to have had an additional note in each line and a completely different final line. The consensus is that Lowell Mason made the necessary alterations which created the present form of the melody, and gave it the name, probably from Mendon, Massachusetts.

Samuel Dyer was born November 4, 1785, and was educated in England. He came to America in 1811 and directed choirs and taught music in New York City and Philadelphia. In 1815 he returned to England for additional study. Upon his return to America and establishing residence in Baltimore, Maryland, he began publishing books of sacred music, one of which is an important contribution to hymnological study. Dyer was much in demand as a conductor of singing schools and traveled extensively between Savannah, Georgia, and Salem, Massachusetts, in response to his invitations. He died in Hoboken, New Jersey, on July 20, 1835.

432   God Be in My Head

LYTLINGTON Irregular

Sarum Primer, 1558
Sydney H. Nicholson, 1875-1947

After appearing on the title page of a *Book of Hours*, 1514, this little prayer became a part of several books of devotion written during the sixteenth century. Our source of the text is the *Sarum Primer*, 1558, a prayer book used at old Sarum which now lies in ruins just outside of Salisbury, England. *The Oxford Hymn Book*, 1908, seems to have been the first to use it as a hymn.

LYTLINGTON, named for Lytlington Tower where the composer lived during his tenure as organist of Westminster Abbey, was first published in 1928 in *The Winchester Hymn Supplement*.

Sydney Hugo Nicholson was born February 9, 1875, in London. He was educated at Rugby, New College, Oxford, and the Royal College of Music. He served as organist of Carlisle Cathedral, Manchester Cathedral, and Westminster Abbey. He left Westminster Abbey in 1927 to become warden of St. Nicholas College at Chislehurst, Kent, where he founded the School of English Church Music. He was knighted in 1937 for his work on behalf of church music. He has published cantatas, hymn tunes, service music, and several books on church music. He died May 30, 1947.

433   The Lord Bless You and Keep You

Numbers 6:24-26
Peter C. Lutkin, 1858-1931

This familiar benediction is from Numbers 6:24-26. The music is given in abbreviated form omitting the amens.

For a note on Peter C. Lutkin see No. 417.

434   To Thee Before the Close of Day

JAM LUCIS L.M.

Latin: c. 7th Century
Tr. John M. Neale, 1818-1866
Plainsong, Mode VI

A translation of the seventh-century Latin hymn, *"Te lucis ante terminum,"* the present hymn makes use of J. D. Chambers' first line from his *Psalter,* 1852, and the remainder of John M. Neale's translation from his *Hymns Noted, 1852.* *"Te lucis"* has appeared in a number of English manuscripts since the eleventh century. Julian lists twenty-five English translations.

For a note on John M. Neale see No. 155.

"Jam lucis ort sidere" is the traditional office hymn with which the tune was used, hence the name JAM LUCIS. It is a syllabic chant arranged by Winfred Douglas for *The Hymnal, 1940.*

435   Thou Wilt Keep Him in Perfect Peace

DUKE'S TUNE 8.6.

Isaiah 26:3
Scottish Psalter, 1615, Abridged

The words of Isaiah 26:3 are used for this benediction.

DUKE'S TUNE is here given in abbreviated form, using only the first and final phrases of the original. DUKE'S TUNE, one of the twelve common tunes in Hart's *The CL Psalmes of David,* 1615, and in Ravencroft's *Psalter,* 1621, was listed as a Scottish Tune.

436 *May the Grace of Christ Our Savior*

OMNI DEI 8.7.8.7.

> John Newton, 1725-1807
> Corner's *Gesangbuch,* 1631
> Harm. Hubert Lamb, 1909-

As a paraphrase of 2 Corinthians 13:14 this short hymn appeared in *Olney Hymns,* 1779. It was written for "the close of Divine Service."

For a note on John Newton see No. 354.

OMNI DEI is named for the opening words of the text with which the tune appeared in the *Grosscatholisch Gesangbuch,* Nürnberg, 1631 edition. David G. Corner (1585-1648) compiled several collections of Catholic hymns and tunes before his death in 1648. The harmonization is the work of Hubert Lamb and was prepared for use with this text in *The Middlesex Hymn Book,* 1952.

Hubert Lamb graduated from Harvard University. From 1934 to 1945 he taught at the Longy School of Music in Cambridge, Massachusetts, and served simultaneously on the faculty of Wellesley College. In 1957 he devoted his time to Wellesley and has become the head of the music department there.

437 *Father, Give Thy Benediction*

ALTA TRINITA BEATA 8.7.8.7.

> Samuel Longfellow, 1819-1892
> *Laudi Spirituali,* 14th Century

This response consists of the first half of an eight-line stanza of a hymn which appeared in *Hymns of the Spirit,* 1864.

For a note on Samuel Longfellow see No. 191.

ALTA TRINITA BEATA, an abridgement of the traditional tune to a hymn to the Trinity said to have been found in a collection of popular devotional songs known as *Laudi spirituali* in a library in Florence, Italy. *Laudi spirituali* were nonliturgical songs cast in the vernacular and set to simple popular tunes.

438-454 Amens and Responses

"Amen" has traditionally been uttered by the people as assent to what has been said or sung. The practice has been traced to ancient Jewish worship where it was used after prayers and meant "So be it," an affirmation of commitment to the words and actions of the worship leaders.

Most of the responses given in this section are well known and have become "traditional" in many Protestant churches in the United States.

The following four responses are from *The Lutheran Service Book and Hymnal,* 1958, where the first two are used as offertory chants, the third is a setting of the *"Venite Exultemus,"* for Matins, and the final one is a twofold amen for use at the conclusion of the benediction.

438—A twofold amen by William Crotch, English musician, who began his colorful career as a mere child.

William Crotch was a musical genius who was playing a homemade organ at the tender age of two and a half years and made a public appearance in London at the age of four. At eleven he was assistant organist at Trinity and King's Colleges, Cambridge. His ability as a composer was demonstrated at the age of fourteen when he composed the oratorio, *The Captivity of Judah.* He spent two years studying for the ministry but apparently lost interest and continued the study of music at Oxford where he was organist at Christ Church and received the Bachelor of Music and Doctor of Music degrees. At the age of twenty-two he was appointed professor of music at the University and organist of St. John's College. He was in great demand as a lecturer on music in London and became the first principal of the newly established Royal Academy of Music in 1822. He was born in Norwich, England, July 5, 1775, and died in Taunton, December 29, 1847.

439 was composed by John Alcock. He was born in London on April 11, 1715, and began playing the organ at the age of fourteen. He held positions as organist in London, Plymouth, and Reading. He became organist, master of the choristers, and lay vicar of Lichfield Cathedral in 1748, took his music doctorate degree from Oxford in 1761. Alcock died at Lichfield on February 23, 1806. He composed many psalms, hymns, anthems, and services.

440—For a comment on William Henry Walter see No. 93.

441—This threefold amen is based on a work by T. Tertius Noble (1867-1953).

For a note on Dr. Noble see No. 338.

442 is said to come from the Greek liturgy.

443 is attributed to Johann Gittlied Naumann (1741-1801), composer of church music and opera. It is commonly called the "Dresden Amen" because of its association with the Royal Chapel of Dresden. Mendelssohn (Reformation Symphony) and Wagner (Parsifal) have contributed to the immortality of this musical idea.

444—We can find no information in this threefold amen.

445 is sometimes called the Danish Threefold Amen because it is believed to have originated in the Lutheran Church in Denmark.

446 is from DeLamarter's *Service Responses,* 1930. Born in Lansing, Michigan, on February 18, 1880, Erik DeLamarter studied music in Chicago and in Paris under Guilmant and Widor. From 1900 until about 1936 he held various positions as organist-choirmaster in churches of Chicago. He was for many years assistant conductor of the Chicago Symphony Orchestra, conductor of the Chicago Civic Orchestra and Allied Arts ballet and concerts. For a time he was music critic for Chicago newspapers. He was in demand as a guest conductor and teacher. His compositions cover a wide field of interest including ballets, symphonies, overtures, organ concertos, chamber music, and church music. He died in 1953. Obituaries appear in the *New York Times* p. 29, May, 1953, *Musical America,* 73:19, June, 1953, and *Etude* 71:56, August, 1957.

447 is adapted (upward progression of final melodic note) from the final phrase of Louis Bourgeois' setting of a metrical version of the NUNC DIMITTIS which appeared in the *Genevan Psalter,* 1549. The present harmony is by Claude Goudimel, except for the positioning of the final chord. The complete tune is given in 292.

For a note on Louis Bourgeois see No. 225.

448 is a fourfold amen by Franklin Elwood Perkins. He was born at Riverside, New Jersey, on March 30, 1929, and graduated from Juniata College (B.A. 1949), Union Theological Seminary School of Sacred Music (M.S.M. 1951), and Washington University (Ph.D. 1968). He has served as minister of music for churches in Huntingdon and Bloomsburg, Pennsylvania, and Springfield, Illinois. At present he is serving the Ladue Chapel, St. Louis, Missouri, and Lindenwood College, St. Charles, Missouri, and is assistant professor at the University of Missouri at St. Louis.

449 is a threefold amen written for the choirs of the First Christian Church at Eureka, Illinois.

For a note on Arden D. Keen see No. 425.

450—See No. 448 for a note on the composer of this twofold amen.

451—This fourfold amen was composed by John Stainer who was born in London, June 6, 1840, and began his musical training in St. Paul's Cathedral. It is said that he was a remarkable player and sight-singer at the age of seven. By 1854 he was already serving churches as organist but in 1859 began his study at Oxford where he earned his Mus. B., B.A., Mus.D., and M.A. degrees. He returned to London in 1872 and succeeded John Goss as organist at St. Paul's Cathedral and earned a great reputation for the high pitch of excellence of the musical services. He was examiner for music degrees at Cambridge and the University of London, professor of organ and harmony at the National Training School for Music and eventually became its principal, and was for a time inspector of music in the English elementary schools. Failing eyesight forced him to resign his position with St. Paul's in 1888, the year he received knighthood. During his life he held many important positions with musical organizations and societies. His last position was professor of music at the University of Oxford. He was buried in the Holywell Cemetery, Oxford, on April

6, 1901. Although Stainer composed a large quantity of church music, he is remembered chiefly for his cantata *The Crucifixion* and the "Sevenfold Amen."

452 is the well-known "Sevenfold Amen" mentioned in Stainer's biographical sketch at No. 451.

453 and 454 are from Vincent Persichetti's *Hymns and Responses for the Church Year.*

Vincent Persichetti is one of America's gifted contemporary composers. His compositions have attracted wide recognition here and abroad. Born in Philadelphia in 1915, he began his musical career as pianist in orchestras and, while still in his teens, was playing the organ in Philadephia churches. He studied at Combs College, the Philadelphia Conservatory of Music, and Curtis Institute of Music. He served as head of the composition department of the Philadelphia Conservatory of Music for 25 years, and for seven years has been head of the composition department at Juilliard School of Music in New York City.

BIBLIOGRAPHY

Bibliography

REFERENCE BOOKS

Baker, Theodore, *Baker's Biographical Dictionary of Musicians*. 5th ed. New York, G. Schirmer, Inc., 1958.

Blom, Eric, ed., *Everyman's Dictionary of Music and Musicians*. 5th ed. London, Macmillan and Co., Ltd., 1954.

Dictionary of National Biography. 68 Vol. London, 1885-1901.

Dictionary of National Biography. Supplements 1 and 2. London, 1901 and 1902.

Diehl, Katherine Smith, *Hymns and Tunes—An Index*. New York and London, The Scarecrow Press, Inc., 1966.

Harvard Alumni Directory. Cambridge, Harvard University Press, 1948.

Jensen, John M., *The United Evangelical Lutheran Church, An Interpretation*, Augsburg Publishing House, Minneapolis, Minnesota, 1964.

Jensen, John M., Giving, Gerald, and Linder, Carl E., compilers, *A Biographical Dictionary of Pastors of the American Lutheran Church*, Augsburg Publishing House, Minneapolis, Minnesota, 1962.

Julian, John, ed., *A Dictionary of Hymnology*. New York, Charles Scribner's Sons, 1892. (New York, Dover Publications, Reprint, 1957).

Mortensen, Enok, *The Danish Lutheran Church in America*, Board of Publication, Lutheran Church in America, Philadelphia, 1967.

New Catholic Encyclopedia. 15 Vol. New York, McGraw Hill Book Co., 1957.

Nyholm, Paul C., *The Americanization of the Danish Lutheran Churches in America*, Institute for Danish Church History, Copenhagen, Denmark, 1963, Distributed by Augsburg Publishing House, Minneapolis, Minnesota.

Scholes, Percy A., *Oxford Companion to Music*, 8th ed. New York, University Press, 1938.

The Union Theological Seminary in the City of New York. *Alumni Directory, 1836-1958.* New York, 1958.

The Universal Jewish Encyclopedia. 10 Vol. New York, 1939-43.

Who Was Who in America, 1607-1963.

Who's Who in America, 1928-33, 1942-43, 1950-53, 1956-57, 1960-61, 1968-69.

Who's Who in the Methodist Church. Nashville, Abingdon Press, 1966.

Zahn, Johannes, *Die Melodien der deutschen evangelischen Kirchenlieder.* Gutersloh, 1889-1895 (Reprint).

HANDBOOKS

Covert, William C., and Laufer, Calvin W., *Handbook to the Hymnal.* Philadelphia, Presbyterian Board of Christian Education, 1935.

Dearmer, Percy, and Jacob, Archibald, *Songs of Praise Discussed.* London, Oxford University Press, 1933.

Farlander, Arthur, Ellinwood, Leonard, and others, *The Hymnal 1940 Companion.* New York, The Church Pension Fund, 1949.

Frost, Maurice, *Historical Companion to Hymns Ancient and Modern.* London, William Clowes and Sons, Ltd., 1962.

Harvard University. Hymnal. *The Harvard University Hymn Book.* Cambridge, Harvard University Press, 1964.

Haeussler, Armin, *The Story of Our Hymns.* The Handbook to the Hymnal of the Evangelical and Reformed Church. St. Louis, Eden Publishing House, 1952.

Hostetler, Lester, *Handbook to the Mennonite Hymnary.* Newton, Kansas, General Conference of the Mennonite Church of North America Board of Publications, 1949.

Lightwood, James T. (ed. and revised by Francis B. Westbrook), *The Music of the Methodist Hymn-Books.* London, The Epworth Press, 1955.

Macmillan, Alexander, *Hymns of the Church, A Companion to The Hymnary of The United Church of Canada.* Toronto, The United Church Publishing House, 1935.

Martin, Hugh, ed., Jones, J. Ithel, *et al., The Baptist Hymn Book Companion.* London, Psalms and Hymns Trust, 1962.

McCutchan, Robert G., *Our Hymnody; A Manual of the Methodist Hymnal,* 2d. ed. New York and Nashville, Abingdon-Cokesbury Press, 1942.

Moffatt, James, and Patrick, Millar, *Handbook to the Church Hymnary with Supplement,* rev. ed. London, Oxford University Press, 1927.

Parry, K. L., and Routley, Erik, *Companion to Congregational Praise*. London, Independent Press, Ltd., 1953.

Polack, William G., *The Handbook to the Lutheran Hymnal*, 3d and rev. ed. St. Louis, Concordia Publishing House, 1958.

Reynolds, William Jensen, *Hymns of Our Faith, A Handbook for the Baptist Hymnal*. Nashville, Broadman Press, 1964.

Ronander, Albert C., and Porter, Ethel K., *Guide to the Pilgrim Hymnal*. Philadelphia and Boston, United Church Press, 1966.

Statler, Ruth B., and Fisher, Nevin W., *Handbook on Brethren Hymns*. Elgin, Illinois, The Brethren Press, 1959.

GENERAL

Bailey, Albert Edward, *The Gospel in Hymns*. New York, Charles Scribner's Sons, 1950.

Baker, Frank, selected and edited, *Representative Verse of Charles Wesley*. London. The Epworth Press, 1962.

Benson, Louis F., *Studies of Familiar Hymns*. First Series, New Edition. Philadelphia, The Westminster Press, 1924.

Benson, Louis F., *Studies of Familiar Hymns*. Second Series. Philadelphia, The Westminster Press, 1923.

Benson, Louis F., *The English Hymn*. New York, George H. Doran Co., 1915. (Reprint, Richmond, John Knox Press, 1962).

Benson, Louis F., *The Hymnody of the Christian Church*. Richmond, John Knox Press, 1956.

Benson, Louis F., *The Hymns of John Bunyan*. New York: The Hymn Society of America. Paper No. I, 1930.

Breed, David R., *The History and Use of Hymns and Hymn-Tunes*. New York, Fleming H. Revell Company, 1903.

Brown, Theron and Butterworth, Hesekiah, *The Story of the Hymns and Tunes*. New York, George H. Doran Company, 1906.

Butterworth, Hesekiah, *The Story of the Hymns; or Hymns That Have A History*. New York, American Tract Society, 1875.

Clarke, William Kemp Lowther, *A Hundred Years of Hymns Ancient and Modern*. London, William Clowes and Sons, Ltd., 1960.

Crawford, Richard A., *Andrew Law, American Psalmodist*. Evanston, Northwestern University Press, 1968.

Dearmer, Percy, Williams, R. Vaughn, and Shaw, Martin, *The Oxford Book of Carols*. London, Oxford University Press, 1928.

Duffield, Samuel Willoughby, *English Hymns: Their Authors and History*, 3d ed., revised and corrected. New York, Funk and Wagnalls, 1888.

Ellinwood, Leonard and Douglas, Anne Woodward, *To Praise God, The Life and Work of Charles Winfred Douglas*. New York, The Hymn Society of America, Paper No. XXIII, 1958.

Foote, Henry Wilder, *Three Centuries of American Hymnody*. The President and Fellows of Harvard College, 1940, reprinted. Hamden, Connecticut, The Shoestring Press, Inc., 1961.

Frost, Maurice, *English and Scottish Psalm and Hymn Tunes, c, 1543-1677*. New York Oxford University Press, 1953.

Gradenwitz, Peter, *The Music of Israel, Its Rise and Growth Through 5,000 Years*. New York, W. W. Norton and Company, 1949.

Gray, G. F. S., *Hymns and Worship*. London, S.P.C.K., 1961.

Hass, Alfred Burton, *Charles Wesley*. New York, The Hymn Society of America, Paper No. XXII, 1957.

Hitchcock, H. Wiley, *Music in the United States: A Historical Introduction*. Englewood Cliffs, New Jersey, Prentice-Hall, Inc., 1969.

Hunter, Stanley Armstrong, ed., *The Music of the Gospel*. New York, Abingdon Press, 1932.

Idelsohn, A. Z., *Jewish Music in Its Historical Development*. New York, Tudor Publishing Company, 1948.

Jackson, George Pullen, *Another Sheaf of White Spirituals*. Gainesville, Florida, University of Florida Press, 1952.

Jackson, George Pullen, *Down-East Spirituals and Others*. Locust Valley New York, J. J. Augustin Publisher, n.d. (Jackson signed the Introduction April 1, 1939.)

Jackson, George Pullen, *Spiritual Folk-Songs of Early America*. Locust Valley, New York, J. J. Augustin Publisher, n.d. (Jackson signed the Introduction April 10, 1937).

Jackson, George Pullen, *White and Negro Spirituals, Their Life-Span and Kinship*. Locust Valley, New York, J. J. Augustin Publisher, n.d. (Jackson signed the Prefatory Acknowledgments August 20, 1943.)

Jackson, George Pullen, *White Spirituals in the Southern Uplands*. Chapel Hill, North Carolina, University of North Carolina Press, 1933. Reprinted by Folklore Associates, Inc., Hatboro, Pennsylvania, 1964.

James, Joe S. and others, ed., *Original Sacred Harp, Revised, Corrected and Enlarged*. Atlanta, Georgia, 1911.

Johansen, John Henry, *The Olney Hymns*. New York, The Hymn Society of America, Paper No. XX, 1956.

Jones, Francis Price, *The Church in Communist China*. New York, The Friendship Press, 1962.

Kelynack, William S., *Companion to the School Hymn-Book of the Methodist Church*. London, The Epworth Press, 1950.

Lightwood, James T., *Hymn Tunes and Their Story*. London, The Epworth Press, 1935.

Lough, A. G., *The Influence of John Mason Neale*. London, S.P.C.K., 1962.

Lowens, Irving, *Music and Musicians in Early America*. New York, W. W. Norton and Company, 1964.

Mason, Henry L., *Hymn Tunes of Lowell Mason*. Cambridge, The University Press, 1944.

McCutchan, Robert Guy, *Hymn Tune Names, Their Sources and Significance*, New York, Abingdon Press, 1957.

Metcalf, Frank J., *Stories of Hymn Tunes*. New York, Abingdon Press, 1928.

Ninde, Edward S., *The Story of the American Hymn*. New York, Abingdon Press, 1921.

Noss, Luther, ed., *Christian Hymns*. Cleveland, Ohio, The World Publishing Company, Meridian Books, 1963.

Noyes, Morgan P., *Louis F. Benson, Hymnologist*. New York, The Hymn Society of America, Paper No. XIX, 1955.

Nutter, Charles S. and Tillett, Wilbur F., *The Hymns and Hymn Writers of the Church*. New York, The Methodist Book Concern, 1911.

Phillips, Charles S., *Hymnody Past and Present*. New York, The Macmillan Company, 1937.

Price, Frank W., *China, Twilight or Dawn*. New York, The Friendship Press, 1948.

Reynolds, William Jensen, *A Survey of Christian Hymnody*. New York, Holt, Rinehart and Winston, Inc., 1963.

Robinson, Charles Seymour, *Annotations Upon Popular Hymns*. New York, Hunt and Eaton, 1893.

Routley, Erik, *Twentieth Century Church Music*. New York, Oxford University Press, 1964.

Routley, Erik, *Hymns Today and Tomorrow*. New York, Abingdon Press, 1964.

Ryden, Ernest Edwin, *The Story of Christian Hymnody*. Rock Island, Illinois, Augustana Press, 1959.

Sankey, Ira D., *My Life and the Story of the Gospel Hymns*. New York, Harper and Brothers Publishers, New York, 1906.

Smith, H. Augustine, *Lyric Religion: The Romance of Immortal Hymns*. New York, D. Appleton-Century Company, 1931.

Stevenson, Robert, *Protestant Church Music in America*. New York, W. W. Norton and Company, Inc., 1966.

Sutherland, Allan, *Famous Hymns of the World: Their Origin and Their Romance*. New York, Frederick A. Stokes Company, 1906.

Sydnor, James Rawlings, *The Hymn and Congregational Singing*. Richmond, John Knox Press, 1960.

The Hymn Society of America. *The Hymn,* Vol. I-XX, 1949-1969.

The Hymn Society of Great Britain and Ireland. *Bulletin.* Vol. IV-VII, 1956-1969.

Thompson, Ronald W., *Who's Who of Hymn Writers*. London, Epworth Press, 1967.

Towle, Eleanor A., *John Mason Neale, D. D., A Memoir*. London, New York, Longmans, Green, and Co., 1906.

White, James F., *The Cambridge Movement*. Cambridge, The University Press, 1962.

Wyeth, John, Repository of Sacred Music, Part Second. Harrisburg, Pennsylvania, 1820. Reprint with Introduction by Irving Lowens, DaCape Press, New York, 1964.

INDEXES

Index of Authors, Composers, and Sources

References indicate hymn numbers.

Biographical comments are shown in boldface type.

Index of Meters

Short Meter
S.M. 6.6.8.6.

Dennis 273
Festal Song 93
Franconia 302
Korea 267
Mornington 341
Platten 198
Potsdam 298
St. Andrew 400
St. Augustine 301
St. Bride 259
St. Michael 266
St. Thomas 348
Schumann 261
Silver Street 254
Southwell 234, 255
Trentham 200

Short Meter
with Refrain

Marion 97

Short Meter Double
S.M.D. 6.6.8.6.D.

Diademata 184, 257
Llanllyfni 215
Terra Beata 5

Common Meter
C.M. 8.6.8.6.

Abbey 84, 276
Antioch 122

Azmon 72, 243
Bangor 169
Belmont 317
Bishopthorpe 12
Blackbourne 313
Christmas 126
Consolation 25
Coronation 284
Crimond 40
Dundee 29, 324, 367
Dunfermline 311
Evan 41
Farrant 387
Irish 80
Isleworth 190
Land of Rest 274
Lobt Gott, ihr Christen 138, 280, 361
Nun danket all' 196, 233
Perry 318
St. Agnes 195, 232, 282
St. Anne 23
St. Flavian 166
St. Mary 386
St. Peter 269, 343
Tallis' Ordinal 55, 402
Twenty-fourth 390
Winchester Old 231

Common Meter Double
C.M.D. 8.6.8.6.D.

All Saints New 351
Carol 119
Ellacombe 4
Forest Green 98, 263
Kingsfold 223, 277

8.6.

Duke's Tune 435

8.6.8.6.6.6.6.6.

Ponden Cote 189

8.6.8.6.7.6.8.6.

St. Louis 120

8.6.8.6.8.8.

O Jesu 239

8.6.8.6.8.8.8.6.

Indonesian Folk Tune 345

8.6.8.8.6.

Lobt Gott ihr Christen 280, 361
Rest 86
Salvation 85, 337

8.7.8.7.

Alta Trinita beata 437
Danish Folk Song 153
Dominus regit me 49
Father, Hear 226
Kingdom 309
Lieben ist mein leben 140
Merton 116
Omni Dei 436
Rathbun 208
Regensburg 204
St. Columba 258
Stuttgart 106
Wellesley 13

8.7.8.7.D.

Austrian Hymn 352, 354
Beecher 297
Bradbury 220
Ebenezer 247, 342
Erie 224
Geneva 203
Hastings-on-Hudson 65
Hyfrydol 79, 294
Hymn to Joy 1, 34

In Babilone 145, 175
Pleading Savior 366
Rex G'oriae 389

8.7.8.7.
with Refrain

Greensleeves 133

8.7.8.7.4.4.7.

Winter 211
Union Seminary 316

8.7.8.7.6.6.6.7.

Ein' feste Burg 31

8.7.8.7.6.7.

Neander 20

8.7.8.7.7.7.

Irby 125
Unser Herrscher 392

8.7.8.7.7.7.8.8.

Psalm 42   110

8.7.8.7.7.8.7.4.

Christ lag in Todesbanden 177

8.7.8.7.8.7.

Cwm Rhondda 186, 245, 251
Dulce carmen 368
Picardy 114
Praise my soul 73
Regent Square 124, 144
St. Thomas (Wade) 187

8.7.8.7.8.7.7.

Divinum mysterium 139

8.7.8.7.8.8.7.

Allein Gott in der Höh 58
Aus tiefer Not 89
Mit Freuden zart 26, 222
Nun freut euch 372

8.7.8.7.8.8.7.7.

Ermuntre dich, mein schwacher Geist 131

8.8.4.4.8.8.
with Alleluias

Lasst uns erfreuen 54, 87

8.8.5.8.6.

Hampton Poyle 347

8.8.6.D.

Cornwall 365

8.8.7.D.

Alles ist an Gottes Segen 107

8.8.7.7.

Mon Dieu, prête-moi l'oreille 430

8.8.7.8.8.7.

Stabat Mater 164

8.8.7.8.8.7.4.8.4.8.

Wie schön leuchtet der Morgenstern 287

8.8.8.

Wulfrun 383

8.8.8.
with Alleluias

Gelobt sei Gott 178
O filii et filiae 179
Victory 182

8.8.8.5.

Cheshire 401

8.8.8.6.

Saffron Walden 217

8.8.8.8.D.

Schmücke dich 310

8.8.8.8.
with Refrain

More about Jesus 206

8.8.8.8.6.

St. Margaret 17

8.8.8.8.8.8.

Leicester 398
Melita 210, 370
Old 113th   74
Sagina 241
St. Catherine 253
St. Chrysostom 238
St. Petersburg 336
South Gore 355
Veni Emmanuel 108, 109

8.8.8.8.8.8.8.

Kirchen den er et 349

8.8.9.8.

Jesus Christus, unser Heiland 321

8.9.8.8.9.8.6.6.4.8.8.

Wachet auf 112

8.10.10.10.

Paris 360

9.8.8.9.

God be with you 44
Randolph 43

9.8.9.8.

Eucharistic Hymn 304
Les Commandmens de Dieu 39
St. Clement 38
Weisse 322

9.8.9.8.D.

Rendez à Dieu 303

9.8.9.8.8.8.

Wer nur den lieben Gott 51

9.9.10.10.

Ostergaard 249

10.4.6.6.6.6.6.10.4.

All the world 83

10.4.10.4.10.10.

Sandon 21, 28, 46

10.6.10.6.8.8.8.6.

All is well 335

10.10.9.10.

Slane 90

10.10.10.
with Alleluia

National City 59

10.10.10.4.

Sine nomine 279

10.10.10.6.

Peace 11

10.10.10.10.

Birmingham 306
Canticum refectionis 314
Ellers 82
Eventide 47
Farley Castle 154
Hall 92
Holborn 305, 323
Morecambe 201
National Hymn 22
O quanta qualia 185
Toulon 149, 334, 369

10.10.10.10.10.

Old 124th   339

10.10.11.11.

Hanover 76
Lyons 67

11.10.11.9.

Russian Hymn 33

11.10.11.10.

Charterhouse 147
Donne secours 225, 236, 312
Faithfulness 14
O perfect love 378
Welwyn 264, 278
Zu meinem Herrn 379

11.10.11.10.
with Refrain

Tidings 330

11.10.11.10.10.

Langham 265

11.10.11.10.11.10.

Thomas Circle 377

11.11.11.5.

Christe sanctorum 62
Flemming 229
Herzliebster Jesu 162

11.11.11.9.

Maddermarket 19

11.11.11.11.

Adoro te devote 319
Cradle Song 128
Foundation 35
Ihr kinderlein kommet 130
St. Denio 75

Index of Tunes

Index of First Lines